THE GULF IN
WORLD HISTORY

Arabia at the Global Crossroads

Edited by Allen James Fromherz

EDINBURGH
University Press

Edinburgh University Press is one of the leading university presses in the UK. We publish academic books and journals in our selected subject areas across the humanities and social sciences, combining cutting-edge scholarship with high editorial and production values to produce academic works of lasting importance. For more information visit our website: www.edinburghuniversitypress.com

Edinburgh University Press Ltd
The Tun – Holyrood Road
12 (2f) Jackson's Entry
Edinburgh EH8 8PJ

Typeset in 11/15 Adobe Garamond by
Servis Filmsetting Ltd, Stockport, Cheshire,
and printed and bound in Great Britain

A CIP record for this book is available from the British Library

ISBN 978 1 4744 3065 4 (hardback)
ISBN 978 1 4744 3067 8 (webready PDF)
ISBN 978 1 4744 3068 5 (epub)

CONTENTS

ILLUSTRATIONS

FIGURES

PLATES
Between pages 182 and 183

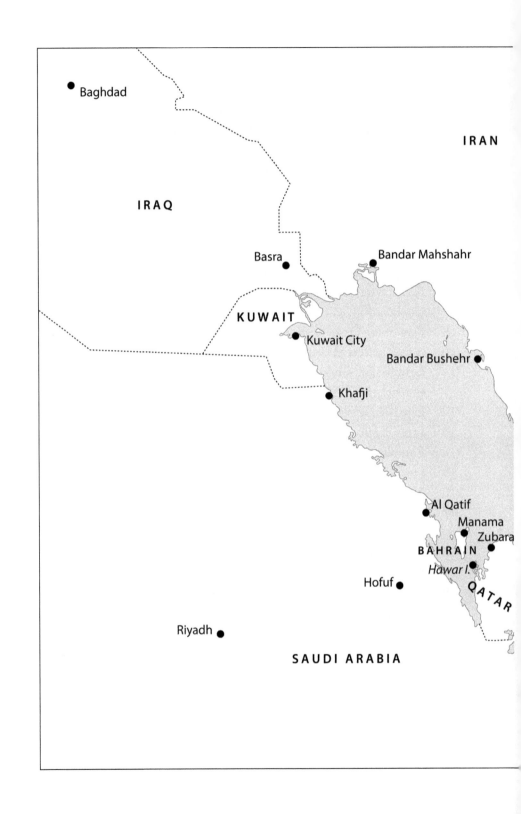

Baghdad

IRAN

IRAQ

Basra

Bandar Mahshahr

KUWAIT

Kuwait City

Bandar Bushehr

Khafji

Al Qatif

Manama

Zubara

BAHRAIN

Hawar I.

QATAR

Hofuf

Riyadh

SAUDI ARABIA

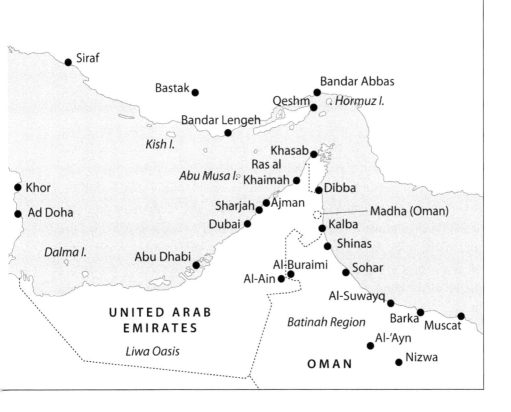

Shiraz

Siraf

Bastak

Bandar Abbas

Qeshm   *Hormuz I.*

Bandar Lengeh

Kish I.

Khasab

Abu Musa I.   Ras al
Khaimah

Khor

Dibba

Ad Doha

Sharjah   Ajman

Dubai

Madha (Oman)

Kalba

Dalma I.

Shinas

Abu Dhabi

Al-Buraimi

Sohar

Al-Ain

Al-Suwayq

**UNITED ARAB
EMIRATES**

Batinah Region

Barka   Muscat

Al-'Ayn

Liwa Oasis

OMAN   Nizwa

ACKNOWLEDGEMENTS

The Gulf in World History is the result of collaborations between scholars, staff, administrators, reviewers and editors from different parts of the planet. It has been a global project since its inception, involving scholars from around the world from differing academic cultures and perspectives. In this way, the book is a reflection of its thesis: the Gulf as a catalyst of global encounters.

I can only attempt to mention some of those from around the world who made this book a reality. The germ for the volume came from a call for fellowships from the New York University Abu Dhabi Institute. It was its support, both of my application for a senior fellowship and of my supplemental application for a major workshop to be held at NYU Abu Dhabi, that provided the original impetus for the book. The Humanities Institute at NYUAD impressed me not simply in terms of its support for this project. Every week there seemed to be a major event, lecture or workshop on some topic related to Gulf heritage, history and culture. In my mind, the NYUAD Humanities Institute is at the vanguard of a new renaissance in Gulf Studies that has swept through universities, both established and new, throughout the Gulf in just the past decade. From Senior Vice Provost Fatma Abdulla to Vice Chancellor Carol Brandt to Dean Robert Young, who attended and presented at our workshop, providing important insights, there was support from every level at NYUAD. Specifically, I want to thank Reindert Falkenburg, Vice Provost for Intellectual and Cultural Outreach. His feedback on my proposal was especially helpful in terms of framing the larger significance of the Gulf as a 'missing link' in world history. Also, I enjoyed our discussions about Dutch masters Bosch and Breughel. I also want to thank the excellent staff at the Institute for their incredible depth of knowledge and support. Nora Yousif, Alexandra Sandu, Nils Lewis, Gila Waels, Antoine El Khayat, Manal Demaghlatrous, thank you not only for making sure everything ran smoothly and efficiently, but also for your friendship and your deep knowledge of the region. Martin Klimke, Cyrus Patell, Yousef Casewit, Giuliano Garavini, Matthew Maclean, Marcel Kurpershoek, Justin Stearns, Philip Kennedy and Michael Cooperson, thank you for your companionship and your many insightful suggestions. Michael and Philip, the library of Arabic Literature is a true lodestone for any scholar who works in the language. I want to thank NYUAD Humanities Research Fellowship Program specifically for the financial support of the book itself, which has allowed us to produce beautiful images for the text. At Dartmouth and at Boston University I wish to thank Gene Garthwaite, Diana Wylie and Dale Eickelman for serving as references and reviewers. At Emory I want to acknowledge Vincent Cornell, who deserves credit for working on an NEH grant with me that was later transformed into the Global Gulf workshop, Rkia Cornell, Scott Kugle, Devin Stewart and Roxani Margariti and the whole MESAS department.

I also want to sincerely thank all of the contributors and all of the people who helped chapter authors complete their work in a timely manner. I am grateful to authors who also provided advice or images during the production phase. The number and quality of chapters has exceeded expectations in almost every way. I have provided more details about the contributors in the introduction. I am particularly proud of the international and interdisciplinary background of our authors, with scholars specialising in literature, medieval astrology, archaeology, Indian history (thank you, Seema Alavi, for your feedback), as well as those subjects more familiar to students of Gulf. We also have contributions from every level of academe, from recent graduates or graduate students to senior professors. Specifically, we all gained from the interventions by Isa Blumi, Richard Payne, Leah Kleinberger, Nathalie

Peutz, Nicolas Purcell and others who attended and presented at the workshop. Especially helpful for contextualising the history of Abu Dhabi and the UAE were Frauke Heard-Bey and her husband David Heard. Ahmed Yaqoub, a graduate student in Abu Dhabi, provided insights on the history of the Baluchi community. We also received honoured guests from UAE University in Al-Ain, including the Dean.

Edinburgh University Press in Scotland, in my view the foremost press on pre-modern Islamic history, publisher of the works of scholars such as Montgomery Watt and Carole Hillenbrand, has been an important partner for the success of this project. I want to thank the EUP editorial board, the senior editor Nicola Ramsey as well as Kirsty Woods, Eddie Clark and Rebecca Mackenzie. Clive Gracey, the photographer of our cover image, deserves special recognition for allowing us to use his stunning images for this text.

I wish to express my sincere gratitude to the Sultan Qaboos Cultural Center, including to Kathleen Ridolfo and Iman Busaidi for providing me with research support that helped me develop the seeds of this project while in Oman.

Another important partner in the success of this book has been Georgia State University and the Global Studies Institute under the leadership of Tony Lemieux and Jennie Burnet. As director of the Middle East Studies Center at GSU, I have been able to work on this edited volume, which includes a chapter by Asian Studies Center director Ghulam A. Nadri, due to the support of the GSI. I want to thank the Provost of GSU, Risa Palm, and the Dean Sara Rosen for the semester leave afforded to recently promoted Professors. This has also allowed me the time and mental space needed to accomplish this major project. I want to express gratitude to my home department for research support and flexibility as I have travelled around the world completing research for this and other books. Thank you Michelle Brattain, Mary Rolinson, Ian Fletcher, Kate Wilson and the whole department, for your encouragement. My graduate students at GSU have been particularly helpful as well. Leah Kleinberger, Dr John Sullivan, Donna Hamil, thank you for working with me either as a GRA or through the Middle East Studies Center and its activities. Dr Patricia Coates, thank you for volunteering to help with indexing and other duties related to the book. It is an honour to work with such an intelligent and engaged graduate cohort.

Finally, I want to thank my close friends and family in Atlanta and in Oregon. William Tomlin and the Law Office of William L. Tomlin, thank you for looking over portions of the text and providing suggestions. Of course, any errors are completely my own. Glenn Faulk, Bill Crawley, Joe Maxwell and Hugh Latta, thank you for being supportive friends. Robin Fromherz, Allen J. Fromherz, Rebecca and Amy Fromherz, Kathy Martin, Emmit, Diesel, Marseille and Daisy, thank you all for your love and care.

CONTRIBUTORS (IN ORDER OF APPEARANCE IN THE VOLUME)

Allen James Fromherz is Professor of History at Georgia State University in Atlanta, where he directs the Middle East Studies Center. In 2016 he was Senior Humanities Fellow at NYUAD.

Richard McGregor is Associate Professor of Religion and Islamic Studies at Vanderbilt University.

Valeria Piacentini Fiorani is Professor of the History of the Muslim World at the Catholic University of the Sacred Heart in Milan, Italy.

Charles Häberl is Associate Professor and Chair of the Department of African, Middle East and South Asian Languages and Literatures at Rutgers, the State University of New Jersey.

Ghulam A. Nadri is Associate Professor of South Asian History at Georgia State University, where he directs the Asian Studies Center.

Abdulrahman al Salimi is an Omani Researcher, Sultanate of Oman.

Johan Mathew is Assistant Professor of the Indian Ocean World at Rutgers, the State University of New Jersey.

Matthew S. Hopper is Professor of History at California Polytechnic State University, San Luis Obispo.

Mark Horton is Professor in Archaeology at the University of Bristol.

Michael A. Ryan is an Associate Professor of Mediterranean and Medieval History at the University of New Mexico.

Eric Staples is Assistant Professor, College of Humanities and Social Sciences, Zayed University.

Timothy Power is Associate Professor, College of Humanities and Social Sciences, Zayed University.

Robert Carter is a Professor of Arabian and Middle Eastern Archaeology at University College London (UCL) Qatar.

Carolyn M. Swan is Barry Curator of Glass at the Chrysler Museum of Art in Norfolk, Virginia.

William G. Zimmerle is a Professor of Humanities at Farleigh Dickinson University.

Karen Exell is an Honorary Senior Research Associate at University College London (UCL) Qatar.

Lamya Harub is an Omani Diplomat who recently obtained her Ph.D. in the political economy of energy security from King's College London.

1

INTRODUCTION: WORLD HISTORY IN THE GULF AS A GULF IN WORLD HISTORY

Allen James Fromherz

Weep not for a friend that is distant, nor for an abode,
But turn yourself about with fortune as it turns.
Consider all humanity your dwelling place,
And imagine all the earth your home.
– Abu Zayd in the *Maqamat* of Al-Hariri[1]

The above passage is from the twenty-eighth assembly by Al-Hariri, part of a series of fifty entertaining stories written in Basra in the eleventh and twelfth centuries CE. Basra at the time was the crucial port on the Gulf linking Baghdad, the capital of the Abbasids, with the Indian Ocean, Africa, even China. It had a striking, cosmopolitan ethos, as this poem suggested. Abu Zayd, the protagonist of this story, rejected any notion of rootedness or singular identity. In fact, he actively uprooted and challenged the past. He used the form of the *qasida*, or the classical Arabic ode, to proclaim a new and surprisingly global sentiment. Instead of the classic *nasib*, the nostalgic 'weeping for the abode' which is the opening used by almost every other Arab poet and is used to display pride in tribe and family, Abu Zayd said here in his poem to 'weep not' for the loss of any one particular place. Rather, he called on his listeners to consider humanity, regardless of creed or race or dwelling place, and see the world as their 'home'. This sentiment even went beyond the well-established Islamic notion of the 'complete person' or the 'perfect human' (*al-insan al-kamil*) elaborated by Sufis such as 'Abd al Karim al Jili (d. 1424 CE) and Muhyi al-Din ibn 'Arabi (d. 1240 CE). Abu Zayd's speech implored his audience to ask not simply about universalism within an Islamic context, but also about a universal notion of humanity, beyond a religious world view.

In the Gulf, as in other parts of the world that the Gulf brought together, was it so surprising that, at certain extraordinary moments, questions went beyond 'What does it mean to be Muslim, Christian or Hindu?' to ask what it meant to be human?[2] On the Gulf, in the close quarters of the ship, one often simply slept outside in the elements with one's passengers from many parts of the world, speaking a Babel of tongues. The ports were filled with people from a great variety and diversity of creeds, languages and cultures, far surpassing the three main faiths of the Mediterranean. When compared to the Gulf, the post-Classical Mediterranean becomes rather less of a diverse space than is often assumed, with only Jews, Christians and Muslims dominating after the seventh century. Is it such a surprise to see instances in the literature and culture and life of the Gulf where the question 'Of human meaning' emerges from under this the sea of faiths and in this Gulf of encounters? What sort of society or culture accounted for a transformation of identity from one bounded by place to one unbounded and unmoored? Of course, there was more to Basra, as there is today more to Dubai, than a projected image or a reputation for cosmopolitanism. A whole complex of local factors and histories, on the ground, are linked to the wider world, the world to which these global spaces turn. This book, a compilation of chapters by the foremost scholars in their fields, as well as new and rising academic stars, examines both this local context of particular places in the Gulf and the links between these particular places and a wider world.

Basra, a global gateway similar to many other such ports before it and after it on the Gulf, accounted for the remarkable ideas expressed by Abu Zayd. After all, the history of the Gulf in its most prosperous ports was, and still is, a history of cross-cultural encounters. These included ancient Dilmun (Bahrain) described in the writings of Ea-Nasir who travelled there on business from Ur,

Siraf in the writings of Abu Zayd al-Sirafi, Hormuz, as described in this book by Prof. Piacentini, and modern Dubai, with port and airport not just for the Gulf but for all of Asia. All of these places revealed a history of humanity and the world both passing through and making a dwelling place.[3] Unlike the Mediterranean, where geography and history have dictated that certain locations and cities (Byzantium, or Rome) establish a type of imperial memory of predominance and a division of Eastern and Western zones, no one particular place along the Gulf has held the position of most prominent port of call for too long. Although increasingly we are seeing translations of the primary sources of Gulf history, much of its exciting past has yet to be fully analysed and contextualised.[4] The global history of the Gulf, often hidden beneath the buildings built from the profits of oil, remains to be written.

The 'Gulf' in World History

The Gulf is a gulf in the writing of world history. So much of the world's history has happened either in the Gulf or through it. Paradoxically, while there is much world history in the Gulf, there is not so much of the Gulf in world history. Geographically, the Gulf is a shallow sea (only around 300 feet at its deepest, compared to the Gulf of Oman at around 12,000 feet), a benefit for pearl divers but also a challenge for transport and invading navies. Unfortunately, studies of the Gulf and its connections to the world have also lacked depth. Historians describe the Gulf as important and original, the body of sea water to lap the shores of the first civilisations. Just as often, historians pass over it, with their attention and focus quickly shifting inland to the empires of Persia or Babylon, or even to the Mediterranean and the Indian Ocean. It would be difficult to find another more famous body of water or cultural space about which we still know so little. While recognised as a key to understanding world history, a missing link between the Mediterranean, the Middle East and Asia, the culture of the Gulf itself has traditionally remained understudied.[5] This occurred even as the great, agrarian empires and peoples that the Gulf connected, from Rome to Babylon to Persia, and even the trails to the Indus Valley and China, received great scrutiny. Ancient history exemplifies the situation that has prevailed until very recently. The historian Herodotus (d. c. 425 BCE), the geographer Strabo (d. 23 CE) and the natural philosopher Pliny the Elder (d. 79 CE) noted the existence of Gulf ports and settlements, but wrote rare bits and pieces about Gulf culture and society. Typically, the ancients mention a few spare scraps about the *Ichthyophagi*, the so-called 'fish-eaters' who were said by these ancient writers to inhabit Gulf shores. Not much is said about these fish-eaters, except maybe that they engaged in pearl fishing as well. 'Fish eating' was hardly a very 'thick description'.[6] Yet Herodotus and the Classical writers managed to narrate the culture and society of the imperial Persians, who claimed parts of the Gulf from their inland capital, with much more detail and dimensionality. Descriptions of the Gulf improved marginally when Alexander the Great recognised the strategic importance of the Gulf and sent his officer named Nearchus to survey its shore. Fortunately, modern archaeology, including discoveries by the many eminent scholars in this volume, has filled in some of the gaps in the ancient written records.[7]

Writing on the Gulf increased during the Islamic period. Literature in both Persian and Arabic, something of an untapped source for the social history of the Gulf, developed even through the waning centuries of the Abbasid Caliphate. We possess important geographies and famous travellers' and geographers' accounts and maps from Abu Ishaq al-Istakhri (d. 957 CE; Plate 1) to Ibn Battuta, Ibn Mujawir, Ambrosio Bembo and Ignazio Danti, which can still be mined for material. The eventual rise of European interest led to the production of lengthy government reports on the region. The thickness of the description and analysis on the Gulf rarely surpassed the utilitarian tone of the secret Civil Service *Gazetteer*.[8] Although valuable for policy analysis and economic studies, many works on the modern Gulf have been written in the context of a new guarantor of Gulf security and an undeniable influence on current Gulf affairs – the USA. These works, focused on policy and petrol dollars over people, are valuable, but lack depth and rarely include the rich cultural and social-historical roots of the present.[9] Gulf history did not start sixty or seventy years ago. There is more to the Gulf than oil, wealthy families and pure, political history. The chapters in this volume, addressing topics from Ikhwan literature, to dancing, to use of Chinese ceramics, to shipbuilding, to glassmaking, attest to the depth of time and perspective needed to understand the global history of the Gulf.

As is often the case in cosmopolitan places, other people's things appear in unlikely places, their original meaning or function long forgotten. The

Figure 1.1   Chinese dish set decorating the mihrab of Al-Masjid Al-ʿAyn. © Clive Gracey.

image on the cover of this book (Figure 1.1) of the Chinese ceramic plate of a Phoenix or Persian Simurgh embedded in the *mihrab*, or prayer niche, of an Ibadi mosque in the town of al-ʿAyn on the other side of the Green Mountains of Oman reveals how goods and materials from across the Indian Ocean came to form a central part of the visual iconography of both daily and, even, religious life in the Gulf. This use of 'other people's dishes' extends to use of 'other people's symbols'. Sometimes there symbols lose their original meaning and are recast, as with the case of the carvings on the back of Baghlas (large boats) in Dubai, called 'Dibai' by Thesiger, in the harbour pictured by the British traveller Wilfred Thesiger (Figure 1.2). The letters IHS, originally

Figure 1.2 Stern of a Baghla at Dubai Creek, 10–18 May 1948. Image from *The Thesiger Collection: A Catalogue of Unique Photographs* by Wilfred Thesiger (Dubai, 1991), p. 47: 'Dhow carvings'.

the Christian monogram symbolising Jesus Christ, are carved on a boat stern likely owned by Muslims for trade in Africa, India and beyond. It is worth quoting Thesiger's commentary from his book *Arabian Sands*:

> Sharja on May 10th . . . I said goodbye to my companions at Sharja, hoping to be with them again in four months' time. I then went to Dibai and stayed with Edward Henderson . . . He lived in a large Arab house overlooking the creek which divided the town, the largest on the Trucial Coast with about twenty-five thousand inhabitants. Many native craft were anchored in the creek or were careened on the mud along the waterfront. There were booms from Kuwait, sambuks from Sur, jaulbauts, and even a large stately baghila with a high carved stern on which I could make out the Christian monograph IHS on one of the embossed panels. This work must have been copied originally from some Portuguese galleon. I wondered how many times it had been copied since, exactly to the last scroll and flourish. Commander Alan Villiers, who had sailed in a boom from Zanzibar to Kuwait, believed that there were only two or three of these baghlas still in

existence. To the English all these vessels were dhows, a name no longer remembered by the Arabs.[10]

The Portuguese are not portrayed favourably in Arab or Persian sources, even as their shipping technology and methods were adapted and adopted by the Khalijis. The IHS symbol probably no longer indicated 'Jesus' but the 'brand' of quality shipbuilding, which had continued well into the dusk of the sailing era, a remnant of Lusitanian culture carved into the fabric of Gulf life. It is only in recent years that some of these 'mixed symbols' have disappeared in favour of a much 'cleaner' notion or even, in some cases, nationalistic notions of the past. It is also only in the past few years that studies of the history of the region have gained urgency and scope.

Recent studies have started to rectify the place of the Gulf in history, revealing the underlying richness of the littoral region and the cultural, economic and social diversity of the Khaliji experience. Many of the scholars represented in this volume, for instance, deserve recognition for their work on the region, uncovering new and surprising facts and histories that have yet to be fully explored. At the same time, important scholars whose work is not represented here have also played an important role. Frauke Heard-Bey and her husband David Heard, for instance, have both written excellent texts on the origins of the UAE that go beyond political chronology and delve into social factors.

There are also writers born in the Gulf, in addition to the authors included in the volume, who have written compelling accounts from a more nuanced or autobiographical perspective. For instance, M. A. Fahim, author of *From Rags to Riches*, spoke to us at the workshop about the rapid economic changes his family experienced over a few decades. There is also the national historical or religious literature, often of good quality, written in Arabic by scholars such as Al-Shaybani in Qatar and the Al-Salami in Oman. The formation of the various Arabian Gulf states led to an initial interest in formulating these notions of a national past. There are also important oral histories and accounts, such as Fahad Bishara's translation of the memories of the pearl trader Al-Hijji in Kuwait, that shed light on older ways of life that remain not so distant from the present.[11]

A Gulf in World History

Lawrence Potter's edited book, *The Persian Gulf in History* (2009) planted the seeds of a chronological approach to the Gulf. Fortunately, Dr Potter, M. A. Fahim, David and Frauke Heard-Bey, Richard Payne, Nathalie Peutz, Justin Stearns, Nicholas Purcell, Michael Cooperson, Robert Young and others were all able to attend and contribute to the Global Gulf Workshop in May 2016 held at New York University in Abu Dhabi. Their comments during the workshop have strengthened this volume. Other scholars who were not able to attend, including Seema Alavi and Roxani Margariti, provided important guidance and suggestions, especially as they related to connections between the Gulf, the Red Sea, the Mediterranean and India. James Onley and the Exeter programme for Gulf Studies deserves special note due to the quality and influence of work coming out of that centre and represented in the footnotes in this volume. In the USA there has been a steady growth of Gulf studies with the success of the Association for Gulf and Arabian Peninsula Studies. Another positive trend is the slow but steady growth of critical Gulf Studies within the Gulf itself. Many of the scholars in this volume are associated with centres and universities that have sprung up in the Gulf over just the past two decades. Mark Beech, for instance, a leading archaeologist in the UAE, was able to contribute to our workshop. The search for the Khaliji past has almost become something of a friendly race, a competition between Gulf States almost as fierce as the common interest in history, heritage and memory. One exciting result of this rise of interest in the history of the Gulf is a new cohort of graduate students or post-doctoral students training in the Gulf. They are receiving advanced degrees and will soon be ready to publish for a wider audience. The internationalising of the Gulf and of Gulf history has started. If support for Gulf Studies holds, we may eventually approach a new, high water mark for the historical study of the region. But even this 'high water mark' would be rather low when compared to the scholarship accumulated on other world-historical bodies of water. It would take multiple generations of Gulf scholars to approach our current knowledge of just a part of the Mediterranean.

Despite the growing body of knowledge and interest in the Gulf, specialists and non-specialists interested in the Gulf recognise that much work needs to be done. Much of our basic understanding of the history of the Gulf, especially the Gulf as a global space, still remains unwritten. Even as the number of archaeological studies, archival publishing and scholarly monographs on specific parts of the Gulf have increased in the past decade, prominent historians of the region recognise 'historical thinking about the Gulf as a whole is still in an embryonic stage'.[12] Also, the basic gathering and compiling of historical sources, from archaeology to private and sovereign archives, has hardly begun.

What the studies in this volume show is that the Gulf of today with its cities that touch the world is not the exception. Instead, the modern Gulf is a result of deep historical patterns of trade and cosmopolitanism. The work of scholars in this volume has started to fill in many of the gaps in the chronology. Most importantly, instead of simply stating the obvious importance of the Gulf and then moving on, we are showing how and in what specific ways the Gulf was a sea connected to the larger trends of World history. Using the methodology of the late world historian Jerry Bentley, the Gulf can be studied as a place of encounters, of 'cross cultural contacts and exchanges' that lead to changes for each side in the contact. Peter Frankopan's new history of the world and silk roads repeatedly mentioned the Gulf as an integral part of Asian and World history, highlighting the spread of Buddhism to its shores.[13] The Gulf was a magnet that pulled peoples from all cardinal directions, including north. Archaeologists have discovered evidence of Vikings in the Qatari desert.[14]

The Gulf today seems to manifest these many global trends. At the same time, there are also trends and tendencies to divide the Gulf into separate cultural zones. Revealing the existence of a Gulfi or *Khaliji* culture, inextricably linked to global phenomena, contrasts with some current attempts, arising since the creation of modern national borders and a resource economy, to divide the Gulf into zones of influence and territorial claims and to partition the common experience of the Khalijis into sectarian or cultural affiliations. Certainly these affiliations existed in the past, Persian, Arab, Shiite, Sunni, or even Hindu, African, Muslim, Mandæan and Christian, but they were far more mobile and fluid, following the freedom and autonomy historically afforded by the Gulf. The aim here is not to deny the historical existence of division or even of violence between different groups. Rather, it is to show that such categories have remained conditional and that the Gulf has thrived the most when it has leveraged its position as a gateway to the world. While present conflicts in the Gulf may lead some to believe in a deeper history of division, this volume questions easy categories. The Gulf, when viewed historically, is neither fully Persian or Arab, nor African or Indian; it is a global space. Gulf geography, isolated by both desert and mountain ranges that come right up to the beach and allow for easy autonomy, has abhorred absolute imperial power even as it has served as the emporium at the doorstep of empire. It is a transit space, but not necessarily transitory. Even as different ports emerged and then declined, many of the social and cultural structures remained over the long term. In this way Khalijis were able and free to spin their own 'webs of significance', and from those webs, create a culture. It is our intent in this volume to interpret, to go 'in search of meaning', tracing the web of Khaliji cultural and social history.[15]

This book peers underneath the surface of 'what happened' in the Gulf, to start examining the 'why' and the 'how' and hopefully to start the processes of revealing more of the long-term and medium-term trends of its history. This requires an array of interdisciplinary tools, one mirrored by the diversity of fields and specialisations of the authors. Arranged thematically, this book focuses on the role of change in culture, society, religion and trade, and the history of cosmopolitanism and trans-cultural encounters.

Gulf Cosmopolitans

Instead of viewing the Gulf as a neglected, transit space, passed on routes between the great civilisations of the Mediterranean of Babylon and of India, this book reveals new research on the Gulf as a place with its own rich cultural history. Despite Western stereotypes about the Gulf as a place of uncompromising religious fanaticism, Khalijis have historically been adept at shifting, adjusting and rehearsing their identity to suit the wider world at their doorstep. Al-Hariri of Basra, the author of the famed *Maqamat*, had Abu Zayd say this about port life near the shores of the Gulf in his last assembly:

> In it meet the ships and the saddle-beasts, the fish and the lizards, the
> camel-driver and the sailor, the hunter and the tiller, the harpooner and the

lancer, the herd and the swimmer, and to it belongs the spectacle of the tide
that rises and the tide that ebbs . . .[16]

Like Abu Zayd, we seem to be at a crucial turning point. Abu Zayd was about
to give up his life as a trickster for the life of a great ascetic and mystic. It was
an apotheosis of sorts, not only for Abu Zayd but for Al-Hariri's home on the
Gulf. For those who study Gulf history, we are also facing an exciting turn, a
re-centring of the Gulf not only to world historians but also to historians of
places and regions influenced by Gulf commerce, culture and society.

Book Themes

The book opens with three chapters on Gulf cosmopolitanism. The first chapter, by Vanderbilt University religious studies scholar Richard McGregor,
introduces the figure of the cosmopolitan exemplar in another great work
of literature that emerged from Basra: the tenth-century encyclopedia of the
Brethren of Purity, a group of worldly merchants who had an ambition
to compile the world's secrets and knowledge. The Ikhwan (the Brethren)
viewed the ideal human as an amalgam of different cultural and religious
identities. The next chapter, by Professor Valeria Piacentini, the prestigious
scholar from the Catholic University of the Sacred Heart in Milan who is
known for her many discoveries and analyses of finds on the eastern side of
the Gulf and Pakistan, examines features of the kingdom of Hormuz in the
late fifteenth and early sixteenth century that made it a cosmopolitan, mobile
society that linked the Gulf to other seas. She proposes that liquid spaces have
never been a barrier to the mobility of the societies settled on their seaboards.
Archaeological evidence and literary sources almost unanimously maintain
this image: political and military upheavals did not hamper the crossing of
the sea and continuous traditional movements of local peoples with their
individual cultural influences. A mobile institutional system developed that
was deeply rooted in the traditional, social and economic forces of the Gulf.
The third contribution takes us back to Mesopotamia, to examine the important question of the origin of the Mandæans, a religious community with ties
throughout the Gulf and the wider Indian Ocean world. Known for their high
level of learning, Mandæans worked as secretaries and bureaucrats for rulers
such as the Omani Sayyid Sa'id bin Sultan (d. 1851 CE). Charles Häberl, an

authority on the language and literature of the Mandæans, discusses the ways in which scholars have constructed different narratives about their origins as a distinct religious community even as their early history remains shrouded in myth and legend, due to a lack of historical sources.

The next theme of the book is the Gulf and the Indian Ocean. In his dialogues Socrates spoke of Mediterranean cities perched like 'frogs' around a 'pond' (Plato, *Phaedo*, 109 a-b), holding tight to the protective shore and, similar in culture, trade and practice around the sea pond of the Mediterranean. The Indian Ocean is no pond. While the Mediterranean is *a* world, even a *Mare Nostrum* for the Roman Empire, in many ways the Indian Ocean was *the* world, or at least much of it. The literature, history and culture of the Gulf reflect this position at the doorstep of the world's wonders. Importantly, like the Gulf itself, the Indian Ocean is hardly possible as a single, 'imperial' space. None has conquered all of the Indian Ocean shores. The Indian Ocean hits the sailor who ventures from the Gulf as an expanse of opportunity which, due to the seasonal monsoon, brings the near far away and the far very near to the majority of the world's population. Indian Ocean trade brought items inland, such as Ming porcelain bowls adorning the most remote of Omani Ibadi mosques, Indus Valley seals in Dilmun, Bahrain, or Chinese pottery shards emerging like mementos of a long-forgotten voyage from excavations in the Buraimi/al-'Ain oasis explored by Timothy Power. If the Mediterranean is a pond and the Indian Ocean is a nexus of the world for a vast portion of the world's population, it is the Gulf that lies between.

The Gulf is an antechamber to the World Sea of the Indian Ocean, but it is also touched by the outer orbits of the Mediterranean. The Roman Emperor Trajan received the submission of Athambelus, ruler of Charax, a classical Gulf port at the mouth of the Tigris/Euphrates. His ambition was to make sacrifices at the house in Babylon where Alexander the Great died. Mediterranean influence exists, for example, in the architecture of the hybrid Ionic/Achaemenid Failaka temples, called a pastiche of Greek and oriental elements (Figure 1.3).[17] Indeed, like many of the islands and religious sites around the Gulf coast, Failaka's status as a holy site continued into the Islamic period. There is also on Failaka the shrine to Al-Khidr, 'The Green One', an Islamic figure endowed with immortal life (Qur'ān 18: 60–82). Al

Figure 1.3 Kuwait archaeological excavations at Failaka Island. Art Directors & TRIP/ Alamy Stock Photo. Alamy Images.

Khidr, according to some traditions, delved into the waters of eternity and is associated with the protection of mariners.

Long after the fall of Rome, Europeans knew of the pearl banks of the Gulf. The pearl divers can be seen in the 1375 CE Atlas of Abraham de Cresques, a geographer from the distant Western Mediterranean Island of Majorca (Plate 2).[18] Such examples of Mediterranean contacts are an invitation to further study. Beyond these connections, however, the Gulf shares elements of both the Mediterranean pond of Plato and the Indian Ocean expanse of monsoon sailors such as Ahmad ibn Majid (d. c. 1500 CE), who wrote just as the Portuguese were venturing around the Cape of Good Hope.[19]

The chapters here focus on the Gulf, the Indian Ocean and the Indian subcontinent after the death of Ibn Majid. Professor Ghulam Nadri, Director of Asian Studies at Georgia State University, examines the archives of the VOC, the Dutch East India Company, and other sources to reveal a rich history of cross-cultural trade between Gujarat, India and the Gulf. Abdulrahman al Salimi studies the surprising role of the Banian, or Banyan Indian merchants who, according to tradition, 'opened the gates' of the city of Portuguese Muscat to the Ibadi, Muslim Omanis. The Banyan are but one example of the vibrant, diverse cultures and religious traditions present in the Muscat suq. Finally, Professor Johan Mathew from Rutgers asks his readers to reconsider and reframe our understanding of Gulf–India connections, showing the pull and importance of India and Indian merchants in the nineteenth century.

Part III turns our attention southward to East Africa, another region of the world connected over the centuries by the monsoon to the Gulf. While studies exist on the role of Arabs on the Swahili Coast, Matthew Hopper provides an important and theoretically insightful understanding of the meaning and identity of the African Diaspora community within the Gulf. Next, Mark Horton connects his work on the archaeology of East Africa to the Gulf and asks his readers to reconsider a new thalassology: a new way of studying the seas.

Part IV returns to the history of Gulf and focuses on the theme of diversity and change in the skies, on land and on the sea. Professor Michael Ryan from the University of New Mexico brings his formidable knowledge of the history of astrology to the Gulf and asks us to consider the astrological connections across a global space. Astrology, far from being simply an exercise of imagination, was a real node of connectivity between thinkers as distant from one another as Basra and Barcelona. Professor Eric Staples, at Zayed University in Abu Dhabi, dives into the taxonomy of ships, arguing quite effectively that ship names and types vary according to port and place. The fluidity and diversity of meaning when it came to maritime topics revealed the central importance of life on the water for Khalijis. Finally, Professor Timothy Power, also at Zayed University, convincingly shows the connections between the Gulf and one of the most important inland Gulf oases: Al-'Ain/Buraimi. Far from being isolated, these Gulf oases were also intricately connected to the sea, showing a zone of influence from the Gulf that expanded and shifted according to changing patterns of trade and dynastic politics. Power, Horton, Zimmerle and Staples are also part of a new wave of Gulf archaeology that is the focus of the next two chapters, grouped together as Part V. Professor Robert Carter at University College London and Carolyn Swan, at the Chrysler Museum of Art, ask us to consider the world history of the Gulf through trade in pearls and glass. For example, beautiful glass flasks in the shape of dates from the Mediterranean have been found in first-century CE Bahraini tombs (Plate 3). This scholarship reveals important new finds that provoke exciting questions about the extent of the Gulf's role in international trade. Archaeology can enlighten our understanding of material life, commodities, imports and exports. As Robert Carter tells us in his chapter, archaeology 'reveals patterns of behavior and consumption that are almost absent from the historical sources'.

The final group of chapters focuses on a recent trend in Gulf studies, one that focuses on themes of heritage, memory and preservation. Professor William Zimmerle at Fairleigh Dickinson University provides important insight into the shifting meaning of the emblematic, cuboid incense burner, prominent in many a Gulf home, museum and city roundabout. Dr Karen Exell, a trailblazer in the field of Gulf heritage studies, asks important questions about memory and history in Doha's Heritage House Museums. Finally, Dr Lamya Harub, who has just completed her Ph.D. in Political Economy at King's College London, uses ethnographic interviews, as well as new data and analysis, to provide compelling insights into the reproduction of an Omani national identity and the Sultanate's cultivation of the Omani *nahdha* (renaissance) even in the wake of lower oil prices and production. In all, these chapters show that we have good reason to be optimistic about Gulf studies, about new ways of describing both the Gulf in the world and the world in the Gulf over the long term.

The Khaliji *Longue Durée*

When we assembled for the Global Gulf Workshop at the new NYU Abu Dhabi campus in May 2016, a simple glimpse outside the window seemed to encapsulate incredible modernity and success. Skyscrapers reaching into the sky confront the viewer almost as a metal screen between 'now' and 'then'. The chapters of this book reveal there is far more to the Gulf than oil, politics and tall buildings. There is also culture, society, archaeology and artistic forms of expression. Indeed, although we should hesitate to reach into the past to explain all contemporary issues, the symbols of modernity in the Gulf are no exception, but an expression of a *longue durée*, of long-term trends.

One of these trends has been a concentration of life in ports looking outward towards the water. There is a need for the history of these Gulf cities not only as a place where people made a living on a short-term basis as traders, but also as a place where people actually lived and established families and lives over the long term. In 1863, Muhammad al Thani remarked to the traveller William Palgrave in 1863, 'We are all from the highest to the lowest slaves of one master, Pearl.' Palgrave elaborated, 'Hence, their real homes are the countless boats which stud the placid pool . . . All thought, all conversation, all employment, turns on that one subject; everything else is mere by-game, and below even secondary consideration.'[20] Al Thani could have just as well have said we are all residents not only of the Gulf, but also *on* the Gulf. Peregrine Horden and Nicholas Purcell said in their monumental and cited study of the Mediterranean, *The Corrupting Sea*, there is a difference between being *of* Mediterranean culture and being simply *in* the Mediterranean.[21] For the Gulf, however, the sea is often an even more central locus of culture.

Unlike the somewhat temperamental Mediterranean, or the consistent monsoons of the Indian Ocean, with its convenient natural path from point A to point B, Gulf waters were, literally, lived upon. Even when the shore was quite near, the pearl divers spent nights and days for months on the *ghaws kabir*, the pearl diving season, in their boats. While fishing for pearls or other fruits of the sea, fresh water could be found in vents welling up and collected in leather bags. Khalijis moved easily to abandoned islands and easily-defended, rocky Bandars, a Persian name for 'protected cove', which became settlements for those avoiding taxation, or wishing to tax others, including imperial agents, as they passed by. In the Gulf much that was stratified in imperial realms became more equal. Khalijis were sometimes dependent on single Gulf resources such as the pearl. They were also vulnerable to geography and the extremes of climate. But they were also often free from direct outside interference. Instead, theirs was often a cosmopolitan, non-centralised, non-stratified society where the free movement of peoples, not the decisions of distant centralised authorities, often mattered most. The Gulf was not merely a transit point but a home, home for large numbers of Gulf men. There are even stories of female *nakhodahs*, pearl captains. While the Mediterranean bound populations to particular cultural zones around its shores and encouraged imperial claims and conquests, the Gulf was a much more fluid place characterised by autonomous or semi-autonomous populations capable of moving to more favourable locations, or locations less vulnerable to outside control, along the shore.

Of course, there is also more to the Gulf than the water. The date palm line on the Gulf may be analogous to the famous olive line (showing the extent of production) used by some to define Mediterranean culture and economy. Through innovative use of water channels, *falaj* and the *qanat*, Khalijis have harvested great quantities of dates for both export and subsistence from plantations such as those on the Batina Coast of Oman or further inland in Liwa, Abu Dhabi, a place of retreat from the humidity of the coast. Lest we assume some ancient division between sea and land, however, there were countless connections between the palms and the prow. Even camels were transported at times from land to the fresh waters that bubble up into the sea off the coasts of Bahrain, source of the ancient legend of paradise and sweet underground waters. Nomadic tribes would consist of sections and families devoted to pearling and, in lean years, Bedouin would even join the *ghaws*, with their very international crews, consisting of peoples from around the world, creating a unique mixture of musical and cultural heritage: cosmopolitanism on the waves. Dried fish fed camels that made the trek across vast spaces to the central Arabian markets and eventually to Mecca.

In the last few decades, the Gulf has moved dramatically from pearls to petroleum and other related industries, almost just in time after the devastating collapse of the market which occurred with the introduction of the artificial Mikimoto pearl from Japan. But focusing on pearls, dates and oil can only take us so far away from the Gulf itself, which has been replaced with internationally disputed and litigated boundaries for oil extraction where once the obsession was with pearl beds. Like pearls, oil price is similarly determined not by local markets but by world appetite. Also, even as there were seasonal migrations and exports of dates from the land, the sea was still a main source of livelihood for most Khalijis. Although modern historians like to exaggerate the difference between 'then' and 'now', changes as a result of oil are easily overstated.

Two deep trends from Gulf social history persist today: relative freedom of the ports, embodied by the customs house, and the *majlis*, the tribal council. They made the Gulf a society distinct from surrounding, interior regions that were more readily dominated by empire. There is still, for instance, the easy embrace of *laissez faire* cosmopolitanism, practised over generations of competitive trade between ports and sheikhs who wanted to maximise the profits from their customs houses or the loyalty of other lineage groups, or of fickle merchants who might leave on a dime. Religion or place of origin did not seem to matter as long as port fees were paid, often not directly to the sheikh but to the banyan, or the Indian merchants in charge of collection. Today expatriates of many faiths are brought in to work. The *majlis*, within the framework of time, identity and place, remains a powerful informal institution, too often underestimated by those focused on quantitative measures.

The Gulf has been modified by oil in image, but lineage history remains, and even, one might argue, grows in importance. It can be seen even in the present patchwork of boundaries that define national identity in places such as Madha, Fujairah and Musandam. Alliances and loyalties, often with distant sheikhs, unite inland settlements and lineage groups across and between and through borders only recently drawn, causing interesting pockets of nations within nations within nations, as is the case of the hill village of Nahwa which is part of the UAE which is surrounded by Madha which is part of the Sultanate of Oman which is itself surrounded by Fujairah near the border of Sharjah, which controls the nearby port of Khor Fakkan. A layered onion of borders is traversed within minutes. Although young Khalijis are facing a large number of challenges, it is hard to argue they are abandoning the past; if anything, there seems to be a renaissance of heritage promotion, from festivals to museums to intangible UNESCO recognitions, to a focus on the local, that has swept the Gulf in just the past few years. As the last of pre-oil living memories begin to fade, Khalijis have an increasing fascination with their own heritage, whether from a national or a more regional perspective.

The uniqueness of the Gulf also lies in its comparative lack of direct imperial or centralised history, even as autonomous Gulf cultures have existed side by side with some of the world's most dominant empires, religions and cultural trends. Except perhaps for some brief windows in the ancient past that are not very well documented or understood, the Gulf was almost always between, but never completely under, particular empires or single civilisations. This does not mean empires did not leave their mark – far from it. Nor were controlling caliphs or shahs always against a more cosmopolitan ethos. Before Islam, Khosrow Anoshirvan actively supported debates and disputations between representatives of the highly varied religious faiths in his lands, claiming in the *Karnamag*, a type of *Res Gestae* of the Shah, 'We have never rejected anybody because of their different religion or origin . . .'[22] Through trade and contact the Persians and subsequent empires left legacies in culture, art and life, often in surprising ways.

Nonetheless, one empire or one claim to civilisational identity, one 'abode' in the words of Abu Zayd, could never dominate the whole cultural scene in the Gulf. There were far too many places in which to hide and far too many resources that had to be expended to control the space. This was due in part to Gulf geography and the Khaliji resilience and determination to resist centralisation. Thus, the Gulf is both tantalisingly close to great empires, from the Persians to Alexander to the 'Abbasids, Portuguese, Dutch, Ottoman and British, but on the very edge of them, as both centre and frontier, as both an ancient nexus of trade and the 'missing link' between civilisations and worlds. Even under the British, Gulf rulers had a great deal of relative autonomy on land, especially when compared to outright colonial possessions. There were some less-known empires that actually emerged from the wider Gulf region, as our authors will explain, even from deep in the Buraimi. Later, Gulf rulers such as Sayyid Said bin Sultan were expert at playing larger empires off one another. Sheikhs and sultans knew the game, even if some played their hands differently from others. Unlike the Mediterranean or Indian Ocean ports, the Gulf, like al-Thani's oyster, is fickle in revealing its secret treasures and the reasons why one place becomes prized while another loses its lustre. Dilmun, Hormuz, Siraf, Basra, Bandar Abbas, Muscat, Qatif, Quriyat, Dubai have all risen at various times to prominence as major entrepôts for Gulf trade. Like the luck of the pearl diver, our search for Gulf history must always be prepared for surprises and disappointments in an environment of extremes and in lands and places forsaken by or forbidden to central authority.

The *longue durée* to Gulf history is not about geography's triumph over humanity. It does not tell a story of the submission of humans to the crushing trends of environment and geography, as described in the final chapters of Fernand Braudel's magnum opus, *The Mediterranean and the Mediterranean*

World in the Age of Philip II.[23] If any place could potentially suppress human-ity under the weight of geography, it might be the Gulf: extreme heat, extreme dryness, extreme height and extreme muggy marshes all surround its shores, both protecting the Gulf from imperial interests and challenging its residents to survive. Instead, the history of the Gulf is about human effort against the extremes of nature both on shore and in the sea in lands on the edge of power. There is a reason why the Gulf has remained on the margins of centralising states and empires; it has to do with an environment that is at once protective if mastered, but also incredibly challenging and deadly if not. Abu Zayd's cosmopolitanism is not an option but a necessity for success, and even for survival. Life along the Gulf is successful because of the relative tolerance needed for trade and because of distant links to the outside world, allowing Khalijis to exist below the radar of imperial concern while hop-skipping over empire to distant lands of opportunity, and bringing the world back to their ports. The history of Gulf citites such as Siraf on the east-ern coast proves this. Their perilous existence, often without ready access to water, suffering extremes of climate, perched unlikely in a comparatively free zone of economy, religion, culture and regional politics, show the triumph of humans against geographical odds.

The history of Gulf must be sought eagerly but with patience, with the same stamina as that of the pearl divers. There may be some false leads and a frustrating lack of evidence for some periods, places and peoples. Often there are rich treasures just waiting to be opened, both from the perspective of the vast imperial archives and travel narratives and from local sources, material evidence and literatures or oral histories, that deserve greater attention. The Gulf is a 'missing link' not only because of its location, but also because of the unique opportunity it presents for understanding a larger, global story.

Engaging the Gulf in World History

As the late C. A. Bayly proclaimed from his post in Cambridge, 'All histo-rians are world historians now . . . though many have not yet realized it.'[24] World historians argue there are three main world history methodologies followed in the academy today. First, there is global history as the history of everything, an omnivorous approach to describing all that happened on Earth. In this category are global biographies of kingship, cotton and tulips.

Second, there is world history that focuses on exchange and connections, and movements of people and ideas, where the interconnectedness of the world is highlighted. The third, arguably more sophisticated and compelling, approach identifies patterns of exchange that were regular and sustained. There have always been cross-border exchanges, but their operation and impact depended on the degree of systemic integration on a global scale. Oftentimes these studies focus on not one or two subjects or regions but three or four, emphasising the larger, global conditions that made change possible. There remain open opportunities for the globalising of Gulf studies using all three methods.

Despite recent advances in our knowledge of the past in the Gulf, for Gulf history the first method, just finding out what happened, still needs to be followed. There remain vistas of scholarly opportunity just waiting to be written about or discovered. This is both challenging and exciting for the field. The same is true of the second method – although there is work being done, there is still so much to be said about cross-cultural exchanges between different points on the map or different cultures and civilisations in the Gulf. The third method of writing world history, one that expands the study of a place to compare it with at least two others and connects it to global trends, can be one result of this book. By bringing together specialists on the Mediterranean, the Gulf and the Indian Ocean, this book aims to show how history, archaeology and recent political and cultural trends in the Gulf are key to a larger global story. The world that the Gulf helped make possible was even broader than the geographical frontiers of this volume. There continues to be ample space for future studies of the Gulf in context. As the late scholar Shahab Ahmed tells us in his magnum opus *What Is Islam?*, 'It has long been recognized that the societies of the geographical, temporal and demographic space that I have been calling the Balkans-to-Bengal Complex, in spite of local variations in language and ethnicity and creed, comprised a relatively distinct and integrated world'.[25] The history of the Gulf can be studied not only as a means of understanding the Gulf but also as a means of understanding that world as well as many others.

The life of the pearl, as told by Basra's Brethren of Purity, is analogous to our search for the world history of the *Khalij*:

The pearl oyster is the smallest sea-animal in bulk, the most delicate, yet the greatest in soul, the most skillful and cunning. She lives in the depths of the sea-bed, minding her own affairs, seeking her food, until, at a certain season, she rises from the sea floor to the surface on a rainy day and opens paired hatches like lips to catch the raindrops. Once she knows this is done, she snaps her hatches tight, careful admits no salty sea-water, and gently returns to the sea floor. Then she patiently waits with closed shell until those water drops ripen and fuse within her to a pearl. What human scholar could do such a thing, tell me if you know?[26]

Like this pearl oyster of legend, Gulf scholars and scholars of the Gulf must remain persistent, opening our shells to new and deeper ways of thinking about the Gulf in world history.

Notes

1. The *Maqamat* of Al-Hariri are notoriously difficult to translate. Michael Cooperson at NYUAD is currently engaged in this task. This translation is my own modernisation of the 19th-century version by Dr F. Steingass, *The Assemblies of Al-Hariri*, Vol. II (Royal Asiatic Society, 1898), p. 13. In lieu of Michael Cooperson's expected, scientific translation, I also consulted some of the Arabic editions available online, including the B. nationale de France edition dated to the 14th century: Manuscript Arabe 3929 and online <http://gallica.bnf.fr/ark:/12148/btv1b8422962f> (last accessed 28 March 2018).

2. For the notion of the 'Perfect Human' see Alexander D. Knysh, *Ibn 'Arabi in the Later Islamic Tradition: The Making of a Polemical Image in Islam* (Albany: SUNY Press, 1999).

3. For the Ea-Nasir merchant tablet see British Museum collections: Museum number 131236. Abu Zayd al Sirafi, *Accounts of China and India*, trans. Tim Mackintosh-Smith (New York: New York University Press, 2017).

4. In addition to exiting series, such as the Institute of Ismaili Studies, the Brigham Young University series, credit for this should be given to the excellent efforts of the New York University Press, Philip Kennedy, Michael Cooperson, Shawqat Toorawa and others involved in the Library of Arabic Literature translation efforts. Especially helpful is the use of parallel English–Arabic texts.

5. I thank Reindert Falkenburg, director of the Humanities Institute at NYUAD, for the idea of the Gulf as a 'missing link'.

6. Clifford Geertz, *The Interpretation of Cultures*, Chapter 1, 'Thick Description: Toward an Interpretive Theory of Culture' (New York: Basic Books, 1977).

7. Although in need of an update, for a survey of important advances in Gulf archaeology see the work of D. T. Potts, *The Arabian Gulf in History*, 2 vols (Oxford: Oxford University Press, 1991).

8. At over 5,000 pages, the *Gazetteer of the Persian Gulf, Oman and Central Arabia*, available in Cambridge Archive Editions, 2015, was written between 1908 and 1915 by John Gordon Lorimer, a member of the Indian Civil Service. It remains an important source and reference, especially for Gulf historians of the 19th and early 20th century.

9. There are some notable exceptions that do explore deeper social structures in the period before oil and after, including Jill Crystal, *Oil and Politics in the Gulf: Rulers and Merchants in Kuwait and Qatar* (Cambridge: Cambridge University Press, 1995); Nelida Fuccaro, *Histories of City and State in the Persian Gulf: Manama Since 1800* (Cambridge: Cambridge University Press, 2012); Michael Herb, *The Wages of Oil: Parliaments and Economic Development in Kuwait and the UAE* (Ithaca: Cornell University Press, 2014) and A. Fromherz, *Qatar, A Modern History* (Washington, DC: Georgetown University Press, 2016).

10. *Arabian Sands* (London: Longmans, 1959), pp. 256–7.

11. Yacoub Yusuf al Hijji, *Kuwait and the Sea: A Brief Social and Economic History*, trans. F. Bishara (London: Arabian Publishing, 2010).

12. Richard Bulliet, professor of Middle East and World History at Columbia University, wrote this review – quoted on the cover of Lawrence Potter (ed.), *The Persian Gulf in History*, 2009.

13. Jerry Bentley, *Old World Encounters: Cross-Cultural Contacts and Exchanges in Pre-Modern Times* (Oxford: Oxford University Press, 1993). Peter Frankopan, *The Silk Roads: A New History of the World* (New York: Knopf, 2015).

14. Guy Isitt, 'Vikings of the Persian Gulf', *Journal of the Royal Asiatic Society*, vol. 17, no. 4, October 2007, pp. 389–406.

15. For this definition and approach to culture see Clifford Geertz, *The Interpretation of Cultures*, 5.

16. Fiftieth Assembly in *The Assembles of Al-Hariri*, trans. Steingass, Royal Asiatic Society, 1898, 177; also, see B. nationale de France edition dated to the 14th century: Manuscript Arabe 3929 and online <http://gallica.bnf.fr/ark:/12148/btv1b8422962f> (last accessed 28 March 2018).

17. D. T. Potts, *The Arabian Gulf in Antiquity*, Vol. II (Oxford: Oxford University Press, 1990), p. 158.

18. See B. Nationale de France, L'Atlas Catalan, <http://expositions.bnf.fr/ciel/catalan/index.htm> (last accessed 10 October 2017).

19. See a translation of his writings in G. R. Tibbetts, *Arab Navigation in the Indian Ocean before the Coming of the Portuguese* (London: Royal Asiatic Society, 1971).

20. William Palgrave, *Personal Narrative of a Year's Journey through Central and Eastern Arabia (1862–3)* (London: Macmillan, 1883), p. 387.

21. *The Corrupting Sea: A Study of Mediterranean History* (Hoboken: Wiley-Blackwell, 2000).

22. Qtd in Josef Weisehöfer, trans. Azizeh Azodi, *Ancient Persia: From 550 BC to 650 AD* (London: I. B. Tauris, 1998), p. 217.

23. 2 Vols (University of California Press, 1996).

24. *The Birth of the Modern World, 1780–1914* (Oxford: Blackwell, 2004), p. 469. Qtd in Sebastian Conrad, *What Is Global History?* (Princeton: Princeton University Press, 2016).

25. Princeton University Press, 2016, p. 73.

26. Brethren of Purity, *The Case of the Animals vs. Man before the King of the Jinn*, trans. Lenn Goodman and Richard McGregor (Oxford: Oxford University Press, 2009), p. 300.

PART I

GULF COSMOPOLITANISM

2

THE COSMOPOLITAN FIGURE AS ETHICAL EXEMPLAR: NOTES FROM A TENTH-CENTURY GULF ENCYCLOPEDIA

Richard McGregor

At the intersection of continents, between Asia and the Middle East, in southern Iraq, Basra, an anonymous group of scholars gathered to record the sciences of their day. This was shortly before the end of the tenth century, when Islamic theology and law had yet to crystallise, and philosophy was as strong as it would ever be. The authors, collectively known as the Brethren of Purity (*al-Ikhwan al-Safa*), produced a fifty-two-volume encyclopedia, which became known simply as their Epistles (*Rasa'il*). The range of the work was truly comprehensive. It was divided into four parts:

1. The mathematical sciences (with volumes on logic, geometry, astronomy, geography and music).
2. The sciences of natural bodies (with volumes on meteorology, minerals, plants and embryology).
3. The psychological and rational sciences (with volumes on movement, epochs and eras, and cause and effect).
4. Theology (with volumes on magic, talismans, prayer and beliefs).

Historians have recognised the wide-ranging sweep of this encyclopedia, which draws upon 'Pythagorean and Nichomachian arithmetic, numerology and music, Hermetic and Indo-Persian magic and astrology, Aristotelian logic and physics, Gnostic esotericism, neo-Platonic cosmology, theory of emanations and metaphysics, Biblical and Qur'anic prophetology, Platonic concepts of law and leadership, and Buddhist, Zoroastrian and Manichean wisdom and allegory'.[1] It also draws upon the beliefs of the Mandæans, a minority religious group discussed by Professor Charles Häberl in this volume. As a collection, the *Rasa'il* provide a unique window onto the formative period of medieval thought, when various pre-Islamic sciences were still contested. The authors aim not only to be exhaustive, but also to present their material in an accessible form, with the intention of facilitating the widest possible reception. By any measure, the tone of the work is strikingly cosmopolitan. While scholarship has established that the authors were likely Isma'ili Shia in their personal commitments, this *Epistle* is neither dogmatic nor exclusivist when treating matters of culture or religion. Shi'a perspectives are represented, but thanks to the work's breadth and openness, its subsequent life in Islamic intellectual history has transcended communal divisions, allowing the encyclopedia an unparalleled role in the transmission of philosophical and scientific ideas. In this spirit the Brethren repeatedly enjoin us to follow their lead, and to draw knowledge from all sources, regardless of origin.

In volume twenty-two, the epistle on ethics, the authors present an innovative paradigm of the highest of possible human virtues, tying it directly to a culturally and religiously diverse vision of humanity. The central argument of *The Case of the Animals versus Man Before the King of the Jinn* is not that animals are superior to humans – we will return to the nature of this relationship below – but rather that there is a moral lesson to be drawn from the relations between animals and humanity. The Brethren make clear their intention to 'consider the merits and distinctions of the animals, their admirable traits, pleasing natures, and wholesome qualities, and to touch on man's overreaching, oppression, and injustice against the creatures that serve him – the beasts and cattle – and his heedless, impious thanklessness for the blessings for which he should be grateful'.[2] The affective impact of the fable is an important dimension of the communication, and thus the authors explain: 'We've put these themes into the mouths of animals, to make the case clearer and more compelling – more striking in the telling, wittier, livelier, more useful to the listener, and more poignant and thought-provoking in its moral.'[3]

The story takes place on the island of the king of the jinn, where a group of humans, of a racial and religious mixture representing the range of humanity, have been shipwrecked. Upon seeing the peaceful and flourishing animals of the island, the humans begin to trap them, harness them and force them into service. Endowed with speech, the animals complain to the king of the jinn, who summons the humans and representatives of all the animals to his court to resolve the matter. The animals are divided up into kingdoms, which include: the predators, who are represented by the jackal; the birds, who send the nightingale; the swarming creatures, represented by the bee; the birds of prey, who send the parrot; the aquatic animals, who send the frog; and the crawling animals, who are represented by the cricket. The kingdoms and species of the animals are many, and the epistle offers an all-encompassing typology. Parallel with this classification are the divisions among humans. Here geography and environment are important identifiers, as is religion. This chapter will briefly outline the suit the animals bring against humans, and explore several dimensions of the cosmopolitanism that is associated with the ideal human life. Of particular significance is the conclusion of the story, which revolves around a fictional composite human figure – who is at once Muslim and Christian, Greek and Arabian, Indian and Sufi – who articulates a clinching argument based on the shared divine nature of all humans.

Writing in the diverse milieu of the Gulf port of Basra, the Brethren offer a vision of human diversity and interconnectedness which spans the boundaries of race, civilisation and religion. The authors' argument operates with a two-fold gesture. On the one hand, they present the diversity of human races and religions, while on the other hand they bridge those differences with a universally applicable religious virtue. The spiritual elite, then, are not confined to one religious tradition or another – exceptional and rare as they might be in history. We will return to this elite, but first let us turn to religious and cultural diversity.

In a long chapter, the court hears from a series of human spokespersons who, in support of their claim to suzerainty over the animals, list the achievements and high-points of their civilisations. An Iraqi is the first. He points to his homeland as the birthplace of many prophets including Noah and Abraham, and the home of many celebrated ancient kings such as Manujahr, Darius and Ardashir, who built cities, administrations and empires. In response to this bragging, however, a wily jinn servant of the king launches a rebuttal. 'This learned body should know that the human from Iraq has omitted crucial matters from his speech.' What might they be?, asked the King. 'He did not say, "On our account the great Flood was sent, drowning all on the face of the earth." Nor did he say, "Nimrod the Tyrant was one of us." Or boast, "We cast Abraham into the flames."'[4]

Looking around the court, the King then spied 'a man with a lean, brown body, long beard, and a great mane of hair. He was wrapped in a waist-cloth tied about his middle.' This was a man from India, the island of Ceylon, and the second human spokesperson. After boasting of his region's climate, which produces abundant riches and huge animals, he notes the divine benevolence that 'sent prophets to our land and made most of our people sages – like the Buddha, the Brahmins, Bilawhar and Budasf'.[5] Not to escape the biting cross-examination, the Indian is dismissed when the King's jinni sage retorts, 'Had you finished your speech, you would have said, "We are also plagued with burning the bodies of our dead, worship of idols, images, and apes . . ."'

A third human spokesperson is a Jewish Syrian, described as tall and wearing a yellow robe, holding a scroll. In defence of human superiority, he notes that God chose Moses from among all of creation, and gave him the miraculous signs of the white hand and the staff – in addition to the Torah and the books of the prophets. The outspoken jinni then counters with hostile passages from the Qur'ān.

Another spokesperson is a man clad in a woolen robe, bound at the waist with a leather belt, swinging a censer to and fro, 'spreading incense smoke as he sonorously chanted . . .'.[6] This is the Syriac Christian, who champions his religion by noting that God joined his divine substance with the son of Mary, who performed miracles, and led his community of disciples, priests and monks into lives of meekness and monasticism. The outspoken jinni then counters with the claim that Christians should instead be reproved for their trinitarianism, and condemned for worshipping the cross.

The Syrian Christian is then followed by an Arab of the tribe of Quraysh, with deep brown skin, lean and tall, wearing the waist wrap and shoulder wrap of a *hajji*. Invited by the King to speak, the Qurayshi begins his case saying, 'Praised be He who chose us for the best of all faiths, made us the folk of the Qur'an, taught us to read its rule, to fast in Ramadan, to circle the sacred precinct', the Black Stone and the maqam Ibrahim. God gave us 'tidings of the first and the last generations, the reckoning of the Day of Judgement, and the reward promised to prophets, martyrs, and godly folk – the *salihin*'.[7] Not missing the opportunity to deflate human superciliousness, the outspoken and critical jinni replies, 'Say also, "Then after our Prophet we rebelled, forsook and spurned the faith . . . We slew our finest, most virtuous leaders, seeking the world through faith."'

A fair-skinned human with an astronomical instrument in his hand then takes the stand. This is a Byzantine from Greece, who begins his disquisition, 'Praised be God who in bounty and grace caused the Active Intellect to flow forth from His goodness, source of science and mysteries, light of lights, and elements of all spirits . . . Praised be God who from the power of the Soul brought forth the elements with matter and essence.'[8] In this passage, the boastful human claims that being 'Greek' is synonymous with human excellence, represented by wisdom and science. '[God] made us natural rulers, for our virtues, our keen discernments, and our just way of life, our overwhelming intelligence, wonderful arts – medicine, geometry, astronomy . . . He gave us the sciences of measurement and movement, the instruments of astronomy, the talismans, and taught us mathematics and logic, physics and metaphysics.'[9] As a retort to these boasts, the jinni cross-examiner then asks the Byzantine, 'Where did you get these sciences and the wisdom you brag of? Didn't you take some from the Israelites in Ptolemy's time, and some from the scholars of Egypt . . . transplant them into your own lands, and then take credit for them?' In response, the Byzantine refocuses his boast to include a wider vision of scientific and intellectual borrowing among nations. He concedes that 'men do adopt the sciences from one another. Otherwise, where would the Persians have gotten astronomy and cosmology and the use of astronomical instruments, if not from the people of India?'[10]

The last in this list is the Shi'ite from Khurasan, who grounds his version of human superiority in the shared devotional, if unsophisticated, instincts of the common adherents of all religions.

The full spectrum of human diversity extends, not surprisingly, into politics, or at least the need for a variety of kingdoms on earth. In Chapter 24 of the epistle, the humans make the case that 'It's because the ends of humans are many. Their inclinations vary. Their conditions are diverse. So men need many kingdoms.' And, 'With all this diversity [of polity and institutions of government], humans need many rulers. In every land or state a king arises to order its affairs and those of all its people . . . For there are seven climes on earth, and each clime has many lands. Each land has many cities. And every city teems with people – God knows how many! – who differ in language, mores, beliefs, ways of thought and practice, values and temperaments.'[11]

On the subject of diversity, the Syrian Jew returns in Chapter 30, providing an overview of religious pluralism among humanity. He declares, 'It was [God] who favored us with prophesy and inspiration, graced us with miracles and revealed books, the unshakeable verses that bear His divers permissions and prohibitions . . . His dreadful threats and His promises of delight . . . He graced us too with ablutions, purifications, fasts, worship, charity and alms, festivals, churches, or synagogues, sanctified house of God. We have pulpits, ritual observances, ceremonies, and the like.'[12]

Later in the disputation, the animals will recognise this very diversity among human religions, but will point to it as a flaw, and evidence of the discordant and conflicting souls that make up humanity. In Chapter 39, the King asks for details about this diversity, at which point he is told the source is: 'Their diverse notions, rival sects, competing schools, and varied religions. Among them you find Jews, Christians, Sabians, Magians, pagan idolaters, and worshippers of the sun and moon, stars and constellations, among other things. And you'll find that the followers of a single faith also split into many sects and schools. There are Samaritans, Ananites, and Exilarchs, Nestorians, Jacobites, and Melkites, Dualists, Khurramites, Mazdakites, and Manichaeans, Brahmins, Buddhists, and Disanites, Kharijites, Nasibites, Rafidites, Murji'ites, Qadarites, Jahmites, Mu'tazilites, Sunnis, Jabrites – among many other opinions and schools, all calling each other unbelievers, cursing, and killing each other.'[13] This diversity, the animals claim, is a sign of confusion and bad theology. In rebuttal, however, the Persian defends the pluralistic nature of human religiosity. When asked by the King why so many doctrines, sects and creeds persist, the Persian provides a teleological rationale: 'Because religion, schools, and sects are just different paths, different avenues of approach. Our goal is one. Whichever path we take, *There is the face of God* (Q 2: 115).[14]

The final chapter of the epistle presents a dramatic denouement. It begins with an Arab Hijazi pointing to the fact that prophets, imams, sages, poets, ascetics and saints are only to be found among humans, as evidence of humanity's superiority. Upon hearing this, the animals concede the point, drop their suit, and declare that this indeed is something extraordinary. This is not the end of the story, however. Along with the jinn, the animals then ask for more information on these saintly persons. The last person to speak is not a representative of one nation or religion, but rather an embodiment of the cosmopolitanism the humans have been celebrating. He is 'Persian by breeding, Arabian by faith, a *hanif* by confession, Iraqi in culture, Hebrew in lore, Christian in manner, Damascene in devotion, Greek in science, Indian in discernment, Sufi in intimations, regal in character, masterful in thought, and divine in awareness'.[15] Perhaps surprisingly, his final statement is quite brief. He tells the court that although many have sought to recount the attributes and noble deeds of the saints, none has managed to do more than scratch the surface. With this abrupt ending, we are left wondering about this elusive attribute, which apparently represents what is uniquely human about humanity. This attribute is clearly 'sanctity' (*walaya*), the Islamic concept of a widened capacity for inspiration, esoteric knowledge and wisdom. This idea of an enlarged capacity for sanctity was not original to the Brethren. It had been key in Shi'ism and Sufism earlier, but its use here in a vision of universal human attributes, psychology and ethics – transcending and yet embracing human cultural diversity – is likely unprecedented.

The resolution of the court case seems to confirm the humans in their superiority to the animals. Due to its capacity to produce inspired saintly figures – if only on rare occasions – humanity can lay claim to a unique spiritual potential. The animals recognise that this is not possible for them. Yet it does not follow that animals are to suffer for ever as slaves of the humans; and certainly there is no licence here for cruelty or abuse. In short, the fable's conclusion is that humanity has a superior capacity, which it should struggle to realise. The court's judgment is not that the animals are mistaken, that their claims are erroneous, or that their beliefs and practices are false. On the contrary, the conclusion points to the overlap and shared sensibilities of animals and humans. The clinching evidence in the case, the final exhibit, was after all a saintly figure whose description defies words: 'Many have cited their virtues, and preachers in public assemblies have devoted their lives down through the ages to sermons dilating on their merits and their godly ways, without ever reaching the pith of the matter.'[16] The significance of this discursive limit should not be overlooked. Humans cannot even describe the deeds, knowledge and character of their saints. Neither can the animals. Indeed, they would like to know more: 'tell us, O humans, of the qualities and lives of these persons, inform us of their insights and ways, their virtues and godly doings, if you know aught of these . . . The whole court fell silent, pondering the question. But no one had an answer' (p. 313).

Notes

1. Abbas Hamdani, 'Religious Tolerance in the *Rasa'il Ikhwan al-Safa*', p. 137.
2. Al-Ikhwan al-Safa, *Epistles of the Brethren of Purity*, p. 65.
3. Ibid.
4. Ibid., p. 205.
5. Ibid., p. 206.
6. Ibid., p. 209.
7. Ibid., p. 212.
8. Ibid., p. 214.
9. Ibid., p. 216.
10. Ibid., pp. 216–18.
11. Ibid., pp. 230–1.
12. Ibid., p. 255.
13. Ibid., p. 302.
14. Ibid., p. 303.
15. Ibid., p. 314. The term *hanif* refers to a believer who is monotheist before having heard the revelation.
16. Ibid., p. 315.

Bibliography

Al-Ikhwan al-Safa (The Brethren of Purity), *Epistles of the Brethren of Purity: The Case of the Animals versus Man before the King of the Jinn: An English Translation of Epistle 22*, ed. and trans. Lenn E. Goodman and Richard McGregor (London: Oxford University Press, 2012).

Hamdani, Abbas, 'Religious Tolerance in the *Rasa'il Ikhwan al-Safa*', in Tzvi Langerman and Josef Stern (eds), *Adaptations and Innovations: Studies on the Interaction Between Jewish and Islamic Thought and Literature* (London: Peeters, 2007), pp. 137–42.

3

THE GULF: A COSMOPOLITAN MOBILE SOCIETY – HORMUZ, 1475–1515 CE

Valeria Piacentini Fiorani

Liquid spaces have never been a barrier to the mobility of the societies settled on their seaboards. The Gulf is no exception. Archaeological evidence and literary sources unanimously maintain this image. Political and military upheavals did not hamper the crossing of the sea or the continuous traditional movements of local peoples sharing their individual cultural influences. Personal relations, and even marriages and ordinary practices, went on in spite of imperial or political upheavals. New political structures and new patterns of peopling were reorganised through new balances and counterbalances of power. Urban centres flourished and decayed. But urban life and traditional activities never came to an end, shaping the deep roots of a mobile, cosmopolitan society that still prospers all along the lands surrounding this liquid region, giving life to a cultural *unicum per se*. [1] The aim of the following chapter is to take a closer look at the 'underground world' of the Gulf and its intrinsic strength and forces.

My chapter will focus on the kingdom of Hormuz. Made famous in Europe at the end of the fourteenth century by the description of Marco Polo (d. 1324 CE), Hormuz was long a great maritime dominion whose magnificent capital city rose on a rocky island, the island of Jarun, located at the entrance of the Gulf, at the crucial strategic Strait of Hormuz. I will examine a particularly critical time for the Hormuz Kingdom: the turn of the sixteenth century. This was just after Europeans had discovered the South African route to India. Locally, it was a time marked by the accession to the throne of Hormuz of Salghur Shah (d. 1505 CE) after a bloody internecine war, and the appearance on the maritime scene of two new dominant and ambitious actors: the Portuguese, newly arrived on the scene with their formidable fleet and firepower, on the one hand, and the Safavids, with their maritime ambitions, on the other. Despite recurrent warfare and spasmodic intrigues, despite tribal strife in Arabia and on some occasions sharp competition between seaboard and hinterland, the crown of Hormuz and its administrative system managed to keep to a pragmatic political strategy rooted in the traditional forces of the Gulf. This ensured a cultural continuity in the region for more than one century.

Here, I will restrict myself to recalling the main stages of this period, keeping one special eye on Hormuz and another on Oman and the Arabian eastern coastal regions. These regions, linked for centuries by personal relations and common interests, after the ravages brought by Portuguese attacks and the conquests of the major ports and strategic strongholds, would soon develop again in a renewed and even tighter network of politics, business and culture, destined to survive the decline and final collapse of the kingdom of Hormuz and its structure, and reorganise and survive elsewhere.

Salghur Shah (1475–1505) and his Omani Great Vizier, *Ḥājjī* 'Attar

The first stage in this history is Salghur Shah's rise to the throne of the Kingdom of Hormuz. He was crown-prince and governor (*wakīl*) of Qalat, son of the Hormuzi Prince Turanshah II (1436–70/1). Hormuz had long been an autonomous domain under the sovereignty of one or other potentates ruling on the Iranian land mass. By the turn of the fourteenth century, two enlightened personalities, Mahmud Qalhati (1242–77/8) and his Turkish slave Ayyaz, regent for the young prince (1291–1311), reorganised the realm, shifted the capital city of Hormuz from *terra firma* to an insular position on the island of Jarun, militarised the Iranian and Arab seaboards, building a chain of fortresses, reinforced matrimonial alliances and allegiances with the Arab neighbours, and introduced new administrative practices in an amalgam of cultural concepts, which, in later centuries, were to give a characteristic stamp to Hormuz government and society. Though regularly paying the owed tributes to the Timurid emperors and the various Turkmen potentates on the Iranian land mass, they ensured for their dominion a de facto independence. Turanshah II's long and enlightened rule allowed the reorganisation and further consolidation of the institutional system of Hormuz and its interlinks with its associated partners (Oman and the Kij-u-Makran realm in the hinterland of present Southern Makran). With the final victory on Qays, the superb harbour-town of the economic/financial empire of Fars rising on an islet facing the latter's seaboard (first half of the 14th century), Hormuz inherited Qays' international maritime dominions and full control over the Strait. Instead of encouraging systemic piracy, robbing and sacking, Hormuz developed a mercantile structure. Turanshah II consolidated his power structure through matrimonial alliances and shrewd balances between the various components of the kingdom. Literary evidence is not ambiguous.[2] His ability was to engage the main Arab groups and their interests (i.e. the tribes of the hinterland and the mercantile, urban milieu of the seaboard) within the Hormuzi system and its society. Convergences and allegiances expanded to other territories, including a vast liquid space beyond the Strait, encompassed by three territorial realities: Hormuz and its dominions; Oman and its coastal sheikhdoms and delicate balances with the hinterland; and the Kij-u-Makran and its well-attended land routes. These were the three axes, whose apexes were the harbour-town of New Hormuz on the island of Jarun, the stunning harbour-town of Qalhat along the Omani seaboard, and Kij along the Kich river with its harbour-town of Tiz, in the Kij-u-Makran. All in all, it was a vast liquid space, a positive mobile, international, cosmopolitan society.[3]

When Turanshah II came to power, new disorders were shaking Arabia: internal strife, disintegration of the Rasulid hold in Yemen, the Sunni Tahirids' seizure of power; religious enmities and feuds between Malikite and Ibadi sheikhdoms; Nabhan princes versus the rising power of the Bani Jabr tribe; raids and pillaging of the coastal centres; disruption of the main pilgrimage routes of Arabia; and so on. Despite all this, the long reign of Turanshah II – he himself a man of learning and a poet – is recalled by literary sources as a period of prosperity and well-being.[4] He used shrewd mechanisms to balance and counterbalance Turkish Lords, who held power de jure on the Iranian mainland, the Arab components of the region, and the arrogant and unreliable Persian landlords and merchant families settled all along the seaboards. He created a pragmatic ruling system based on a written bureaucratic apparatus, an autonomous military structure and a formidable economic force. The bureaucratic apparatus was bilingual (Arabic and Persian), and represented the spine of the institutional administration. The military structure was based around the geography of the Gulf, independent from the powerful armies running on the mainland. The economic structure was represented by the merchant families and their entourage settled on one or the other region of this dominion, and the main land and sea trade routes of their vast range of international business and their financial-economic empires.[5]

These articulated structures of bureaucracy, military and economy were well supported by a calibrated system of negotiations and compensations. In times of disorders and ravages on one or the other side of the sea, people could find safe shelter, sanctuary and military support, too, on the other side. Land troops were generally supplied by the tribal communities of Arabia; when in danger of raids and attacks, the 'military' fleet was supplied by the ships of the merchant families settled all along these liquid spaces. All in all, we are confronted with a well-attuned balance between complementary powers and related forces: a flexible system, that was ready to pay special duties to the lords in command on the land mass, without implying any permanent vassalage, in order to have safe passage (and escorts when needed) for caravans and merchants, and thus access to the markets of the interior. In addition, cultural links between the various shores of the seas had created a variegated artistic and intellectual cultural atmosphere, which enlivened the court and the main centres of this particular maritime structure and its urban milieu.[6]

The accession to the throne of Hormuz by Salghur Shah marked a turning point in these equilibriums and a sharp diversion in favour of Arabia. Previously, after the enthronement of his brother, Shihab al-Din, Salghur had been appointed as *wakīl* of the rich province of Qalhat, and married to a Nabhan princess (The Nabhan were an elite family who had ruled large parts of Oman for centuries). He began to rise in power and reputation as a powerful pretender to the throne. The Iranian elite, however, disliked him: 'he wore Arab dresses . . . spoke Arabic . . . and behaved according to Arab customs.' Nimdihi states that he 'emanated the strength and determination of a tyrant'.[7] Be that as it may, he certainly emerged as a capable character, supported by the Arabs, determined to become ruler of Hormuz. His land-troops were the Bani Jabr; his fleet was provided by the two raises (commanders, military superintendents) of the fortress of Shilav/Siraf on the Iranian coast. And he won access to the throne at Julfar, through what the scholar Christian Velde called a well-planned co-ordination between Bedouin troops and marine units.[8] The city of Julfar succumbed politically to the new ruler of Hormuz, and with Julfar also Bahrain, Qatif and other rich ports inside and outside the Gulf.[9]

However, the wider political context was rapidly changing. In 1503, the Qizilbash of Isma'il Shah had conquered Semnan and Fars with its capital city Shiraz. Thence, they continued to push southwards to Yazd and the sea. But at the time, the sea was still beyond their reach; Safavid interest for the sea will come later. Be that as it may, Salghur hurried to pay tribute, since his reign was facing a phase of political changes and adjustment in the organisation of the whole state-apparatus (military, economic and administrative). The main target was to overcome the problems posed by his accession to the throne, and, in particular, to put an end to the interminable fights between the various components of the social milieu. Therefore, though hard-pressed by the Safavid might and the ambitions of the Laris' dervish order (*tariqa*), his priority went to the continuous feuds between the Arab component of his kingdom and the Iranian one. As a result, the Iranian elements, still prominent at court and in the institutional organisation of the reign (administrative as well as mercantile), became more and more unreliable; distrusting Salghur's Arab feelings, they were inclined to come to political terms with the new Turkish power on the Iranian land mass. This will be a constant political factor for the following century, that will affect on more than one occasion the Gulf's balances. It was at this point that Salghur abruptly changed his policy. Realising the seriousness of the situation, he turned his back on the treacherous Iranian components of his realm and sought to offset them by favouring the Arab component. He claimed to be a descendant of Hud, and that his lineage was from Qahtan (progenitor of the South Arabs);[10] then he gave a drastic response to the Iranian disloyalty, and at the same time challenged the Safavid arrogance, too, by putting into force an embargo on Iranian harbours. In other words, he forbade ships to enter or leave Iranian harbours loaded with strategic raw material – such as pitch, wood, rope, iron, copper – essential for the building or repair of local vessels. The consequence was that the Iranian harbours and the merchant families settled there lost their naval independence, since they were no longer able to depend on a fleet of their own. At the same time, the Safavid ambitions and their thrust to the sea lost a precious ally.[11]

Shipping activity and related wealth were diverted towards the Arabian coast, its harbours and outlets to the sea, which rose in mercantile and military/strategic importance: Baleed, Sur, Qalhat, Quriyat, Tibi, Muscat,

Rustaq and Nahal, Julfar, Khawr Fakkan, Daba, Bahrain and Qatif stood out in this period as the main ports of call and shipyards along the maritime routes to and from the Gulf. The loyalty of the Arabian seaboard continued, ensured by a canny matrimonial policy and a no less clever policy in appointing officials in the most strategic ports and fortresses.[12]

This phase of this crucial historical period is well documented by Nimdihi, who was employee and historian at the Hormuzi court. Personal *kātib* (secretary) to the great vizier of the ruler of Hormuz, he never overemphasises his patrons' policy. His brisk chronicle gives a first-hand narrative of the events taking place in and outside the Gulf; particularly informative is the vizier's correspondence with the Arab tribal chiefs and the peoples of the hinterland. On the whole, Nimdihi's report and correspondence give an objective inside view of the time, which allows us to clearly perceive, beyond the resolute temperament of Salghur, the shrewd personality of his vizier, an Omani character, *Hājjī* 'Attar, destined to forge Hormuz's and the Gulf's destiny in the following years up to Hormuz's capitulation to a new actor on the Gulf stage, the Portuguese.[13] Salghur's rule and, after his death, *Hājjī* 'Attar's practical running of all public affairs for the weak young successors, managed to keep alive the essence of the cultural atmosphere so far preserved by Hormuz's dynasty through a policy based on a sensible equilibrium between the Iranian component of the realm and the foreign new Turkish aristocracy looming in Iran, on the one hand, and the Iranian component and the Arab populace and its various social segments and interest groups on the other. With particular regard to the Arabs, 'Attar carried out a well-attuned policy of conciliation between the Arab population of the interior and that of the coast, where, in particular, the Arab populace was mixed with Iranian enclaves and families. The vizier's correspondence reported in Nimdihi's chronicle is particularly telling, and becomes a major source with regard to the actual components of the social milieu of the time all along the Iranian and Arabian seaboards. These connections are also well evidenced by the family names of prominent merchants settled all along the Arabian coastal region, and officials appointed by the Crown in the main harbour-towns and strongholds there. Often there recur names such as Tarumi, Khunji, Fali, Abzari, Iji – from Iranian place names along its coastal areas – or that of Shabankara'i (these latter, Kurdish peoples who played a major role in the Fars' events) and others. All of them are mentioned and stem out when referring to the most wealthy communities of Arabia.

Europe in Search of Spices: The Portuguese and Hormuz

As mentioned above, the Portuguese opened a new phase in the life and activities of the Gulf.[14] They are called 'faranghi' (that is, foreigners), or, in some cases, 'masihi' (Christians); however, their presence did not impress the official writing at the court of Hormuz. They were not perceived as a threat to the realm but as a new powerful actor, one that could be played as a counterbalance against the rising might of the Safavids and the intrigues of their Turkish aristocracy and ferocious militias. Salghur was assassinated by his own son and successor, Turanshsh IV, one of the few members of the royal family not to be murdered or blinded; but he was destined to reign for only a few months. New rivalries and feuds followed until the end of the 1507, when the young Sayf al-Din Aba Nadar became *malik* of Hormuz. Sayf al-Din was an irresolute character, completely under the sway of his omnipotent Omani minister, *Hājjī* 'Attar: 'Cojeattar, wazir y mouro principal', as the Portuguese sources define him. A true Arab, however. As long as he lived he never trusted the Iranian component of the realm (officials, aristocracy, merchants), whom he considered ready to sell themselves at any opportunity to the more powerful rival. But he did not trust the Turks, either, sly and superior.

Thus, when in 1507 Alfonso d'Albuquerque arrived with his fleet in front of the island of Jarun, 'Attar opened for the infant prince a subtle game between the Safavids and the Portuguese, playing the one against the other, a game that would succeed as long as he lived, but at the end would completely unbalance the already delicate balance between the Turkish and Iranian component on the one hand and the Omani and Arab one on the other. Realistic and lucid, he will run the realm for another decade; his death will sign a harsh set-back in the 'diplomatic' game of the crown of Hormuz. But, on a closer reading of the events and how they are depicted by contemporary literary sources, it is possible to state that it did not signal the end of that cosmopolitan milieu and mobile society typical of the Gulf and its very strength.

According to the strategy planned by Albuquerque, the Lusitanian dominion in the Indian Ocean should be based on a form of supremacy and control of the sea, based on a number of military strongholds, in practice a triangle with its points in Goa, Malacca and Hormuz to the west. The vast liquid region thus delimited followed the laws imposed by the monsoons and by the ships that followed the routes imposed by these seasonal winds. At the terminals of these maritime routes were the ports and outlets of a commercial network that went back thousands of years. The three strongholds, adequately fortified, would represent as many bases of military support and supplies for the Portuguese fleet. Territorial conquest was not part of this plan, but rather the establishment of treaties of friendship and commerce with the local rulers, once their military and defensive structures had been dismantled. Then, once the military action and the disruption of the conquest would be over and done, the regional traditional patterns of life, with their systemic structures and balances, would start and prosper again under the Lusitanian military shield.

A more accurate analysis, and archival sources, today allow us to affirm that Albuquerque's project was based on the body of scientific, astronomical and cartographic information that the Portuguese crown prince, the *Infante* Henry the Navigator, had collected at Sagres when he formulated also his famous theories and plans for the Ocean's travel and discovery. Undoubtedly, these extraordinary elements of scientific knowledge inspired the rounding of Africa and the long sea routes from Europe to India and China, and discovered the way to master the monsoon winds and their challenges, mortal to any fleet not familiar with these traitorous winds. And there is no doubt, either, that at the time these were major achievements. But Alfonso d'Albuquerque's plans were even more daring. The naval Portuguese officers – well-trained and skilled in the new nautical sciences and supported by experienced pilots – could well succeed in outflanking the Ottoman Empire and its arrogant supremacy in the Levant and the Eastern Mediterranean waters. And, as would be clear soon afterwards, they could also succeed in outflanking the Venetians, thus winning for the Lusitanian Crown and its fleet full control over the Ocean and its two branches to the west, the Red Sea and the Gulf, and with them immense wealth in terms of spices. The Crown approved the plan and gave its support to Alfonso d'Albuquerque. In the official view, it had the advantage of limited costs and only relative risks, insofar as it did not imply the conquest of lands so far virtually unknown – if not for travellers' accounts and literary circles' talk – and did not imply the 'acquisition' of foreign and potentially 'unfaithful subjects'. Success depended on naval and nautical experience and superiority, which Portugal at the time undoubtedly held given its advanced nautical techniques and cartographic knowledge. In return, the Crown could well see the advantages and profits that such an empire could give: if the project were successful, Portugal would, while the Great European Powers were involved in fighting each other on the continent and the Baltic region, hold the monopoly over an extremely profitable trade in spices and other commodities much wanted in Europe.

So, the Lusitanian fleet, under the authoritative command of Albuquerque, on the trail of Vasco da Gama, outflanked the Ottomans in the Mediterranean Sea and their control of the land-routes from/to the Levant, outflanked the Arabs too, and put in check the Venetians and Genoese financial and maritime power, throwing itself into the overseas adventure.

Goa and Malacca were to be easy acquisitions compared to New Hormuz and its maritime, mercantile dominion. The latter succeeded in barring the way to Alfonso d'Albuquerque's great project for almost two decades. In addition, in the Red Sea the Portuguese found firm resistance from the last Mamluks and then, after 1517, from the Ottomans (for the occasion allied with Venice), who barred that sea to their ambitions and plans. Consequently, the Gulf acquired a centrality of its own. Military control and dismantlement of the chain of fortresses and strongholds of Hormuz on both coasts became a strategic imperative. Only thus would the Ocean's maritime trade be secured to the Lusitanian Crown, and with it would access to the rich markets of Persia and Central Asia become a reality. Albuquerque soon realised that control of the access to the Strait meant also the possibility – when convenient – of closing this liquid route to any other foreign economic-financial rival. In any case, without control of the Gulf the Portuguese plans for a monopoly over given goods and markets could not be achieved.[15]

The First Siege (1507)[16]

After a first siege and a naval battle (more a skirmish than a battle), *Hājjī* 'Attar advised Sayf al-Din to come to an agreement with the Portuguese and start negotiations. The young ruler agreed to pay tribute in return for Portuguese protection. At this point, an event happened without precedent: the Portuguese disembarked to seal the pact, and, instead of withdrawing after the customary banquet, they began to reorganise the city. The sovereign and his court were confined to a residence on the island, and the royal palace-castle was taken by the Portuguese, who started to refurbish it into a mighty sea-front fortress – known as the *Fortaleza*, a structure typical of the Portuguese colonial military architecture. The local inhabitants were initially shocked; then, a growing hostility spread in reaction to a behaviour that went against every custom. The atmosphere was tense, but there was no insurrection – perhaps due to fear produced by the new military techniques of these foreigners and, likely, also the strength of their warships (*nãos*) and their cannons. The astute *Hājjī* 'Attar advised the king to adopt a strategy of cautious watching and waiting. On the Iranian mainland there were always the Safavids, now well established in Fars. Conversely, all around the island of Jarun there were its two insular sentinels – Kishm and Larak – and along the seabords its fortresses and garrisons, vigilant custodians of the realm's security and prosperity. Sayf al-Din could always ask the Shah of Persia to intervene – since, in effect, he was still his vassal – or appeal once again to the solidarity of his own peoples. Secret negotiations were started with the Safavid governor of Fars, to whom Hormuz continued to pay regular tribute 'for the *castella* which were on terrafirma', and at the same time garrisons and raises were put on alert. The population's sentiments on the island became increasingly intolerant; open revolt could be expected every moment.

And revolt broke out – not, however, between the people of Hormuz, but between the Portuguese, in the form of a real mutiny. The troops of Albuquerque – already severely strained – mutinied. A violent outbreak of dysentery, responsible for numerous victims among the Portuguese contingent, was the catalyst which set off the revolt. Yet, other causes can be sought in a combination of unfavourable circumstances: the unbearable climate, shortage of water, difficulty in obtaining supplies of foodstuffs, the hard work of building the *Fortaleza*, the discomfort the troops had suffered over years and years of campaigning on the seas and far from their homeland and families, the hostility of the populaces they had met and fought against and the relatively few advantages so far enjoyed, and – not least – the poor booty obtained from the campaign against Hormuz, it having been strictly forbidden to sack the city, and any contact with the local population being punished by hanging.

Thus it was that three Portuguese captains deserted with their ships. At this point, the Governor and Viceroy of the Portuguese Indies, who from 1505 on was the Duke of Almeida, repudiated the action taken by his admiral, Alfonso d'Albuquerque, and ordered him to leave the island. Thus ended the first Portuguese siege and occupation of the island of Hormuz.

The Second Siege of New Hormuz (1508–9)

Despite all, Albuquerque did not abandon his project of giving life to a Portuguese mercantile empire in the Indian Ocean. In 1507, Alfonso d'Albuquerque had bound his head and obeyed the orders of the Viceroy. But this did not mean that he had also abandoned his plans. Strengthened by his previous experience, he decided to adopt the same policy of waiting and boycotting, exploiting the superior firepower of his fleet. He left two captains, Martim Coelho and Diego de Mello, heading a fleet in the Gulf with the task of systematically blocking the island of Jarun and boarding all convoys to/from New Hormuz. At the same time, he ordered them to wage co-ordinated attacks on the islands of Kishm and Larak, on which Hormuz depended for supplies in water, and to fire their cannons against the coastal strongholds so as to weaken any military resistance outside the capital city. The objective was to harass Hormuz's business and break down the morale of its population until it was ready to surrender.

These orders were promptly obeyed, thanks also to the fact that sacking and taking booty was allowed. In 1508, Qalhat was bombarded from the sea, taken and heavily sacked; the city was devastated and all fortifications torn down. A similar fate awaited Socotra, Sohar, Muscat, Rustaq and other ports at the entrance to the Gulf. The blockading of the convoys also met with success.

At this point, Sayf al-Din once again opened negotiations with the Portuguese, offering to pay them tribute and give them access to Hormuz's markets, in line with the local custom. However, and despite the heavy losses suffered, on the advice of his vizier, the *malik* refused Albuquerque permission to land on the island and take up again the work on the fortress, which in the meantime had been completed and occupied by the young ruler and his court. Albuquerque rejected these conditions, and resumed his activities at sea. Hostilities broke out again. But that 'underground world' which embodied the backbone of the system set up by Hormuz, based on the very components of the Gulf, held out.

I have indulged in these facts because in these precise circumstances it is well possible to perceive the real strength of this maritime dominion, the rationality and soundness of its organisation and structures, and the determination of its cosmopolitan, mobile society. In other words, apart from the official events as recorded by chronicles and preserved in archives, we are confronted with another reality; we are confronted with the features typical of this branch of the Indian Ocean, the Gulf's very forces, which, for centuries if not millennia, had ruled the life of these liquid spaces, surviving domestic feuds and foreigners' arrogance and ambitions, wars and disruptions.

First of all, we can see the tenacity of Hormuz's ruling class – not only the ruling class on the besieged town on the island of Jarun, but all the commanders throughout Hormuz's dominions, the raises of the fortresses along the seaboards and on the mainland, the governors of the provinces, and the allied partners of the kingdom. Still, even more notably, we can also witness the loyalty and faithfulness of this populace of navigators and merchants which, when confronted with direct attacks, despite severe losses and devastations was capable of overcoming internal rivalries and feuds, and providing the Centre (in this case the Hormuzi crown) with ships, land troops, foodstuffs and supplies, and support in human and natural resources. All in all, it is possible to say that, more than the difficulties of the sea and the terrain, it was this unexpected resistance that defeated the firepower of the Portuguese and forced Albuquerque to suspend the siege for the second time, withdrawing the ships under Coelho and de Mello's command. Thus ended the second attempt of the Portuguese to force an entry into the Gulf.

The third siege and capitulation (1515)

The situation continued in much the same way until 1514, the year in which *Hājjī* 'Attar died. As long as he lived, the minister had always refused to cede in any way; rather, with his firm stance, he had succeeded in restoring order to the realm and in rallying its forces – the very forces of the Gulf – around the Crown.

Having in his turn, in 1509, become second Governor and Viceroy of the Portuguese Indies, Alfonso d'Albuquerque again took up his great project. While New Hormuz continued to hold out, other strongholds and fortresses were attacked. On 25 November 1510 Goa fell, and Malacca succumbed the following year. Hormuz obstinately continued to resist and to block access to the Gulf, thus preventing the Portuguese from 'closing' their strategic triangle. With even greater determination, the boycotting of Hormuz's convoys was taken up once more, along with attacks on the land-based fortresses. But no tangible success was attained. Hormuz (and its allies) remained the unquestioned master of the region.

In 1514, with the death of *Ḥājjī* ʿAttar, things changed. Sayf al-Din found himself surrounded by untrustworthy and greedy ministers. These were mainly of Iranian extraction and determined to overthrow the policy of the Omani vizier, in order to place power and wealth in Iranian hands again. Their first move, therefore, was to turn to the Lord on the Iranian land mass and, unlike the political line followed by ʿAttar, they started negotiating with Ismaʿil Shah, aiming at a positive alliance with the Safavid emperor in exchange for the payment of heavier tribute by Hormuz.

Albuquerque, having learnt from the experience of his previous failures, decided to play the same game as the locals. Rather than attempting yet again to land on the island of Jarun, he turned his attention against the coastal and inland system of fortresses, leaving the petty local power to destroy itself from within.

Thus, a new military action began in the Gulf. The coastal and island defences of Hormuz were, one by one, systematically isolated, attacked, conquered and ferociously sacked and dismantled. The capital city was deprived of regular supplies of foodstuffs and drinking water. Mercantile convoys were intercepted, attacked and sacked. And then a subtle game of cunning began. Informed by spies of the real situation of rivalries, ambitions, greed, and groups of power at court, Albuquerque in his turn opened secret negotiations with the ruler.

In the space of nearly one year, Sayf al-Din, deprived of his Arab support, had found himself practically at the mercy of his entourage, his power and very life in serious danger. Crushed between the intrigues of his new ministers and counsellors and the ever-looming threat of the Portuguese fleet, he decided that Albuquerque represented the lesser of the two evils. After the conquest of the strongholds of Suru and Gamrun on the Iranian coast (practically the place where Bandar Abbas today rises), New Hormuz lay virtually at the mercy of the Governor and Viceroy of the Portuguese Indies. At this point, he had no alternative, and turned to Albuquerque.

He accepted all conditions imposed. He asked only one pledge in return, and this was satisfied during the solemn banquet with which the Hormuzians and the Portuguese celebrated the agreement: the dangerous counsellors were slaughtered at the very feet of Sayf al-Din, it would seem by the very hand of one of the nephews who accompanied Alfonso d'Albuquerque to the meeting. Thus, the capitulation of Hormuz was signed with blood, and with blood was the Treaty of Friendship and Trade signed between the realm of Hormuz and Portugal.

The local population was disarmed, opponents were allowed to leave the island unhurt, and the fortress begun some years earlier was evacuated by the *malik* and his court and definitely occupied by the Portuguese, the artillery – probably provided by the Ottomans – being dismantled.[17] The princes and rebels were captured and sent to the Indies. Sayf al-Din, in exchange, was assured that his own life would be safe under Portuguese protection, together with legitimate succession for his heirs. However, nobody was allowed to leave the island without a special patent from the Portuguese Captain of the *Fortaleza*, permanently posted there. For his part, the Captain of the *Fortaleza* severely forbade his own men to leave the fort or to have any contact or intercourse with the local population.

Here, I wish to hang on some terms of the Treaty that, in my personal view and within this context, deserve a closer look. The Crown's sovereignty over his own traditional subjects was guaranteed, with specific regard to personal statute and religious affairs, in particular where Islam was concerned. In exchange for the payment of tribute, commercial traffic was allowed to return with the same frequency and intensity as in the past, and according to the traditional codes. The monopoly of only a few goods passed from the ruler and merchants of Hormuz into the hands of the Portuguese: spices and drugs. Otherwise, business could be resumed as in the past.

With this treaty, Albuquerque finally had the missing ring of his empire, and crowned his project in the Indies. However, he also achieved other, no less interesting goals: Persia was in check, and he could oblige the Safavids – who had no fleet and no outlet to the sea – to pay a special toll and depend on Portugal for all transactions by sea, and the impressive volume of traffics which the rebirth of a market economy in Iran had brought to unprecedented rates with the Ottoman empire, the European courts and Asia. Furthermore, with this treaty Albuquerque also held Europe in check, a new and rapidly expanding Europe of conquests and markets which, for a century and more, would attempt in vain to wrest from Portugal – and the Spanish crown for the brief period of the union – its superiority in the Indian Ocean and its monopoly over spices.

It is also worth noting that this Treaty – with its final clauses – did not interrupt the traditional political-institutional and cultural system that had always animated the life of the Gulf and adjoining waters. In other terms, the final clauses allowed the system set up by the Hormuzi ruling class to survive for one century ahead in name of what can be called the 'reorganisation of a pre-existing structure of relations'. It is a fact that – with the Treaty of Friendship and Trade – Hormuz had de facto and de jure lost its independence. It is also a positive fact that, for the first time, a foreign garrison was permanently established in the capital city of the realm and in other once-renowned harbour-towns and strongholds which once had been powerful allies and vigilant sentinels of the splendid centre of the realm. Yet it is also a positive fact that this Treaty did not signal the cultural and mercantile decline of the Gulf – anything but.

The realm of Hormuz still had a fleet, strategic links and allegiances, personal connections inside and outside the Gulf: a de facto power, which was both cultural and economic. Hormuz still had mercantile allies and personal relationships along the main commercial routes. On a closer analysis, we are still confronted with a system based on the very forces of the Gulf and its seas, a system that Salghur Shah had inherited from his father and that he had further reinforced, a system well tested during the Portuguese sieges, when the light fleets of the Gulf easily sailed in rocky shallow waters and were master of those routes that the galleys and *nãos* of Albuquerque could not follow. And it is a positive fact that after 1515, once again the very forces of the Gulf rallied. Once again merchants would unite and give money, men and ships in the name of a common cultural unity and defence, imposing their own rules. Settled life with its characteristic aspects (hydraulic agriculture, mercantile activities, craftsmanship and speculative undertakings) would reorganise and flourish again.[18]

The 'Underground World' and the Deep Forces of the Gulf

A closer look at the events which took place during the short span of time here under consideration has allowed us to see the regional mechanisms of power and to perceive the very forces behind them, apart from the official façade. And here, a feature typical of these liquid spaces emerges with great clarity. The arrival of new conquerors and foreign powers with their formidable armaments and technologies did not succeed in shattering what can properly be called, in the words of C. E. Bosworth, the 'underworld' of the Gulf. Today, this world is no longer mere conjecture. It is a definite 'underground' world, which existed not only within crowded towns, busy markets and well-fortified fortresses, or out in countryside and villages and in the vastness of the desert, but on the seas also. A world of which we do have information in written and oral sources, and in archaeological evidence. A world that embraces a mobile, cosmopolitan society with its own traditions and customs. A world where merchants and bureaucrats ('men of pen'), artists, poets and 'men of science' and law were highly influential, not only at court but also among the common people. A world of fishermen and sailors. A world with its own traditional activities and patterns of living deeply rooted in a remote past. And, on a closer analysis of the available material and literary evidence, it is also possible to glimpse another dimension of this underworld: a social dimension where popular entertainers and story-tellers, popular preachers, *pir*, sellers of relics of Muslim martyrs, ascetics and mystics of different religious creeds had a role to play. They could bring to the masses a more comprehensible and palatable version of the faith, fulfilling an educational role that, in given circumstances, gained them prestige and influence. They could also rally popular consensus and support around the Crown. This is what happened during these thirty years or so, and this makes it possible to give a reasonable explanation for the events taking place in the Gulf and its adjoining waters. We are confronted with a de facto power: the very gears that made facts turn and allowed Hormuz and its system to survive the ominous military strength of the various powers that held de jure control of the Iranian land mass countering those powers.

As was said above, this underworld is no longer mere conjecture. It is a precious cultural legacy that, during periods of disruption, swiftly shifted to new niches, under the aegis of some other regional actor. Nevertheless, it survived, as it had survived centuries before in the time of the Buhids and their impressive land troops in the tenth century, or the Turks and the Mongol armies with their fearful archers soon afterwards, or Tamerlane and after him others until the arrival on the scene of the European powers.[19] It always survived, through the centuries if not millennia, despite political and military upheavals. This underground world is the very backbone of these waters. And when dealing with the history of the Gulf, we must always bear in mind the perennial rhythms of these forces. Coming to Hormuz, its rulers had a clear perception of this reality when – at the start of the thirteenth century – they reorganised their small dominion. Enlightened princes structured it into a political flexible complementary system of balances and counterbalances, reinforced it with occulated and well-calibrated matrimonial alliances and no less calibrated relationships within its various 'social' components. It was not an easy task, and the dramatic struggles for power within the dynastic family are a proof of the fragility of the institutional system and its structures. This was a system that Salghur Shah had inherited from his father and that he had further reinforced, a system well tested during the Portuguese sieges, when the light fleets of the Gulf easily sailed in rocky shallow waters and were master of those routes that the galleys and *naos* of Albuquerque could not follow.

Although this system seemed more than once on the verge of disintegrating, it regenerated itself 'from within' and survived, and endured.[20] The 1515 Treaty of Friendship and Trade is emblematic. Hormuz lost its political and territorial integrity; yet, in the shadow of the Portuguese fortresses and their cannons and firepower, the Muslim merchants and their fleets united again and continued to control an impressive volume of trade and transactions along the maritime routes linking Europe, Africa and Asia. At the same time, the underground world regenerated itself from within, too, and despite dynastic crises, despite the ambitious plans of the Ottomans and the Safavids, despite the Turks' united or disunited adventurous expeditions into the Gulf up to Hormuz itself (which in 1552 underwent a new siege), to Bahrain (1559), Socotra and other strategic targets, despite the Basra action, once again the strength of these very forces rallied around the Crown and supported the Portuguese fleet, enabling it to check the Safavid enterprises aimed at securing a direct outlet to the Gulf and tighter control of the rich commercial opportunities offered by this sea. Despite new dynastic crises, local feuds and endless warfare, it was this mobile society and its underworld that allowed the reign of Hormuz to survive the Lusitanian yoke, and at the same time allowed the system to survive the traumatic event of the Portuguese loss of Hormuz after one century of presence in the Gulf, when its power would be definitely crushed in 1622 by joint English–Safavid forces. These social groups reorganised there or elsewhere as in the past, without losing the memory of their culture and identity. And, as in the past, they reorganised and interacted in a closely interwoven network of inter-ethnic, inter-religious, cultural local forces.

Notes

1. Piacentini Fiorani, V., 'When Hormuz was the Hinge of a New Land and Maritime System, and Oman was its Pivot: The Hormuz–Oman–Kij Mercantile Dominion', in A. Al Salimi and E. Staples (eds), *The Ports of Oman* (Hildesheim: Olms, 2017), namely Part 2, pp. 323–33 and Part 3, pp. 339–51.

2. Kamal al-Din 'Abd al-Razzaq Samarqandi, *Matla'a al-sada'yn*, 2 vols, Tehran: Shafi 1941; Wassaf, Shihab al-Din 'Abdallah ibn 'Izz al-Din Fadl Allah Shirazi, *Kitab tajziyat al-ansar wa tazjiyat al-a'sar*, better known as *Tarikh-i Wassaf*, 2 vols, lithographic print pers. text. Bombay: 1852–3; Natanzi, Mu'in al-Din, *Muntakhab al-tawarikh-i Mu'ini*, ed. J. Aubin, Tehran: 1335/1957, hence cited as Natanzi/Aubin; Ja'fari, Ja'fari bn Muḥammad Ḥusayni, *Tarikh-i Ja'fari*, ed. V. V. Barthold from a MS at Leningrad, Zap. Inst. Vost. Akad. Nauk S. S. S. R., 5 (1935): pp. 5–42, ed. E. Hinz, 'Hormuz', *Zeitschrift der Deutschen Morgenländischen Gesellschaft* 90: 379–83 (cited in this text as J'afari/Hinz); Nimdihi, 'Abd al-Karim, *Tabaqat-i Mahmudshahiyyah*, ed. and comm. J. Aubin, *Revue des Etudes Islamiques*, 34 (1966) hence cited as Nimdihi/Aubin. Fiorani Piacentini, V., *L'Emporio ed il Regno di Hormoz (VIII–fine XV secolo D. Cr.) Vicende storiche, problemi ed aspetti di una civiltà costiera del Golfo Persico*, Istituto Lombardo di Scienze e Lettere – Classe di Lettere – Scienze Morali e Storiche, vol. XXXV – Fasc. 1 (Milano 1975); idem, *Beyond Ibn Hawqal's Bahr al-Fārs – 10th–13th Centuries AD. Sindh and the Kīj-u-Makrān region, hinge of an international network of religious, political, institutional and economic affairs*, BAR International Series 2651 (Oxford: Archaeopress, 2014).

3. Piacentini Fiorani, V., 'The Eleventh–Twelfth Centuries: An 'Umān-Kīj-Kirmān/Harmuz axis?' *Proceedings of the Seminar for Arabian Studies*, vol. 43 (2013), pp. 261–76.

4. Kamal al-Din 'Abd al-Razzaq Samarqandi, *Matla'a al-sada'yn*, vol. 1: pp. 271–4 ff., vol. 2: pp. 321 ff., vol. 2: pp. 716, 767–8. Diplomat of the Timurid Court, in the fourties Samarqandi was special envoyé to the Court of Hormuz.

5. Here, I refer in particular to the 'families' and to a subtle network of special officials in their service. Namely: the wakils (*wakīl*, pl. *ūkalā'*: agents with delegated powers, authorised representatives of a given personality) and the 'bankers' (*sarrāf*, pl. *sarrāfūna*, financial agents, brokers, who were entitled to represent their lords in full capacity). At that time, it was a solid, well-structured international economic-financial system, which contemporary written sources have well stated and documented since Seljuk times.

6. Piacentini Fiorani, V., 'When Hormuz Was the Hinge of a New Land and Maritime System', Part 3, pp. 349 ff.

7. Nimdihi/Aubin, pp. 879, 880 ff.

8. Piacentini Fiorani, V. and Velde, Ch., 'The Battle of Julfar (880/1475)', *Proceedings of the Seminar for Arabian Studies*, vol. 39 (2009), pp. 321–36, and here given literary sources and bibliographical references.

9. Nimdihi/Aubin, *Tabaqat-i*, pp. 870, 879, 880, 904; Ibn Majid al-Najdi, *Kitab al-fawa'id fi usul al-bahr wa al-qawa'id*, ed. G. R. Tibbets, Oriental Translation Funds, n.s. vol. XLII (repr. London: Royal Asiatic Society, 1981), pp. 222 ff. See also Piacentini Fiorani, V. and Velde, Ch., 'The Battle of Julfar', pp. 332 ff.

10. Nimdihi/Aubin, p. 716.

11. Fiorani Piacentini, V., 'Salghur Shāh, Malik of Hormuz, and His Embargo of Iranian Harbours', in D. Couto and R. M. Loureiro (eds), *Revisiting Hormuz. Portuguese Interactions in the Persian Gulf Region in the Early Modern Period* (Wiesbaden: Calouste Gulbenkian Foundation–Harassowitz Verlag, 2008), pp. 3–12.

12. Bahrain makes an interesting exception within this well-calibrated policy. See Piacentini Fiorani, V., 'The Ports of Oman', pp. 352–4.

13. Piacentini Fiorani, V., 'When Hormuz Was the Hinge of a New Land and Maritime System', Part 3, pp. 354 ff.

14. This historical period is well-documented. With regard to the Safavid rise on the Iranian land mass, the subjugation of the Caspian provinces of Mazandaran and Gurgan and the capture of Yazd (1504), the end of the Aq-Qoyunlu (1503), the annihilation of the last forces of the Qara-Qoyunlu and the clash with Bayazid II in Anatolia (1505–7), the capture of Baghdad and the conquest of South-Western Iran (1508), the death of the last Timurid rulers in Inner Asia and the collapse of the Shaybanids (1510–15), and, lastly, the taking of power of the leader of the Safavi confraternity and his enthronement as *shāhinshāh* of Persia, there is a rich literature. See in particular Savory, R. M., *Iran under the Safavids* (Cambridge, London, New York, New Rochelle, Melbourne and Sydney: Cambridge University Press, 1980); idem, *Studies on the History of Safavid Iran* (London: Variorum Reprint, 1987) and here given literary sources. About a Persian fund in the Torre do Tombo and its relevance for the history of the Gulf from the 16th to the 17th century, see Naser Nasiri-Moghaddam, 'Les documents persans dans les Archives Nationales du Portugal (Torre do Tombo) et leur importance pur l'histoire du golfe Persique aux XVIe–XVIIe siècles', in D. Couto and R. M. Loureiro (eds), *Revisiting Hormuz. Portuguese Interactions*, pp. 13–27.

15. This does not mean that the Gulf will become a Portuguese inland lake. The Gulf, although a branch of the Indian Ocean, had a special physiognomy. There

were some reasons (economic and strategic) why the Ottomans could have tried to bring it, too, under their control, and, with some proper planning, they might have had it. Actually, according to Svat Soucek – and I largely agree with his analysis – the Ottomans between 1517 and 1528 had no known preparation for confronting the enemy in the Indian Ocean. At the same time, after Jedda's conquest, the Portuguese were realistic enough to concede that the whole Red Sea was beyond their reach, just like the Ottomans, too, who afterwards never dared to seriously challenge their Lusitanian opponents in a full-scale confrontation on the Ocean. Soucek, S., 'The Portuguese and the Turks in the Persian Gulf', in D. Couto and R. M. Loureiro (eds), *Revisiting Hormuz. Portuguese Interactions*, pp. 29–55, namely 31 ff.

16. *Història da Expansão Portugueza no Mundo*, eds A. Baião, H. Cidade and M. Mùrias (Lisbõa: 1937–9, 3 vols); *Commentarios de grande Affonso Dalbuquerque, Capitão geral y governador da India, collegidos par seu filho Affonso Dalbuquerque das proprias Cartas que ella escrieria ao . . . Rey Manoel o premeiro deste nome* (1st edn Lisbõa: 1557, 8 vols; 4th edn by A. Baião, Cohimbra: 1923); *Roteiro de Dom Joam de Castro de viages que os Portuguezes fizeram des a India ate Soez*, with a commentary in Latin by Antonio Nunez de Carvalho (Paris: 1833); *Commentarios do Grande Capitão Rui Freire de Andrade*, ed. J. C. Leite (Lisbõa: 1940 – this book includes a long monography on Hormuz: pp. 138–231); Gaspar Correira, *Lendas da India*, ed. Manuel Lopes de Almeida (4 vols, Porto: Lelloe Irmão, 1975). D. Couto and R. M. Loureiro (eds), *Revisiting Hormuz. Portuguese Interactions*.

17. Lizardo, J., 'The Evolution of the Fortress of Hormuz up to its Renovation by Inofre de Carvalho', in D. Couto and R. M. Loureiro (eds), *Revisiting Hormuz. Portuguese Interactions*, pp. 135–47; Campos, J., 'Some Notes on Portuguese Military Architecture in the Gulf: Hormuz, Keshm and Larak', ibid., 149 ff.

18. Indeed, the evidence provided by other authors in this book, in particular the rich archaeological record described by Mark Horton (Chapter 9), Eric Staples (Chapter 11), Robert Carter (Chapter 13) and Carolyn M. Swan (Chapter 14), as well as Abdulrahman al Salimi's note on Banyan commerce, all confirm the existence of connections, both cultural and economic, between the Gulf and the Indian Ocean world. The chapters of this book provide material evidence of the 'underground forces' of the Gulf, the forces that make it an open space.

19. Piacentini Fiorani, V., *Beyond Ibn Hawqal's Bahr al-Fārs*, esp. pp. 83–98, 99–143 ff.

20. Piacentini Fiorani, V., *Beyond Ibn Hawqal's Bahr al-Fārs*, pp. 131–74 and herewith given literary sources.

Bibliography

Campos, J., 'Some Notes on Portuguese Military Architecture in the Gulf: Hormuz, Keshm and Larak', in D. Couto and R. M. Loureiro (eds), *Revisiting Hormuz. Portuguese Interactions in the Persian Gulf Region in the Early Modern Period* (Wiesbaden: Calouste Gulbenkian Foundation–Harassowitz Verlag, 2008).

Commentarios de grande Affonso Dalbuquerque, Capitão geral y governador da India, collegidos par seu filho Affonso Dalbuquerque das proprias Cartas que ella escrieria ao . . . Rey Manoel o premeiro deste nome (1st edn Lisbôa: 1557, 8 vols; 4th edn by A. Baião, Cohimbra: 1923).

Commentarios do Grande Capitão Rui Freire de Andrade, ed. J. C. Leite (Lisbôa: 1940).

Coreira, Gaspar, *Lendas da India*, ed. Manuel Lopes de Almeida (4 vols, Porto: Lello e Irmão, 1975).

Couto, D. and Loureiro, R. M. (eds), *Revisiting Hormuz. Portuguese Interactions in the Persian Gulf Region in the Early Modern Period* (Wiesbaden: Calouste Gulbenkian Foundation–Harassowitz Verlag, 2008).

Historia da Expansão Portugueza no Mundo, eds A. Baião, H. Cidade and M. Murias (Lisbôa: 1937–9, 3 vols).

Ibn Majid al-Najdi, *Kitab al-fawa'id fi usul al-bahr wa al-qawa'id*, ed. G. R. Tibbets, Oriental Translation Funds, n.s. vol. XLII (repr. London: The Royal Asiatic Society of Great Britain and Ireland, 1981).

Ja'fari ed. E. Hinz, 'Hormuz', *Zeitschrift der Deutschen Morgenländischen Gesellschaft* 90, Wiesbaden: Harrassowitz; Stuttgart: Steiner, 1847.

Ja'fari bn Muhammad Husayni, *Tarikh-i Ja'fari*, ed. V. V. Barthold from a MS at Leningrad, Zap. Inst. Vost. Akad. Nauk S.S.S.R., 5 (1935).

Kamal al-Din 'Abd al-Razzaq Samarqandi, *Matla'a al-sada'yn,* 2 vols, Tehran: Shafi, 1941.

Lizardo, J., 'The Evolution of the Fortress of Hormuz up to its Renovation by Inofre de Carvalho', in D. Couto and R. M. Loureiro (eds), *Revisiting Hormuz. Portuguese Interactions in the Persian Gulf Region in the Early Modern Period* (Wiesbaden: Calouste Gulbenkian Foundation–Harassowitz Verlag, 2008).

Naser Nasiri-Moghaddam, 'Les documents persans dans les Archives Nationales du Portugal (Torre do Tombo) et leur importance pour l'histoire du golfe Persique aux XVIe–XVIIe siecles', in D. Couto and R. M. Loureiro (eds), *Revisiting Hormuz. Portuguese Interactions in the Persian Gulf Region in the Early Modern Period* (Wiesbaden: Calouste Gulbenkian Foundation–Harassowitz Verlag, 2008).

Natanzi, Mu'in al-Din, *Muntakhab al-tawarikh-i Mu'ini,* ed. J. Aubin, Tehran: 1335/1957.

Nimdihi, 'Abd al-Karim, *Tabaqat-i Mahmudshahiyyah,* ed. and comm. J. Aubin, *Revue des Études Islamiques,* 34 (1966).

Piacentini Fiorani, V. and Velde, Ch.,'The Battle of Julfar (880/ 1475)', *Proceedings of the Seminar for Arabian Studies,* vol. 39 (2009).

Piacentini Fiorani, V., 'The Eleventh–Twelfth Centuries: An 'Uman-Kij–Kirman/ Harmuz axis?' *Proceedings of the Seminar for Arabian Studies,* vol. 43 (2013).

Piacentini Fiorani, V., 'Salghur Shāh, Malik of Hormuz, and His Embargo of Iranian Harbours', in D. Couto and R. M. Loureiro (eds), *Revisiting Hormuz. Portuguese Interactions in the Persian Gulf Region in the Early Modern Period* (Wiesbaden: Calouste Gulbenkian Foundation–Harrassowitz Verlag, 2008).

Piacentini Fiorani, V., *L'Emporia ed il Regno di Hormoz (VIII–fine XV secolo D. Cr.) Vicende storiche, problemi ed aspetti di una civiltà costiera del Golfo Persico,* Istituto Lombardo di Scienze e Lettere – Classe di Lettere – Scienze Morali e Storiche, vol. XXXV – Fasc. 1 (Milano: 1975).

Piacentini Fiorani, V., *Beyond Ibn Hawqal's Bahr al-Fārs – 10th–13th Centuries AD. Sindh and the Kīj-u-Makrān region, hinge of an international network of religious, political, institutional and economic affairs,* BAR International Series 2651 (Oxford: Archaeopress, 2014).

Piacentini Fiorani, V., 'When Hormuz was the Hinge of a New Land and Maritime System, and Oman was its Pivot: The Hormuz–Oman–Kij Mercantile Dominion', in A. Al Salimi and E. Staples (eds), *The Ports of Oman* (Hildesheim: Olms, 2017).

Roteiro de Dom Joam de Castro de viages que os Portuguezes fizeram des a India ate Soez, with a commentary in Latin by Antonio Nunez de Carvalho (Paris: 1833).

Savory, R. M., *Iran under the Safavids* (Cambridge, London, New York, New Rochelle, Melbourne, Sydney: Cambridge University Press, 1980).

Savory, R. M., *Studies on the History of Safavid Iran* (London: Variorum Reprint, 1987).

Soucek, S., 'The Portuguese and the Turks in the Persian Gulf', in D. Couto and R. M. Loureiro (eds), *Revisiting Hormuz. Portuguese Interactions in the Persian Gulf Region in the Early Modern Period* (Wiesbaden: Calouste Gulbenkian Foundation–Harrassowitz Verlag, 2008).

Wassaf, Shihab al-Din 'Abdallah ibn 'Izz al-Din Fadl Allah Shirazi, *Kitab tajziyat al-ansar wa tazjiyat al-a'sar,* better known as *Tarikh-i Wassaf,* 2 vols, lithographic print pers. text, Bombay:1852–3.

4

FROM JERUSALEM TO THE KARÛN: WHAT CAN MANDÆAN GEOGRAPHIES TELL US?

Charles Häberl

The subject of this chapter is a small ethno-religious community, a single thread running through the rich tapestry of the Gulf region, from which it has roughly been plucked.1 As elaborated in its sacred texts, the core of this community's faith is a doctrine known as *Nāṣirutā* or 'Nazorenism', the adherents of which are called 'Nazorenes' (*nāṣorāyi*), who include among their number John the Baptist and his followers in Jerusalem. Within this group of people, these texts further distinguish between a priesthood, *tarmidutā*, and a laity, *mandāyutā*. The latter word, which comes from their word for knowledge (*mandā*), furnishes us with a useful term for the entire complex of beliefs, culture, faith and practices associated with this doctrine, namely 'Mandæism'. Thus its followers are often called Mandæans, although we could just as easily refer to them as 'Nazorenes' or even 'Gnostics', using the Greek word for knowledge (*gnōsis*) in place of an Aramaic one. To their non-Mandæan neighbours, they are most commonly known as *Ṣubba* or Sabians, employing a term lifted from the religious vocabulary of the Qur'ān.

Before they were ethnically cleansed, the bulk of their community was to be found in and around the marshy regions at the head of the Gulf, in what is today southern Iraq and south-western Iran. They also spread widely throughout the Gulf system and the Indian Ocean, sometimes even becoming ministers and elite officials to Muslim rulers such as Sayyid Said bin Sultan of Zanzibar and Muscat. But they have always maintained that they had emigrated to the Gulf from somewhere else. Stefana Drower, their premier ethnographer throughout the twentieth century, collected oral traditions situating this territory 'to the west' of the then current distribution of the Mandæans, in and around a legendary 'Mountain of the Mandæans', also known as *Jabal Maddāʾi*, 'for Arabs call the Jebel Mandai [*sic*] the Jebel Maddai [*sic*]' (Drower 1937: 316).

Although these oral traditions have not received as much attention as the written sources concerning the origins of the Mandæans, it bears noting that oral traditions can sometimes manifest a surprising antiquity. The Africanist Jan Vansina relates (1985: 17–18) an account collected in 1954 from a caravan guide in southern Libya:

> He said that west of the Teda (Libya/Chad) live people who do not know how to make fire. They are called the sun-fire-people. They live around a big well into which the sun sets every night. Then the water gets hot and they can cook their food. Thus they only eat once a day. Confirmation of this was given three weeks later by another guide. I cite this bit of gossip rather than another because it has already been told for the same general area by both Herodotus and Pliny. This bit of gossip then is 2,500 years old, and dispels the notion that gossip must be ephemeral.

Likewise, the first-century CE Greek geographer and historian Strabo noted that Piraeus, the port of Athens, had previously been situated upon an island. A group of French and Greek geologists and archaeologists conducted soundings to extract sediment cores, and demonstrated that the peninsula on which Piraeus is currently located had indeed once been an island – between 6,000 and 4,000 years before the present date, which means that the oral traditions upon which Strabo drew had already persisted for over two thousand years before being recorded (Goiran 2011: 531).

Considerably less time separates Drower from the subjects of the traditions that she has recorded, so we cannot cavalierly disregard the testimony of her informants, at least not without significant proof to the contrary. Furthermore, the oral accounts of their origins are consistent with their literary accounts, including the *Great Treasure*, their most sacred religious text, and the *Scroll of the Great Revelation*, also known as the *Scroll of Inner Harrān*, a collection of legends first published by Drower in 1953, which details their settlement in a territory identified as 'Inner Harrān' (*Harrān Gāweytā*), during the first century of the Common Era.

According to the latter text, Harrān, also called *Ṭurā d-Maddāyi*, the 'Mountain of the Maddæans', is a country beyond the lands of Islam in which Mandæans live free from the domination of other races, comparable in this respect to the medieval European legend of Prester John's Kingdom. It was to this refuge that the ancestors of the contemporary Mandæan community were led by an Arsacid ruler named Ardawān, and it is from it that Mandæans are occasionally brought forth to re-enter the rest of the world. Drower, her contemporaries Rudolf Macuch and Kurt Rudolph, and her successor Jorunn J. Buckley – which is to say all the scholars who are most familiar with Mandæans and have worked directly with their community, their language and their texts – all accept this legend as an authentic Mandæan representation of their own origins. To what degree should we be prepared to accept the Mandæans' own accounts of their origins, as opposed to external accounts and those constructed for them by scholars? This question – often implied, but seldom articulated – lies at the heart of all scholarship on the Mandæans over the last hundred years or more.

Much of the debate over Harrān in particular has revolved around whether the term refers to a physical location, and if so, where it might lie. Various sites have been proposed for it, including a mountain (Jabal Ḥawrān in Syria), a city (Ḥarrān in Turkey), a mythological location, and, most recently, a seasonal watercourse (the Wādi Ḥawrān in Iraq). The present study examines potential candidates for this territory, assesses them in the light of existing sources for the geography of the region, both written and oral, and identifies the most plausible among them. It analyses the larger context of Mandæan sacred texts in an attempt to define the boundaries of the Mandæan world, and situates it within these boundaries.

'Sabian' and 'Chaldæan': Two Problematic Categories

Whether we date Mandæan contact with Europeans to Riccoldo da Monte de Croce's *Peregrinations* at the end of the thirteenth century (Lupieri 2002: 63–6) or the Portuguese mission in the middle of the fifteenth (Lupieri 2002:

67–9), it is clear they were already well-known as Sabians prior to that time, as both they and their non-Mandæan neighbours consistently represented them as such to Europeans. Indeed, they were apparently the only group so designated at the time of contact. This term is not only the oldest recorded by European scholars, but it has also outlasted all other competing representations from that same period, such as 'St John Christians'. Its durability can perhaps be attributed to the fact that it circumscribes significant aspects of their public identity, and continues to have personal significance to Mandæans even today. Despite this (or perhaps, perversely, because of its centrality to Mandæan self-representations), scholars have aggressively developed the case that the Mandæans are not who they claim to be, from the latter half of the nineteenth century and continuing to the present date. How did this state of affairs come to be?

Although earlier references to Mandæans have survived (van Bladel 2017: 26–36), the earliest substantive and unambiguous account of the history and beliefs of the community we today call Mandæan appears in the final chapter of the *Book of the Scholion* by the eighth-century Christian scholar Theodore bar Kōnay. Identifying them explicitly as Mandæans (Syriac *Mandāye*), he notes that they exist in *Bet Arāmāye* (that is, central Mesopotamia), and mentions that they were still known in that region as Nazorenes (Syriac *Nāṣrāye*) rather than Sabians. As unusual (and uncomplimentary) as his account of their origins is, bar Kōnay demonstrates a surprising familiarity with their doctrine, even including a brief extract from the *Great Treasure* (Pognon 1898: 245–55; Kruisheer 1993–4: 163–8). Although he writes shortly after the advent of Islam, he assigns their arrival in central Mesopotamia unambiguously to the pre-Islamic period.

After bar Kōnay, 'Mandæans' and 'Nazorenes' virtually disappear from the historical record until their encounters with European missionaries in the sixteenth century, but it is clear that this same group became one of several groups indiscriminately identified as 'Sabian' by historians throughout the Muslim world, principally the tenth-century Baghdadi scholars Abu al-Ḥasan ʿAlī b. al-Ḥusayn b. ʿAlī al-Masʿūdī and Abūʾl-Faraj Muḥammad b. Isḥāq al-Nadīm, the eleventh-century Andalusian scholar Abū Muḥammad ʿAlī b. Aḥmad b. Saʿīd b. Ḥazm, and his near-contemporary from the province of Khwarazm, Abū Rayḥān Muḥammad b. Aḥmad al-Bīrūnī. From the start, these scholars attempted to identify Sabians among different groups, including (but not limited to) Babylonians, Chinese, Christians, Egyptians, Greeks, Indians, Jews and Persians. Of particular interest, in connection with the discussion of Mandæan origins, are their attempts to identify the inhabitants of the city of Ḥarrān near Şanlıurfa in Turkey as Sabian. The tenth-century Church of the East scholar al-Ḥasan ibn Baḥlūl, better known as Bar Bahlul, uniquely identified a group that resembles Mandæans in nearly every particular as authentically Sabian (van Bladel 2017: 47–56), and takes pains to distinguish them from these other Sabians, but it must be acknowledged that most of the subsequent scholarship on Sabians has been concerned with the Sabians of Ḥarrān rather than with any of these other groups.

Many of these scholars, but most particularly al-Bīrūnī and b. Ḥazm, emphasise the hybrid nature of Sabians and their religion. In the words of the former (ed. Sachau 1879: 188), they arose from a mixture of the Jews who settled in Babylonia and local Magians, whom he identifies as practising the 'religion of Nebuchadnezzar'. The latter scholar contrasts (ed. Ibrāhīm Nāṣir and ʿAmīrah 1996: 88) his reconstruction of a pure Sabian religion with the mixed religion of the contemporary Sabians of Ḥarrān. According to this reconstruction, Sabians originally kept ḥalāl, fasted during the month of Ramaḍān, and prayed five times a day in the direction of the Kaʿbah, precisely in the manner of his own community, but their depictions of the stars and their reverence for them eventually led them into idolatry.

All these scholars deliberately connect these diverse 'Sabians' with a group mentioned within the Qur'ān (e.g. 2: 62, 5: 69, 22: 17), where the term makes its first appearance in the literature. These are, in fact, their first principles, namely that the Qur'ānic term 'Sabian' refers to a specific and discrete group that must have existed at some point, and that other groups so designated must either be related to this group or not, in a strictly genealogical sense. Both propositions are potentially problematic, because the Qur'ān also situates supernatural beings such as Jānn (e.g. Sūrat al-Jinn 72) and ʿAfārīt (e.g. 27: 38–40) in the very same world as Jews, Christians and Sabians. This is not necessarily a problem for Muslim scholars, who embrace all such references as equally valid and further develop these categories on that principle, but non-Muslim scholars and those who reject the existence of djinnis and ifrits as fictive categories have thus far failed to articulate why Qur'ānic references to Jews, Christians and Sabians should be any less factitious. The proposition that Sabians cannot be a discursive construct but must really have existed as a specific entity, simply because the Qur'ān mentions them, is thus a product of the sort of extreme realism that has always characterised the study of religious texts.

It is, in any case, clear from these descriptions that the reference to this term was contested practically from the moment it first emerges into discourse; our earliest extra-Qur'ānic authority, al-Mas'ūdī, ascribes four different groups to that category (ed. Ismā'īl Sāwi 1938: 4, 18, 101, 138–9), and one of the earliest surviving Qur'ānic commentaries, that of his contemporary Abū Ja'far Muḥammad ibn Jarīr al-Ṭabarī (ed. Shakīr 2001: 252), offers us no fewer than ten different opinions about them, of which three characterise them as a hybrid of two other religions. This emphasis on hybridity reflects the perennialist doctrine, expressed repeatedly in the Qur'ān (e.g. 5: 41–8), that Allāh has revealed His laws at multiple times in the past, but that His followers had subsequently distorted them, producing different religions. Any similarities between them must reflect these revelations, whereas any differences between them (and particularly with the latest and final revelation, which is the standard against which other claims to divine inspiration are measured) must therefore be attributed to human agency.

Non-Muslim scholars do not share these same theological constraints, and are therefore not similarly obliged to distinguish these groups according to their quanta of divine revelation. The twelfth-century Andalusian Jewish theologian Mūsā ibn Maymūn, better known as Maimonides, and the thirteenth-century Syrian Orthodox historian Abū'lfaraj ibn al-'Ibrī, better known as Barhebraeus, both elaborate upon this category, following al-Nadīm (ed. Fouad Al-Sayed 2009: 383) in identifying them as 'Chaldæans' (Syr. kaldāye, Arab. kaldāniyūn); none of the other authorities explicitly characterises its subjects as such. This is a term of biblical origin that primarily signifies 'astrologers' (cf. Dan. 2: 10; 4: 7; 5: 7, 11), and only secondarily those who spoke various forms of what we today call Aramaic (cf. Dan. 1: 4) and were not otherwise distinguished as 'Syrians' (Syr. suryāye, Arab. suriyāniyūn) or 'Palestinians' (Syr. Palesṭināye, Arab. Falasṭīniyūn). When describing the Sabians of Ḥarrān in his Compendious History of the Dynasties (ed. Ṣāliḥānī 1890: 265–6), Barhebraeus characterises their 'profession' (*di ͨwah*) – not in the sense of an occupation but rather in the sense of an open but transparently false claim – as *di ͨwat al-kaldānīyīn al-qudamāʾ*, 'the profession of the ancient astrologers'. In this, he agrees with al-Nadīm and the other Muslim sources who identify the Sabians of Ḥarrān as worshippers of the stars and the planets, even though he does not share their perennialism.

Among the Europeans belonging to their early modern period, on the other hand, the term 'Chaldæan' had a subtly different meaning. In its broadest sense, it referred indiscriminately to different forms of Aramaic and their speakers, and in a narrower sense to Christians adhering to the East Syrian Rite, namely those belonging to the Church of the East (Lupieri 2002: 72, fn. 20). Barhebraeus also occasionally uses this term in its latter, strictly sectarian sense. When he refers to contemporary 'Chaldæans' as opposed to ancient ones (e.g. Assemani 1725: 214), he exclusively intends members of that denomination, and never himself or his fellow 'Syrian' Christians. In any case, these are clearly not the senses of the word 'Chaldæan' that he intends in his discussion of the Sabians of Ḥarrān and their profession, as Ḥarrān is no more located in Chaldæan territory than his own native Malatya is, and the ancient Chaldæans were no more adherents of the Church of the East than he was. Additionally, in their earliest accounts of the Sabians or 'St John Christians' of Basra, European missionaries and travellers consistently distinguish 'Sabians' from 'Syrians', 'Chaldæans' and other Christian communities, at least until the mid-seventeenth century (Lupieri 2002: 72–3).

Then, in 1650, the English theologian Edward Pococke first translated Barhebraeus for a European audience, remarking that 'the one thing clear to us concerning the sect of the Sabians is that their profession is absolutely the same as the profession of the ancient Chaldæans' (165). Here, we see the beginnings of a semantic shift, from Chaldæans and Sabians as two distinct religious communities, to two synonyms for a single community. Citing Pococke, his Swiss contemporary Johann Heinrich Hottinger expanded the range of the term Sabians (Arabic *al-Ṣābiʾūn*, with a *ṣād*) to encompass other completely unrelated peoples in other times and other places, such as the ancient Sabaeans of southern Arabia (Arabic *al-Sabaʾiyūn*, with a *sīn*) in his *Historia orientalis* (1658: 165), ascribing any differences in the spelling of the two names to 'Mohammedan ignorance'. As these scholars expanded the horizons of these terms, they came to develop their own referential and representational powers, such that by the end of the eighteenth century the Swedish scholar Matthias Norberg could put a factitious Chaldæism on an equal footing with Judaism and Christianity in the history of religions (1780: 4–5), even as he ultimately discounts theories of a Chaldæan origin for the Mandæans:

> But since in these books are teachings about stars, angels and demons, counterfeit histories of Adam, Seth, Noah, Enoch, Abraham, and others, and stories made conspicuous by the appearance of John and Christ, it is doubtful whether we ought to attribute their birth first to a Judaism slightly tinged by Chaldæans, or to a Chaldæism slightly tinged by Jews. I shall conclude, however, that they came to light at a time when Judaism was drawing its last breaths. For it was during that time that books bearing the names of illustrious men went out among the common people, some Gentile, others Jewish, others Christian, to whose abilities this religion's claim to deceive rational beings seems to owe its origin. Insofar as is consistent with what is described in these books, I can perceive that the Sabians ought not to be considered Chaldæans, since they do not worship the sun, the moon, and the stars, nor Jews, since they do not await the Messiah, nor Christians, since they claim that Christ is a false messiah; but their religion is bundled up with the teaching and the rites of these peoples.

By this point, the Chaldæans had acquired a national identity very much in the contemporary romantic vein, with all the trappings of European nationhood, including a national language (Chaldaic), a national religion (Chaldæism) and a national homeland (Chaldæa). This passage is significant on many levels, not merely because it bears witness to the emerging synthesis of classical Islamic ontologies with those of Romantic nationalism, but also because a footnote to this very passage identifies the Mandæans as latter-day Gnostics, and their books with those the fourth-century Christian heresiologist Epiphanius attributed to the Gnostics, for the very first time. As the first European scholar to engage with Mandæan texts, Norberg was the starting point from which all subsequent scholarship throughout the nineteenth century departed. It was therefore he who introduced this powerful new frame of reference, that of 'the world's only surviving Gnostic religion'. In time, this frame also developed its own referential and representational powers, and it continues to be the frame within which Mandæans are most popularly known and understood today.

Thirty-five years later, Norberg published the first translation of any Mandæan scripture, an edition of the *Great Treasure* under the name *Codex Nasaraeus*. Significantly, this text explicitly repudiates the worship of the stars and the planets, once again emphatically disassociating the Mandæans from these other groups categorised as Sabian and Chaldæan, who are defined primarily and indeed rather exclusively by their worship of these entities. Confronted with these new data, scholars nonetheless failed to re-examine these categories, and continued to deploy them uncritically, as this passage from the German theologian Johann Georg Sommer (1846: 310–11) demonstrates some decades later:

> Among the Zabians or Sabians, also well-known as Sabæans – among whom we intend the adherents of the Chaldæan religion, namely star-worshippers (for which reason they are called Chaldæans, and also Harrānians, with respect to their chief sanctuary in Harrān) diffused widely from Babylon, even as far as the ancient Arabs – we find interesting parallels with the observances of the Hebrews.

This is none other than the typology that Hottinger had already proposed two centuries earlier in his *Historia orientalis*, namely the wholesale identification of the Qur'ānic Sabians with Sabians of Harrān, the Sabians of the marshes of southern Iraq, the Arabian Sabæans, and all four with the star-worshipping Chaldæans – even though Norberg had already demonstrated that the sole surviving group of Sabians emphatically rejects the worship of the stars, and in any case such an identification would have been complete anathema to the Muslim scholars who had originally introduced this category. In their accounts, such worship was a wholly incidental and often external influence upon the original Sabian religion, rather than its essential and defining feature, as non-Muslim scholars have so often construed it.

This process, by which the category 'Sabians' expanded to delimit more and more groups, including those against which it had formerly been contrasted, was first documented by the Russian Orientalist Daniil Avraamovich Khvol'son. He was the first to address 'Sabians' as a discursive construct, which is to say a product of the very scholarship that sought to explain it, anticipating the work of Edward Said 122 years later. Even though he uncritically embraces his predecessors' ontological realism, he is nevertheless surprisingly prescient in acknowledging the representational powers of scholarship. In discussing the relationship between the Mandæans and other groups called Sabian, he concludes (1856: 310):

> We have seen that originally only the Mandæans and their religion were known as Sabians and Sabism, but other Sabians, who differed quite distinctly from those Sabians in locality, history, and religion, have come to the fore since Caliph al-Maʾmūn; furthermore, that Muslims, knowing well that these Harrānian Sabians were pagans, increasingly called other pagan peoples, whose cults they believed to be related to that of the Harrānians, Sabians as well; and furthermore, they gradually ceased to distinguish one pagan from another, and came to consider paganism chiefly as the worship of the stars, and therefore considered all the pagan nations of the ancient world, and those of their time, as Sabians, and their religion as Sabism, so that Sabian and pagan, Sabism and paganism, became identical concepts.

Khvol'son has rightly been criticised (e.g. de Blois 2001) for too readily identifying Mandæans as 'the original Sabians', on the grounds that the sources cannot be reconciled in such a way as to reflect the Mandæans, *or for that matter any other community*. Furthermore, once Khvol'son had introduced the concept of 'the original Sabians' into the scholarly discourse, his critics felt obliged to introduce their own candidates, including (but not limited to) Harrānians, Elkesaites, Nisibenes, 'Gnostics in general', and more recently 'non-monotheists, but in a theologically neutral way' (Gutas 1988: 44), despite never having established with any certainty what the Qur'ān really intends by it (Greene 1992: 104–19). This 'uncritical reading of medieval sources, sources that themselves reflect a mythical conception of the Sabians' is what Sarah Stroumsa (2011: 90) calls 'the modern Sabian myth'.

Following the whole span of this debate, it is hard not to conclude that this term 'Sabian' is anything other than a blanket category, much like 'Oriental', initially imposed by Muslim scholars upon the complex religious situation in Mesopotamia that they had inherited through its conquest, in order to understand the multiple faiths of their new subjects and situate them within the framework of their own theology. This same blanket was subsequently appropriated by non-Muslims for similar purposes, to designate different parties in different places and at different times. The question we should be asking ourselves is what work this blanket continues to do for us now; it has obvious potential to elucidate how we scholars of these religions have viewed our subjects across an extremely long period of time, but it also undeniably obscures their own beliefs and conflates their separate histories in a fundamentally anachronistic and intellectually dishonest way.

Today, Chaldæism has completely vanished from discourse, even though scholars from Edward Pococke to Adolf von Harnack have accepted its reality as a matter of faith, referencing it and elaborating upon it through their scholarship. This is not unexpected, considering that socially constructed categories such as Chaldæans and Sabians can be surprisingly evanescent and require constant attention on the part of their communities to maintain. In the absence of this effort, the impressive edifice of scholarship on Chaldæism has now completely collapsed, and ownership of the discursive construct 'Chaldæan' has reverted to the one community still engaged in maintaining it, the Chaldean Catholic Church, descendants of those pre-1650 Chaldæans who entered into full communion with the Roman Catholic Church but continue to follow the East Syrian Rite.

The same has obviously not happened to the discursive construct 'Sabian' and the communities still engaged in maintaining it. Its continued relevance as a subject of discourse is ensured by their appearance in the sacred literature of Islam and by the living example of the Mandæans, even though the scholarly debate over their meaning in the former has brought the continued existence of the latter into question in a very real way. Unlike Chaldæism, however, many Muslim and non-Muslim scholars alike still maintain that Sabism was once a specific religion, one whose tenets and history can be discerned through careful analysis – not of the texts of the Mandæans themselves, which are generally disregarded as self-interested, but rather those of Islamic and Christian heresiologists, even though these are by no means disinterested accounts.

Despite a growing recognition that any attempt to recover the Sabians as 'a single people with a single religion' would be pointless and futile, Stroumsa's 'modern Sabian myth' obviously still has legs. As a consequence of this myth, Mandæans – who obviously exist in the real world, follow a real religion and are today the only real community that still identifies as Sabians – find themselves accused of not really being authentically 'Sabian' – which is to say, members of a socially constructed category not unlike 'Oriental', the parameters of which have never been fully defined, and which has demonstrably referred to different groups at different times. At the very least, they find themselves accused of not being authentically 'Sabian' in the ways that matter to those who are even today still engaged in the work of elaborating what 'Sabian' signifies. That is, Mandæans are not doing their fair share of the discursive work that these scholars expect 'Sabian' to do for them.

This scholarly hand-wringing over whether Mandæans are the original Sabians or merely another group of the same name brings to mind the old quip that 'the Homeric Poems were not written by Homer, but by another man of the same name'. The legendary poet is celebrated as the father of Greek literature, even though the origins of the name 'Greek', and the process by which it came to be attached to the citizens of the Hellenic Republic, are every bit as convoluted as those of 'Sabian'. Despite this complicated history, or perhaps because of it, most of us are content to acknowledge the useful work that the term 'Greek' does for us when identifying figures like Homer, Herodotus and Alexander. Only the most contrarian of scholars object when contemporary Greeks recognise them retrospectively as their own, despite the obviously anachronistic nature of this recognition, which collapses three millennia into a single chronotope of 'Greek' history. As Stephan Palmié notes (2013: 35, fn. 3), 'human social interaction could not be apprehended as "continuous" in the complete absence of such retrospective mechanisms'. It is precisely this continuity that scholars seek to deny to Mandæans.

Under scrutiny, the socially constructed and ahistorical nature of these representations quickly becomes apparent. For example, until their War of Independence inaugurated an entirely new discourse about them in 1821, our prospective Greeks did not delimit themselves in the manner now familiar to us. Instead, they were subsumed under a different identity, one reflected by the now obsolete autonyms *Romaíiki* for their language and *Romaíoi* for themselves, and by prior retrospective recognitions of figures like 'Alexander the Roman'. Absolutely no one, to my knowledge, argues that they had claimed this 'Roman' identity for the purpose of self-legitimation; yet when it comes to the most recent summation of the *status quaestionis sabiorum*, van Bladel (2017: 5) professes that the original 'Sabians' were a single people with a single religion, even if Muslims had 'obscured or forgotten' their identity 'within a short time after Muḥammad's death', and that Mandæans have since taken advantage of their ignorance by appropriating that identity. Obviously, a spectre is haunting scholarship – the spectre of Hottinger. The only explanation for this highly uncharitable account of 'Mohammedan ignorance' and Mandæan cunning is simply that the very real Mandæans have not had the courtesy to fit within the neat lines that we have drawn for the very fictive Sabians over the centuries.

Mandæan Accounts of their Own Origins

The attentive reader will no doubt have already noted the absence of an important voice from the preceding account of thirteen centuries of scholarship on Mandæans – that of the Mandæans themselves. Edmondo Lupieri has documented how Roman Catholic missionaries at first enthusiastically embraced Mandæan traditions about their origins from the middle of the sixteenth century, but by 1622 these missionaries had become increasingly sceptical of their claims (2002: 89). Mandæans preserve their doctrines and beliefs in an extensive collection of manuscripts, but extremely few non-Mandæans have ever acquired even a modest fluency in their language, and even fewer of these manuscripts have circulated outside of their community. After Norberg published his Latin translation of the *Great Treasure* in 1815, scholars finally had access to Mandæan accounts of their own origins. By that time, however, what Palmié (2013, 7) calls the 'ethnographic interface' between what scholars wanted to discover and what Mandæans wanted them to find had already been thoroughly inscribed, and the challenge of inscribing these 'new' texts and all that they entail into this interface remains with us even today.

The following represents a modest attempt. The very first chapter of the *Great Treasure*, which again was the only Mandæan text available in translation for much of the nineteenth century, concerns historical and cosmological matters. As this chapter draws to its conclusion (Norberg 1815: 100–3; Lidzbarski 1925: 30), we find a short account situated in Jerusalem, in which a supernatural figure appears during the time of Pontius Pilate, performs miracles such as healing the sick and raising the dead, and converts Jews to 'the name of the Lofty King of Light'. Jerusalem is destroyed, and the Jews go into exile, but this same supernatural figure lifts 360 prophets up from Jerusalem and sets them down at a place called 'the diverter, Truth', *Məšonni Košṭā*.² The chapter then ends with the arrival of Muhammad.

While Mesopotamia has not thus far appeared anywhere in this chapter, the name of the final destination of the Jerusalem community, 'the diverter, Truth', provides us with a potential connection. The Aramaic word *məšonni* ('diverter') ultimately derives from an Akkadian word *mušannitu*, 'diverter; dam', and is likely related to an Arabic word with the same meaning, *al-musannāh* (Kaufman 1974: 73). The only other reference to this location comes from a legend related in the Babylonian Talmud, in Tractate Sanhedrin (97a), concerning the death of Rabbi Tabuth's two sons (Kiperwasser 2014: 296–7). According to this legend, a certain R. Tabuth (or perhaps Tabyomi) once lived in a place called Truth (*qušṭā*),

> which does not differ [*lā məšanne*] in its words [that is, no one tells lies], and where no man dies before his time. There, he married a woman, and she bore him two sons. One day, while his wife was bathing, a neighbour came looking for her, and out of his concern for etiquette R. Tabuth told the neighbour that she was not there. His two sons died, and the inhabitants of Truth drove him out of town for inciting death against them.

For ever more, R. Tabyomi (whom Kiperwasser connects with a Babylonian sage of the fifth generation, which is to say the mid-fourth century CE) refused to tell a lie, 'even if he were given all the empty spaces of the world'.

Given the Mandæan penchant for wordplay, it is probably not coincidental that this defining characteristic of the people of Truth is echoed in the Mandaic place name *Məšonni Košṭā*, as Kiperwasser notes in a personal communication (23/3/2014). In addition to sharing a name, the people of Truth share another quality with the Nazorenes. Twice, the colophons with which Mandæan copyists conclude their scriptures include the following petition: *u-zāki ammā d-nāṣorāyi d-lā šannon mendi d-Heyyi paqqed* ('May the Nazorene people, who did not change (*lā šannon*) anything that Life has commanded, win'). If these two legendary places called Truth, in which live people who do not change their words, can be identified with one another, then the ending to the first chapter of the *Great Treasure* must reflect a legend about the Nazorenes that has circulated in the region since the mid-fourth century, if not before.

Truth appears once again in the nineteenth-century French scholar Nicolas Siouffi's *Études sur la religion des Soubbas ou Sabéens*, in an account collected from his informant, a Mandæan convert to Christianity named Adam. He begins his account of their origins (1880: 3) with Truth, describing it as a physical location rather than a spiritual one, and

> an immense country, even larger than the one we inhabit, but unknown to us. It is better than our world, which is considered in relation to it as the left hand to its right. The inhabitants of this mysterious world are all Sabians. They are all human like us, but because they always remain pure without a trace of sin, after they die they go directly to *Olmi-Danhouro* [the lightworld], which is their paradise, without passing through any place of punishment.

Drower collected further information about Truth (1937: 55–6) during the course of her own fieldwork in Iraq. According to her informants, it is an exact likeness of this world, located somewhere far to the north, beyond the snow and ice. Everything here is represented by a perfect likeness there, and when people die, their doubles ascend immediately to the lightworld, but their souls assume their doubles' bodies, and go through a process of purification before eventually ascending to the lightworld, where they are reunited with their doubles.

Just as Khvol'son was writing his *Ssabier und Ssabismus* in Saint Petersburg, the German Orientalist J. Heinrich Petermann collected a legend similar to the one related in the *Great Treasure*, in which a demon saves a portion of a community of Mandæans from religious persecution by lifting up them up into the sky and setting them down in a kind of terrestrial paradise (1861: 100–1). In one version of this same legend (Häberl 2010, 2013), they are taken north, directly to Truth as in the *Great Treasure*'s account, but in Petermann's version they are taken instead to a country called Beyādhiye, which lies to the west.

This same legendary refuge also appears repeatedly in several Mandæan legends collected by Drower, 'Concerning the Mountain of Maddai [*sic*] and How the Turks Came to Take It' and 'How the Maddai [*sic*] and Their

Ganzibra Left the Mountain of the Maddai [sic] for a Better Country, Farther North' (1937: 309–25) and in the tale of 'The Appearance of the White Cat', which can be found in the newly enlarged edition of her *Folk-Tales of Iraq* edited by Jorunn Buckley (2007: 443–8). In these tales, it is explicitly identified as the 'Mountain of Maddai [sic]' or 'Jebel Mandai [sic]', and always situated in the far west. The connection between Petermann's Beyādhiye and Drower's Mountain of the Maddæans is not immediately obvious, but Drower (1937: 287) notes that the Mountain of the Maddæans is also known as *Harrān Gāweytā*, 'Inner Harrān'. The Arabic *Bayāḍīyah* or 'White (Country)' would then appear to represent a calque upon the Mandaic name *Harrān*, assuming a folk etymology from the Mandaic word *həwārā* 'white'.

This name is familiar from one of the *Great Treasure*'s accounts of the flood. In this particular account (Petermann 1867: 380, ln. 11; trans. Lidzbarski 1925: 409), Noah chops down cedars from *Harrān* and fir trees from Lebanon, paralleling another account (Petermann 1867: 265, ln. 12; trans. Lidzbarski 1925: 263) in which he is commanded to chop down cedars from the land of Lebanon and firs from a third mountain, *Ṭurā d-Yatur*. Lidzbarski was justly sceptical that the authors of this passage would ever have considered the city of Ḥarrān to be an appropriate source of cedars, and so emends *Harrān* to the otherwise unattested form **Hāmān*, situating it far to the north, in the Amanus mountains. He was perhaps too hasty to emend this text, as the traditions collected by Drower (1937: 258, 259) clearly and unambiguously identify the source of Noah's wood as Jabal Ḥawrān near the Syrian border with Jordan and Israel, formerly known to the Romans as Auranitis, and today known as the Jabal al-Durūz or Jabal al-ᶜArab.

Another clew guiding us to this location is the name of the third mountain, *Ṭurā d-Yatur*. Lidzbarski emends this to *Ṭurā d-Atur*, Mt Athur or 'the mountain(s) of Assyria'. This phrase would likewise be unique within Mandæan literature, and perhaps any other literature from the region. Certainly, neither the ancient city of Aššur nor the territory of the diocese of Mosul, to which the word *ʾAtur* strictly corresponded until the archaeological discoveries of the nineteenth century expanded its reference to encompass the territory imagined by Lidzbarski, was any more mountainous or thickly wooded than the city of Ḥarrān. *Yatur* likely corresponds to Jathur, the tenth son of Ishmael and therefore one of the twelve tribes of Hagarites which settled somewhere in the vicinity of the Israelite tribes of Manasseh, Gad and Reuben, in the mountainous region known as Ituræa,[3] again in close proximity to Lebanon.

In short, there is no compelling reason to emend either *Harrān* or *Yatur*, as there are very plausible candidates for both in the vicinity of Lebanon. If the evidence for Harrān in the *Great Treasure* therefore seems reasonably secure, perhaps it is worth revisiting the location of Inner Harrān.

Towards a Mandæan Geography

Knowing how ancient peoples like the Mandæans perceived and regarded the spaces they occupied is as critical to understanding their texts as simply identifying these spaces, and in some respects even more critical. In the exhibit 'Reconstructing Ancient Geography', at the Institute for the Study of the Ancient World at New York University, banner 11 reads:

> Geography is central to the investigation of ancient cultures. Humans are spatial creatures, and their activities and interactions in antiquity were embedded in spatial contexts ranging from the physical layout of the smallest private home to the grandest public spaces of the city-state or imperial capital, and beyond. Consequently, we can better understand the thoughts and actions of ancient people if we can identify the places and spaces they occupied, and explore the challenges and successes they encountered there, traveling, living, and at times exploiting resources.[4]

Thus, ancient 'geographies' are as conceptual as they are physical, which is to say that they are informed as much by abstract concepts (such as social, ethnic, political and cultural boundaries, the limits of the known world) as they are by physical locations (including features like rivers, mountains and settlements). While these particular scriptures contain no charts (or indeed illustrations of any sort), we can derive a sense of the parameters of the Mandæan *mappa mundi* from the place names embedded within them. By contrast, if we fail to ascertain (or even attempt to ascertain) how Mandæans perceived the world around them, we cannot read their texts as they would have, but rather anachronistically impose our own perceptions of the geography of the region upon their texts.

The fact that the Mandæan scriptures refer to the geography of the 'Holy

Land' of the Hebrew Bible is particularly significant, because it speaks to these same perceptions. To give one example, at the beginning of Chapter 18 of the Mandæan *Book of John*, which is the first of several chapters dedicated to John the Baptist, the text introduces us to the full sweep of this geography with the verses

> Upon the Eulæus, a silence descended; a silence descended upon
> Jerusalem.

The parallel of *Ulāy*, likely to be identified with the river Karûn in Iran, and *Urašlam*, Jerusalem, suggests a merism, a popular literary device in ancient Near Eastern poetry (and as much at home in the Mandæan scriptures as in the Hebrew Bible). Thus, in my reading, the stupefaction of the entire world on the eve of the prophet's birth is conjured by the listing of these two geographic locations, conspicuous in both their assonance and their location at the opposite ends of the Mandæan world.[5] The Book of Daniel (8: 2, 16) similarly invokes this same river as the setting of one of Daniel's own apocalyptic visions.

The *Book of John* contains both mythical and legendary content (Figure 4.1 overleaf). The former unfolds in the worlds of light and darkness, and strictly involves supernatural beings, whereas the latter is consistently and unambiguously situated within the material world, and involves humans and animals as well as supernatural beings. Among the physical locations mentioned within the *Book of John* are four bodies of water, the Jordan or *Yardnā* (x 61), the Euphrates or *Paraš* (x 12), the Eulæus or *Ulāy* (x 1) and the *Yammā Rabbā d-Sup* (x 10), a single body of water historically known as the Erythræan Sea, which from our vantage point comprises three separate bodies of water, namely the Indian Ocean, the Red Sea and the Gulf. Additionally, the *Book of John* includes two cities, Jerusalem or *Urašlam* (x 87) and Babylon or *Bābel* (x 1); a mountain, Mt Carmel or *Ṭurā Ṭur Karemlā* (x 3); and two peoples, the Jews or *Yahuṭāyi* (x 22) and the Arabs or *Arbāyi* (x 2). As can easily be seen, the overwhelmingly largest number of these references relate to 'western' people and places.

The *Great Treasure* contains a much larger number of people and place names, including rivers, adding the Tigris or *Deglāt* (x 3); mountains, adding Mt Sinai or *Ṭurā d-Sināy* (x 1), Mt Judi or *Ṭurā d-Qardun* (x 2) and Mt

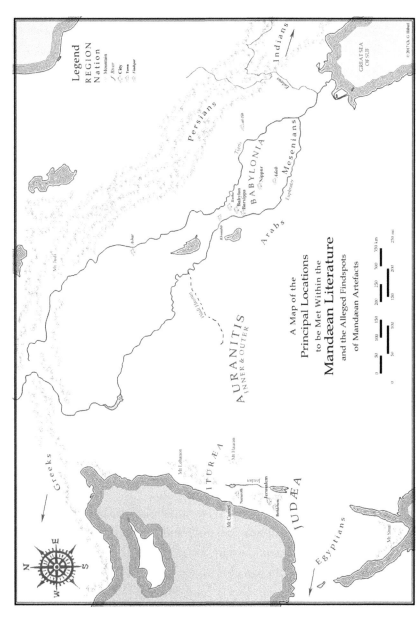

Figure 4.1 A map of the principal locations to be met with within the Mandæan literature. © 2017 Ch. G. Häberl.

Lebanon or *Lebnān* (x 2); cities, adding Bethlehem or *Bet Lahmi* (x 1) and Borsippa or *Borṣep* (x1); and entire regions such as Judaea or *Yahud* (x 3). Some of the landmarks of the city of Jerusalem are included as well, such as the Temple (*Bet Məqaddəši*, x 2) and possibly Mt Moriah (*Ṭurā d-Mārā*, x 1 cf. S 2 Chron. 3: 1). Other regions are referenced through gentilics, such as Indians (*hendəwāyi*), and perhaps even *ekuri* 'demons', literally denizens of the É.KUR or temple of Nippur, although the last noun, much like 'Chaldæans', had likely come to refer to a class of beings independent of geography rather than the inhabitants of a particular place.

Just as in the *Book of John*, the Jordan (x 185), Jerusalem (x 44) and the Jews (x 44) constitute the overwhelming number of references to people and places in the *Great Treasure*, which is to say that these two texts are as familiar with 'western' peoples and places as they are seemingly unfamiliar or unconcerned with other parts of the ancient world. There is absolutely no reason to assume that any of these places are anything other than what they appear to be, and certainly not deliberately cryptic names or ciphers. While the 'western' focus of these texts does not in itself constitute proof of 'western' origins, it certainly cannot be said that the Mandæans' own texts situate their origins anywhere else, and logically it is therefore to the west that we must first look in any discussion of these origins, at least insofar as such discussions are based on their own accounts and not those of others, as McGrath (2013: 373) notes in his discussion of Jerusalem in these accounts. This probably goes without saying, but if we choose to discard these accounts in our attempts to construct a narrative about Mandæan origins, then the only limits are those provided by our imagination.

Situating the Mandæans and Harrān

Over the course of the twentieth century, seven scholars situated the Mandæan Harrān in three different physical locations and one imaginary location. In his edition of the *Great Treasure*, Mark Lidzbarski (1925: VI) proposed the region around Jabal Ḥawrān, despite having emended the sole instance of *Harrān* in this same text to *Hāmān*. Stefana Drower (1937: XVI) and J. B. Segal (1956: 375) both proposed the city of Ḥarrān on the Turkish border with Syria, south-east of Şanlıurfa, although they felt that the 'Mountain of the *Maddāyi*' with which it is frequently identified lay not to the west, as the texts and the traditions suggest, but rather to the east in Iran. Jorunn Buckley has recently (2010: 293) proposed the Wādi Ḥawrān, the principal effluent of the Euphrates in the Syrian desert, reviving the thesis of the nineteenth-century American orientalist Samuel Fales Dunlap (1861: 13), who first suggested this same *wādi* as the means by which the Mandæans attained the Gulf. Against all these other scholars, Macuch (1954: 360) claims that the references to *Harrān* in their sacred texts are purely mythical, a rather original claim that van Bladel (2017, 82) has recently revived.

So, which, if any, of these corresponds to the Mandæan Harrān? What clews run through the Mandæan traditions to guide us to this place? We can rule out the city of Ḥarrān on several grounds:

- The *Harrān* of the *Great Treasure* is described as being in the vicinity of Lebanon and Iturǣa, and as the source of cedars, details which match Jabal Ḥawrān but not the city of Ḥarrān.
- In the *Scroll of the Great Revelation*, *Harrān Gāweytā* is specifically called the 'Mountain of the *Maddāyi*', but the city of Ḥarrān is located in the centre of a level plain, rather than in mountain country.
- The city of Ḥarrān was once served by two seasonally spring-fed brooks, the Jullāb (Cüllab) and the Daysān (Deysan), but proper rivers, so prominent in the liturgy and literature of the sect, are absolutely nowhere to be found within a 120 km radius.
- Finally, as shown above, the Mandæan sources demonstrate considerable familiarity with the territory around Palestine and Babylonia, but are completely mute about the territory around the city of Ḥarrān.

At this point, one might reasonably ask why anyone might identify *Harrān*, apparently from the geminate root √*ḥ-r-r* 'to be arid' after the lenition of the pharyngeal, with *Ḥawrān*, presumably from the hollow root √*ḥ-w-r* 'to be white'. A cognate of the latter form does indeed appear in the Mandaic liturgies, in the form *Hawrān u-Hawrārān*, a lightworld location; Jabal Ḥawrān, here in the material world, is otherwise represented by the form *Harrān*, as we have seen above. The identification of these two is made possible by the complete collapse of the paradigms of geminate and hollow verbs, already in the classical texts, and the Mandæan tradition that identifies *Harrān* with *al-Bayāḍīyah* 'the white country' requires us to privilege a derivation from √ḥ-w-r, particularly since √ḥ-r-r has left no other traces within the classical texts.

Lest we jump to the assumption that the collapse of these two roots is an indication of the relatively recent vintage of these Mandæan traditions, evidence suggests that these two names are likewise equated in the Hebrew Bible. In the Book of Genesis (28: 10), Jacob, son of Isaac, travels from Beersheba towards a place called *Ḥārān* in Hebrew, when he has a vision in which he is granted all the land that would later bear his name. Beersheba is repeatedly identified as the southern extent of the land of Israel (e.g. Jud. 20: 1; 2 Sam. 17: 11; 2 Chron. 30: 5), but in the Book of Ezekiel (47: 16–18) it is not *Ḥārān* but rather *Ḥawrān* that is identified as its northernmost extent. In the following chapter (Gen. 29: 1), Jacob encounters the nomadic Qedemites or the 'children of the east', who tell him (29: 4) that they are from *Ḥārān*. Why exactly would these *eastern nomads* tell Jacob that they have come from *a city far to the north*? The most famous of the 'children of the east' is, of course, Job, who, we are told (Job 1: 1–3), resides in the land of Uz, to the east of the river Jordan, and pointedly not anywhere near the city of Ḥarrān. All this points towards identifying the *Ḥārān* of Genesis with the *Ḥawrān* of Ezekiel, and it seems that the Mandæan scriptures are merely agreeing with the Hebrew ones in this regard.

The ensemble of this physical and textual evidence suggests not only that the city of Ḥarrān is a poor candidate for the Mandæan Harrān, but also that it and its environs were completely alien and unknown to their own conception of the world that surrounded them. Leaving aside Macuch's intriguing but ultimately unsubstantiated hypothesis, namely that it was not a physical location, as it is otherwise consistently described in the Mandæan texts and the biblical ones with which they are clearly engaged, the exclusion of the city of Ḥarrān leaves the Jabal Ḥawrān as the only plausible candidate for the Harrān of the *Great Treasure*. Given the facts listed above, the former would be the obvious candidate for 'Inner Harrān' as well, if it were not for the fact that it was never under Parthian rule and therefore no Parthian ruler could possibly have provided a refuge to the Mandæans there (Buckley 2010: 297).

The problem of resolving the two different Ḥarrāns would seem to be intractable, until we consider that the term 'Inner Harrān' implies the existence of an 'Outer Ḥarrān' as well. *Paulys Realencyclopädie der classischen Altertumswissenschaft* informs us that the term 'Auranitis' (s.v.) did possibly refer to two separate regions in antiquity: a Palestinian Auranitis and a Mesopotamian Auranitis, which appears in some manuscripts of the *Geography* of Claudius Ptolemy as a variant form of 'Auchanitis' (s.v.). Was this indeed its original name, confused by subsequent copyists with the similar-sounding Auranitis, or is Auranitis the form to be preferred? The *Realencyclopädie* is non-committal.

Ptolemy situates his Auranitis or Auchanitis along the west bank of the Euphrates, and lists four towns within it. Travelling down the river, they are Idikara, which Pauly-Wissowa inform us is another name for Is (the modern Ḥīt), Duraba, Thakkona and Thelbenkane. Apart from Ḥīt, which is located immediately south of where the Wādi Ḥawrān joins the Euphrates, none of these towns has been satisfactorily identified. Other towns in their vicinity along the east bank have, however; Neharde'a, one of the earliest centres of Babylonian Judaism; Seleucia, the Seleucid capital; the ancient site of Sippar, today Tell Abu Habbah; and finally Babylon and Borsippa, which are the two Mesopotamian cities mentioned in the *Great Treasure*.

Relative to these other sites, Ptolemy's Duraba, Thakkona and Thelbenkane were located along the Euphrates in precisely the region defined to the north and east by that river, to the south by the Arabian desert, and to the west by the Wādi Ḥawrān, which slopes from the summit of Jabal Lahā, close to where the present borders of Jordan, Iraq and Saudi Arabia converge, to the Euphrates, for a distance of about 300 miles. In his *Notes on the Bedouins and Wahabys*, the Swiss explorer Jean Louis Burckhardt (1830: 217) describes this part of the desert as

the 'low-grounds', so called in the Desert, between Tedmor [Tadmūr, also known as Palmyra] and Anah [ʿĀnah, on the Euphrates immediately north of Hit]. Those low grounds, which are denominated 'wádys', and of which the Bedouins distinguish eight as the principal in this direction, are the pasturing places of all the great Aeneze tribes in winter time, and extend for a distance of five day's journies [*sic*] from west to east. Wady Hauran, which has been mentioned in a preceding account of this Desert, forms a part of those wadys. During the last century [the seventeenth] this ground was the continual scene of conflict between the Mowaly Arabs, who were then very powerful, but at present inhabit the desert around Aleppo, and the Beni Khaled tribe from Basra. On those grounds both tribes were accustomed to meet in winter, and contend for the right of pasture.

It would appear, therefore, that this region was actually quite heavily travelled in the pre-modern period, from the direction of the Levant as well as Lahsa (al-ʾAḥsāʾ, the traditional territory of the Banī Khālid at the head of the Gulf). If the Palestinian Auranitis never fell within the orbit of the Parthian empire, the same cannot be said of the Mesopotamian Auranitis; indeed, it is a strategically important location between the Parthian capital and the Parthians' Roman adversaries in Syria, and therefore demanded their attention. Furthermore, the Mesopotamian Auranitis is directly adjacent to sites such as Khoaubir, Kutha, Nippur and Adab, where the incantation bowls, which are the earliest Mandæan artefacts, were discovered, and was also an integral part of the territory of the Lakhmid 'Kings of the Arabs', whom the *Great Treasure* records among the last rulers of the Mandæans prior to the advent of Islam (Petermann 1867: 387, ln. 8–10; trans. Lidzbarski 1925: 414).

It is clear that the name of the *wādi* preserves the ancient name of the region, and that the textual variant 'Auranitis' is therefore to be preferred over 'Auchanitis'. Is the similarity between the names of the two regions more than a happy coincidence? Anne Blunt (1881: 235–40) described the Syrian desert as 'a plain of sand-stone grit, or gravel, unbroken by any considerable range of hills, or by any continuous watercourse, if we except the Wady Hauran, which traverses it in the extreme north and in rainy seasons forms a succession of pools from the Harra, east of Jebel Hauran, to the Euphrates'. Her claim was later repeated verbatim in the 1910 *Encyclopaedia Britannica* (s.v. 'Arabia', 257–8). Gertrude Bell (1911: 131–2) was more circumspect about the Wādi Ḥawrān, describing it as 'one of three valleys that are reputed to stretch across the Syrian desert from the Jebel Hauran to the Euphrates'. Blunt and Bell were merely reporting what they had heard from their local informants, but in reality 'the great Wadi Hauran and other effluents of the Euphrates . . . rise, not as Arab report had it on the Jebel Druze, but on the Jebel ʿAneiza and Laha, the most important divide in "Arabia Deserta"' (C. 1928: 278–80).

What is most important for our purposes is not that the Wādi Ḥawrān doesn't actually begin in the Jabal Ḥawrān, but rather that local tradition places its source there, effectively making the two Auranitides contiguous in the mental geography of the region, even if they are not contiguous in its physical geography. As I mentioned earlier, the existence of two separate but contiguous territories both named *Harrān* is suggested by the epithet 'inner' (*gāweytā*), which presupposes an 'outer' (*bāreytā*) territory, with which it is contiguous, along the same lines as Mongolia, formerly known as 'Outer Mongolia', and the Inner Mongolia Autonomous Region of China, 内蒙古 *Nèi Měnggǔ*. If the Mandæans identified the Palestinian Auranitis simply as *Harrān*, then that would logically make the Mesopotamian Auranitis *Harrān Gāweytā*.

One other possible ramification of adopting Ptolemy's Mesopotamian Auranitis as the location of Inner Harrān is that the name *Ṭurā d-Maddāyi* logically cannot refer to the 'Median hill-country' as it has traditionally been translated by Drower and her followers, including me. In identifying the *Maddāyi* with the Medians (*Mādāyi*) rather than the Mandæans (*Mandāyi*), both Drower (1953: ix) and Segal (1956: 375) cite the research of Henry Field (1949: 301–28). It should be mentioned in this context that Henry Field's conclusions concerning the Mandæans in the *Anthropology of Iraq* are derived exclusively from the now-deprecated science of anthropometrics. The following passage, from the page cited by Segal, is representative of Field's approach:

> In stature the Subba were tall, the result of long trunks. The head and forehead were wide, although the bizygomatic breadth (136.05) was not unusually large. The bigonial breadth (104.66) was exceptionally narrow so that the face tended to have an ovoid or even triangular appearance. Since the upper and total facial heights were long, the cephalic index (78.39) is misleading unless examined in relation to the Keith classificatory system (p. 308). There appeared to be both dolichocephalic and brachycephalic elements present.

Field's approach is an inheritance from nineteenth-century scientific racism, and most particularly Georges Vacher de Lapouge's 1899 *L'Aryen et son rôle social*. In the social and political climate of the 1930s, his conviction that Mandæans were of Iranian and therefore 'Aryan' stock easily found its way into the ethnographic interface, such that even Drower, who was easily the most sympathetic researcher of Mandæan traditions in her time, could compare Mandæan self-representations to contemporary 'Nordic' propaganda (1937, 9). Drower had accompanied Field on his tour of southern Iraq, and deemed his research 'painstakingly thorough' (1953: ix). In this manner, the Iranian hypothesis of Mandæan origins first entered into the ethnographic interface, where it has been endorsed and elaborated by Geo Widengren (1960: 89–108) and other Iranists.

Field also moots a potential connection with the 'Hairy Ainu' of the Japanese island of Hokkaido (310), but ultimately rejects it on these same anthropometric grounds. The grounds on which he attributes the Mandæans to a 'Iranian Plateau Race', and therefore Drower and Segal's identification of Mandæans with the Medians, are equally suspect. Nor can we still seriously entertain the prospect that Mandæans ever represented the city of Ḥarrān as their hometown. Instead, their traditions about the *Jabal Mandā'i* or 'Mandæan Mountain' refer to the *Ṭurā d-Maddāyi* of the *Ḥarrān Gāweytā*, and both are to be identified with the Harrān of the *Great Treasure*, which is to say, the region around Jabal Ḥawrān. In this regard, it is worth noting that the 'black stony fastness' to the north-east of the latter is even to this day known as *al-lajāh*, 'a refuge – as its Arabic name indicates – at all times to turbulent tribes', in the words of Philip Hitti (1951: 42).

Conclusions

Whether it be traditional or postmodern, religious or secular, Jewish, Christian or Muslim, outside scholarship has obviously played an oversized role in the representation of the Mandæans. With the exception of the earliest missionary accounts (Lupieri 2002), scholars of the Mandæans have traditionally worked in complete isolation from their subjects, effectively denying them any voice in the way they are represented. Despite Drower and Buckley's critical interventions, when Mandæan texts directly contradict the convictions of centuries of scholars (such as the frequently cited but improbable claim that Mandæism derives from the ancient Mesopotamian astral cults), we still tend to summarily disregard these texts rather than embark upon the challenging but intellectually honest labour of returning to our own hypotheses and revising them in light of the evidence.

The contemporary debate among Muslim and non-Muslim scholars over their own representations of Mandæans has had real-world consequences for this community, which has been ethnically cleansed from Iraq due at least partially to this debate, as evidenced by the fact that the fatwas issued against them since 2003 cite the lack of clarity over their status as a protected faith, their putative connections to those astral cults and their supposed Iranian origins. Although these fatwas represent themselves as the products of traditional Islamic scholarship, all of these claims can be directly attributed to repeated European interventions into the literature on the Sabians since the mid-seventeenth century, as mediated by Muslim scholars such as ʿAbd al-Razzāq al-Ḥasanī (1931, 1955, 1963).

Looking back on the long span of European scholarship on Mandæism, it is hard not to conclude that it represents a textbook example of 'How Not to Study Religion'. Although it is now too late to undo the very real damage that has already been done, it is never too late to call for reassessment of our representations of Mandæans, beginning with a more charitable treatment of their own texts. Within these texts, the 'known world' consists of a narrow band running from roughly 28° to 34° N and from 33° to 48°E, describing a rough trapezoid with its corners defined by Mt Lebanon, Baghdad, the Karūn River and Mt Sinai. Beyond this band, the world as described grows more abstract, defined by distant peoples rather than specific geographic features such as cities, mountains and rivers. To the north, there were Greeks; to the south, there were Arabs; to the east, there were Persians and Indians; and to the west, there were Egyptians. Within the band, two areas stand out as being described in considerable detail: the regions of Palestine and Babylonia. It is only within these two areas, and particularly in Palestine, that the texts demonstrate any familiarity.

For this reason, it stands to reason that the referents of place names found in the texts should be sought first in these regions before they are subjected to unnecessary emendations and forced to correspond to places much further afield, such as upper Mesopotamia or the Iranian plateau, regions of which the texts and the communities who preserve these texts otherwise reveal no direct knowledge. Furthermore, when these texts and communities plainly situate these places in the material world, there can be absolutely no justification for reading their referents as mythical or cryptic in lieu of a straightforward and charitable reading of the sources. When we employ such dubious strategies, we do a grave disservice to our scholarship by engendering a justified and healthy scepticism not only among our subjects but also among our scholarly colleagues in other fields.

Finally, oral traditions about this region, and particularly the Mandæans' own oral traditions, are critical to understanding the context within which these sources have been interpreted – not least that of the community that has sustained them for many centuries. The textual and oral traditions situating Harrān as a place of refuge linking Palestine and Babylonia are corroborated by abundant external evidence from multiple sources: Ptolemy's *Geography*, which situates twin Aurantides adjacent to these two regions; the archaeological record, which furnishes us with the earliest material evidence for the Mandæans precisely opposite the Mesopotamian Auranitis, along the east bank of the Euphrates; and other local but non-Mandæan oral traditions, identifying the Wādi Ḥawrān as a conduit between the two. In light of all this evidence, the Mandæans' own accounts of their origins, as recorded in the *Great Treasure* and in the *Scroll of the Great Revelation*, should not be cavalierly disregarded, as they have been by generations of scholars, and other (ultimately unsustainable) attempts to situate their origins in upper Mesopotamia or the Iranian plateau can safely be discounted. Instead, the Mandæans can be seen as a link between the Mediterranean and the world of the Gulf. Although misunderstood by outside sources and variously protected or persecuted, the Mandæans lived and navigated within the cosmopolitan milieu of pre-modern Gulf society.

Notes

1. All non-Latin script languages are transcribed and normalised according to widely accepted standards (SBL for Aramaic, Hebrew, and Greek, DIN 31635 for Arabic), with the exception of Mandaic, as its script represents neither consonant length ('gemination') nor phonemic contrasts in vowel tenseness ('length'). Thus **haran** could represent *hārān, *harrān, *hāran, *hārran, *haran, and *harran, even if only the first three patterns are attested (Macuch 1965: 171–87), and if we recognise **-an** as the suffix *-ān* (193–6), then only the first two are feasible. I have normalised these forms according to either the received pronunciation or established comparative linguistic principles. All translations from various Aramaic languages, Arabic, Latin, French and German are my own unless otherwise noted.

2. The syntax of the phrase is characteristic of Mandaic place names (Macuch 1965, 396), e.g. *arā Bābel* 'the land, Babylonia', *kokbā Bel* 'the planet, Jupiter', *mātā Urašlam* 'the city, Jerusalem'.

3. The Hebrew equivalent in 1 Chron. 1: 31 and 5: 19 is *yəṭur*, hence the *Jetur*, but the Vulgate has *Jathur*, reflecting Jerome's 5th-century Palestinian informants, and likely the Nabatæan personal name *yṭr*, which is rendered *iatour* in Greek transcriptions. Already in the Septuagint (G 1 Chron. 5: 19) the territory of Jathur is identified with the classical Ituræa (JBA *ʾiṭur*, Syriac *ʾiṭuryā*, with an emphatic *ṭ*), albeit not uncontroversially. The identification of *Yatur* with Jathur and Ituræa is likewise not without its problems; for example, the Mandaic form has a *t*, corresponding to the form *Jathur*, but the Hebrew and the Syriac have a *ṭ* (even if S 1 Chron. 1: 31 has *nṭyr* in place of *yəṭur*).

4. Available at <http://isaw.nyu.edu/exhibitions/space/banner11.html> (last accessed 20 December 2016).

5. Lidzbarski (1915: 75, fn. 1) considers the possibility of **eulh** being the river *Ulāy*, but rejects it in favour of the reading *olli* 'his embryo(s)', which he himself deems to be unsure and even doubtful.

Bibliography

Assemani, G. S. (1725), *Bibliotheca Orientalis Clementino-Vaticana: In Qua Manuscriptos Codices Syriacos, Arabicos, Persicos, Turcicos, Hebraicos, Samaritanos, Armenicos, Aethiopicos, Graecos, Aegyptiacos, Ibericos, & Malabaricos, [. . .]: T. 3, Ps. 1. De Scriptoribus Syris Nestorianis/Recensuit, digessit & genuina scripta à spuriis secrevit, Addita Singulorum Auctorum Vita Joseph Simonius Assemanus Syrus Maronita Sacrae Theologia Doctor, atque in eadem Bibliotheca Vaticana linguarum Syriacae & Arabicae Scriptor*, Rome: Typis Sacrae Congregationis de Propaganda Fide.

Barhebraeus, G., a.k.a. Abū'lfaraj ibn al-ʿIbrī (1890), *Tarīkh Mukhtaṣar al-Duwal*, ed. A. Ṣāliḥānī, Beirut: Catholic Press for the Fathers (for the Jesuits in Beirut).

Bell, G. L. (2002), *Amurath to Amurath*, Piscataway, NJ: Gorgias.

Bladel, K. T. van (2017), *From Sasanian Mandæans to Ṣābīans of the Marshes*, Leiden: Brill.

Blois, F. de (2006), 'Ṣābīʾ', in P. Bearman, Th. Bianquis, C. E. Bosworth, E. van Donzel and W. P. Heinrichs (eds), *The Encyclopædia of Islam*, Leiden: Brill.

Blunt, A. and Blunt, W. S. (1881), *A Pilgrimage to Nejd: the Cradle of the Arab Race*, London: John Murray.

Buckley, J. J. (2007), *Drower's Folk-Tales of Iraq*, Piscataway, NJ: Gorgias.

Burckhardt, J. L. (1830), *Notes on the Bedouins and Wahabys*, H. Colburn and R. Bentley.

C., D. (1928), 'Review: Musil's Arabian Journeys', *The Geographical Journal* 72(3): 278–80.

Drower, E. S. (1953), *The Haran Gawaita and the Baptism of Hibil-Ziwa*, Città del Vaticano: Biblioteca Apostolica Vaticana.

Drower, E. S. (1937), *The Mandæans of Iraq and Iran*, Oxford: Clarendon Press.

Dunlap, S. F. (1861), *Sōd: The Son of the Man*, London and Edinburgh: Williams & Norgate.

Fahd, T. (2006), 'Ṣābi'a', in P. Bearman, Th. Bianquis, C. E. Bosworth, E. van Donzel and W. P. Heinrichs (eds), *The Encyclopædia of Islam*, Leiden: Brill.

Field, H. (1949), *The Anthropology of Iraq, The Lower Euphrates-Tigris Region*, *Fieldiana, Anthropology*, vol. 30, Part 1, No. 2, Chicago: Field Museum.

Goiran, J.-P. (2011), 'Piraeus, the Ancient Island of Athens: Evidence from Holocene Sediments and Historical Archives', *Geology* 39(6): 531.

Green, T. M. (1992). *The City of the Moon God: Religious Traditions of Harrān*, Leiden: Brill.

Gutas, D. (1988), 'Plato's "Symposion" in the Arabic Tradition', *Oriens* 31: 36–60.

Häberl, C. G. (2013), 'The Demon and the Damsel: A Folktale in Iraqi Neo-Mandaic', in R. Voigt (ed.), *'Durch Dein Wort ward jegliches Ding!'/'Through Thy Word All Things Were Made!' – II. Mandäistische und Samaritanistische Tagung/2nd Conference of Mandaic and Samaritan Studies*, Mandäistische Forschungen 4, Wiesbaden: Harrassowitz, pp. 97–116.

Häberl, C. G. (2010). 'Flights of Fancy: A Folktale in Iraqi Neo-Mandaic', *ARAM Periodical* 22: 549–72.

Hämeen-Anttila, J. (2006), *The Last Pagans of Iraq: Ibn Waḥšiyya and His Nabatean Agriculture*, Leiden: Brill.

b. Ḥazm, Abū Muḥammad ᶜAlī b. Aḥmad b. Saᶜīd (1996), *al-Fiṣal fī'l-Milal wa'l-ʾAhwāʾ wa'n-Niḥal*, eds Ibrāhīm Nāṣir and ᶜAmīrah, vol. 1, Beirut: Dār al-Jīl.

Henrichs, A. and Koenen, L. (1970), 'Ein griechischer Mani-Codex (P. Colon. inv. nr. 4780)'. *Zeitschrift für Papyrologie und Epigraphik* 5: 97–216.

Hitti, P. (1951), *History of Syria: Including Lebanon and Palestine*, New York: Macmillan.

Kiperwasser, R. (2014), 'The Misfortunes and Adventures of Elihoreph and Ahiah in the Land of Israel and in Babylonia: The Metamorphosis of a Narrative Tradition and Ways of Acculturation', in R. Nikolsky and T. Ilan, *Rabbinic Traditions between Palestine and Babylonia*, Leiden: Brill, pp. 232–49.

Kruisheer, D. (1993–4), 'Theodore bar Koni's Keṭābā d-ʾEskolyon as a Source for the Study of Early Mandæism', Jaarbericht 'Ex Oriente Lux' 33: 151–69.

Lidzbarski, M. (1925), Ginza, der Schatz oder das grosse Buch der Mandäer, Göttingen: Vandenhoeck & Ruprecht.

Lidzbarski, M. (1915), Das Johannesbuch der Mandäer, vol. II, Giessen: Alfred Töpelmann.

Lupieri, E. (2002), The Mandæans: The Last Gnostics. Trans. Charles Hindley. Grand Rapids, MI: Eerdmans.

al-Masʿūdī, A. H. (1938), al-Tanbīh wa-ʾl-Išrāf, ed. A. I. Sāwi. Cairo: The Islamic East.

McGrath, J. F. (2013), Polemic, Redaction, and History in the Mandæan Book of John: The Case of the Lightworld Visitors to Jerusalem, ARAM Periodical 25(1–2): 375–82.

Morony, M. (2005), Iraq After the Muslim Conquest, Piscataway, NJ: Gorgias.

al-Nadīm, M. I. (2009), Kitāb al-Fihrist, ed. A. Fouad Al-Sayed. London: al-Furqān Islamic Heritage Foundation.

Nöldeke, T. (1875), 'Zur Topographie und Geschichte des Damascenischen Gebietes und der Haurângegend', Zeitschrift der Deutschen Morgenländischen Gesellschaft 29: 419–44.

Palmié, S. (2013), The Cooking of History: How Not to Study Afro-Cuban Religion, Chicago: University of Chicago Press.

Pauly, A. G. Wissowa, W. Kroll, K. Witte, K. Mittelhaus and K. Ziegler (eds) (1894–1980), Paulys Realencyclopädie der classischen Altertumswissenschaft: neue Bearbeitung, Stuttgart: J. B. Metzler.

Petermann, J. H. (1861), Reisen im Orient, vol. II, Leipzig: von Veit.

Petermann, J. H. (1867), Thesaurus s. Liber magnus vulgo, Liber Adamiʿ appellatus opus Mandaeorum summi ponderis/conscripsit et edidit H. Petermann, Leipzig: Weigel.

Pococke, E. (1663), Historia compendiosa Dynastiarum, autore Gregorio Abul-Pharajio Malatiensi, historiam complectens universalem, a mundo condito, usque ad tempora autoris, res Orientalium acuratissime discribens, Arabice edita et Latine versa, Oxford.

Pococke, E. (1650), Specimen Historiae Arabum, sive Gregorii Abul Farajii Malatiensis, de Origine et Moribus Arabum succincta narration, in linguam Latinam conversa, Notisque illustrata, Oxford.

Pognon, H. (1898), Inscriptions mandaïtes des coupes de Khouabir, Paris: Imprimerie nationale.

Ptolemy, C. (1991), *The Geography*, New York: Dover.

Sachau, C. E. (1879), *The Chronology of Ancient Nations: An English Version of the Arabic Text of the Aṯâr-ul-Bâkiya of Albîrûnî, or 'Vestiges of the Past'*, London: W. H. Allen.

Scher, A. (1912), *Theodorus bar Koni. Liber Scholiorum, vol. 2, Corpus Scriptorum Christianorum Orientalium, Scriptores Syri 26 = Syri II, 66*, Amsterdam: Peeters.

Scher, A. (1910), *Theodorus bar Koni. Liber Scholiorum, vol. 1, Corpus Scriptorum Christianorum Orientalium, Scriptores Syri 19 = Syri II, 65*, Amsterdam: Peeters.

Segal, J. B. (1956), 'Review of Drower, *The Haran Gawaita and the Baptism of Hibil-Ziwa: The Mandaic Text Reproduced, Together with Translation, Notes, and Commentary*', *Bulletin of the School of Oriental and African Studies*, University of London 18(2): 373–5.

Sommer, J. G. (1846), *Biblische Abhandlungen*, Bonn: H. B. König.

Stroumsa, S. (2009), *Maimonides in his World: Portrait of a Mediterranean Thinker*, Princeton: Princeton University Press.

al-Tabarī, M. J. (2001), *Jāmiᶜ al-Bayān fī'l-Tafsīr al-Qurʾān*, ed. Maḥmūd Shakīr, 30 vol., Beirut: Dār ʾIhyāʾ al-Turāṯ al-ᶜArabī.

Vansina, J. (1985), *Oral Tradition as History*, Madison, WI: University of Wisconsin Press.

Widengren, G. (1960), *Iranisch-semitische Kulturbegegnung in parthischer Zeit*, Geisteswissenschaften Heft 70, Düsseldorf: Arbeitsgemeinschaft für Forschung des Landes Nordrhein-Westfalen.

PART II

THE GULF AND THE INDIAN OCEAN

5

MERCHANT COMMUNITIES AND CROSS-CULTURAL TRADE BETWEEN GUJARAT AND THE GULF IN THE LATE SEVENTEENTH AND EIGHTEENTH CENTURIES

Ghulam A. Nadri

Introduction

This chapter explores the commercial and social dynamics of maritime trade between Gujarat in India and the Gulf in the late seventeenth and eighteenth centuries. Maritime trade between the ports of Gujarat, such as Cambay and Surat, and those on the Arabian and Persian coasts of the Gulf grew exponentially following the early sixteenth century. While the significance of this trade in the overall maritime economy of the Indian Ocean in general and that of Gujarat in particular is well recognised in the existing literature, the mechanics of this trade, merchant networks, commodities exchanged between the two regions, and many other interesting aspects have not been fully explored. This is primarily due to the lack of indigenous sources on merchants and trade and the scant references to Indian or Asian merchants and their trade in European records including those of the English and the Dutch East India Companies (EIC and VOC respectively). Most merchants mentioned in European sources were prominent shipowners and influential traders in Surat, many of whom were associated with the European companies. As shipowners were predominantly Muslims, it was generally assumed that the maritime trade was the domain of the local Gujarati and West Asian

Muslim merchants. So pervasive was this assumption that, for some scholars, the Indian Ocean was an 'Islamic lake', and many understood the Portuguese encounter with Asians in the Indian Ocean in the sixteenth century as a clash between Portuguese and Muslim maritime trading interests.[1]

The literature on Gujarat's maritime trade in the seventeenth and eighteenth centuries also reinforces the notion of a Muslim predominance, and some scholars have even equated the early eighteenth-century loss of Muslim shipping in Gujarat with the decline of Surat, the main trading port of the Mughal Empire in western India.[2] A close look at the mechanics of trade, however, shows that the maritime trade in the western Indian Ocean was not a monopoly of the Muslims. It was more cosmopolitan. Merchants of diverse ethnic and regional origins, such as the Hindu and Jain Banias, Armenians, Jews, Kachhi Bhatias, Arabs, Turks, Persians and the local Gujarati Muslims, shared this trading domain. This social and ethnic mix of merchants trading between Gujarat and the Gulf reveals the multicultural character of port cities and markets in Gujarat and the Gulf. This chapter explores the commercial dynamics of this trade and the ethnic diversity among merchants trading between the two regions, and the nature and extent of cross-cultural interaction among them.

The Gulf–Gujarat Trade: An Overview

Gujarat's Surat-based maritime trade in the seventeenth and eighteenth centuries was primarily oriented towards the Red Sea and the Gulf. In the historiography of Surat's maritime trade with West Asia, a major focus has been on the Red Sea segment. Not very much, therefore, is known about merchants and their trade between Gujarat and the Gulf. We do know, however, that in the seventeenth century, the Gulf ports, such as Basra, Bandar Abbas and Muscat, were major destinations for commercial ships sailing from Surat. Extant shipping lists from the middle of the century indicate that some fifteen to twenty ships sailed (or returned) from the Gulf to Surat every year. It has been argued that Gujarat's trade with the Gulf declined in the second half of the seventeenth century and that with the Red Sea expanded towards the end of the century.[3] The extant shipping lists show that Surat's trade with the Red Sea ports increased in the late seventeenth century but there was no decline in trade with the Gulf. On the contrary, the number of ships sailing between Surat and the Gulf ports shows that the maritime trade in this sector flourished well up to the early eighteenth century and remained substantial until the 1760s. The fall of the Safavid dynasty in 1721–2 and the political instability that it caused, and the crisis in the middle decades of the eighteenth century, seem to have caused a decline in the Gulf–Gujarat trade. There was certainly a drastic fall in the volume and value of imports into the Gulf by the Dutch VOC and the English EIC, but these political events did not totally disrupt shipping and trade between western India and the Gulf. In the early 1720s, the trade was still impressive. In 1721–2, at least fifteen out of a total of forty-five ships arriving in Surat came from the Gulf ports. One major change, however, was that the number of European ships visiting the Gulf ports increased while the number of ships owned by Muslim merchants remained the largest. Bandar Abbas seems to have suffered more than other Gulf ports as Surat ships were no longer sailing to that port from the mid-eighteenth century onwards. The cities of Basra and Muscat retained some vitality during this period even though they received fewer ships from Surat than in the preceding period. In 1763–4, for example, three ships returned from Basra to Surat bringing, in addition to merchandise, a large quantity of gold and silver species (ducats and reals of eight) that amounted to around one million Mughal silver rupees.[4]

The Mechanics of the Gujarat–Gulf Trade

The Gujarat and Gulf regions were already well-connected both through maritime and overland trade routes. Surat's trade with West Asia and especially the Gulf rapidly increased after the Safavid takeover of Hormuz and the Portuguese withdrawal from the port in 1621. Merchants and shipowners of Surat began to trade with Basra, Bandar Abbas and Kung in the Gulf. The shipping transport capacity of Surat's merchant fleet increased in the 1640s and continued to do so subsequently.[5] The Surat fleet in the mid-seventeenth century comprised ships belonging to Surat merchants, the Mughal imperial household and the European companies. The Mughal imperial ships initially provided freight services to merchants mostly on the Surat–Mokha–Jeddah route, which also carried on board pilgrims to the Islamic holy cities of Mecca and Medina. This hajj traffic also had some economic importance; the pilgrims carried with them a basket of goods for sale in Jeddah and at the annual markets of the holy cities.[6] The imperial interest in the freight trade grew in the 1650s when Emperor Shahjahan (1628–56) got four to six new large ships built to facilitate transportation of goods to the Gulf and Red Sea ports. An expansion of available tonnage caused a reduction in freight costs, which may have further induced merchants to export and import merchandise to and from West Asia. The scholar Van Santen has argued that Surat–Basra trade expanded after the mid-seventeenth century Mughal imperial initiatives to provide freight services to merchants trading with the Gulf.[7] Evidence from the shipping lists prepared by the VOC officials in Surat, Gombroon or elsewhere does not support this. The fleet that serviced this sector in the 1650s was almost entirely merchant-owned. Thus, in 1654–5, fourteen out of thirty-four ships arriving in Surat were from the Gulf and were owned by Surat merchants, including three vessels owned by the Bania merchants.[8] Surat's merchant fleet rapidly expanded with the withdrawal of the Mughal imperial interest in shipping and freight trade in the early 1660s.[9] The expansion in shipping led to a medium-sized merchant-owned commercial fleet coming into prominence. This fleet, in the early 1700s, consisted of some 112 ocean-going vessels.[10] The Gulf ports and their extensive hinterlands continued to attract merchants and merchandise from Gujarat. In the late seventeenth and early eighteenth centuries, the largest number of ships arriving in Surat came from the Gulf ports.[11] The cost competitiveness (lower freight charges, sometimes half of those charged by the European ships) and general merchants' preference for Gujarati ships on account of their availability as and when required, as well as their reliability and other advantages, have been suggested as the causes of the Surat fleet's continued prominence in the Arabian Seas.[12]

Every year, the Gulf received the largest number of ships and valuable merchandise from Surat. Gujarati ships visited Bandar Abbas and Basra, where many Surat merchants had their resident agents or partners to look after their businesses. The merchandise supplied to these ports included fine spices, pepper, cotton, textiles, indigo, high value grain such as rice and wheat, and sugar. These commodities were in high demand in the interior that constituted the hinterland of the Gulf ports. Some were also transmitted overland via Baghdad to Aleppo and further on to Europe via the Mediterranean Sea. It was primarily through this re-export trade to the Levant that the Gulf received precious metals – gold and silver. Gujarati merchants exchanged their goods for gold ducats, silver *abbasis* and reals of eight and a variety of merchandise. Return cargo lists show that dates, raisins, linen, almond, rosewater, pistachio, leather, pearl and glass were prominent items imported into Surat. Among these, dates, raisins and linen accounted for the largest proportion of the total value of imports. Some merchants also brought horses from the Gulf, especially the ones trading with Basra. In the mid-seventeenth century, several ships coming from Basra including some imperial vessels had horses in their cargo.[13] Most merchants, it seems, were interested in gold and silver species, pearl and other merchandise.

Long-distance trade on a large scale was made possible by an elaborate institutional infrastructure. Banking and brokering or agency services were crucial for a successful commercial enterprise in the long run, as was the political stability and relative peace that the Mughal and Safavid Empires were able to provide over a fairly long period.[14] Gujarati Hindu Banias and some Armenians and Parsis ran an efficient banking network that rendered financial intermediation to merchants who needed any monetary credit or exchange services. Most maritime merchants had to deal with money-changers (*sarraf/wisselaar*), bankers (*sahukars*) and brokers or agents (*dalal*).[15] All merchants importing gold and silver from the Gulf or other places had to go through money-changers and bankers associated with the mint to convert their gold and silver into Mughal rupees. Freight services between Surat and the Gulf ports played a vital role in facilitating maritime trade, as the merchants freighting their merchandise were far more numerous than ship-owners. Almost all ships sailing in the Arabian Seas carried freight goods. In the seventeenth and eighteenth centuries, the European companies (the EIC and the VOC) offered their ships' tonnage to other merchants on payment of freight charges.[16] The companies benefited from merchants' demand for cargo spaces and earned considerable income by providing this service to a multitude of merchants. This was so lucrative that, in the late eighteenth century, EIC officials in Surat and Bombay adopted measures to control and monopolise Surat's freight trade with the Gulf and the Red Sea.[17] They even, sometimes, extended respondentia loans to merchants as working capital with which the latter purchased merchandise and freighted it to the intended port of destination, including the Gulf ports.[18]

The prominence of Surat merchants in the Gulf–Gujarat trade may be attributed to their access to these facilities and services. Most shipowners and large-scale traders carried out their enterprise with the help of brokers and agents. A number of Surat merchants were resident in Basra, Bandar Abbas and other places and had their partners or agents in Surat to transact business, or they acted as agents of those based in Surat. Our knowledge of their networks and the dynamics of their relationship is rather limited. Rare but detailed lists of merchants and their cargo of merchandise on some VOC ships sailing from Gombroon to Surat are useful as they provide interesting information on some important aspects of maritime trade, such as partnership, agency, family firms and inter-community networks.

There are two detailed lists of cargo of goods freighted by a number of merchants in two VOC ships, the *Moercappel* and the *Schoonderloo*, compiled in 1698 and 1699 respectively, which not only mention the names of merchants and their correspondents in Surat but also illuminate many of the important aspects of trade mentioned above.[19] A close look at the lists reveals that a number of merchants, Banias, Muslims, Jews and Armenians, had their residence in the Gulf (Gombroon/Bandar Abbas) and consigned their money and merchandise to their agents or partners in Surat, or they worked as resident agents for Surat merchants. Many merchants freighted their merchandise and travelled to Surat, possibly in the same ship, to collect it. It also reveals the scale of trade carried out by merchants individually or in partnerships as well as the range of commodities they traded in. The values of the merchandise are not mentioned in the lists, but the amounts paid as freight charges do indicate a broad range of scale on which merchants were trading between Surat and the Gulf. Khwoja Jacob Jan Waledd Phanos and Khoja Katiel Waledd Avanos, for example, freighted 137 packs and chests of merchandise and paid 5,322 *mahmudis* as freight charges. At the lower end of the spectrum were merchants like Khwoja Kalbali Waledd Aga Abda, who had only two packs of raisins and paid just seventy-two *mahmudis*.[20] This differentiation among merchants is clear if we look at the amount of money (gold and silver coins) they brought to Surat. Thus, the Jewish merchants Khwoja Magaki and Agabab Waledd Mirza Terki freighted two bundles of ducats that amounted to 227,932 *mahmudis*, whereas a Bania merchant, Pitaldas Jivanmal, carried one chest of *abbasis* amounting to 3,271 *mahmudis*.[21]

A majority of merchants mentioned in the lists seem to have traded individually, which also reflects the overall nature of Indian/Asian maritime trade in the western Indian Ocean. Such merchants usually travelled with their merchandise to the Gulf ports and returned with money and goods for which they had exchanged their merchandise. Even those who did not seasonally travel from one port to the other had their agents carry out the transaction. Our sources are not explicit as to whether their relationship was that of patron and agent or that of joint owners and partners. A merchant in Bandar Abbas sending money and goods to another merchant in Surat could have been an agent or a business partner. Some certainly worked for their family/household firms, as the family names of the senders in the Gulf and the recipients in Surat might indicate.[22] There are several examples of joint or partnership trade like the one involving two Jewish merchants mentioned above. For example, Haji Ibrahim and Haji Mohammad Shafi traded in partnership, and so did Haji Mohammad Tahir and Haji Mohammad Taqi. In 1699, they freighted their merchandise jointly and travelled to Surat on the VOC ship, the *Schoonderlos*.[23] While in most cases partners belonged to the same community, there are nevertheless a few examples of inter-community relationships of trust and partnership. Mia Sultan Ali, a Muslim merchant, and Kapurchand Tejpal, a Hindu Bania, jointly freighted a sack of silver money to Surdas Akai and Sultan Ali Karimji in Surat.[24] To what extent were the partnerships and the patron–agent relationships exclusively based on cast, clan, or community considerations? This dimension is explored in the following section.

Diversity in the Gulf–Gujarat Trade

Merchants of different ethnic and religious backgrounds were involved in the Gulf–Gujarat trade. Contemporary European sources generally identify them according to their religious or regional affiliation. They were often broadly categorised as Banias, Muslims, Jews, Armenians and Parsis in our sources. 'Bania' is an umbrella term used for Hindu and Jain merchants of Gujarat, and included people from some eighty-four different castes and sub-castes.[25] The Muslim merchant community was made up of the Arabs, Persians, Turks and local Gujarati Muslims, among whom the most prominent were the Bohras. The Bohras were made up of two sects, the majority

Sunnis and minority Shias. Among the Shiite Bohras were different sects, among which the Ismailis were the most numerous and most affluent. The Parsis, who were apparently considered to have enjoyed a remarkable cultural cohesiveness in Gujarat, were nevertheless divided into two sects, the Shahanshahi and Kadami. Besides them, there were also Armenians, Jews and European merchants (both company officials with a privilege to trade on their private account and free European merchants) who played a prominent role as much in the Gulf–Gujarat trade as in Indian Ocean trade.

The presence of such a diverse community of merchants reveals the cosmopolitan character of the Gulf–Gujarat trade. The domains of maritime trade and its allied professions were shared by members of various communities of merchants mentioned above. There was nevertheless a greater participation by some communities in certain commercial activities. This relative predominance gained by a particular community in a particular trade was simply a matter of technical and other logistical expertise acquired by merchants of that community. Muslim merchants, for example, were predominant in shipping. This did not imply a total exclusion of others. A number of Bania and Parsi shipowners could be discerned from some seventeenth-century VOC shipping lists. Other Bania and Parsi merchants sailed to almost all overseas destinations as freighters. As mentioned above, the impression that the overseas trade in the Indian Ocean, and particularly in its Arabian Sea segment, was Muslim-dominated, or 'Islamic trade', needs to be questioned. The presence of Gujarati Banias, both as residents at the Gulf ports and in Yemen, Habsh, Hadramaut and other places in the Red Sea region and as itinerant traders visiting the ports in the season, invalidates the notion of 'Islamic trade'.[26] The impression of the Banias' exclusive control over inland trade, banking and brokering too is problematic. Since a large number of Banias in Surat/Gujarat had acquired expertise in banking services and had the potential to serve others, especially Europeans, as brokers and agents, they tended to dominate these activities. This was not, however, to the total exclusion of all others. Whereas some Armenians were also bankers, the Parsis, since the late seventeenth century, extended brokering services to European companies and other merchants.[27] These activities required a network of trustworthy persons at numerous trading stations and deploying a large capital. Some merchants, especially the Banias and Parsis, could combine all these factors, hence their prominence in such professions. Clan and caste loyalties might have helped them build sustainable networks at least initially, but such networks were not always dependent on familial affiliations. A number of Bania and Parsi merchants combined trading overseas with banking and brokering as a measure to maximise trade benefits and also possibly as a survival tactic. Trade in the Indian Ocean arena was, thus, shared by a heterogeneous community of merchants, each of which was in a complex relationship of complementarity and competition.

This heterogeneity is very well reflected in the composition of merchants – both shipowners and freighters – in the Gulf–Gujarat trade. The owners of a large number of ships sailing between Surat and the Gulf were mostly Surat-based Muslim merchants, including some Turkish merchants of Baghdad and other parts of the Ottoman Turkey. Haji Salim Baghdadi, Mohammad Chelabi, Ahmad Chelabi, Saleh Chelabi and Usman Chelabi were among the leading merchants and shipowners of Surat. Abdul Ghafur, a Bohra Muslim of Surat, was the richest of all merchants and, in the late seventeenth and eighteenth centuries, he owned some nineteen or twenty ocean-going ships. Other leading Muslim ship-owning merchants of Surat mentioned in our sources are Haji Zahid Beg, Sheikh Hamid, Haji Ghyas Beg, Mohammad Taqi and Mirza Mohsen. The shipping lists mention some Arab ships arriving from Muscat – mostly belonging to the Imam or ruler of Muscat. In 1681, four Arab ships arrived in Surat, three of which were owned by the Imam of Muscat.[28] There were a few prominent Bania merchants who also owned ships and were active in the maritime trade between Surat and the Gulf ports.[29] Ships owned by Bania merchants such as Mohandas Naan, the broker of the VOC, Achi Parekh, Shambhu, a broker of the French, Kashi Das and Rupji Raghav sailed between Surat and Basra and Bandar Abbas.

In the eighteenth century, some Parsi merchants rose to prominence in Surat's maritime trade both as shipowners and brokers. Rustam Manikji, Mancherji Khursheji, Dhanjishah Manjishah, Manik Dada, Dadabhai Manikji, Mancherji Bomanji and Rustam Jesso were prominent ship-owning merchants and dominated the maritime arena of Surat for much of the eighteenth century, especially in its second half.[30] They carried out an extensive trade with the Gulf ports, even though Mokha and Jeddah in the Red Sea had by then become the most attractive destinations for Surat merchants. It is evident from the shipping lists of the 1750s and 1760s that some Parsi-owned ships regularly sailed to Muscat and Basra. In 1759, two ships sailing from Surat to Muscat with a cargo consisting mainly of cotton and textiles belonged to Parsi merchants, Mancherji Bomanji and Manik Dada.[31] The number of ships sailing to the Gulf had decreased in the second half of the century and many of those still sailing to Basra and Muscat were owned by the Parsis.

The composition of merchants who freighted their goods on Gujarati or European ships was highly diverse. The 1698 and 1699 lists of merchants freighting their money and merchandise from Bandar Abbas to Surat show an overwhelming presence of Bania and Jewish merchants in this sector. There are only a few Armenian and Muslim merchants on the lists, while there are no Parsis. The information on the composition of freighters between Surat and Gombroon (Bandar Abbas) invalidates the notion of a Muslim-dominated maritime trade in the Arabian Sea. Parsis seem to have entered this commerce in the eighteenth century, and certainly by the 1750s they had gained some prominence in it. Many Parsi and some Armenian merchants, who freighted their merchandise to West Asia, were among the signatories of a certificate that the merchants of Surat issued to the EIC chief in support of the latter's endeavour to regulate freight trade.[32] Parsi merchants of Surat also facilitated the Gulf–Gujarat trade by servicing other Gulf-based merchants as agents and brokers. Manikji Pestonji, for example, served as an agent of Muscat-based merchants Bhimji Hirji and Mowji Rowji, taking care of the vessels that the latter sent to Surat and looking after their businesses.[33] The Parsis had by then earned the reputation of trustworthy agents and brokers because of their close association with the European companies, especially the EIC. Most shipowners and freighters to the Gulf ports had their representatives/agents at those places whose identity is not known to us. Mancherji Khurshedji, Manik Dada, or other Parsi merchants, who never travelled on their ships, had their agents take care of their businesses. There existed a complex network of trust and reliance that transcended caste and community boundaries. A Bania merchant at Bandar Abbas, Mohan Ramji, served as agent to several Muslim and Hindu merchants of Surat.[34] Similarly, a Jewish merchant, Khoja Kalbali Chiragi (Shirazi?), sending ten packs of coffee to Abdul Ghafur and Morardas Khambayati in Surat reveals the transcultural nature of merchant networks and shows that trust and reliance in trade transcended community and cultural boundaries.[35] Abdullah ibn Yusuf, a Jewish merchant of Basra, had his co-religionist Ishaq Daud as his agent in Surat, while at the same time he acted as a commercial agent for Tipu Sultan, the Muslim ruler of Mysore, in Basra.[36]

Conclusions

The data culled from the Dutch VOC documents show how significant the Gulf trade was for Gujarat/western India and its merchant communities. Several important aspects of the Gulf–Gujarat maritime trade have eluded scholars' attention, mainly because of the lack of primary sources on merchants and merchandise in this segment of Indian Ocean trade. The data contained in the shipping list used in this chapter provide crucial information on merchants, their networks and commodities. The Gulf was seemingly the most important segment of Surat's maritime trade in the seventeenth and early eighteenth centuries. It shows that Gulf trade did not simply decline in the late seventeenth century as some scholars have suggested. The data are also helpful in revisiting some of the assumptions in the literature about the nature of trade in the Arabian Seas. The diversity among merchants and their complex networks of agency, trust and reliance in commercial matters invalidate the notion of Gujarat's maritime trade with the Gulf or the Red Sea as being exclusively Muslim or Islamic trade. Instead, merchants trading at successful Gulf ports reflected the variety and cosmopolitan diversity of the Indian Ocean system.

Notes

1. Although the literature acknowledges the presence of some non-Muslim shipowners and freighters in Indian Ocean trade, in the description of the Portuguese encounter Muslim merchants and shipowners are almost always the adversaries. Michael Pearson, *The Indian Ocean* (Routledge, 2003), pp. 95–6; M. N. Pearson, 'India and the Indian Ocean in the Sixteenth Century', in M. N. Pearson and Ashin Das Gupta (eds) *India and the Indian Ocean, 1500–1800* (New Delhi: OUP, 1987), pp. 71–92; Pius Malekandathil, *Maritime India: Trade, Religion and the Polity in the Indian Ocean* (Delhi: Primus, 2010), chs 6 and 10.

2. Ashin Das Gupta, *Indian Merchants and the Decline of Surat, 1700–1750* (Wiesbaden: 1979); Ruby Maloni, *Surat: The Mughal Port City* (Bombay: Himalayan Publishing House, 2003).

3. Rene Barendse, *The Arabian Seas: The Indian Ocean World of the Seventeenth Century* (New York: M. E. Sharpe, 2002), pp. 203–5.

4. VOC 3122, Shipping list, Surat, 1764, ff. 3299r–3305r.

5. Van Santen has illuminated this aspect of Surat's trade with the Gulf and the Red Sea in the seventeenth century. H. W. Van Santen, 'De Verenigde Oost-Indische Compagnie in Gujarat en Hindustan, 1620–1660' (Ph.D. dissertation, Leiden University, 1982), pp. 63–74.

6. Van Santen, 'De Verenigde Oost-Indische Compagnie in Gujarat', pp. 69–70. For an analysis of the various dimensions of the hajj, see M. N. Pearson, *Pilgrimage to Mecca: The Indian Experience, 1500–1800* (Princeton: Princeton University Press, 1996).

7. Van Santen, 'De Verenigde Oost-Indische Compagnie in Gujarat', p. 67.

8. VOC 1208, Shipping list, Surat, 1655, ff. 456^r–459^v.

9. Van Santen, 'De Verenigde Oost-Indische Compagnie in Gujarat', p. 67.

10. VOC 1666, Resoluties, Surat, 23 February 1702, pp. 689–95.

11. In 1683, fifteen out of forty-four ships arriving in Surat came from the Gulf ports. VOC 1383, Shipping list, Surat, 1683, ff. 630^r–631^v. In 1720–1, fifteen out of 52 and, in 1721–2, twenty out of 45 ships arriving in Surat came from the Gulf ports. VOC 1963, Shipping list, Surat, 1721, pp. 158–64; VOC 1983, Shipping list, Surat, 1722, ff. 127^r–129^v. A number of ships owned by merchants sailed regularly to Basra in the early 18th century. Ghulam A. Nadri, 'Merchants in Late Mughal Gujarat – Evidence from Two Major Persian Sources', *Proceedings of the India History Congress* (Bangalore, 1997), pp. 382–90.

12. Ashin Das Gupta, 'The Early Seventeenth-Century Crisis in Western Indian Ocean and the Rise of Gujarati Shipping in Early Eighteenth Century' in Ashin Das Gupta, *The World of the Indian Ocean Merchant, 1500–1800*, compiled by Uma Das Gupta (New Delhi: Oxford University Press, 2001), pp. 310–11.

13. In 1651, several ships coming from Basra had horses among the cargo and the ship owned by a merchant, Syed Sana had 16 horses. VOC 1188, Shipping list, Surat, 1651, ff. 567^r–572^v.

14. Some scholars have attributed the rise of Surat and its exemplary success as a trading hub of the western Indian Ocean to the political stability created by these empires in large parts of South and West Asia. Gupta, *Indian Merchants and the Decline of Surat.*

15. See for details Ghulam A. Nadri, *Eighteenth-Century Gujarat: the Dynamics of Its Political Economy, 1750–1800* (Leiden: Brill, 2009), pp. 66–76.

16. The freight charges varied according to the weight or size and contents of the pack. A pack of dates or raisins, for example, paid 29 or 36 *mahmudis* and the VOC charged 40 *mahmudis* for a pack of almonds. A pack of linen was charged at 140, glasses at 60, and leather at 50 *mahmudis*. Passengers were charged separately and the standard rate for a trip from Gombroon to Surat seems to have been 100 *mahmudis*. VOC 1626, Specification of goods freighted by Muslim and Bania merchants on Moercappel to Surat, Gombroon, 20 November 1698, pp. 32–48.

17. Michelguglielmo Torri, 'In the Deep Blue Sea: Surat and its Merchant Class During the Dyarchic Era, 1759–1800', *Indian Economic and Social History Review*, vol. 19, nos 3–4 (1982), pp. 267–99; Ghulam A. Nadri, 'Sailing in Hazardous Waters: Maritime Merchants of Gujarat in the Second half of the Eighteenth Century', in Om Prakash (ed.), *History of Science, Philosophy and Culture in Indian Civilization, vol. III, part 7: The Trading World of the Indian Ocean 1500–1800* (New Delhi: Pearson, 2012), pp. 255–84.

18. Nadri, *Eighteenth-Century Gujarat*, pp. 67–9.

19. VOC 1626, Specification of goods freighted by Muslim and Bania merchants on Moercappel to Surat, Gombroon, 20 November 1698, pp. 32–48; VOC 1626, Specification of goods freighted by Muslim and Bania merchants on Schoonderlos to Surat, Gombroon, 6 February 1699, pp. 64–73.

20. VOC 1626, Specification of goods freighted by Muslim and Bania merchants on Moercappel to Surat, Gombroon, 20 November 1698, pp. 38–9.

21. Ibid.

22. Chaudhuri Sukanan Hargopal sending merchandise to Chaudhuri Hergopal or Anandji Andarji sending goods to Ranchod Anandji in Surat seem to be examples of family/household businesses. VOC 1626, Specification of goods freighted by Muslim and Bania merchants on Moercappel to Surat, Gombroon, 20 November 1698, pp. 38–9.

23. Haji Ibrahim and Haji Mohammad Shafi jointly freighted 4 chests of rose-water and 3 packs of dry fruits to Surat and Haji Mohammad Tahir and Haji Mohammad Taqi jointly freighted 33 chests of dry fruits to Surat. VOC 1626, Specification of goods freighted by Muslim and Bania merchants on Schoonderlos to Surat, Gombroon, 6 February 1699, p. 66.

24. Ibid., p. 70.

25. Ali Mohammad Khan, *Khatma Mirat-i Ahmadi*, ed. Syed Nawab Ali (Baroda:

Gaikwar Oriental Studies, 1930), pp. 132–8. Irfan Habib, 'Merchant Communities in Pre-Colonial India', in James D. Tracy (ed.), *The Rise of Merchant Empires* (Cambridge: Cambridge University Press, 1990), pp. 351–99.

26. Ashin Das Gupta, 'Gujarati Merchants and the Red Sea Trade, c. 1700–1750', in Gupta, *The World of the Indian Ocean Merchant*, pp. 376–88. René Barendse attributes a dominant role to the Banias in Surat's trade to the Persian Gulf. Barendse, *The Arabian Seas*, p. 178.

27. David L. White, 'Parsis in the Commercial World of Western India, 1700–1750', *Indian Economic and Social History Review*, vol. 24, no. 2 (1987), pp. 183–203; idem, *Competition and Collaboration: Parsi Merchants and the English East India Company in 18th Century India* (Delhi: 1995); Ghulam A. Nadri, 'Commercial World of Mancherji Khurshedji and the Dutch East India Company: A Study of Mutual Relationships', *Modern Asian Studies*, vol. 41, no. 2 (2007), pp. 315–42.

28. VOC 1379, Shipping list, Surat, 1682, ff. 2555^r–2564^v.

29. Prominent among them were Mohandas Naan, a broker of the VOC in Surat, Nagji Dharmadas and Achi Parekh. Their ships frequently sailed to Basra and Gombroon. VOC 1157, Shipping List, Surat, 1645, ff. 810r–815v; VOC 1224, Shipping List, Surat, 1657, ff. 196r–197v.

30. Nadri, 'The Commercial World of Mancherji Khurshedji and the Dutch East India Company', pp. 315–42; Nadri, *Eighteenth-Century Gujarat*, pp. 54–8.

31. VOC 2967, Shipping list, Surat, 1759, pp. 195–200.

32. Maharashtra State Archives, Mumbai, Surat Factory Diary, vol. 17, no. 1 (1763–5), pp. 210–11.

33. British Library, Factory Records: Surat, 67, Proceedings of the Chief and the Council in Surat, 13 April 1789, pp. 138–9.

34. In 1699, Mohan Ramji freighted four sacks of silver species to Surat, each for Mohammad Hussain, Mirza Ibrahim, Nagardas Sunderdas and Nattenji Biegla. VOC 1626, Specification of goods freighted by Muslim and Bania merchants on Schoonderlos to Surat, Gombroon, 6 February 1699, p. 68.

35. Ibid., p. 70.

36. Thabit A. J. Abdullah, *Merchants, Memluks, and Murder: The Political Economy of Trade in Eighteenth-Century Basra* (New York: State University of New York Press, 2001), 94.

6

THE BANIANS OF MUSCAT: A SOUTH ASIAN MERCHANT COMMUNITY IN OMAN AND THE GULF, c. 1500–1700[1]

Abdulrahman al Salimi

'Banian' is derived from '*vaṇija*' or '*baṇij*', which are Sanskrit words meaning 'merchant'.[2] The Arabs adopted the term 'Banian' from the fourteenth century onwards when the term was first mentioned in legal documents to describe the Hindu merchants from Gujarat in the Arabian coastal ports of southern Yemen and Oman. Then when the Portuguese arrived in the region in the sixteenth century they also referred to them as 'Banian/Banyan'. The term was later used by the Dutch, English and French when they arrived in the western Indian Ocean in the seventeenth century. This chapter is about the Banian – or Banyan – merchant communities in the western Indian Ocean, particularly those on the Omani coast and in the Gulf before the al-Bu Sa'īdī era in Oman. Recently, we have seen increasing interest in research into this community, its economic influence in the Indian Ocean and its traditions and social structure.[3]

Most of the Banian merchants were Hindus of the Vaishya caste (the third caste, also called the *Vani* or *Vania* in western India). The Persian term for a Hindu merchant was *gaur/gur* (pl. *gauran/guran*) – which means 'infidel' – or *gabr* (pl. *gabran*) ('fire-worshipper') – the word used to describe Zoroastrians.[4] The Banians, however, were not Zoroastrians. It was possible they were identified as such in order to provide them with protected status under Islam.

We can best understand the history of the Banian community in the Gulf region and in Oman if we consider it within the context of three periods:

1. The pre-Portuguese era. Studies on this period are mainly based on historical or archaeological sources. They are usually sketchy because, as the Banians' primary interest was in business and trade between the Indian Ocean ports (they would often return back to India after making their fortunes), they appear to have left few buildings or physical traces of their presence in other lands.
2. The Portuguese era during the sixteenth and seventeenth centuries. The role of the Banian in the events of this period can be studied through documents and other archival materials which are still a significant source of information on the European presence in the region at the dawn of the sixteenth century.
3. The British era from the eighteenth to the twentieth century. During this period relations blossomed between the Banian communities and the British as a result of their close ties with the British Empire's trading stations. Consequently, most information about these communities can be found in chronicles or other British sources.

The main focus of this chapter will be on the Banian presence in Oman and the Arabian Gulf during the second period (i.e. the Portuguese-Ya'riba era, 1624–1741 CE) before the Al-Bu Sa'id dynasty, still the ruling family in Oman, came to power in the 1740s. Our primary sources are Omani and Portuguese documents containing information about the local Banians and their socio-economic systems. In his 1981 paper on the Indian merchant community in Muscat, Calvin H. Allen Jr discussed the Banians in Muscat who had established an economic power base there, particularly during the reign of Sultan Ḥamad b. Sa'īd al-Bu Sa'īdī (r. 1786–92).[5] After Sultan Ḥamad took power in Muscat from his father Sayyid Sa'īd b. Ahmad in 1785, he made it his capital, while his father kept the old capital, Rustaq in the interior of Oman. Ḥamad operated a firm policy of securing trade routes to and through the Arabian Peninsula, particularly the route between Oman and Afghanistan via the Indus river, where the Sindi Bhattias were in direct competition with Ḥamad's state commercial activity.[6]

During the Portuguese-Ya'riba period another group of merchants also arrived in Muscat. Commonly known as 'Hydrabadis', these were the Lawatiya – a community who had formerly been Ismaili Shiite Muslims and later became Twelver Shiites.[7] (This change of sectarian allegiance attracted the interest of the Sunni and Ibadi schools.[8]) Cosmopolitanism, and the coexistence between the different communities that was a feature of life in Muscat during the sixteenth to seventeenth centuries, are recorded in Portuguese documents, where we read that Christians, Jews, Armenians, Hindus, Sindis, Persians, Africans and Arabs lived inside the Muscat walls, with each group residing in its own quarter. This intriguing fact offers an important clue to researchers investigating the reasons behind Muscat's transformation into Arabia's main port on the Indian Ocean.

Of the Omani material available to us on the Banians during the post-Ya'riba period (1624–1721), the writings of Ibn Ruzayq (d. 1874) are an invaluable source. While on the one hand informing his readers that he benefited personally from his close relationship with the Al-Bu Sa'īdī dynasty, Ibn Ruzayq also documented the establishment of the different religious and merchant communities in Muscat during the Ya'riba and post-Ya'riba periods. In his description of the recapture of the last Portuguese strongholds by the Omanis and the Portuguese expulsion from Oman (1649–50) during the reign of Imam Sultan b. Sayf Al-Yar'ubī in his books '*Al-Fath Al-Mubin fi sīrat Al-Sādah Al-Bu Sa'īdiyyin*', '*Al-Ṣaḥīfa al-Qaḥṭāniyya*' and '*Shi'ā' al-Shā'i b. lama'ān bi sirat āhl 'Umān*',[9] he stated that the Banians supported the Omanis during the capture of Muscat.

Ibn Ruzayq reported that his account of the capture of Muscat by the Omanis was taken orally from Ma'ruf b. Salim al-Ṣā'ighī, Ḥumayd b. Sālim and Khāṭir b. Ḥumayd al-Badā'ī. According to him, the account (which he paraphrased in his book) was passed on by word of mouth from what these men had heard from their ancestors, who had heard it from eyewitnesses.[10]

Banians, Omanis and the Conquest of Muscat: Legend and History

The story goes that the Banians began helping the Omanis when the Portuguese garrison commander – a man called Pereira – tried to marry the daughter of the head of the Banian community. His efforts were rejected because the Portuguese drank alcohol and ate meat – habits that the Banian religion regarded as profane. After Pereira (or in Arabic 'Farira') made it clear that he insisted on marrying the Banian girl, her father managed to persuade him that it would be advisable to drain the water from the garrison and discharge the gunpowder since its 'shelf-life' had expired. He (the head of the Banians) then told the Omanis what he had done, and this enabled them to capture the garrison after they had laid siege to Muscat for some time. Surrounded by high cliffs and guarded by formidable defences they had themselves established, the Portuguese were then unable to recapture the city. Thus, if we are to believe the story, the Omanis were able to expel the Portuguese from Oman only with the assistance of the Hindu Banians.

Remarkably, neither of the two most renowned historical works of the later Ya'riba period during the eighteenth century – Sarḥān al-Sarḥanī's' *Kashf al-Ghumma* and Muhammad al-Ma'walī's '*Qiṣaṣ wa ākhbār jarat fī 'Umān*' – reported this incident.[11] In fact, this story did not appear in Omani historical literature for nearly one and a half centuries. Ibn Ruzayq recorded it in around the third decade of the nineteenth century during the reign of Sultan Sa'īd b. Sulṭān (r. 1804–56). Nūr al-Dīn 'Abd Allah b. Ḥumayd Al-Sālimī (d. 1914) also reported it, apparently quoting from Ibn Ruzayq, since he refers to the three men who gave Ibn Ruzayq the details of what had happened.[12]

This story was also not mentioned in the Portuguese documents that have come into our possession so far.[13] The British Captain Alexander Hamilton (c. 1688–1733 CE) stated that details of the Omanis' capture of Muscat are mentioned in British and early European sources,[14] though his account of the incident does not suggest that the Banians played a role. Instead, he referred to the part played by Imam Sultan b. Sayf (r. 1649–80)'s wife, who he claimed was descended from 'the Prophet's house' (presumably he meant the Prophet's tribe Quraysh). According to Hamilton's version, the war started because the Portuguese governor of Muscat sent pork as a gift to the Imam, which angered him; the Imam's wife then swore she would never move until Muscat was back in Omani hands. The Imam's army was stirred to action by her oath and battled its way into Muscat. This cost the Omani army the death of thousands of men.[15]

Later, however, in his commentary and introduction to his translation of Ibn Ruzayq's *K. al-Fatḥ al-Mubiyn*, G. Badger, who named the Banian leader as 'Narutem', tells a different story from Hamilton's and agrees with the Omani historians that the Banian helped the Omanis from the inside.[16] The British traveller Grattan Geary's account of his Muscat trip in 1878 mentioned the name Narrotum.[17] However, although the Banian leader appears as Narutem in Badger's translation, Ibn Ruzayk called him Sakabīlla. This discrepancy could be explained by the fact that Badger's footnotes refer to early European sources which give an account of the capture of Muscat, so the name Narutem could have come from there.[18]

By contrast, Nūr al-Dīn Al-Sālimī (d. 1914) mentioned that there were two Banians working as agents for the Portuguese – Purshottam/Narrottum and the head of the Banian community, who was called Sakkabilla. However, in this version of events it was Narrotum's daughter (not Sakkabilla's) that the Portuguese commander proposed to marry. Although I have not been able to identify the source of Nūr al-Dīn al-Sālimī's reference to the two names, his account appears more likely to be correct since it is compatible with several other accounts.[19] Possibly due to its assistance against the Portuguese, the Banian community was exempted from paying the poll tax (*jizya*) by Imam Sulṭān b. Sayf Al-Yarabi (r. 1649–80), who also gave the community certain privileges. This situation continued under subsequent rulers.[20]

The Open Gate: The Banian Legend in Omani Literature

This was the inspiration for a story by the famous writer Abd Allah al-Ṭa'ī (d. 1972), who retold it in *'Al-Shira' al-Kabir'* ('Big Sail') in a fictionalised version in which the Banian leader's daughter – Tchandra/Tshandra – opened the gate of the garrison for the Omanis. In writing this story, Abd Allah al-Ṭa'ī's intention was to highlight the blend of traditions and peoples among the Gulf population as well as the way the Gulf tribes co-operated to expel the Portuguese during the reign of Imam Sayf b. Sulṭān. At the time he wrote it, al-Ṭa'ī was inspired by Arab nationalism and its goal of Arab unity, which was a major feature of the region's politics in the 1950s and 1960s.[21] In addition to the sources mentioned previously, Al-Ṭa'ī also used Portuguese documents to illuminate the role of Banians in Muscat society.

Banian in the Sixteenth-century Gulf

If we examine the Portuguese documents that have been published recently, they will reveal the cosmopolitan relationships described by al-Ta'ī and enable us to trace the way they developed. On the basis of the recorded documents currently available to us, we can conclude that these connections and working relationships between diverse peoples and Gulf tribes began in 1522 and continued until the defeat of the Portuguese in the Battle of Diu in 1669.[22] Although aspects of the story of the Banian helping the Omanis may have been fictional, they were probably based on a very real set of relationships of mutual dependence and co-operation between Omanis and Banians that had continued for centuries.

A report issued in Hormuz covering the period from 29 November 1521 to 23 July 1522 lists the booty seized by the Portuguese fleet under the command of the 'Captain-Major of the Sea of Hormuz/Sea of Oman' D. Luis de Meneses. In this document, which is highly significant in view of its content, all the booty seized by the Portuguese from Masirah Island, off the coast of Oman, to Bahrain is described. Included in the documents were twenty-two Banian prisoners. The report gave their total value as 59,400 Ryan. According to the report, D. Luis de Meneses sold two Banian prisoners in Hormuz for 30,000 Ryans, which was equal to 100 Pardaus. He then sold another Banian prisoner for thirty Pardaus, which was equal to 9,000 Ryans.[23] This showed that Banians were very much a part of Omani society in this early period.

According to available documents dating from the beginning of the sixteenth century, there appeared to have been Banians living in Oman's coastal cities well before the arrival of the Portuguese. Portuguese often treated the Banians as prisoners and sold them as slaves. The reason for this was that the Portuguese saw them as allies with the Portuguese adversaries. Banian fighters actively engaged in hostilities against the Portuguese and other outsiders alongside the Omanis. Thus, Banians were, in many cases, treated as combatants, not as vassals or protected subjects.

At this early stage, it seems the Portuguese vision of empire was still evolving and their overall objectives were not yet determined. We have not come across any documents which can cast much light on the Gulf Banian situation in the sixteenth century; those that we have found generally suggest that the Portuguese were trying to devise the most effective way of achieving supremacy in the western Indian Ocean region over rival powers such as the Ottomans and Persians and that the Banians were one piece on the strategic chessboard.

Banian in the Seventeenth-century Gulf

From the seventeenth century onward, the Portuguese attitude to Muscat and its residents reflected Portugal's ambitions for greater overseas expansion. A major factor was the impact of economic and political events in Western Europe. Importantly, many Portuguese rivals were beginning to embrace the capitalist system, and the imperial Portuguese system now faced rivals for markets and influence. In particular, the Portuguese faced competition from the Dutch and the British, who were using the power and influence of their respective East India Companies in order to mould the trade system in the region in accordance with their own rules.

The Portuguese had imposed a system of citizen taxation in which residents under their colonial rule had to pay tax, regardless of their ethnic or religious affiliation; indeed, the tax regulations were the most important issue dealt with in the documents in our possession. According to a document issued in Goa on 26 October 1620, separate rules applied to the levying of taxes upon residents, settlers and foreigners. Portuguese who were coming from India paid a 5 per cent tax, while Portuguese resident in Muscat paid 3.5 per cent; Muslims and Banians paid 8.5 per cent in Muscat and on the coast, 7.5 per cent of which was payable to local sheikhs. This was a clear indication that the Portuguese established a direct relationship with the country's sheikhs, who became their agents and direct employees alongside those state officials who were Portuguese or other European nationals. In classic colonialist fashion, they co-opted the local leadership. This resulted in a broad partnership of interests; the sheikhs, for instance, used to deliver grain grown in Oman to the Portuguese.[24]

Dynamic Catholic missionary activities were also highly effective in spreading Portuguese influence. A document issued in Muscat on 22 August 1626 listed the names of people who had converted to Christianity through the preaching of the Augustinian order during the previous three years. The list of converts – including, among others, Arabs, Persians, Armenians, Jews,

Turks, Sindis, Malabaris, Dius, Goans and Bengalis – reflected the ethnic and religious diversity of Muscat's residents at that time. The list also included Banians who had converted to Christianity, though the majority of converts were coastal dwellers from Persia.[25]

During this period a gradual shift was seen in the relationship between the Portuguese and many of the Banians. Muscat fortress had become a significant centre of military and naval funding for the Portuguese, as well as a hub for trade and the distribution of medical and food supplies, and this encouraged close interaction between all the resident communities. A document issued in Goa on 10 October 1624 shows that a Banian named Raghau was financing Muscat fortress by selling opium (a piece of opium was worth 35 Ashrafis). This was the first tangible sign of the Banian community's gradual rise to prominence as merchants. The opium had not been produced in Oman; it appears that it had been imported from north-western India.[26]

The Banians were becoming major financial players in Muscat port, where the local Portuguese authorities employed them as collectors of customs and anchorage duties. Interestingly, a document issued in Goa on 12 April 1628 noted that the Portuguese captain Luis de Sequeira refused to pay 1,009 Pardaus in dues to a Banian because of a cash loan. This shows that the Banians were actively involved in banking just years before the fall of Muscat to the Omanis.[27]

The struggle against the Portuguese in Oman began in the 1630s, according to a report issued in Goa in January 1636. Gaspar de Melode Sampaio, a Portuguese writer, spoke of the possibility of creating the office of Castellan (Castle Governor) in Muscat. The report, which was sent to the King of Portugal, contained references to the following:

1. The Omani revolution and the Omanis' siege of the Portuguese fortress.
2. A misunderstanding between the Captain-Major of Muscat and the Captain-Major of Muscat fortress that had led to commercial unrest.

The document also pointed out that Muscat had a large population of Muslims, Christians, Jews and Banians, all of whom coexisted peaceably in the city, and that each religious community had its own quarter inside

Muscat's city wall.[28] The Portuguese Captain-Major of Muscat's responsibilities included dealing with these groups on a day-to-day basis as well as protecting them. The major topic in this document was taxation, especially the issue of how to deal with the multiplicity of Muscat's religious and ethnic groups, including converts; in particular, who should be treated as protected subjects and who should come under the direct authority of the Portuguese administration in Muscat.

On 12 February 1636 a Portuguese Royal Decree was issued in Lisbon in the name of King Philip, laying down the regulations for Muscat fortress, its factory, the tax and how to implement it.[29] This decree was among the most significant documents to be issued on administrative regulation in the western Indian Ocean during the seventeenth century, particularly since it showed the impact of changes taking place in Europe upon Portuguese colonies overseas. We shall here consider the following items or clauses in the Royal Decree that concern the Banians:

1. Arab Muslims or Banians were of the same class, quite distinct from the Portuguese living in Muscat: *'The clerk of the said customs house, my accountant, the remaining Moorish officials and banyans of the said sheikh.'*
2. Tax revenue mentioned the Banians. *'As for the tax collected and the revenue from rice output and from the custom of the banyans [Banians], residents of the villages of Kalbuh [and] Riyam in Muscat.'* However, the Banians became the region's major rice suppliers.
3. Banians were involved in the reform of financial control and supervision on how the money is spent: *'When the dispatches of the said customs house are issued the overseer of the treasury, if any, will always be present, and in his absence my factor, and Sheikh Keys, the judge and vizier, or whoever succeeds them.'*
4. Fraudulent behaviour by Portuguese businessmen to evade custom duties involved Banians. The Royal Decree said: *'I have been informed that some Portuguese merchants or captains of vessels dispatch under their titles and names some goods belonging to banians and heathens to help themselves of the two and a half percent that banians and other people wearing turbans pay in excess of the Portuguese, because the Portuguese pay five percent, as stated above, and the banians pay seven and a half percent. From now on, when*

the officials of the customs house believe and assume that some people do such collusion they will swear them in to declare if those goods are theirs, and they will open some fardels [and] search for the loading passes that usually are inside [penned] in banian writing or in Portuguese, and in which the name of the owners are declared. And the same procedure will be followed as regards the burghers of Muscat, who also do the same in collusion with the banians, to receive four percent.'

5. The Decree appointing the Sheikh of Muscat, Sheikh Rashid, to be the overseer of non-Portuguese, both Arabs and Banians, and to be responsible for them before the authorities.

6. The tax law distinguished between Muslim and Banian merchants living in Muscat and those outside Muscat. Customs duties for exported goods belonging to a Banian merchant living outside Muscatare were to be charged at the rate of 0.5 per cent according to the assessment made by the custom house.

7. Customs duties on ships at the port are to be paid to the Muscat Sheikh, whether the ships come from the Arabian Peninsula or India, and whether they belong to Muslims, Banians or others.

Another remarkable Portuguese document from this period was on the pearl trade in the Gulf. Pearls were the Gulf's major export commodity in the pre-oil era. A document issued by the Kunju commercial centre on 26 October 1648 showed that a boom was taking place in the Gulf region's pearl trade, particularly between the Gulf and the Indian sub-continent. The trade was controlled by the Banians, since they were the people who actually exported the pearls to India. Despite differences with the Portuguese mentioned above, the Banians also acted as fund-raisers for the Portuguese and financed their expansion in the Gulf in the face of competition from their Dutch and British rivals.[30]

According to the account of the British writer J. G. Lorimer, there were two types of pearl merchants in the Gulf: the *musaqqim* and the *tawwāsh*. The *musaqqim* funded the pearling expedition, either partly or wholly, and took a usurious rate of interest from the divers or the ship owner, while the *tawwāsh* was the merchant who bought the pearls directly from the pearling dhows. Both functions were dominated by Banians until the nineteenth century, when they were gradually replaced by Persians or local Arabs. The trade continued to be run by both these types of merchants – *musaqqim* and *tawwāsh* – until recently.[31]

According to records, after the Muscat incidents a co-operative relationship developed between the Banians and the Omanis. This could be mainly because the Banians were the responsibility of the regional sheikh, who was also responsible for delivering the taxation money collected from the other ethnic groups in Muscat.

The Portuguese presence in Muscat came to an end in the mid-seventeenth century, due to an alliance between Banians and Omanis. However, that was not the end of the story of conflict and interaction between Portugal and Oman. A document from 1669 written by an Augustinian missionary and containing a report on the Battle of the Port city of Diu showed that the Portuguese were still wishing to expand over the western Indian Ocean. The document notes that in the battle for Diu there was clear co-operation between the Omanis and the Banians, to the extent that the latter opened up access to part of their district in the city to enable the Omanis to enter it.[32] The Banians helped the Omanis break the outer wall of their quarter in Diu. The Omanis then brought a large number of ladders and scaled another section of the wall of the Banian settlement through to the new St Sebastian bulwark. They seized the parapet walks of the fortress and stationed twenty pieces of artillery along the wall of the Banian settlement. According to the reports, the attitudes of the city's Muslims and Christians were anti-Omani.[33]

According to the accounts mentioned above, the Omanis captured around two hundred Banians and took them to Muscat. The Omanis refused ransom. The Omanis may have been keen to re-establish Banians in Muscat, reviving it as a city with an ethnically diverse merchant and trading community, as had been the case during the Ya'riba and Portuguese eras. The Banians, whether captured or not, certainly played an important role during the nineteenth and twentieth centuries in administering the customs in the port of Muscat.

The British and the Gulf Banians

By the beginning of the nineteenth century the British arose as the rulers of the Indian subcontinent. Indians of all religions and castes migrated within the British Empire over the Indian Ocean and across the Pacific, employed and protected under British rule. Under the protection of the British, the Banians, like the Jews of Iraq, had the opportunity to invest their experience and expertise in order to benefit from the emerging modern financial and marketing systems. Meanwhile, the Omanis and Portuguese saw their scattered empires in the Indian Ocean gradually disappear. They yielded to the rising power of the British.

Notes

1. My thanks go to Pedro Pinto, Universidade NOVA de Lisboa.
2. Monier Monier-Williams, *A Sanskrit–English Dictionary Etymologically and Philologically Arranged with Special Reference to Cognate Indo-European Languages* (Oxford: Oxford University Press, 1992), p. 915.
3. Antunes, LuísFrederico Dias, 'The Trade Activities of the Banyans in Mozambique: Private Indian Dynamics in the Portuguese State Economy (1686–1777)', in Mathew, K. S. (ed.), *Mariners, Merchants and Oceans: Studies in Maritime History* (New Delhi: Ajay Kumar Jain, 1998), pp. 301–32; Pearson, Michael N., 'Banyas and Brahmins: Their Role in the Portuguese Indian Economy', in *Coastal Western India: studies from the Portuguese records* (New Delhi, Concept Publishing Company, 1981 (XCHR Studies series, 2)), pp. 93–115; Gommans, Jos and Kuiper, Juitske (eds), 'The Surat Castle Revolutions: Myths of an Anglo-Banian Order and Dutch Neutrality, C. 1740–1760', *Journal of Early Modern History*, vol. 10, no. 4 (2006), pp. 361–89; Subramanian, Lakshmi, 'Capital and Crowd in a Declining Asian Port City: The Anglo-Banian Order and the Surat Riots of 1795', *Modern Asian Studies*, vol. 19, no. 2 (1985), pp. 205–37; Torri, Michelguglielmo, 'Trapped Inside the Colonial Order: The Hindu Bankers of Surat and their Business World during the Second Half of the Eighteenth Century', in *Trade in Politics in the Indian Ocean : Historical and Contemporary Perspectives* (New Delhi: Manohar Publications, 1990), pp. 47–79; Antunes, LuísFrederico, 'Osmercadoresbaneanesguzerates no comércio e a navegação da costa oriental africana (Século XVIII)', in *Actas do SeminárioMoçambique: Navegações, Comércio e Técnicas: Maputo, 25 a 28 de Novembro de 1996* (Lisbon: ComissãoNacionalpara as Comemorações dos DescobrimentosPortugueses, 1998), pp. 67–93; Antunes, LuísFrederico Dias, *A actividade da companhia de comércio: Baneanes de Diu emMoçambique 1686–1777* Lisbon, s.n., 1992); Antunes, LuísFrederico Dias, 'A actividade da Companhia de Comércio dos

Baneanes de Diu emMoçambique: a dinâmicaprivadaindiana no quadro da economiaestatalportuguesa (1686–1777)', *Mare Liberum*, vol. 4 (1992), pp. 143–64; Antunes, LuísFrederico Dias, 'A Crise no Estado da Índia no Final do século XVII e a Criação das Companhias de Comércio das ÍndiasOrientais e dos Baneanes de Diu', *Mare Liberum*, vol. 9 (1995), pp. 19–29; Lobo, Almiro, 'Baneanes de Diu emMoçambique: fragmentos de um auto-retrato', in Laborinho, Ana Paula *et al.* (eds), *A vertigem do Oriente: modalidadesdiscursivas no encontro de culturas* (Lisbon: Cosmos, 1999 (Viagem, 7)), pp. 185–215; Monteiro, Ana Rita Amaro, 'InfluênciasBaneane e IslâmicanaIlha de Moçambique, nosfinais do Século XIX', *Africana*, vol. 19 (1998), pp. 193–226; Zamparoni, Valdemir, 'Monhés, Baneanes, Chinas e Afro-maometanos. Colonialismo e racismoemLourenço Marques, Moçambique, 1890–1940', *Lusotopie*, 2000, pp. 191–222.

4. James Onley, Indian Communities in the Persian Gulf, c.1500–1947, in Lawrence G. Potter (ed.), *The Persian Gulf in Modern Times: People, Ports, and History* (New York: Palgrave Macmillan, 2014), pp. 231–66.

5. Calvin H Allen, The Indian Merchant Community of Masqat, *Bulletin of the School of Oriental and African Studies*, vol. XLIV (1981), pp. 39–53.

6. Calvin H Allen, The State of Masqat in the Gulf and East Africa 1785–1829, *International Journal of Middle East Studies*, vol. XIV (1982), pp. 117–27.

7. Abbas Mustafa Al-Lawati, 'The Lawatiya of Oman: The Identity Transformations of an Ethno-Religious Minority', MA dissertation, Exeter University, 2012.

8. Laurence Louër, *Transnational Shia Politics: Religious and Political Networks in the Gulf* (Columbia University Press, 2008), p. 147,

9. Ḥumayd b. Muhammad Ibn Ruzayq, *Al-Fatḥ Al-Mubīnfīsīrat Al-Sādah Al-BūSaʾīdiyyin*, ed. ʿAbd al-Munʿim ʿĀmir and Muhammad Mursī ʿAbd Allah (Ministry of Heritage and Culture: Muscat, 1977), p. 262; Ḥumayd b. Muhammad Ibn Ruzayq, *Al-Ṣaḥīfa al-Qaḥṭāniyya*, ed. Hasan Muhammad al-Nābūdha, vol. 2, pp. 544–6, Dār al-Bārūdī: Beirut, 2009; Ḥumayd b. Muhammad Ibn Ruzayq, *Shuʾāʾ al-Shāʾiʾ biʾ lamaʾān bi Dhikr Āʾ ʾimmat ʿUmān*, ed, ʿAbd al-Munʾim ʿĀmir (Muscat: Ministry of Heritage and Culture, 1987), p. 255,

10. Ḥumayd b. Muhammad Ibn Ruzayq, *Al-Ṣaḥīfa Al-Qaḥṭāniyya*, vol. 2, pp. 544–6.

11. Sirḥān b. Saʿīd al-Sarḥanī, *Kashf al-Ghumma al-Jāmiʾ li-Akhbār al-Umma*, ed. Hasan Muhammad al-Nabudha (Beirut: Dār al-Bārūdī, 2006); AbūSulaymān Muhammad b. ʿĀmir b. Rāshid al-Mawalī, *Qiṣaṣwaākhbārjarat bi-ʾUmān* (Muscat: Ministry of Heritage and Culture, 1979).

12. Nūr al-DīnAbd Allah b. Ḥumayd al-Sālimī, *Tuḥfat al-Ā'iyān bi-sīratāhl 'Umān*, vol. 2, pp. 64–7, Maktabat al-Istiqāma (Muscat, 2002).

13. *Portugal in the Sea of Oman – Religion and Politics*, ed. Abdulrahman al-Salimi and Michael Jansen (Philipp von Zabern, 2012) (16 vols); with translation see *Portugal in the Sea of Oman: Religion and Politics. Research on Documents: Part 2: Volumes 1–10. Transcription, English Translation, Arabic Translation*, ed. Abdulrahman al-Salimi and Michael Jansen (Hildesheim: Olms, 2016).

14. Alexander Hamilton, *A New Account of the East Indies* (London: C. Hitch & A. Miller, 1744), pp. 60–77.

15. Ibid.

16. Salil Ibn Razik, *History of the Imams and Seyyids of Oman, from A.D. 661–1856*, trans. George Percy Badger (London: Hakluyt Society, 1871), p. xxvi, p. 87.

17. Philip Ward, *Travels in Oman* (Cambridge: Oleander Press, 1987), pp. 35–8.

18. Salil Ibn Ruzik, *History of the Imams and Seyyid of Oman*, p. 84; Ibn Ruzaykh, *Fatḥ*, p. 262.

19. Al-Salimi, *Tuḥfa*, v. 2, pp. 64–7.

20. Salil Ibn Ruzik, *History of the Imams and Seyyids*, p. 87; al-Salimi, *Tuḥfa*, v. 2, pp. 64–7.

21. Abd Allah Muhammad al-Ṭā'ī, *al-Shirā' al-Kabīr*, Muscat, p. 98; In fact this novel was the last work of al-Ṭā'ī and completed in 1973.

22. Portugal in the Sea of Oman (v. 1–16). 2011.

23. Portugal in the Sea of Oman, v. 1, p. 295; *Núcleo Antigo*, N.º 592, Hormuz, 29/11/1521–23/07/1522.

24. Portugal in the Sea of Oman, v. 5, p. 2,065; *Junta da Real Fazenda do Estado da Índia*, Livro 4, fol. 45v.º–47, Goa, 26/10/1620.

25. Ibid., v. 6, p. 2,531; *Manuscritos da Livraria*, 731, fol. 287–290, Muscat, 22/08/1626.

26. Ibid., v. 12, p. 5,259; *Fundo Geral*, Códice 1784, fol. 103v.º–104, [Goa], 10/10/1624.

27. Ibid., v. 12, p. 5,607; *Fundo Geral*, Códice 1986, fol. 32–34, Goa, 12/04/1628.

28. Ibid., v. 7, p. 3,119; *DocumentosRemetidos da Índia*, Livro 35, fol. 60–60v.º [Goa, 01/1636].

29. Ibid., v. 7, p. 3,181; *DocumentosRemetidos da Índia*, Livro 45, fol. 309–333v.º Goa, 12/02/1636.

30. Ibid., v. 9, p. 4,213; *DocumentosRemetidos da Índia*, Livro 59, fol. 94, Bandar-e Kong, 29/10/1648.

31. J. G. Lorimer, *Gazetteer of the Persian Gulf, Oman and Central Arabia* (Cambridge: Archive Editions, 1986), pp. 2,225–7.

32. Ibid., v. 10, p. 4,629; *Manuscritos da Livraria*, 1699, fol. 1–146, Goa, 24/12/1669.

33. Ibid., v. 10, p. 4,677, 4,685, 4,693; *CartórioJesuítico*, Maço 27, N.º 6, fol. 17–20, Goa, 03/06/1676; *CartórioJesuítico*, Maço 27, N.º 6, fol. 21v.º–24v.º, Diu, 13/06/1676; *CartórioJesuítico*, Maço 27, N.º 6, fol. 25v.º–29, Diu, 03/07/1676.

7

KHALIJI HINDUSTAN: TOWARDS A DIASPORIC HISTORY OF KHALIJIS IN SOUTH ASIA FROM THE 1780s TO THE 1960s

Johan Mathew

The relationship between South Asia and the Gulf today is sometimes reduced to an image of exploited migrant labourers. Whether it is construction work under the scorching Khaliji sun or sleeping in filthy and overcrowded dormitories, we imagine the South Asian experience in the Gulf as one of oppression and immiseration. However, if you had presented this image to a resident of the Gulf a hundred years ago he or she may have doubled over with laughter. Such a future would have seemed unimaginable. Indeed, at the beginning of the twentieth century, Indian residents in the Khalij would have been far wealthier than the average Arab (or Iranian or African). Those from the subcontinent also enjoyed special privileges and protections provided by the British Raj that were not necessarily extended to the Gulf. In this period, India similarly stood in relationship to the Gulf not as a supplier of cheap labour but as an imperial metropole and beacon of modernity.

The Gulf has long been a neglected corner of the Arab world, and historians in particular often saw the region as an unrewarding site of inquiry. In recent years, however, historians have increasingly turned to the Gulf as a space worthy of historical study. These scholars have uncovered rich histories of urban life, piracy, empire and, of course, oil production in the region.[1]

With good reason, these scholars have focused on events occurring between the Shatt al-Arab and the Straits of Hormuz. There is no escaping the numerous groups that enter and leave the Gulf, from Ottoman and British administrators to Indian merchants to African slaves. Yet Khalijis themselves appear to be somehow circumscribed by the Straits of Hormuz.[2] The standard image of Khalijis before the era of oil remains that of the *bedu*, or Bedouin, who at most shepherded his flocks to Mecca or Basra. In this conventional wisdom, the Indian Ocean world came to the Gulf but not vice versa.

However powerful this image appears, it is false. Omanis ruled a vast empire down the Swahili coast, and Kuwaiti and Bahraini sailors and merchants were regular visitors as far south as Madagascar and as far east as Calicut. Abdelrahman Munif's classic novels either created the conventional narrative of Khaliji history, or consolidated this narrative as the accepted history.[3] Munif most likely inherited some of his feel for Khaliji history from the narratives constructed by British colonial officials. In this telling, Khalijis were parochial, primitive and isolated from the world until the arrival of British traders and diplomats. The convenient erasure of the Gulf's connections to South Asia, Africa and the wider Ottoman and Persianate worlds was a classic move of orientalist scholarship. Conceiving of a static and immobile Orient highlighted the progressive and technologically superior nature of European civilisation. Munif's depictions of Khaliji communities seem very much caught up in this vision of the Arabian Desert. The shock of the seaside community of Harran at seeing a steamship, and European women, in what would have been the 1930s makes little sense even for the more remote fishing communities of the al-Hasa coast. For at least a century, they had been seeing British and Ottoman officials, and since the 1860s steamships were a regular presence in the Gulf.

Contrary to this vision of an immobile and isolated Gulf, this book seeks to place the region in a long history of communication and interaction with the wider world. We are pushed to contemplate and excavate the cosmopolitan qualities of the Gulf that precede and shape the cosmopolitan population that arrives with petro-capitalism. This of course raises the question of what we mean by cosmopolitanism: does it still carry with it Euro-centric and elitist connotations? Or perhaps a Khaliji cosmopolitanism was more working-class and less pretentious: a cosmopolitanism of sailors and traders. One could not get very far in the commercial world of the Gulf without dealing with merchants from Iran, East Africa, Yemen and British India, as well as Europe. Foreign commodities, from rice to timber to guns, made their way into the Gulf from across the globe, but, just as importantly, dates, pearls and fish from the Gulf were sent across the globe in the nineteenth century. Dhows from Kuwait, Bahrain and the Omani coast made their way to every corner of the western Indian Ocean.

Far from being isolated, the Gulf has always been an important part of a *longue durée* history of globalisation, as other chapters in this volume make clear. Labourers from Africa have travelled across these waters from at least the eighth-century Abbasid Caliphate. Over its waters is the path of the oldest maritime trade route in human history, connecting the Indus valley civilisations to that of ancient Mesopotamia. Moreover, it is no coincidence that the Gulf's oldest trading connections are to South Asia. Proximity obviously plays a central role in this connection, but as important is the fact that these regions have very different climatic conditions and consequently agricultural products. This difference, predicated on the divergent geographies produced by the moisture-rich monsoon winds, was an essential component to productive exchange. Thus while the Gulf has engaged in productive exchange with the Swahili coast, Japan, Britain and the Americas, South Asia has always held a position of prominence.

The following pages will focus on Khalijis in South Asia. I hope to illuminate the history of this admittedly small community, but also to argue for its significance to both the Gulf and the urban life of western Indian cities. The majority of Khalijis residing in British India were sailors and small-scale merchants, or indeed sailors who were also small-scale merchants. But the nature of the historical record leaves only the smallest traces of their presence, so they will unfortunately only be discussed in passing here. This chapter will focus first on the ruling elites of the Gulf, and the ways in which British India provided a space of exile and escape from the frustrations of rule within Britain's informal empire. Secondly, we will turn to the more prominent Khaliji merchant families, their lives in South Asia and their impact on the urban life of cities like Mumbai (known as Bombay until 1995). A history of the Khaliji diaspora in South Asia brings into relief the transnational dynamics of political power in the Gulf and the cosmopolitanism of Khaliji society well before the impact of oil wealth.

Exile and Escape

Mumbai's most iconic street is Marine Drive, a broad thoroughfare reclaimed from the Arabian Sea in the early twentieth century. If you walk along with the crowds of amorous couples and middle-aged joggers you may just notice, among the Art Deco facades from the 1930s and 1940s, 'Al-Sabah Court' and 'Al-Jaberiya Court'. These exemplars of Bombay's architectural heritage and two prime pieces of Bombay real estate are, of course, owned by the ruling family of Kuwait.[4] They are certainly the most visible evidence of the long history of Khalijis in India, and particularly of the presence of Khaliji royalty in India's urban fabric. These iconic buildings were most likely purchased with the proceeds of the Al-Sabah's burgeoning revenues from oil. However, Khaliji sheikhs and sultans had been influencing the urban geography of South Asia for centuries.

The history of the port of Gwadar, in present-day Pakistani Baluchistan, is tied to almost two centuries under the rule of the al-Bu Saʿidi Dynasty of Oman. It is particularly appropriate that the port city began its colonial existence as the home for an exile from the Omani throne. Sayyid Sultan bin Ahmed had hoped to become the next ruler in the al-Bu Saʿidi Dynasty, but lost out to his brother and escaped across the Gulf of Oman to the territories of the Khan of Khalat. In 1783, the Khan granted Sayyid Sultan the port of Gwadar as a temporary measure until he could retake Oman. Gwadar was strategically located, just within striking distance of the Bu Saʿidi capital in Muscat. It was only after the death of his brother that Sayyid Sultan returned to Muscat, most likely backed by a group of Baluchi mercenaries, and finally succeeded in taking the throne from his brother's son. While there were continuing disputes over the legitimacy of Omani rule, Gwadar would continue to be administered by a *wali* appointed by the descendants of Sultan bin Ahmed until 1958.[5] The port-colony of Gwadar is the perhaps the most prominent mark of the Khalij on the geography of South Asia, and the only impact of Khalijis on the region that actually shows up on geopolitical maps. Furthermore, it is not a coincidence that Gwadar was founded as a place of exile for an aspirant to the Bu Saʿidi throne. Its close proximity to Muscat, the long history of Baluchi soldiers in the Bu Saʿidi military and dense trading connections made the South Asian coastline a natural place of exile for an Omani royal.

Sayyid Sultan's successor Saʿid would come to rule over the zenith of the Omani Empire in the Indian Ocean world. But unlike their grandfather, Saʿid's sons would not have an opportunity to fight it out to establish who would rule this great empire. Instead, British officials divided the Bu Saʿidi empire between two sons. The elder Sayyid Thuwaini would rule in Oman itself. He was born to Sayyid Saʿid's concubine Khurshid, who was from Malabar in the west coast of India.[6] It is impossible to tell precisely what impact this had on Thuwaini, but it is hard to imagine that she did not leave some impression on the life of her son. Indeed, there was a clear cosmopolitan character to the household of the rulers of Muscat, with numerous concubines from Circassia and Ethiopia also becoming the mothers of sultans. After the death of Sayyid Thuwaini bin Said, Muscat entered a period of turmoil when several different members of the family jockeyed to assume power, and India would serve as both waiting room and retirement home for failed aspirants to the Bu Saʿidi throne.

First, Thuwaini's son Salim took power in 1866, allegedly as a result of parricide. This power grab sent his uncle Turki bin Saʿid and his family into exile in Bombay.[7] Salim was then overthrown by a cousin, ʿAzzan bin Qais, who was supported by the more conservative Ibadhis of the Omani hinterland. Meanwhile, Turki's exile in Bombay allowed him to consolidate British support against ʿAzzan and eventually retake his brother's throne. After solidifying his position, Sayyid Turki sought to eliminate his competitors, but they escaped to British protection in India. The deposed Salim found refuge in the commercial centre of Hyderabad in the Sind province of western India.[8] Turki's brother Abdul Aziz cooled his heels in Bombay, until he appeared less a threat than an asset and was recalled to Muscat.[9] Indeed by 1875, Sayyid Turki was feeling the frustrations of rule, particularly under the pressure of British influence. He asked the local British agent if he might abdicate in favour of his brother Abdul Aziz and retire to Karachi with an allowance for his expenses. After some negotiation he in fact did abdicate, only to return a few months later having changed his mind and exiling his brother back to Karachi.[10] On the death of Sayyid Turki, his brother Abdul Aziz would leave Bombay one last time and try to assume their father's throne, but he failed and eventually died not in Oman but in India.[11] This game of musical chairs between Muscat, Bombay and Karachi reflects the dense political, social and economic connections between these cities. Bombay and Karachi, rather than Baghdad, Tehran or Mecca, were the places where an Omani could stay out of trouble and yet remain closely connected to events back in Muscat.

One of the more interesting members of the Bu Saʿidi family also made her way to Bombay and while there linked up with the Al-Khalifas of Bahrain. Naz al-Bustan was a Circassian slave purchased by Sayyid Thuwaini in Istanbul and brought to Muscat. In her account, his brother Turki married Naz al-Bustan, but after seven years of marriage he divorced her and she went to live with Thuwaini's daughter. Then she was aggressively courted by the *wali* of Dhofar, Suleiman ibn Suweilim, also allegedly a former slave. She felt, however, that he was merely a servant of the sultan and thus was beneath her. But with much pressure from the royal family she eventually married Suleiman, settled in Dhofar and bore him a son.

Not surprisingly, after a few years Naz became unhappy with her life in the wilderness of Dhofar. She particularly complained that her husband had taken away the jewellery given to her by Sayyid Thuwaini and Sayyid Turki. She decided to leave her husband and returned to Muscat, seeking refuge with Thuwaini's daughter. But Naz had miscalculated; the princess rebuffed her, saying that Naz was not Suleiman's wife but his slave and so she had no choice but to return to Dhofar. A less self-confident woman would have accepted her fate, but Naz al-Bustan was clearly a force to be reckoned with. She surreptitiously escaped from Muscat, and found a place on a dhow going to Bombay for herself, her child and even her *ayah* (nanny). After arriving in a city where she lacked both social networks and social status, Naz had to somehow find a means of support. She asked around the Arab community in Bombay and was directed to appeal to Sheikh ʿIsa ibn Khalifa.[12] Now it is not certain that this Sheikh ʿIsa ibn Khalifa is the same man as the one who was ruling Bahrain at this time, but it is hard to imagine that Naz would have been directed to another Sheikh ʿIsa ibn Khalifa who also happened to be staying in Bombay and had the economic wherewithal to support a woman, her child and *ayah* without difficulty. Like his fellow royals the Bu Saʿidis, Sheikh ʿIsa was apparently escaping the Khaliji summer in an Indian hill station. But when he returned to Bombay he was happy to take on the responsibility of supporting Naz and her small family. In the late nineteenth century, Bombay was not only an important centre for British imperial influence over Bahrain, but also the most important market for Bahraini pearls. In this context it is not surprising that Sheikh ʿIsa seemed to maintain almost a second home in the city.

As the twentieth century opened, Bombay would only become a stronger magnet for Khaliji royalty. Sayyid Turki's son Faisal was in fact born in Bombay during his father's exile. Faisal ruled over a slow decline in the power of the Bu Saʿidi Sultans in the interior of Oman, but also a rejuvenation of Muscat as an important Indian Ocean entrepôt. Taimur bin Faisal (now fully adopting the title of Sultan) harboured the same dreams of a quiet retirement in India as his grandfather Turki. But Taimur was rather more successful, most likely because British imperial influence over Oman was far more substantial in the inter-war period than it had been in the 1870s. It is not clear when Sultan Taimur first visited India, but certainly by the 1920s he was spending substantial amounts of each year in India, much to the chagrin of his imperial minders. Sultan Taimur was spending four to five months a year travelling around India and even purchased a house in the hill station of Dehradun.[13] He complained regularly of the oppressive heat in Muscat, and complained of ill health that could only be cured by cooler climes in India. Yet his ill health was not merely physical, but also mental. Taimur seemed to relish the opportunity to escape the demands of power, the expectations of his subjects and, according one colonial official, the complaints of his formidable wife.[14] In 1920 he was starting to trim his beard, and dress in European clothes and a fez instead of the traditional Omani robes and turban. On the eve of his abdication, he was clean-shaven, smoked cigars, and even wore shorts![15] Colonial officials finally relented regarding Taimur's pleading for abdication, justifying the decision with the hope that his young Western-educated son would prove a more ambitious and energetic ruler than his father.

The future Sultan Saʿid bin Taimur was sent by his father to Mayo College in Ajmer, the school for Indian princelings established to serve as the Indian equivalent of Eton.[16] As James Onley and others have shown, the Gulf was ruled through an extension of the British Raj in India.[17] Arab sheikhs would be present at the darbars in Delhi, and their sons would be educated along with those of Indian nawabs rather than Ottoman pashas. After assuming power, Sultan Saʿid would return to India relatively frequently to meet with British officials as well as to visit his blissfully retired father.[18] To a Khaliji ruler within the orbit of the British Empire, Delhi was an inescapable metropole. To gain the ear of higher-level decision makers and to appeal the decisions of local British agents, a visit to Delhi or Bombay was invaluable.

So why was India such an attraction to the ruler of a substantial state like Oman? Well, certainly an important part of the story was the push factor of Sultan Taimur's increasingly constrained rule and the enervation of Muscat's economy. British pressure to curtail the arms trade had destroyed the economic lifeline of the port of Muscat and the Sultan's territories more generally. It also helped prompt a revolt against the Sultan in the Omani hinterland, the historic centre of Omani power and the Ibadhi faith. So the desire to leave Muscat was clear, but why India, and not Iraq, Egypt or indeed Britain? I would argue that it was part proximity, part climate, part modern technology and urban life, but mostly a long-standing Khaliji experience of India as a gateway to the wider world. From India, Sultan Taimur could regularly meet his son and other Omanis, but then turn around, put on his shorts and live a westernised lifestyle. He could also travel to many parts of the globe, visiting the USA with his son the Sultan and apparently heading to Japan and even taking a Japanese wife. Colonial Bombay was one of the best-connected entrepôts in the world and a truly cosmopolitan city. If Bombay was the Gateway of India, it was also the Khalij's gateway to the globe.

Diwāniyyas and Diasporas

Today, one cannot avoid Arabs and the shops catering to them on a particular stretch of Colaba Causeway in the tourist heart of South Bombay. This district is likely a post-1973 development specifically for tourists enriched by the oil boom, but Khalijis have lived here from at least the early twentieth century.[19] Through the twentieth century Khalijis seem to have been distributed in different neighbourhoods of South Bombay, including Colaba, Marine Drive and Churchgate. But at the end of the nineteenth century it seems that the Arab population lived in closer quarters. So many Arabs had settled in a street near the Grant Road commuter rail station that the streeet became known as Arab Galli (similar to 'alley'). On this street, in a recently gentrified part of the city, Arab merchants would have been able to purchase houses and create a small diasporic social world. Furthermore, this was probably where exiled Khaliji royals and notables could congregate at arm's-length from machinations at home and yet in the company of their fellow Arabs.[20] While the commercial diaspora of Khalijis in India was never very large, in the nineteenth century it was wealthy and substantial enough to give its name to certain neighbourhoods. For Khaliji merchants, South Asia was not a place of exile but a central node in networks of Khaliji commerce.

Bombay's commercial connections to the Gulf begin as early as the 1790s when the Sayyid Sultan al-Bu Saᶜidi obtained the monopoly concession to provide salt to the still-nascent colonial port of Bombay.[21] By the early nineteenth century there was a well-established community of Khalijis in Bombay, prominent enough to even show up in tourist souvenirs. In 1811, a British artist named R. Temple produced a series of early postcards of the city. These were hand drawn and coloured cards depicting different 'views' of the city of Bombay. The views include quasi-anthropological representations of different communities and occupational groups within the city. Among these are three (possibly four) cards depicting 'Arabs'. There is an image of a turbaned and robed man with prayer beads who represents an Arab, and in another depiction a group of Arab women. Interestingly, these women wear the 'burqa' or falcon-shaped face-mask typical of Bedouin women from Oman and Musandam. There is also a separate card depicting 'Muscat Arabs' wearing *khanjars* and their characteristic red and blue plaid turbans.[22] That Omani Arabs should be familiar enough to merit a stereotypical scene from the city of Bombay is a testament to the size and prominence of this Khaliji diaspora. Thus from a very early period Khalijis – and Omanis in particular – were deeply integrated into the urban fabric of Bombay.

A collection of merchant correspondence from Khaliji merchants provides clear evidence of the importance of the Khaliji diaspora in British India, and its impact on political and commercial affairs in the Gulf. Abdullah al-Tabur has written several books tracing the history of the UAE and one concerning nationalism in particular.[23] The extraordinary collection of correspondence that he has assembled demonstrates that Khaliji merchants were in contact with Arab nationalist leaders and were engaged with the political currents flowing through the Arab world at the beginning of the twentieth century. What is particularly striking, both in the correspondence preserved in al-Tabur's monographs and in the copies held at the Jum°a al-Majid Library, is the central place of India and Khaliji merchants based in India in the circulation of these ideas. The correspondents receiving news and journalism from Cairo, Damascus and even Jeddah were often based in Bombay or Calicut, and from India relayed commercial information as well as nationalist ideas to Khaliji ports like Sharjah.[24]

By the 1940s and 1950s the Khaliji diaspora in India seemed to be reaching an apogee. On the one hand, the Indian rupee continued to function as legal tender in the Gulf, and increasing oil revenues facilitated increasing purchases of consumer goods from India. On the other hand, postcolonial India was placing increasing restrictions on Khaliji trade because of the fear of smuggling, and oil profits were undercutting the impetus for a new generation to take up the mantle of long-distance trade. This particular conjuncture led to one final flourishing of the Khaliji diaspora in India in the middle decades of the twentieth century.

Oil revenues permitted the creation of institutional infrastructures for the Khaliji diaspora in India that had previously remained informal. The most prominent Khaliji merchants in Indian cities opened part of their homes as *dīwāniyyas* where men could regularly meet and discuss commercial affairs. Visitors might stay in the houses of these leaders of the community, and their *dīwāniyyas* served as key nodes of cultural and political life for the diasporic community.[25] By the 1940s this had blossomed in Bombay into a formal institution, the Indo-Arab Cultural Association, which had regular meetings and even its own stationery.[26] By this point, the Khaliji *dīwāniyya* in Bombay was located in the Kuwaiti consulate, which soon after would host a school for the children of Khaliji merchants. The Kuwaiti consulate, expanded and funded by the growing oil revenues of the Al-Sabah, helped give a stronger institutional basis to diasporic life in Bombay.[27]

A wonderful collection of oral histories recounts the family lives and particularly the experiences of the daughters of Kuwaiti merchants growing up in India in these decades. These women were born into the well-established Khaliji merchant families in Bombay and Calicut. Almost all these merchant families were important figures in local trade and prominent members of the Arab community in these Indian cities and hence they often left other traces in the colonial archive.[28] But where official archives only pay attention to men, and particularly their trading activities, oral histories can give us a sense of family lives, gender relations and how it felt to live in a diasporic condition. These oral histories describe the classic diasporic sentiment of living in two worlds simultaneously, though with variations depending on the city lived in and the particularities of the families.

The Khaliji community in Bombay was large enough to support diasporic institutions like the Indo-Arab Cultural Association, and an 'Arabic School'. Bombay had a particularly cosmopolitan flavour for Khaliji children. Most of them attended convent schools and spoke English better than they spoke Arabic. They were exposed to different religions, cuisines and climates. The cinema, both Bollywood and Hollywood, seemed to feature prominently in their memories. One interviewee suggested that for Kuwaitis, it was like Paris with all its wealth and cosmopolitan sophistication.[29] Bombay's large Khaliji community meant that the Arab diaspora created its own institutions, and children could be raised with a distant Kuwait or Bahrain continually in their lives through the Arabic school and their many diasporic friends. But Bombay was also still a deeply colonial city in which the diasporic Khaliji experience had as much to do with Hollywood films and convent schools as it had to do with eating *bhel puri* and celebrating Diwali. It represented a space in which diasporic identity could be maintained precisely because the community was large enough to maintain a distinct existence. This was not as true of Khaliji families that had settled in other cities along the western Indian coastline.

Khalijis were a vital part of the urban life of a number of cities along British India's western coast. Khaliji traders regularly visited ports along the Gujarat coast and established stable communities down the Western Indian coast, including in ports like Karachi, Porbandar, Goa and Calicut.[30] Karachi was western India's second metropolis, and a number of families had branches of the business and relatives in the city. Karachi had a large Hindu trading population, but was in the Muslim majority province of Sind and would later become Pakistan's first capital. Thus, following the partition and independence of India and Pakistan there was a slight bump in the number of Khaliji merchants shifting to Karachi. But the appeals of the new Muslim state seemed to be relatively minimal when compared to long-standing ties and larger markets in Indian cities.[31] So for the Khaliji diaspora religion was not a major factor in where they settled, who they traded with or how they integrated into South Asian urban spaces.

Calicut, on the other hand, provides an important counter-example to the diasporic experience of Khalijis in Bombay. Calicut had old and important trading connections with the Khalij, but it had declined in importance by the late nineteenth century. It was a smaller city with a smaller foreign trading community. Just a handful of Khaliji families truly settled in Calicut, with most Khaliji visitors being seasonal. Those families that did settle appeared to be more integrated and indeed entrenched in the Malayali social world of Calicut and Kerala. Even the most stable and wealthy Khaliji traders married into local Indian families. Frequently, the Khaliji father might be away for many months in Kuwait or handling business in Bombay or Karachi. Without a critical mass of settled families there was less of a diasporic experience for these Khalijis, and certainly none of the formal institutions that existed in Bombay. One prominent family maintained Calicut's Khaliji *dīwāniyya*: they would host visiting merchants and provide a social space for ship captains and other visiting Khalijis.[32] Unlike the Khaliji children in Bombay, Khalijis who grew up in Calicut saw Kuwait as a cosmopolitan and liberal space compared to the conservatism of Muslim Calicut. Children who grew up in Calicut had a difficult transition when arriving in Kuwait, understanding little Arabic and confused by the customs as they had been quite integrated and had normalised 'Indian' or Malayali customs as the norm. Moreover, the transition back to Kuwait often involved the dividing up of families. Indian women had married Khaliji traders and raised their children, but they themselves never felt Khaliji or could conceive of moving to a new country late in their lives. As the diasporic families returned to Kuwait, such mothers would stay in India.[33] In this sense, the separation that characterises diasporic communities was not present in Calicut. Unlike Bombay, it might be more appropriate to resist calling the Khaliji community in Calicut or other small cities a diaspora because they were more integrated and acculturated, and frequently it was just an often-distant father who connected these families to the Khalij.

The impact of Khaliji diasporas on the society and geography of British India or postcolonial India and Pakistan was admittedly small. But it was nonetheless significant, particularly in Bombay where sufficient numbers of Khalijis had an important role to play in the economic life and cosmopolitan flavour of these urban centres. Certain families were known to locals and to British administrators as the pillars of these small communities and they hosted *dīwāniyyas* in their homes to serve the diaspora. By the 1940s, institutions had been established in India that transcended any particular family and strengthened ties to the Gulf. But by the 1960s the struggles and the attendant profits of trading in India seemed meagre compared to the opportunities proliferating back in the Gulf. Few from the new generation followed their fathers to Calicut, Karachi or Bombay.

If the stable and growing revenues from petroleum production enticed merchants away from their trade in India and Pakistan, it turned the tables for Khaliji rulers and their relationship with the British Empire. The al-Khalifas needed to spend time in Bombay supervising the trade in Bahraini pearls, but as the pearl trade declined and oil revenues rose, their time in India dissipated. Bu Saʿidis plotted in Indian exile for their return to power, or were desperate to escape the heat and the impotence of their rule in their own country. Sultan Saʿid bin Taimur was educated in India but was able to draw on his oil revenues to eliminate Oman's debts to Britain and cut the apron strings of empire. In the process, the Bu Saʿidis also sold their last imperial possession, Gwadar, for 3 million dollars. Sultan Qaboos would be educated not in Mayo College with Indian royalty but in Sandhurst along with British royalty. Similarly, students from across the Gulf would look not to British India but to Egypt, the UK and the USA as centres of education and capitals of consumption. Until the 1960s, cities like Bombay and Karachi were commercial and cosmopolitan centres of which Khalijis formed an integral part. Throughout these two centuries, Khalijis were polyglot and enterprising, but their horizons usually ended in South Asia. Oil wealth did not bring globalisation to the Gulf, it merely altered the networks in which Khalijis operated and shifted the horizons to which they aspired.

Notes

1. There are too many works to list here, but see e.g. Jill Crystal, *Oil and Politics in the Gulf: Rulers and Merchants in Kuwait and Qatar* (Cambridge: Cambridge University Press, 1995); L. Potter, *The Persian Gulf in History* (New York: Palgrave Macmillan, 2009); Nelida Fuccaro, *Histories of City and State in the Persian Gulf: Manama Since 1800* (Cambridge: Cambridge University Press,

2009); Robert Vitalis, *America's Kingdom: Mythmaking on the Saudi Oil Frontier* (Stanford: Stanford University Press, 2007); James Onley, *The Arabian Frontier of the British Raj: Merchants, Rulers, and the British in the Nineteenth-Century Gulf* (Oxford: Oxford University Press, 2007); Charles E. Davies, *The Blood-Red Arab Flag: An Investigation into Qasimi Piracy, 1797–1820* (Exeter: University of Exeter Press, 1997); Frederick F. Anscombe, *The Ottoman Gulf: The Creation of Kuwait, Saudi Arabia, and Qatar* (New York: Columbia University Press, 1997).

2. There are of course important exceptions, particularly works on Oman, but also Yacoub Yusuf Al-Hijji, *Kuwait and the Sea: A Brief Social and Economic History* (London: Arabian Publishing, 2010).

3. Abdel Rahman Munif, *Cities of Salt* (New York: Vintage, 1989).

4. Siddarth Bhatia, 'The Making of Marine Drive', *The Indian Quarterly*, September 2014, available at <http://indianquarterly.com/the-making-of-marine-drive> (last accessed 7 April 2017).

5. Beatrice Nicolini, *Makran, Oman, and Zanzibar: Three-Terminal Cultural Corridor in the Western Indian Ocean, 1799-1856* (Leiden: Brill, 2004), pp. 32–3.

6. Christopher Buyers, 'The Al-Busaid Dynasty Genealogy', *Royal Ark*, available at <http://www.royalark.net/Oman/oman6.htm> (last accessed 1 June 2016).

7. British Library, India Office Records (Henceforth IOR): R/15/6/1 Political Department Memorandum No. 3419, Bombay Castle 7 November 1867.

8. IOR: R/15/6/8 Undersecretary to Government of India to E. C. Ross, Political Resident in the Persian Gulf (Henceforth: PRPG), 10 January 1876.

9. IOR: R/15/6/7 Sayyid Turki to S. B. Miles, Political Agent (Henceforth: PA) in Muscat 16 June 1874; S. B. Miles, PA Muscat to E. C. Ross, PRPG, No. 288/121, 26 June 1874, p. 57.

10. IOR: R/15/6/7 S. B. Miles, PA Muscat to E. C. Ross, PRPG 28 May 1875; Sayyid Turki to S. B. Miles, PA Muscat 20 December 1875 p. 312; S. B. Miles, PA Muscat to E. C. Ross, PRPG 17 December 1875, p. 356.

11. IOR: R/15/6/53 Sayyid Abdul Aziz to Col. E. C. Ross, PRPG, 15 June 1888.

12. This entire account is taken from the petition found in Maharashtra State Archives Political Department Records, for the year 1889, Vol. 220, Compilation 440. (Henceforth denoted in this format: MSA: P1889-220/440.) Petition of Wazil Bistan to the Commissioner of Police, Bombay, 11 February 1889; also see Johan Mathew, *Margins of the Market: Trafficking and Capitalism across the Arabian Sea* (Berkeley: University of California Press, 2016), pp. 70–2.

13. IOR: R/15/6/53 Sultan Taimur bin Feisal to Major G. P. Murphy, PA Muscat, 15 April 1930.
14. IOR: R/15/6/53 Major T. C. Fowle, PA Muscat to PRPG No. K28, 4 September 1930; T. C. Fowle, Officiating PRPG to Foreign Secretary Government of India, No. 558-S, 31 August 1931.
15. IOR: R/15/6/53 Fowle, Officiating PRPG to Foreign Secretary Government of India, No. 558-S, 31 August 1931.
16. IOR: R/15/6/54 H. Biscoe, PRPG to Foreign Secretary, Government of India, No. 789-S, 23 November 1931, p. 365.
17. See Onley, *The Arabian Frontier of the British Raj* (Oxford: Oxford University Press, 2007); John M. Willis, *Unmaking North and South: Cartographies of the Yemeni Past, 1857–1934* (New York: Columbia University Press, 2012).
18. IOR: R/15/6/200 Note by C. G. Prior, PRPG, 7 April 1941.
19. Rasha al-Duwaisan, 'How Far Did Kuwaitis Integrate into Indian Society?', MA thesis, Harvard University, 2008, pp. 36–43.
20. MSA: P1906-124/369 Report by residency interpreter Agha Mahomed Khalil regarding Sheikh Ali, 30 November 1905.
21. IOR: F/4/72/1595 Extract of Political Letter from Bengal, 11 September 1797.
22. IOR: WD315 'Views' R. Temple, Cards 46, 47 and 51.
23. ʿAbd Allah ʿAli Muhammad Tabur, *Rasaʾil al-Raʿil al-Awwal min Ruwad al-Yaqzah fi al-Imarat al-ʿArabiyah al-Muttahidah* (Sharjah: Daʾirat al-Thaqafah wa-al-Iʿlam, 1999).
24. Archive of ʿAbd Allah al-Tabur, copies held at the Jumaʿa al-Majid Library, Dubai: No. 24 – ʿAbd al-Rahman bin Hassan al-Madfaʿ, Bombay to Jumaʿa Muhammad al-Mutawwaʿ, 22 Shawwal 1356 (25 December 1937); No. 28 – Yusuf Abd al-Rahman al-Mutawwaʿ, Calicut to Ahmed bin ʿAbd al-Rahman bin Hadid, Sharjah, 26 May 1930; No. 25 – Hassan bin ʿAbd al-Rahman al-Madfaʿ, Bombay to Ibrahim bin Muhammad al-Madfaʿ Sharjah, 31 Jumada al-Awwal 1346 (25 November 1927).
25. Al-Duwaisan, 'How Far Did Kuwaitis Integrate into Indian Society?' p. 59.
26. Tabur Archive: No. 15, Indo-Arab Cultural Association to Sheikh Mubarak al-Nakhi, 7 April 1946.
27. Al-Duwaisan, 'How Far Did Kuwaitis Integrate into Indian Society?' pp. 29–34, 44–52.
28. See National Archives of India, Foreign Department 1936, File 583-N and IOR: R/15/5/309 Collector of Central Excises and Salt Revenue, Madras, Order No.

D351, 28 May 1943; Censor intercept – Fahad Khalifah Shaheen Alghanim, Bombay to Abdul Latif Mohammed Thuniyan, Kuwait, 25 March 1944.

29. Al-Duwaisan, 'How Far Did Kuwaitis Integrate into Indian Society?', p. 38.

30. IOR: R/15/3/309 Collector of Central Excises and Salt Revenue, Madras, Order No. D351, 28 May 1943, apparently a Nejdi family was the only Arab trader in Calcutta, see National Archives of India, Foreign Department 1936, File 583-N; al-Duwaisan, 'How Far Did Kuwaitis Integrate into Indian Society?' p. 19.

31. Al-Duwaisan, 'How Far Did Kuwaitis Integrate into Indian Society?' pp. 19–20, 45, 53–5.

32. Ibid., 21–5.

33. Ibid., 21–9.

PART III

EAST AFRICANS IN THE KHALIJ AND THE KHALIJ IN EAST AFRICA

8

AFRICANS AND THE GULF: BETWEEN DIASPORA AND COSMOPOLITANISM

Matthew S. Hopper[1]

Visitors to the popular Al-Satwa quarter of Dubai are frequently treated to Laiwa performances by local musical and dance troupes. Most of these Laiwa performers, who have an identifiable African appearance, do not identify themselves as African. Ethnomusicologists agree that Laiwa is an African import, but French ethnomusicologist Maho Sebiane's interviews with members of the quarter's performers' association indicate that most identify themselves as Baluchi (from the Province of Baluchistan) rather than African, and most share the same last name, Al-Baluchi. Sebiane calls the performers an 'enigma' – their appearance is African, but their surname implies an Asiatic origin. Language provides little assistance, as the performers are as likely to speak some Baluchi, Hindi and Urdu in addition to their first language of Arabic, and they tend to know only the few Swahili words included in the songs they perform. Sebiane hypothesises that freed slaves may have taken the surnames of their masters, who may have been Baluchi or *'ajam* immigrants from across the Gulf. Alternatively, he speculates that the ancestors of these performers may have settled first on the Irano-Pakistani coast before making a second migration to the Arab coast and valuing their Baluchi migration experience more highly than their African origins.[2] Still another possibility is that the performers have chosen to call themselves Baluchi in an effort to deliberately obscure their African ancestry. A similar phenomenon occurs elsewhere in the Gulf. Anie Montigny finds that in Qatar, descendants of enslaved Africans identify as Arab rather than as African and claim lineages of prominent Qatari tribes.[3]

Sebiane's and Montigny's research highlights a challenge facing historians of the African diaspora in the Gulf: unlike with many other branches of the global African diaspora, identification with Africa is not a common feature among the descendants of enslaved Africans in Arabia. In fact, today, many of the characteristics associated with diasporic identity, including 'a collective memory and myth about the homeland . . . an idealization of the supposed ancestral home' and 'the presence of a return movement or intermittent visits to home' are absent among many established members of the African diaspora in Arabia.[4] This chapter explores the question of African identity in the Gulf.

Real, Invisible, Mythical?

Is there an African diaspora in the Arabian Gulf? Today, individuals of African ancestry are observable at every socioeconomic level and make up a particularly recognisable minority among the Gulf's most popular celebrity athletes and musicians. Yet the vast majority of people of African descent in eastern Arabia today speak Arabic as their primary language and self-identify as Arabs rather than Africans. A significant African presence has been evident in the Gulf since at least the early nineteenth century. Foreign visitors such as William Heude (1817) and George Keppel (1824) described sizeable African populations in Muscat and were eyewitnesses to public slave auctions in the bazaar.[5] By 1905, the British writer J. G. Lorimer estimated that Africans made up roughly 17 per cent of the total population of coastal eastern Arabia between Oman and Kuwait. This included 11 per cent of Kuwait's population, 22 per cent of Qatar's population, 11 per cent of Bahrain's population and 28 per cent of the Trucial Coast's population. Africans also made up 25 per cent of Muscat and Mutrah's population. By contrast, African Americans made up 10–12 per cent of the US population according to the censuses of 1900 and 1910.[6]

In each of the Arab states of the Gulf, a substantial African presence remains visible today, even if few Africans in the Gulf identify themselves as

African. Most Gulf inhabitants with African ancestry can trace their lineage to ancestors forcibly removed to the Gulf through the nineteenth-century slave trade from East Africa. Enslaved Africans were in demand in Arabia to perform a variety of tasks ranging from the maritime (divers, sailors, fishermen, stevedores and crewmen) to the agricultural (irrigating, pollinating, harvesting and maintaining orchards, date groves, and fields of various crops, and animal husbandry) to the domestic (cooking, cleaning and childcare) to the elite (soldiers and retainers). Many men also worked in construction and in the gathering and hauling of construction materials. Many women hauled water, prepared meals, produced handicrafts, and worked in childcare and as attendants and domestics for households. Many enslaved Africans worked at a variety of tasks over the course of a year, and a lifetime, but the two biggest sectors of the economy that demanded African labour were pearl-diving and date production. Many African boys worked in date gardens when they were first imported to the region and were then moved into the pearl diving industry when they reached their early teens. Pearl divers (Figure 8.1) and pearling crewmen often worked at their primary tasks during the main pearling season (April through September) and at other tasks such as fishing, hauling or construction in the off-season, although many others were taken to more remote pearling waters, like Socotra or the Red Sea at the conclusion of the annual season in the Gulf.[7]

In the late nineteenth century, slave traders, primarily from Sur and Batinah in Oman and Qasimi ports on the Trucial Coast, increasingly exported young boys from East Africa for work in the pearl industry. By the 1870s, the ratio of male to female slaves among slave dhows captured by the Royal Navy on the Arabian coast contained overwhelming majorities of young males. In 1872, the HMS *Vulture* captured a large slave boat off the coast of Ras al-Hadd at the entrance to the Gulf of Oman. That dhow was carrying 169 captives from Pemba to Sur and Batinah; 124 were males and 45 were females, and the majority were children.[8] The HMS *Philomel*'s capture in 1884 had 77 men, 14 women, 51 boys, and 12 girls (128 males and 26 females), mostly Wazaramo, aboard. That dhow was bound for Batinah from Dar es Salaam, having collected the captives by canoe between Ras Ndege and Kunduchi in East Africa.[9] In November 1885 the HMS *Osprey* captured a 42-ton dhow around Ras Madraka in Oman bound from Ngao

Figure 8.1 'Pearl Divers at Work' (Persian Gulf, c. 1903). *London Magazine*, Vol. XI (January 1904), p. 717.

Figure 8.2 'Men Pollinating Date Palm' (Oman, 1912). Courtesy American Heritage Center, University of Wyoming. Paul Popenoe Collection, Box 177, Folder 2.

in East Africa to Sur with 49 male and 24 female slaves (8 men, 12 women, 41 boys and 12 girls).[10] In fact, in the last quarter of the nineteenth century, it is virtually impossible to find evidence of any dhow captured off the Arab coast carrying more female captives from East Africa than males. There are no reliable statistics for the volume of the slave trade from Africa to Arabia in the nineteenth century, but the best estimates place the numbers between 150,000 and 805,000, although they could well have been higher.[11]

Despite their significant presence in the Gulf and economic and cultural contributions to the region, communities of Africans in the Gulf lack many of the key elements usually associated with the concept of 'diaspora'. Many of the conventional characteristics of the diasporic experience, according to the scholar Robin Cohen's classic survey of global diasporas, are largely missing in the Gulf, including 'a collective memory and myth about the homeland', 'an idealization of the supposed ancestral home' and 'the presence of a return movement or intermittent visits to home'. In fact, beyond the first characteristic, 'dispersal', the African diaspora in the Gulf seems a poor fit for Cohen's ideal type of diaspora.[12]

In the Gulf today the descendants of enslaved Africans typically identify themselves as Arabs. The Gulf has not produced a popular pan-African movement or a large group of intellectuals who call for reparations for slavery. There may be several reasons for this. A leading scholar of the African diaspora in the Indian Ocean has noted that unlike the Atlantic world, the Indian Ocean world has not had a Western-educated class of African individuals and has therefore not produced an Equiano, a Cesaire, a Garvey or a DuBois. 'In sharp contrast to the situation in the Atlantic world', Edward Alpers notes, 'there is no literary tradition struggling either to recall African origins or to understand the retention and transformation of African ways in the new world in which Africans found themselves as a consequence of the slave trade'. Furthermore, 'not a single spokesperson has yet emerged from within the region to articulate the history or contemporary situation of any of these communities'. In much of the Indian Ocean world, he concludes, 'Africans have been made "invisible" to all but the most interested outsiders'.[13] Gwyn Campbell has even gone as far as suggesting that the concept of an African-Asian Diaspora may be a 'myth', in part because of the absence of diasporic consciousness and the degree of assimilation of Africans into their Asian host societies.[14]

Some scholars of the Indian Ocean (and many residents of the Gulf) attribute an absence of African diasporic identity to the homogenising influence of Islam or the race-blind tolerance produced by the region's cosmopolitanism. For example, to illustrate the traditions of cosmopolitanism and tolerance in the Indian Ocean, the Zanzibari historian Abdul Sheriff recounts the story of his visit to a mariner's family home in Sur. Portraits of a man's relatives and a former African slave hung side by side on the wall and all of them were identified as Arab.[15] From this perspective, scholars who view the Indian Ocean with an Atlantic lens may be appear to reify essentialist notions of ethnic or racial identity and seek diasporas in places where assimilation has made such notions irrelevant. By contrast, scholars of the African diaspora may highlight the centrality of race, the embodied expression of African culture, the retention of African cultural traits, and the shared history of victimisation and experience of discrimination.[16] At times, scholars with this point of view may even articulate a frustration towards Africans in the Indian Ocean world for being 'in denial' of their Africanness (as viewers of Henry Louis Gates' *Wonders of the African World* series will recall in his encounter with Shirazis in East Africa). Such frustrations may even lead Atlantic scholars to see the absence of conscious diasporic identity as 'false consciousness'.

Defining Diaspora

Can we speak of an African diaspora in the Gulf, where most of the group's members do not self-identify as African? To put the question another way, can there be a diaspora without self-identification? The answer, of course, depends on how one defines diaspora. The term *diaspora*, as Brent Hayes Edwards convincingly illustrates, has a particular etymology linked to the nationalism of African American formations of black internationalism and pan-Africanism, and was only popularly invoked in the post-Second World War world. Edwards notes that the 'accepted risk' in using *diaspora* is that 'the term's analytic focus "fluctuates". Like *Pan-African*, it is open to ideological appropriation in a wide variety of political projects . . . articulations of *diaspora* that collapse the term into versions of nationalism or racial essentialism.'[17] Diaspora, like cosmopolitanism and nationalism, can be invoked for both cultural and political purposes by groups that employ them as both concepts and projects that both include and exclude.

Edwards' reminder of the shared histories of diaspora and nationalism is useful. Pioneering historians of nationalism such as Friedrich Meinecke long ago (1907) acknowledged the possibility – and even the productiveness – of national groups within cosmopolitan environments. In his classic analysis of the origins of German nationalism, Meinecke argued that 'cosmopolitan thinking' not only 'preceded the awakening of the national idea' but helped to produce it. He argued that, while the conventional view sees 'cosmopolitanism and national feeling as two modes of thought that mutually exclude each other, that do battle with each other, and that supplant each other', such a view 'cannot satisfy the historical mind'. A more 'subtle' view, he argued, 'is that the true, the best German national feeling also includes the cosmopolitan ideal of a humanity beyond nationality and that it "is un-German to be merely German"'. In his exploration of the origins of German nationalism, Meinecke came to embrace a Rankean primordialist view that cultural nations were not based on 'self-determination' but on 'pre-determination'. He argued that 'a nation simply is, whether the individuals of which it is composed want to belong to that nation or not'.[18] Meinecke's work reminds us that diaspora, including the Gulf and Indian Ocean African diaspora, may be defined in terms of either 'self-determination' or 'pre-determination'.

Building on such earlier models, recent work by Vinay Dharwadker identifies a tension among scholars of diaspora stemming from the divergent trajectories of two academic projects: (1) postcolonial writers and scholars of the African diaspora working primarily in the humanities, who established 'broad connections between migration and diaspora, on one hand, and the hybridisation of languages, identities, aesthetic forms, and cultural practices on the other' leading to a 'general equivalence between diaspora and cosmopolitanism'; and, at the same time, (2) scholars working in diaspora studies, 'working chiefly in the social sciences and on a range of diasporas, [who] suggested that certain core features render diasporic formations anticosmopolitan'.[19] Dharwadker argues convincingly that the contradiction between diaspora as 'inherently cosmopolitan' and 'intrinsically anticosmopolitan' has become a central paradox for scholars of diasporas. His analysis of migration and hybridity and diaspora and creolisation in the works of Salman Rushdie, Homi Bhabha, Stuart Hall and Paul Gilroy leads Dharwadker to conclude that although cultural theorists of the 1980s and 1990s did not explicitly attribute cosmopolitanism to diaspora, the primary association in the field remains 'diaspora and hybridity', such that recently 'most scholars simply reinterpret hybridity as cosmopolitanism, assuming that both equally represent a condition that combines elements from two or more sources'.[20]

Dharwadker notes that the definition of diaspora in the inaugural issue of the journal *Diaspora* did not foresee 'the political, ethical, and moral complications created by a diaspora's 'double consciousness' of belonging both here and there – by division of loyalties between hostland and homeland'. He argues: 'locating the characteristics of diaspora in the subjectivity of its members . . . jeopardizes not only the potential connection between diaspora and cosmopolitanism, but the very existence of diaspora itself.'[21] Dharwadker critiques the definition of diaspora provided by Robin Cohen, which is modelled on the archetypal Jewish diaspora, and echoes Steven Vertovec's criticism that the 'over-use and under theorization' of the notion of diaspora threatens the term's descriptive usefulness. Dharwadker further challenges the normativity of the Jewish diaspora noting the peculiarity of the selection of the Greek term *diaspora* as the translation of the Hebrew term *galut* from the Book of Deuteronomy.[22] Subsequent definitions of diaspora have allowed for both 'diasporic cosmopolitanism as syncretism, creolization, or hybridity' and 'exclusionary anticosmopolitanism'.[23]

Dharwadker concludes with a rejoinder that offers potential for studies of the African diaspora in the Gulf: 'The relation of diaspora to cosmopolitanism frequently depends on how diasporas creolize in particular circumstances, what kinds of diaspora consciousness and double consciousness they develop, and especially what their economic and class dimensions are.' In light of these dimensions, 'it may be especially productive to redefine cosmopolitanism as cultural ambidexterity, which cannot merely be equated with either hybridity or creolization'.[24]

Between Atlantic History and World History

Part of the problem with studying the African diaspora in the Arabian Gulf stems from the preeminence of the Atlantic in slavery studies and African diaspora studies, or what Edward Alpers has called the 'tyranny of the Atlantic'.[25] Scholars with an Atlantic bias are unlikely to find the kind of African diaspora they hope to find in the Gulf. Recently, however, scholars of the Indian

Ocean have offered useful correctives to Atlantic dominance.[26] These scholars have shown that, when seen in the broadest context of the global African diaspora, the fact that diasporic Africans in the Indian Ocean have not always identified themselves through a continental (if anachronistic) concept of an African homeland, joined pan-African intellectual currents, identified as part of a global dispersed community or formulated a return movement should not be surprising. These are features distinct to the American branch of the global African diaspora but are not normative features of the diaspora in its entirety. Pier Larson has cogently argued that 'experiences of enslavement . . . are not universal sites for historical memory and identity formation in the diaspora'. Although 'experiences and memories of enslavement and racial oppression are key to African identities in the Americas, similar trauma has been purposefully forgotten or differently remembered in many other parts of the diaspora'. In other branches of the African diaspora, including much of the Middle East and the Indian Ocean world, there have been good reasons for descendants of enslaved Africans – as well as their enslavers – to employ what Larson calls 'countervailing forces of historical amnesia'. Although commemorating enslavement is characteristic of the Atlantic branch of the diaspora, we must be careful not to expect to find that characteristic universally throughout the global African diaspora.[27] In fact, even the Atlantic experience of the African diaspora cannot be taken as static and monolithic. Experiences in some parts of South America display similarities to the Gulf. Tanya Maria Golash-Boza's recent work on Afro-Peruvian communities in Ingenio indicates that 'blackness' there is primarily a discourse on skin colour rather than slavery. Her work challenges scholarship on the black diaspora that points to the 'centrality of slavery for defining blackness in the diaspora'.[28]

Pier Larson reminds us that 'the Indian Ocean is not the Atlantic'.[29] Although the Atlantic world dominates scholarship on the African diaspora, the American creole experience is but one of many contexts for the dispersion of Africans around the world. In spite of the enormity of the transatlantic slave trade – which coercively removed more than 12 million Africans by the best estimates – Africans who were enslaved in the Americas were actually outnumbered by those who were internally displaced within the African continent and dispersed through the Trans-Saharan and Indian

Ocean slave trades between the seventh and eighteenth centuries. The African diaspora in the Americas dominates scholarship on the diaspora, but its experiences of slavery are not normative.[30] Internal displacement within Africa accounted for a much larger and more important part of the African diaspora. Martin Klein has estimated that even at its peak, the Atlantic slave trade produced more enslaved Africans who were relocated and kept within Africa than were sent abroad. Abdul Sheriff and Ralph Austen have drawn similar conclusions about the Indian Ocean and Trans-Saharan slave trades. If there is a normative experience of slavery in the global African diaspora, it may be the intra-continental experience.[31] Seen within the broader context of the African diaspora both within and outside of the African continent, the Atlantic experience may actually prove to be exceptional, not normative. To understand African diasporic identity in the Gulf we need to answer Larson's call for 'recentering the global African diaspora onto the African continent and creating theories of diaspora that are Africa-centric and based on captives' subjective experiences'. With the growth of our knowledge of the African diaspora in other parts of the world 'it is no longer possible to think of the African dispersions of the western Atlantic as constituting either the demographic center of the African diaspora or as providing its core models of cultural adaptation, self-consciousness, and community formation'.[32]

Genealogies of Invisibility

Why has there been so little diasporic consciousness in the Gulf? Why are Africans in the Gulf unlikely to identify as African? There are at least three reasons why Africans have been made, in the words of Edward Alpers, all but 'invisible' to all but the most interested outsiders. First, there is little encouragement on the part of the Gulf states for recognition of any claims to minority identities. Instead, Gulf state governments generally prefer their subjects to embrace the ideals of cosmopolitanism and, therefore, promote these ideals through official displays, publications and museums. In July 2011, the Smithsonian Institute's National Museum of African Art in Washington, DC partnered with the Sultan Qaboos Cultural Center (SQCC) to host Al Najoom, a traditional Omani dance group. Following a live performance featuring Afro-Omani musicians and dancers, a member of the American audience inquired about the African origins of the troupe's music and dance. In response, a representative from the SQCC explained:

> Oman is an Arab country. It's not an African country. But Oman, through-out its history, was a crossroads to many cultures because it was on the east-ern corner of the Arabian Peninsula. It is a seafaring country, and so a lot of people traveled back and forth and traveled through Oman. So, of course, we have taken a lot of different cultures and we have intertwined them with our own and that's why you can feel some of the African rhythms in our music. However, this is very particular to Oman.[33]

The governments of Oman and other Gulf countries have adopted cos-mopolitanism as their preferred mode of national expression in part because it offers a convenient method of masking the real and often uncomfortable history of slavery and tensions that might arise from differences between the various cultures represented within the recently constructed nation states: for example, when the Oman Ministry of Heritage and Culture's third volume of its Contemporary Forms of Omani Folk Arts series discusses Laiwa and other forms of song and dance in the Batinah region with origins in East Africa. The official volume is vague about the ways in which these traditions came to Oman. The volume says that Omanis who travelled, traded and settled in East Africa 'carried back' these traditions to Oman from Omani ter-ritory in East Africa, along with indigenous African religious traditions from 'ancient times'. Although the text describes the songs and dances in detail and gives several possible meanings for the word 'Laiwa', it says little else about the process by which the musical form came to Oman. Readers could be left with the impression that Omani traders witnessed the dances from the safe distance of their ships rather than the uncomfortable reality that they carried back thousands of young Africans to labour on their own shores.[34]

Second, there is a stigmatisation of African ancestry and servile line-age. The descendants of enslaved Africans in the Gulf run the real risk of experiencing discrimination as a result of identification with enslavement. Despite cosmopolitan ideals, there remain strong factors influencing the exclusion of and discrimination against the descendants of enslaved Africans in the Gulf. During his fieldwork in the city of Sohar on the Batinah Coast of Oman in the 1970s, Fredrik Barth identified descendants of Africans slaves as a 'stigmatized' group that experienced 'strong social pressures to isolate them as an endogamous unit' and that functioned as 'a kind of de facto ethnic group'.[35] The Exeter University scholar Marc Valeri notes that today descendants of African slaves are often kept both geographically and symbolically distinct in Oman, with some districts of Salalah, Suwaiq, Sur and Sohar exclusively populated by slave descendants.[36] Certain stigmatised labour has also been associated with Africans. Barth noted that the descendants of slaves in Batinah commonly engaged in playing music in public for money and singing as public entertainment at weddings, two occupations popularly regarded as dishonourable in Oman.[37] Barth found descendants of slaves still popularly called *khadim* (slave), and Valeri notes that the term is still used today, and slave descendants are 'also called '*abid* (slaves) or *zunuj* (black; sing. *zinj*) in the city of Sur and in the Dhofar region'.[38]

While it is true that in the Gulf today one's racial identity is most often determined by that of one's father and paternal grandfather rather than one's skin colour, skin colour *does* matter. Put simply, in the Gulf race matters alongside genealogy. Arabs in the Gulf who espouse notions of racial equality under Islam can also have strong social expectations and feelings related to race at particular times, including the selection of marriage partners. Because many Arab males from the Gulf enjoyed widespread mobility around the Indian Ocean world and frequently married into families beyond the shores of the Gulf, their descendants have often retained Arab identities whether their mothers were African, Baluchi or Indonesian. But this Arab identity contains an internal hierarchy that influences perceptions of acceptable marriage arrangements. Jane Bristol-Rhys has identified numerous barriers between marriages of Arabs and various minority groups in the UAE.[39] Further afield, the Israeli filmmaker Uri Rosenwaks has documented experiences among the descendants of enslaved Africans in Rahat, a town in Israel's Negev Desert, where few Afro-Arab Israelis knew of their slave lineage, although they experienced forms of racism in their communities, especially when seeking marriage partners from other groups.[40]

Some of the most important anthropological work on identity in the Gulf was pioneered by the anthropologist Mandana Limbert, who sensitively explores the delicate subjects of marriage and social hierarchies in Oman among other themes in her book *In the Time of Oil*. Limbert notes that

despite religious admonitions that race does not 'officially' matter, real barriers remain for marriages between Arabs and the descendants of ex-slaves.[41]
She tells the story of a young Arab woman in the 1990s who, by family
accounts, 'almost "accidentally" married a man of a servant family'. The man
had originally come from another town, and despite the initial blessing of
the young woman's grandfather, the approval of neighbours and the man's
reputation as an educated, good and hardworking person, the wedding was
called off after someone from the groom's hometown informed the bride's
family that the man was in fact of slave lineage. Limbert explains that while
official discourses 'maintain that rigid class and race separations are anti-
thetical to Omani history and Ibadism, in practice, some notion of race,
specially in reference to color, mattered'.[42] Limbert argues convincingly that
race and paternal genealogy have been in tension in Oman since at least the
1970s and that old notions of 'Arabness', defined as a class or caste category
inherited through paternal descent, have recently begun to be overtaken by
notions of 'Arabness' defined as a racial or ethnic category, particularly as
Oman has defined itself as an Arab nation with growing connections to the
rest of the Arabian Peninsula and the Gulf Cooperation Council in particular.[43] Limbert explains that Oman's official interpretations of its history
in Zanzibar emphasise relationships between Arab-Omanis and Africans as
peaceful and part of a 'civilizing process' through which Arabs and Africans
remained distinct. 'The relationship between the two groups is conceived as
brotherly, and "neighborly", yet clearly hierarchical. Through the paternalis-
ing and patronising care of the Arab-Omanis, the "Zinjis" could become
brothers; brothers, however, who would never be allowed to forget that they
had been slaves, that they had known nothing, and that they had had to be
cultured.'[44]

Jonathon Glassman, in his recent incisive analysis of creolism and cosmopolitanism, highlights one of the most significant reasons for the obscur-
ing of ancestral lineages in the western Indian Ocean. In his path-breaking
study of revolutionary Zanzibar, Glassman notes that islanders invoked real
or imagined claims to foreign (Arab or Shirazi) origins in order to distinguish
themselves from the more recent arrivals from the mainland, many of whom
were slaves. By invoking a heritage of Arabness or *ustaarabu* (Swahili: civilisation), islanders invoked a conscious sense of difference from the *ushenzi*

(barbarism or unbelief) of the mainland interior. *Ushenzi* imparted a certain 'slavish' quality to individuals that could be inherited and that was associated with lower social rank. Arab families who settled in East Africa reckoned their descent along the patriline and also, in theory, followed the principle of *kafa'a*, or female hypergamy, such that 'so long as women married only at their rank or above, Arab families would not lose children to families of lesser ranks'. The twin principles of patrilineal descent and *kafa'a* marriage allowed Arab men in the Indian Ocean diaspora to 'have children with non-Arab wives without endangering the Arab status of their "creole" children' or being tainted by *ushenzi*, which was increasingly 'understood in racialized or quasi-racialized ways'.[45] Glassman's argument may apply equally to the Gulf, where the obfuscation of African lineage stems from efforts to disassociate from the *ushenzi* or 'slavishness' of the African interior and the legacy of the slave trade. In his study of Batinah, Fredrik Barth likewise identified something he referred to as 'the taint of slave admixture'.[46]

Thirdly, there are contemporary social, political and economic factors at work. Racial relations in the Gulf are complicated by the fact that many of the descendants of Oman's most successful families who had settled over generations in Zanzibar and East Africa fled to the Gulf during the racial turmoil in Zanzibar and East Africa in the 1960s and 1970s. Descendants of the Swahili-speaking branches of elite Omani families today live alongside descendants of enslaved Africans who may not seem to outsiders considerably different in appearance. Add to this complex diversity of populations the recent trends of urbanisation, dislocation, internal migration, and the tradition of homogeneity promoted by national dress, and there remains little incentive for those with servile ancestry to highlight this part of their family history.

In addition, descendants of slaves have been extended citizenship and have been co-opted into the national identities of monarchial states, which concentrate political power in ways that benefit the minority citizen community over largely single, male migrant workers from South Asia. Descendants of slaves can receive financial benefits of citizenship in a rentier state that are withheld from the region's newer and largely South Asian underclass of guest workers who today perform many of the tasks formerly performed by slaves for low wages and in often coercive circumstances.[47] Descendants of slaves may experience forms of discrimination, but economic opportunities in Gulf monarchies are disproportionally skewed in favour of members of the ruling families and their allies, so they are not alone. Economic dynamics are further complicated by the contemporary poverty of Africa relative to the Gulf states. These combined factors may contribute to the development of a kind of 'contradictory consciousness', described by Gramsci, that can produce the state of moral and political passivity similar to that which Eugene Genovese identified among enslaved Africans in North America and which may work against the formation of diasporic identification in the Gulf.[48]

Likewise, the shared historical experience of poverty in the twentieth century, when former slaves and former masters were forced to live side by side through decades of depression following the collapse of the date and pearling industries, may have reduced the significance of differences between African and Arab identities. It is perhaps this common experience of poverty – the families of former masters and slaves scratching out a living in the decades after pearling and before oil – that most profoundly differentiates the legacy of Gulf and Atlantic slavery for the lives of their descendants today. The two regions that imported the greatest numbers of enslaved Africans – Oman and the Trucial States – were also the last two in the Gulf to develop significant oil industries. In the decades between the collapse of the date and pearl industries and the rise of the oil industry, the descendants of former slaves and former masters shared a common experience of destitution that must certainly have shaped the relationships between the region's ethnic majority and minorities. And it is perhaps this experience – more than religion, race or culture – that helps explain the seeming difference between the Gulf and the Atlantic with respect to race relations.

Towards an African Diaspora in the Cosmopolitan Gulf

To locate the African diapora in the Arabian Gulf and in the Indian Ocean more broadly, we will be well served to answer Larson's call to 'recenter', not reject, the concept of African diaspora and embrace his suggestion that our use of the term 'diaspora' must be 'expanded, geographically recentered, and reworked'. Campbell's useful rejoinder that the African-Asian diaspora may be seen as 'mythical' on account of the absence of diasporic consciousness and the degree of assimilation in the Indian Ocean world hinges on his choice to define diaspora as 'self-determination' rather than 'pre-determination', to borrow Meinecke's terms. To move beyond strict and narrow definitions of diaspora, historians of the African diaspora in the Indian Ocean will be wise to take note of the recent approaches to diaspora employed by scholars of literature, language and performance, and the work of anthropologists who stress concepts of diaspora such as 'practice', 'embodiment' and 'social memory'. These scholars offer at least three alternative methods with which to see diasporas in unconventional places.

First, literary scholars have permitted us to see diaspora as 'practice', as shown most forcefully in the work of Brent Hayes Edwards. In his examination of the notion of 'articulation' and the diversity of perspectives on diaspora, Edwards looks to Stuart Hall, who contends that 'ideology must be considered the key site of struggle over competing articulations'. In a transnational circuit, Edwards explains, articulation offers us the means to account for 'the diversity of black takes on *diaspora*'. Diaspora may be determined 'not through "return" but through difference', and citing Hall, 'not by essence or purity but by the recognition of a necessary heterogeneity and diversity; by a conception of "identity" which lives with and through, not despite, difference'.[49] Edwards advocates for a use of diaspora that 'implies neither that it offers the comfort of abstraction, and easy recourse to origins, nor that it provides a foolproof anti-essentialism: instead, it forces us to articulate discourses of cultural and political linkage only through and across difference in full view of the risks of that endeavor'.[50] He argues that articulations of diaspora demand to be approached through their *décalage* – 'the work of "differences within unity"' – because 'in the body it is only difference . . . that allows movement'.[51] His study of black internationalism from 1900 onward, from DuBois to Padmore, is thus focused on the multiplicity of meanings of *Nègre*, blackness, and diaspora as 'practice'.

Second, recent scholarship on performance and memory, much of it by anthropologists, also offers avenues for scholars of the African diaspora in the Indian Ocean. Helene Basu's important critique of scholarship on Sidi performance and questions of diaspora in India will be well-known to readers.[52] To this significant work we must add Nicolas Argenti's recent work on memory, masked dances and commemorative ceremonies in north-west Cameroon, which identifies in myths and 'nondiscursive bodily practices' to be 'impregnated with veiled references to the institutions of slavery'. Whereas the complete 'silence' on the issue of slavery, which devastated the region known as the 'Grassfields', constitutes an 'obstinate discursive absence', Argenti finds masked dances 'encapsulated the oppositions, struggles, and tensions of the slave trade'. In these 'embodied' traditions, the 'mythic memories' and the 'bodily practices' of the Grassfields together 'form a body of social memory'. Argenti's perspective allows us to see memories of slavery in environments dominated by 'discursive absence' such as the Arabian Gulf, where the history of slavery is often deliberately silenced or forgotten. For slavery 'might not constitute a body of verbal knowledge in the Grassfields today', Argenti explains, but

> the contemporary social relations of inequity and exploitation that still bind youths and elders to one another in the present perpetually recall the past by reinscribing its social polarisation in the present, giving to long-standing embodied practices a contemporaneity that makes of them not merely a body of social memory but the site of an ongoing struggle between the generations – a struggle in which contemporary oppression is inscribed and reified in the bodies of the people by means of dances that were first inspired by the extreme violence of the eras of the slave trade and forced labor.[53]

Finally, Rosalind Shaw's work on ritual and the historical imagination in Sierra Leone offers opportunities to explore the 'embedding of histories in meanings and practices that are not discursively "historical"'. Following the Comaroffs, Shaw argues that histories can be embedded in everyday habits in which 'the body is implicitly recognized as a mnemonic entity', and following Bourdieu, that we can identify tacit apprehensions of practical memory, 'forgotten as history' precisely 'because they are embedded in habits, social practices, ritual processes, and embodied experiences'.[54] Although the slave trade – like in the Cameroon Grassfields – is not often addressed discursively, Shaw argues that 'practical, nondiscursive forms of memory' may have 'at least as much importance as those that are discursively "about" the past'. Thus, while researchers in Sierra Leone (or Cameroon, or, perhaps, the Arabian Gulf) may not find eager and open dialogue about the history of enslavement, forced migration, and African origins, one may yet find significance in seemingly unlikely sources such as rumor, utterances about the politics of the present and traditions of divination. Shaw's perspective may provide a lens through which to examine forms of contemporary political protest as social memory or, most compellingly, forms of African musical tradition as 'embodied memories'. French ethnomusicologist Maho Sebiane's recent work on the Laiwa tradition in Oman and the Gulf is a powerful step in this direction.[55]

Conclusion

Although it may be 'invisible' to outsiders or even appear 'mythical' from the perspective of some scholars, an African diaspora does exist in the Gulf even within the context of cosmopolitanism. Seeing it may require some adjustment of our conceptions of diaspora and approaching it may require new methods, but historians do not need to invent these methods. They may follow the path already forged by scholars of literature and performance to answer Pier Larson's call to 'recenter', not reject, the concept of African diaspora and 'expand', geographically 'recenter' and 'rework' our terminology. When defined in terms of 'pre-determination' rather than 'self-determination', the African diaspora in the Gulf may be found hiding in plain sight.

Notes

1. Presented to 'Global Gulf Workshop', NYU Abu Dhabi (7–10 May 2015). Author address: History Department, Cal Poly, 1 Grand Avenue, San Luis Obispo, CA 93407. Author email: mshopper@calpoly.edu. An earlier version of this paper was presented to 'Cosmopolitan Currents in the Indian Ocean: New Conceptual Models for Studying Cultural Integration and Change', NYU Abu Dhabi (15–17 March 2015). I am indebted to participants in that workshop and to Dr Sandra L. Richards for invaluable comments on earlier versions of this paper.
2. Maho Sebiane, 'Le statut socio-économique de la pratique musicale aux Emirats arabs unis: La tradition du leiwah a Dubai', *Chroniques Yemenites*, vol. 14 (2007), pp. 117–35.
3. Anie Montigny, 'L'Afrique oubliée des noirs du Qatar', *Journal des Africanistes*, vol. 72, no. 2 (2002), pp. 213–25.
4. Robin Cohen, *Global Diasporas: An Introduction* (New York: Routledge, 2008), pp. 162–7.

5. Lt William Heude, *A Voyage Up the Persian Gulf and a Journey Overland from India to England in 1817* (London: Longman, Hurst, Rees, Orme & Brown, 1819), pp. 24–5; George Keppel, *Personal Narrative of a Journey from India to England* (London: H. Colburn, 1827), pp. 19–23.

6. J. G. Lorimer, *Gazetteer of the Persian Gulf, Oman and Central Arabia*, Vol. 2 (Calcutta: Superintendent Government Printing, 1908), pp. 238–41, 489–90, 1,058–77, 1,382–451. For US statistics see: Campbell Gibson and Kay Jung, 'Historical Census Statistics on Population Totals by Race, 1790 to 1990', *US Census Bureau Population Division Working Paper Series* no. 56 (September 2002). A. S. G. Jayakar, 'Medical Topograhy of Muscat by Surgeon A. S. G. Jayakar', in *Administration Report of the Persian Gulf Political Agency for the Year 1876–77*, Abu Dhabi: Centre for Documentation and Research, ND 1/H, pp. 96–102.

7. Matthew S. Hopper, *Slaves of One Master: Globalization and Slavery in Arabia in the Age of Empire* (New Haven: Yale University Press, 2015), pp. 18–50.

8. Senior Naval Officer in Persian Gulf (and Commander HMS *Vulture*) to Rear Admiral Arthur Cumming, Commander in Chief, East Indies (10 September 1872), PRO ADM 1/6230; Lt C. M. Gilbert-Cooper, 'Capture of a Slave Dhow: Or the Vulture and Its Prey', (n.d.), Lt C. M. Gilbert-Cooper Papers, National Maritime Museum, London (NMM) BGY/G/5.

9. Commander HMS *Philomel* to Commander in Chief, East Indies (15 October 1884), PRO ADM 1/6714.

10. Herbert W. Dowding, Commander HMS *Osprey*, to Rear Admiral Frederick W. Richards, Commander in Chief, East Indies (19 September 1885), PRO ADM 1/6758.

11. Hopper, *Slaves of One Master*, p. 39.

12. Cohen, *Global Diasporas*, pp. 162–7.

13. Edward A. Alpers, 'Recollecting Africa: Diasporic Memory in the Indian Ocean World', *African Studies Review*, vol. 43, no. 1 (2000), pp. 83–99.

14. Gwyn Campbell, 'The African–Asian Diaspora: Myth or Reality', *African and Asian Studies* vol. 5, nos 3–4 (2006), pp. 305–24.

15. Abdul Sheriff, *Dhow Cultures of the Indian Ocean: Cosmopolitanism, Commerce and Islam* (New York: Columbia University Press, 2010), pp. 53–64.

16. See e.g. Shihan de Silva Jayasuriya, *African Identity in Asia: Cultural Effects of Forced Migration* (Princeton: Markus Wiener, 2008), pp. 111, 135.

17. Brent Hayes Edwards, 'The Uses of Diaspora', *Social Text* 66, vol. 19, no. 1 (Spring 2001), p. 54.

18. Friedrich Meinecke, *Cosmopolitanism and the National State* (Princeton: Princeton University Press, 1970), pp. 21, 205. [Originally pub. 1907.]

19. Vinay Dharwadker, 'Diaspora and Cosmopolitanism', in Magdalena Nowicka and Maria Rovisco (eds), *Ashgate Companion to Cosmopolitanism* (Farnham, UK: Ashgate, 2011), p. 125.

20. Ibid., p. 129.

21. Ibid., pp. 130–1.

22. He notes that '[t]he canonical Greek translation of the Book of Deuteronomy, prepared in the second century, picked *diaspora* to correspond to *galut* because the Greek term had been used as early as Thucydides' *History of the Peloponnesian War* (circa 400 BC) to describe the scattering of the Aeginetan people across Hellas after the Athenian army forcibly expelled them from their native island of Aegina'. He explains that for 'the translators who produced the Old Testiment, a dispersion of a people from their homeland . . . was not exclusively a Jewish experience, which is why it was translatable in the first place. In short, the ancient Greek term, diaspora, was a cosmopolitan, inclusive, and universalizing rendering of galut'.

23. Ibid., pp. 133–4.

24. Ibid., pp. 141–2.

25. Edward A. Alpers, 'The African Diaspora in the Northwestern Indian Ocean: Reconsiderations of an Old Problem, New Directions for Research', *Comparative Studies in South Asia, Africa and the Middle East*, vol. 17, no. 2 (1997, pp. 61–80.

26. See e.g. Paul Tiyambe Zeleza, 'African Diasporas: Toward a Global History', *African Studies Review*, vol. 53, no. 1 (2010), pp. 1–19.

27. Larson, 'Reconsidering Trauma, Identity, and the African Diaspora'.

28. Gloash-Boza, *Yo Soy Negro*, pp. 1–58.

29. Larson, *Ocean of Letters*, p. 350.

30. Larson, 'Horrid Journeying'.

31. Klein, Sheriff and Austen, cited in Larson, 'Horrid Journeying', p. 439.

32. Larson, 'Horrid Journeying', p. 442.

33. Smithsonian Institution, 'Connecting the Gems of the Indian Ocean: From Oman to East Africa', <http://africa.si.edu/50years/oman/> (last accessed 28 May 2014).

34. Sultanat 'Omān, *Ashkāl Mu'āsira li-Alfunūn Al-Sha'bīyat*, vol. 3, pp. 14–15, 31–2.

35. Barth, *Sohar*, p. 48.

36. Valeri, *Oman*, p. 15.

37. Barth, *Sohar*, p. 48.

38. Valeri, *Oman*, p. 15.

39. Bristol-Rhys, *Emirati Women*, pp. 99–102.

40. Rosenwaks, *The Film Class*.

41. Limbert, *In the Time of Oil*, pp. 143–8.

42. Ibid., p. 147.

43. Ibid., p. 143.

44. Ibid., pp. 144–5. See also Limbert, 'Marriage, Status and the Politics of Nationality in Oman', pp. 167–79.

45. Glassman, 'Creole Nationalism'. See also Glassman, *War of Words*, pp. 23–64 and Ho, *The Graves of Tarim*.

46. Barth, *Sohar*, p. 46.

47. Montigny, 'L'Afrique oubliee des noirs du Qatar', *Journal des africanistes*, vol. 72, no. 2 (2002), pp. 213–25. For an excellent discussion of the South Asian diaspora in the Gulf see: Pardis Mahdavi, *Gridlock: Labor, Migration, and Human Trafficking in Dubai* (Stanford: Stanford University Press, 2011); Neha Vora, *Impossible Citizens: Dubai's Indian Diaspora* (Durham: Duke University Press, 2013); Laavanya Kathiravelu, 'The Other NRIs: The Case of Low-Wage Indian Migrants in the Gulf', in Jayati Battacharya and Coonoor Thadani (eds), *Indian and Chinese Immigrant Communities: A Comparative Approach* (London: Anthem Press, 2015).

48. Gramsci, *Prison Notebooks*, p. 333; Genovese, *Roll, Jordan, Roll*, p. 147.

49. Brent Hayes Edwards, *The Practice of Diaspora: Literature, Translation, and the Rise of Black Internationalism* (Cambridge, MA: Harvard University Press, 2003), p. 12.

50. Ibid., p. 13.

51. Ibid., pp. 13–15.

52. Helene Basu, 'Drumming and Praying: Sidi at the Interface Between Spirit Possession and Islam', in Simpson and Kresse (eds), *Struggling with History*, pp. 291–322.

53. Nicolas Argenti, *Intestines of the State: Youth, Violence, and Belated Histories in the Cameroon Grassfields* (Chicago: University of Chicago Press, 2007), pp. 2–6.

54. Rosalind Shaw, *Memories of the Slave Trade: Ritual and the Historical Imagination in Sierra Leone* (Chicago: University of Chicago Press, 2002), pp. 4–7.

55. Maho Sebiane, 'Entre l'Afrique et l'Arabie: les esprits de possession sawahili et leurs frontiers', *Journal des Africanistes*, vol. 84, no. 2 (2014), pp. 48–79.

9

EAST AFRICA, THE GLOBAL GULF AND THE NEW THALASSOLOGY OF THE INDIAN OCEAN

Mark Horton

Introduction

In recent years, there has been a revival in our understanding of the inter-relationship between sea and land. Stemming originally from Braudel's classic study of the Mediterranean World (Braudel 1976), and refined as the 'new thalassology' by Peters (2003) and Horden and Purcell (2006), these new approaches have largely focused on the Mediterranean and Atlantic worlds (Cunliffe 2001; Broodbank 2013) while the Indian Ocean has often lagged behind (Vink 2007). There is still lacking a comprehensive under-standing of the Indian Ocean World that is able to transcend borders and periods in a convincing way (Figure 9.1).

The role of the Gulf in particular in the articulation of the Indian Ocean World has been neglected. While the Gulf in the pre-modern period was gen-erally known for the supply of dates and pearls (Carter, Power this volume), the role of Gulf traders and their port cities in earlier centuries has centred on the spectacular voyages of the Abbasid period (750–1258 CE), with long-distance voyages to India, South East Asia and China in search of ceramics, cloth and spices for the courts of the Caliphate (Hourani 1995), celebrated in ship reconstructions such as those of the *Sohar* (Sevrin 1983) and the *Jewel of*

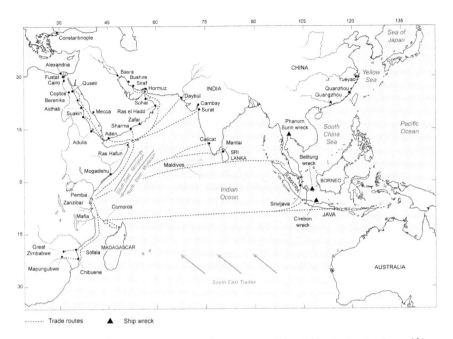

Figure 9.1 Map of the Indian Ocean with routes out of East Africa in the eighth–twelfth centuries. Shipwrecks noted in the text marked.

Muscat (Vosmer *et al.* 2011). The excavations in the two key port cities in this Indian Ocean trade, Siraf (Iran) and Sohar (Oman), have only been partially published, and neither is fully understood (Whitehouse 2001; Kevran 2004; Priestman 2014).

Our understanding of the Indian Ocean World is often presented as a largely Eurasian-centred view – in which connections have been followed across an Asian world (typically between Western Asia, India and South East Asia), with links to Europe through either through the Red Sea or Gulf routes, either in Classical antiquity or from the early modern period (Chaudhuri 1985, 1990; McLaughlin 2014). When it has been visualised as a world system (Abu Lugard 1989), or as networks (Wink 2002), the entire western seaboard of the Indian Ocean is normally omitted – thus excluding the eastern African coast, typically from Ras Guardafui to Madagascar and southern Africa.

In this chapter, I want to argue that, rather than being irrelevant, the eastern African coast played a vital role connecting the Gulf with the Indian

Ocean World and creating a form of proto-globalisation. This occurred through the supply of tropical raw materials – both precious and mundane, minerals and labour. With this economic activity came a long and complex cultural engagement that was a two-way process, in which elements of Middle Eastern and Indian cultures were adopted within the coastal settlements of East Africa, while African elements found their way into Gulf and Indian cultures.

One of the features of the new thalassological thinking is an acknowledgement of the intellectual debt made by World Systems Theory (Vink 2007: 43), as originally proposed by Immanuel Wallerstein (1974–80) and others. While the temporal limits of the original conception (essentially a post-1492/8 world) have been largely abandoned, the idea of 'core and periphery' that underpinned it has remained current. The notion of colonial empires – European or other – exploiting peripheries for their raw materials or labour – still remains (Rodney 1972: 158). Such exploitation took place through technological superiority or, occasionally, military force. In the case of East Africa, the region could be seen as classic 'periphery', supplying raw material to a 'civilised' world (Classical, Sasanian, Arab, Portuguese, Dutch, British and German). Often, colonial models have been invoked to explain this – for example the numerous port cities along the East African coast were 'claimed' to owe their origins to colonial settlement from the Middle East. Arab and Gulf traders came to East Africa on the monsoon winds and 'married' local African women, so introducing features of civilisation (in particular Islam) to an African world (Chittick 1975: 40–3; 1977: 218–19). In this view, the indigenous inhabitants, for unexplained reasons, were more than happy to give up their valuable commodities and labour, in exchange for the gift of Islamic civilisation.

But to Africanists, such models fit poorly with our empirical evidence and ignore the very complex dynamics of African societies. They deny any African agency in the process; they leave Africans with little or no participation, leaving them as only passive consumers. Why would African societies be happy to part with their valuable minerals such as gold or iron, or ivory tusks in exchange for some simple glass beads and a few ceramic vessels, as if they were simple-minded and naive about the benefits of civilisation? Historical archaeologists have shown elsewhere in the world that there are often deep ambiguities about material objects in indigenous and colonial spaces, and often very different understandings of value (Stillman 2010). As Presthold (2008) showed for the nineteenth-century cloth trade in East Africa, the relationship between traders and commodities and consumers was a highly complex one, in which the changing fashions of the consumers in Africa had a major effect on the fortunes of the producers, be it in New England, Manchester or Mumbai. So it was in earlier periods that the African ports and their hinterlands had a very clear idea of what they required from visiting traders, and had strict rules as to how trade was to be conducted. These rules often relied on a patron–client relationship – where the local merchants protected the traders (and provided hospitality and gifts) in exchange for their goods. The goods could only be exchanged on an agreed and fixed price (Horton and Middleton 2000: 90–2; 2004: 83–6).

Eastern Africa and the Global Gulf: North v. South

Several hundred sites have been surveyed, some excavated, along some 3,000 km of the eastern African coast, with archaeological evidence indicating a long and complex sequences of interaction spanning East and Southeast Asia, India, the Middle East and the Eastern Mediterranean from the sixth century CE into the Portuguese period. However, it is materials with a Gulf origin that dominate the assemblages of glass and ceramics found on these sites. This strongly suggests that the relatively straightforward monsoon-driven voyage out the Gulf and onto the Swahili coast with its islands and estuaries was the most frequent for over a millennium (Horton 2017a; Priestman 2013). It was a journey, memorably recorded by Alan Villiers in the dhow the *Triumph of Righteousness*, from Kuwait to the Rufiji Delta to trade mangrove poles in 1939 (Villiers 1940).

Sailing south, with the winds blowing largely astern – sailing ideally suited for sewn boats with square sails, ships regularly made the journey to East Africa in less than a month. The south-westerly inclination of the African coast meant that vessels had only a short sea-crossing of the Gulf of Aden before they were able to follow the African coast and navigate using a series of well-known landmarks – some of which were first noted in the first-century CE *Periplus Maris Erythraei* and were still observed by nineteenth-century navigators (Casson 1989; Guillan 1856: 134–5). Numerous inlets and harbours provided shelter, while the western shores of the offshore islands – Pemba, Zanzibar, Mafia, Comoros and Madagascar, provided safe anchorages. This south-west/north-east route had one important drawback for navigators. While it was ideal for connecting East Africa and the Gulf, sailing from the Red Sea was more difficult, as boats typically sailed outwards on the south-west monsoon from the Bab el-Mandeb, the very monsoon on which boats would sail north, rather than south, along the African coast. While sailing between the Gulf and East Africa could be undertaken in a single monsoon, sailing between the Red Sea and East Africa required two monsoons, making the round journey take nearly two years. For this reason, the southern Arabian coast, and the islands in the outer Gulf (such as Kish and Hormuz), acted as an entrepôt for African goods that could be stored and trans-shipped into the India/Mediterranean trade.

This voyage down to East Africa was part of a network of 'northern' routes driven by the seasonal monsoons – the north-east and south-west – that also provided an east–west corridor between Arabia and the Red Sea, the Gulf, and western and southern India, and extended beyond into southeast Asia and even southern China. The first part of this route was 'discovered' by Hippalus in the first century BCE (Warmington 1974: 45–6; Sheriff 2010: 143) (although in reality had probably been in existence for millennia) and was employed during the Classical spice trade, as recorded in the *Periplus Maris Erythraei*. It was then continued by Sasanian merchants, and with the arrival of Islam in the western Indian Ocean became the focus for Islamic long-distance trade, in which ships from the Gulf evidently reached southern China. There is good evidence for this Gulf trade, both in contemporary accounts (Mackintosh-Smith and Montgomery 2014) and with the discovery of the Belitung wreck, discussed below (Krahl *et al.* 2010). The monsoon winds facilitated the transit of ships which, while modest in size, were able to carry enormous cargos of valuable commodities. With a stable wind on the beam, or beam-reach and competent navigation, these vessels were able to cover considerable distances in relative safety. The distance across open water was relatively limited – to the western Indian Ocean and the Bay of Bengal. The remainder of the voyage could be undertaken along coastlines.

But there were also other, less-well documented transoceanic voyages, where longer distances were covered out of sight of land and connected the peripheral parts of the Indian Ocean, which fed commodities into these northern networks. These can be broadly described as a 'southern' network. These transoceanic voyages were important as alternative routes, in which transit times could be reduced and dangerous coastlines avoided, and ships were more likely to avoid coastal piratical activity. For these southern routes the East African coastal communities acted not only to supply African commodities, but as an entrepôt for south, southeast and even East Asian commodities brought across the ocean to be traded to the Gulf or the Red Sea.

The monsoons were employed for direct sailing between East Africa, southern India and Sri Lanka, and possibly the Maldives – routes recorded in late fifteenth-century navigational treatises (Tibbetts 1971) and taken by Vasco da Gama, guided by a local pilot (sometimes claimed to be Ahmed Ibn Majid, though this is disputed by Tibbetts 1971: 9–11), when he sailed from Malindi to Kappad near to Calicut in 1498. Sailing from southern Asia, it was also possible to follow the mid-oceanic island chains of the Maldives and the Chagos islands to reach the southern end of the African coast and Madagascar, via the Comoros. This has been proposed as the likely route taken by Austronesians from southeast Asia who reached Madagascar (Shepherd 1982: 137; Vérin 1986: 39), with the maximum extent of open ocean being around 1800 km.

Another more extreme southerly route, entirely in the southern hemisphere, connecting southeast Asia with the southern Swahili coast might also explain the Austronesian presence in Madagascar. This involved sailing directly across the ocean from the Sunda, Bali or Lombok straits following approximately the 12° latitude across the Indian Ocean, reaching the northern tip of Madagascar or the Comoros – a distance of between 6,500 and 7,000 km and requiring around 30–40 days at sea. In fact, this voyage has been attempted twice in modern times using Indonesian replica craft. One voyage, in 1985, left the Lombok straits and used a 20 m outrigger canoe, and achieved the journey successfully in 47 days, leaving Bali on 3 June (McGrath 1988; Lübeck and Wiebeck 1994: 34) and employing navigational techniques of latitude sailing using star observations. Another expedition built a replica of the Borobudur ship in 2003, also around 20 m in length, leaving the Sunda straits, and would have made the journey in around 25 sea-days between August and October if it had not diverted to the Seychelles (Beale 2006).

The timing of this route is fairly critical. It needs to be undertaken after the Intertropical Convergence Zone moves north, following the south-east trade winds – June to October being the ideal time. This coincided with the south-west monsoon, blowing along the African coast, allowing for a return journey directly to southern India from around the latitude of Pemba island. Ships could return to Indonesia after the change in monsoon in November, to pass through the Malacca straits. The round trip would take less than a year, and could be achieved in 6–9 months. The same ships could also use the south-west monsoon to sail to the Gulf, and then to India.

East Africa and the Gulf in the *Book of Curiosities*

In 2002, the Bodleian Library in Oxford acquired an important Arabic manuscript, known as the *Book of Curiosities of the Sciences and Marvels for the Eyes* (MS Arab c.90). While the manuscript is a late twelfth- or early thirteenth-century copy, it contains material collected in Fatimid Egypt in the ninth–eleventh centuries and probably before 1050 (Rapoport and Savage-Smith 2014: 1, 32). The manuscript contains much of importance, with both annotated maps and texts, on celestial and geographical matters, and five chapters on curiosities. Among this material is an important map of the Indian Ocean (A Folio 29B–30A), and in particular references to the East African coast (Horton 2018).

The map shows an oval space in which the countries of the Indian Ocean are displayed along the borders (Plate 4). Within the ocean are depicted the key islands of the Indian Ocean – at least as perceived by the author (Rapoport and Savage Smith 2014: 156–7). The depiction of the Indian Ocean is very similar to how the author shows the Mediterranean – but with many fewer islands. Both represent a classic thalassological view of a sea and its rim around the edge. In reality this image may be a little deceptive in that it was drawn in two halves, and the geography in the eastern and western sections does not line up. In the world map in the same manuscript, the Indian Ocean is also shown as open-ended (folio 27b–28a), comparing closely with al-Idrisi's view of the world. The left-hand side of Folio 29B–30A follows the eastern side of the Indian Ocean from the Arabian Peninsula and the Bab el-Mandeb straits, to the southern coasts of Mozambique as a single curving coastline.

The particular importance of this map is in the detail that it provides for the African coast, and the place names it supplies for the first time in the historical literature. There are few surviving detailed accounts of the topography of East Africa, and only one single eyewitness – the historian al-Masudi – who last travelled there in 916 from Sohar and Siraf – until the visit of Ibn Battuta in 1331 (Freeman-Grenville 1962: 14–17, 27–32). Tenth-century and earlier sources provide general regions (such as Zanj, Sufala, Berbera), but only two actual place names, Qanbalu, most likely the island of Pemba, and where al-Masudi travelled to, and Languja, recorded by al-Jahiz in the ninth century, as the island of Zanzibar (Unguja in Swahili). Folio 29B–30A provides many additional names and details. Unjuwa island has several anchorages around it, and a town called A-k-h – this is clearly a reference to Unguja Ukuu, a major site which we have been investigating since 2011 that was the port city of the coast from the eighth to the eleventh century (Crowther *et al.* 2015; Crowther *et al.* 2016; Horton *et al.* forthcoming). The map also marks another island, Jazirat Qanbalu, al-Masudi's destination in 916 and most likely Pemba island. Archaeological investigations at the sites of Tumbe, Ras Mkumbuu and Mtambwe Mkuu have revealed important eighth-to-eleventh-century sequences (Fleisher and LaViolette 2013; Horton *et al.* 1986; Horton forthcoming), although the actual site of the main port city has not yet been satisfactorily located. To further stress the importance of the East African islands and ports, the map includes an itinerary along the coast; places named for the first time include Malindi, Mtwapa, Unguja, Mafia, Kilwa, the island of d-l-h, Q-d-x-h (a bay), Khawr al-amir (the Bay of the Amir), K-l-n-k-w (a stronghold) and Susmar (Crocodile, ?Bazaruto) island at the end of the itinerary. The map also shows the Islands of the Waqwaq 'whose inhabitants engage in piracy' (Madagascar), the Island of Sofala (on the Mozambique coast) and the islands of Dibajat – probably the Comoros (Rapoport and Savage Smith 2014: 444–5).

The particular significance of this list is that it takes the voyages to the southern end of the Swahili coast, and connects this area with the ports in southern Arabia and the Gulf. It is most likely based on genuine itineraries and seems not to be derivative of earlier sources. Given the Fatimid origins of the manuscript, and the difficulties of sailing from the Red Sea, it suggests an active connection from the Arabian or Gulf coasts by the eleventh century, as far south as Mozambique. This has been termed the 'Swahili corridor' (Horton 1987), and may have featured trade in ivory and gold from southern Africa and rock crystal from Madagascar – a trade in high-value luxuries. Recent work in Madagascar has pinpointed the source of rock crystal that was exported both to the Gulf and later to the famous Fatimid workshops in Cairo (Horton *et al.* 2017). From Iron Age sites in the interior of southern Africa are found 'Zhizo'-type glass beads of the eighth to mid-tenth century, which scientific analysis has suggested have a Gulf origin (Wood *et al.* 2017), implying that Gulf and Arabian ships reached as far south as the Mozambique channel in order to trade with the African interior.

By the eleventh century, the southern coast of Arabia may have acted as a staging post for these extreme southerly voyages. Recent work and the comprehensive publication of the site of Sharma in coastal Yemen have helped to locate one such place, with what appears to be an African community resident on the coast of Arabia, between c. 980 and 1050 (Rougeulle 2015). Sharma was founded by merchants who left the port of Siraf, possibly after a series of earthquakes in the late tenth century. They took advantage of the renewed Egyptian interest in the India trade – a trade that is well documented, for example in the Geniza papers (Goitein and Friedman 2011). What is exceptional is that Sharma contains a high proportion of African ceramics, both 'graphite-red slipwares' and 'developed Tana' wares – in places up to 17 per cent of the total – and these can be directly compared to tenth- and early eleventh-century ceramics from the Pemba island site of Mtambwe Mkuu, where a large hoard of Fatimid coins was also excavated in 1984 (Horton *et al.* 1986). Sharma is not alone in containing African communities on the Arabian coast – the site of Ras al-Hadd (Whitcomb 1975: 148, Figure 9, d, e, f) at the entrance to the Gulf contains an East African assemblage of the same or slightly earlier date.

The *Book of Curiosities* and the Sharma/Ras el-Hadd finds thus provide a particular insight into the organisation of Indian Ocean trade in the tenth and early eleventh centuries. It shows that there were already-established long-distance networks extending from the Arabian and Gulf coasts to the far south of the African continent – and with the chronology of the Zhizo beads commencing in the eighth century, possibly as early as this. One of the key sites to confirm this is Chibuene, on the Mozambique coast, near to Vilanculos and Bazaruto island, where there is not only pottery, closely reminiscent of the Swahili coast further north (known as Tana tradition or TIW), but also blue splashed white glaze pottery (of Mesopotamian origin) of the early ninth century (Sinclair 1982: 152) as well as Zhizo glass beads. Chibuene, as far south as Lat. 22° south, lies adjacent to a route into the southern African interior and the Limpopo valley and was most likely the southernmost entrepôt for the Gulf trade with Africa.

One of the motives for sailing so far south was undoubtedly ivory. The ivory trade is well described by al-Masudi on his visit to Qanbalu, including details of how the elephants are caught, and how 'from this country . . . come tusks weighing fifty pounds or more. They usually go to Oman, and from there are sent to China and India. This is their chief trade route, and if it was not so, ivory would be common in Muslim lands' (Freeman-Grenville 1962, 15). Al-Masudi then describes how African ivory was especially prized in China as the officials required straight tusks for their ceremonial staffs. Southern Africa with its open landscape and easy connections to the coast was a practical source of elephant ivory.

Southeast Asian Shipwrecks

The waters of southeast Asia are particularly rich in shipwrecks. While unfortunately many have been uncovered and excavated by commercial divers in less than ideal conditions, they nonetheless throw particular light on global Gulf connections, the routes and commodities that were followed as well as the types of ships involved. Tantalisingly, several other ships are known along the coast of Vietnam, still being pillaged (Staniforth 2012), including a sewn boat of Gulf origin apparently associated with Changsha stoneware, from 'central Vietnam' (Dissanayake 2014).

The most recent discovery, in 2013, the Phanom Surin wreck, was found while excavating tanks for a shrimp farm in Samut Sakhon province of lower central Thailand some 25 km south-west of Bangkok. The excavation and recovery project has been undertaken by the Department of Fine Arts since 2013, and is thus a rare example of a scientific investigation of a shipwreck. The site has been briefly reported in Thai (Preecharpeechacupt 2014) and

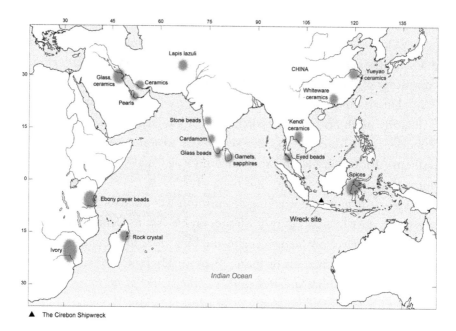

Figure 9.2 The world of the Cirebon ship, c. 970, showing the location of the origin of the cargo recovered from the vessel.

English (Guy 2017). Because the wreck was found on land there is a better opportunity to study the structure of the vessel, although the bulk of the cargo had been salvaged in ancient times. The vessel is a typical sewn boat, with internal and external wadding – a particular feature of early Gulf boats. However, recent identification of the timbers used in the vessel's construction points to a Thai or southeast Asian origin. The keelson of 17.65m has been recovered, and has two masts, one with an in-situ pulley block and complete at 17.35m long (Plate 5). The vessel size is estimated to be around 35 m in total length and about 14 m wide (Guy 2017, 180). This compares to the size of the two carricks used by Vasco da Gama to sail to India in 1498 of around 25 m in total length.

The vessel was probably wrecked in the second half of the eighth century. Unpublished radiocarbon dates suggest an earlier eighth-century construction, with repairs in the mid-eighth century. Relatively few ceramics have been found, but these include Chinese olive green stoneware jars ('Dusun' jars), Mon earthenwares from Thailand and, from the Gulf, turquoise-glazed earthenwares ('Sasanian-Islamic' wares) and torpedo jars, lined with bitumen, as liquid carriers; one had a Pahlavi inscription, 'Yazd-bōzēd', probably a personal name (Guy 2017: 188). Also among the cargo were aromatic woods, an ivory tusk and deer antlers, all of which could have been obtained from Thailand. It has been suggested that the vessel was lost in the river deltas of the Tha Chin and Chao Phraya rivers, visiting the Thai kingdom of Mon, and its cities that flourished in the eighth century. Two of these cities, Khu Bua and Nakhon Pathom, have graffiti and terracotta reliefs that show Western Asiatic traders in the eighth century (Guy 2017: 191–2). This shipwreck shows that Gulf ships sailed beyond the Malacca straits by the mid-eighth century, and may well have reached southern China, but also traded with the emerging states of southeast Asia. Even by this early date these sewn boats were very substantial in size and were capable of carrying enormous cargos.

The Belitung shipwreck was half the length of the Phanom Surin wreck, dates to around sixty years later, and had its cargo largely intact. It was found and excavated by commercial divers in the 1990s off the coast of Sumatra (Flecker 2000, 2001, 2008; Burger *et al.* 2010, Krahl *et al.* 2010). The ship went down shortly after 826 CE, according to a single dated stoneware vessel. It was around 18 m long and 6 m wide. The vessel was carrying as its principal cargo stoneware ceramics, upwards of 57,500 pieces of Changsha stoneware packed inside similar olive green stoneware jars ('Dusun' jars) as at Phanom Surin. Not published, but on display in Singapore, is a torpedo jar similar to that found on the Thai wreck. There were also a number of personal crew items, as well as southeast Asian spices and aromatic resins, eleven Chinese bronze mirrors and a small number of pieces of Chinese gold and silver work.

While the work was largely devoted to the recovery of the many artefacts, some rudimentary recording of the ship's hull was undertaken, which formed the basis for the reconstruction, the *Jewel of Muscat*, that successfully sailed from Oman to Singapore in 2010 (Vosmer *et al.* 2011). The vessel was a western Indian Ocean sailing boat, with double wadding sewn planks, one or two masts and square, possibly matting sails – very similar to the Phanom Surin ship. Remarkably, much of the timber for the construction of the vessel was of African origin – *Afzelia africana* was used for the stern post frames, hull planks, anchor shank and dunnage, *Afzelia bipindensis* was used for the keelson, and the ceiling planks were probably from *Juniperus procera*, or African Juniper. Only the through beams were made from Indian teak, *Tectona grandis* (Krahl *et al.* 2010: 117). The three African species could have been sourced from the coastal forests or hinterland. It has been suggested that vessel was re-sewn while in southeast Asia (Flecker 2008: 386), a common occurrence while awaiting the change in monsoon (Guy 2017: 180). Given the African and India origin of the timber, it has been suggested that the vessel was built in the Gulf, probably in Oman (Vosmer *et al.* 2011).

The third wreck dates to around 140 years later that the Belitung wreck, and was found only 320 km away, 140 km north of the Javanese city of Cirebon. The Cirebon ship was also excavated by commercial divers, between 2004 and 2005, who recovered the cargo and allowed for the hull to be recorded in detail (Anon 2009; Harkantiningsih *et al.* 2010; Leibner 2014). It dates to after 968 (on a dated bowl fragment), was between 32 and 35 m long and was constructed by the 'lashed lug' method, rather than sewn, indicative of a southeast Asian origin for the ship. There is no evidence it had outriggers – indeed it was most likely too large to need them (Liebner 2014).

On board were enormous quantities of Chinese stoneware (maybe as many as 400,000 pieces), mostly Yue wares, some Lio porcelain, and fine paste earthenware, of which at least some originated in mainland southeast Asia, a similar area visited by the Phanom Surin ship (Figure 9.2). However, also in the cargo were significant quantities of Middle Eastern material including an important group of glass (Plate 6) (Guillot n.d.) and sherds of turquoise-glazed wares (Plate 7) (Sasanian Islamic). Several hundred kilogrammes of crude lapis lazuli were also found, suggesting some contact with Afghanistan, either through Gulf or Indian ports. Significant quantities of rock crystal were also present in the wrecked hull; 42 pieces were recorded in total, including carved crystal, a crystal ball, beads and gaming pieces (Plate 8). Four blocks of unworked raw material were found, three of which weighed 125 kg (Liebner 2014: 173). Madagascar was the principal source of rock crystal at this date (Horton *et al.* 2017). Other artefacts from around the Indian Ocean include ebony prayer beads and ivory (East Africa or southeast Asia), pearls (Gulf), stone beads (western India), glass beads (southern India), garnets and sapphires (Sri Lanka), eyed beads (Malay peninsula), *kendi* ceramics (Thailand) and spices (island southeast Asia).

This diverse collection of material is from a vessel that had access to the goods of the entire littoral of the Indian Ocean. Two interpretations can be suggested – the ship obtained these goods in the port cities of southeast Asia, and was trading its way around the ports of the region (Leibner 2014; Guy 2004) as has been surmised from the slightly later Intan shipwreck (Guy 2004, Flecker 2002: 121–5). However, these vessels may also have been bound for the western Indian Ocean (Shen 2017: 208). The presence of western Indian Ocean items such as turquoise-glazed ceramics and Islamic glass might also indicate that the vessel traversed the entire Indian Ocean, calling in to East Africa, the Gulf and India, as well as eastern and southeast Asia, and the excavation recovered small quantities of leftover pieces in the hull that provide a record of its journey across the oceans. The Cirebon wreck provides some credence for the 'China ships' (mostly likely southeast Asian) noted by Masudi in Kalah Bar, located on the Bay of Bengal side of the Kra Peninsular in the mid-tenth century, where they met with Arab ships.

There Masudi noted that 'in most ancient times it was different; for the Chinese vessels used to come to Oman, Siraf, to the coasts of Fars, Bahrain, Ubullah and Basra; and in the same way the vessels went from the ports mentioned as far as China' (Pellat 1962: 325; Hourani 1995: 75–6). The enormous size of the southeast Asian vessels such as the Cirebon ship would pose no problems in the long-distance transoceanic voyages required.

The existence of a China trade during the Tang dynasty has long been known (Figure 9.3). Ships from the Gulf, particular Siraf and Sohar, sailed to Chinese ports, as is described by Abu Zayd as Sirafi – especially Guangzhou in the period up until the massacre of the foreign merchants in 878 (Mackintoch-Smith and Montgomery 2014). After this date, much of the trade was taken over by southeast Asian vessels. These shipwrecks fit closely into this narrative, but indicate the sheer size and scale of this trade, as well as the relatively early eighth-century date when it began. The excavation of key port sites in the Gulf, particularly Siraf and Sohar, which played such an important part in this trade include Chinese and Islamic ceramics represented on these three shipwrecks (Priestman 2013).

East Africa and the Global Gulf

The Phanom Surin, Belitung and Cirebon ships and the *Book of Curiosities* offer a substantially different picture of the Indian Ocean world in the ninth

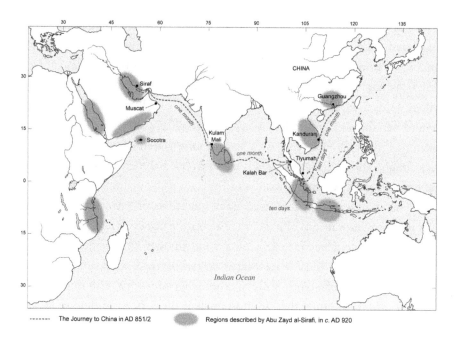

Figure 9.3 Map of the Indian Ocean showing the route of an anonymous voyage to China in 850/1, and the regions described by Abu Zayd al-Sirafi (in c. 920), in the same manuscript.

and tenth centuries from the one normally presented (Abu Lugard 1989; Hourani 1995; Chaudhuri 1990). Large ships were sailing around the rim of the Indian Ocean as well as across it, and to remote areas that are otherwise poorly documented. One particular window into this trade comes from the excavations of the port sites along the eastern African littoral that extends far into the southern hemisphere. Some idea of the complexity of these exchange networks can be gleaned; the Gulf ships sailing to China may well have been loaded with African ivory, as there was little that the Chinese required from the Gulf that they could not manufacture or grow themselves. Chinese ceramics and other goods hinted at in the Belitung wreck, as well as silks and lacquer, may well have been in significant demand in the Middle East and were exchanged for the African ivory (Horton 2017b: 269–71).

Given the quantity of ceramics (including Changsha and torpedo jars), glass and beads found at Unguja Ukuu (Priestman 2017; Horton *et al.* forthcoming), and probably also including cloth, this ivory was by no means cheaply obtained. The African merchants were themselves involved in complex networks to obtain the ivory from the continental sources, and hints of these networks come from the glass beads from India and the Gulf, found in the far interior of southern Africa (Wood *et al.* 2017). Southeast Asian vessels also visited the African coast, and may not have been an unfamiliar sight in the Gulf. The recent identification of rice cultivation on the Comoros and Madagascar suggests that direct maritime links existed with southeast Asia on a substantial scale (Crowther *et al.* 2016) that included also the movement of large numbers of people, suggested by both genetics and linguistics (Adelaar 2009; Cox *et al.* 2012; Boivin *et al.* 2013; Kusuma *et al.* 2015). Excavations at Membeni on Grand Comore (Comoros), a possibly landfall for some of these transoceanic voyages that may well have followed the southern hemisphere route, recovered torpedo jars as well as Changsha stoneware, of types very similar to bowls found on the Belitung wreck.

There does remain an outstanding issue as to why the Belitung wreck was found at the southern end of Sumatra, and well off course for the Straits of Malacca. Maybe it was driven south in a storm, or was en route to trade with Palambang, the capital of Srivijaya. Another possibility is that it was avoiding the Straits of Malacca, and was planning to enter the Indian Ocean via the Sunda straits and sail up the west coast of Sumatra. A further idea may be that the ship was intending to sail along the southern hemisphere route, directly to the African coast, possibly via the Comoros. While there is no documentary evidence that Arab ships undertook such voyages at this date, it would considerably reduce the journey time back to the Gulf by around a year, and avoid the piratical infestations of the Straits of Malacca.

In developing any new thalassology of the Indian Ocean, archaeological evidence is as important as any reassessment of the documentary sources. This chapter has looked at a map and three shipwrecks in the operations within the Indian Ocean. Documents – be they narratives of voyages or Geniza letters – can be valuable, but their interpretation must rely upon a proper understanding of geography and the nature of the winds and currents. Significant areas of the Indian Ocean World may have escaped documentary evidence, but this does not mean that they were unimportant. Our challenge is to work out how to synthesise the various streams of evidence into a convincing understanding of one of the first and most remarkable global systems.

Acknowledgements

I am grateful to Emilie Savage-Smith for drawing attention to the importance of the *Book of Curiosities* for the African coast, and to Yossef Rapoport for discussions about its interpretation. Through the kindness of Erbrem Vatcharangkul, I was able to visit the Phanom Surin wreck site during excavation in 2014; I was also able to discuss the significance of the site with John Guy and Henry Wright. For the Cirebon wreck, I am very grateful to Qatar National Museums for allowing me to view the collection during their cataloguing process. Recent fieldwork on the Comoros and on Zanzibar was part of the Sealinks project, now located in the Max Planck Institute, Jena and directed by Nicole Boivin. Versions of this chapter were delivered at lectures at New York University Abu Dhabi and UCL Qatar in 2016–17, building on the paper given at the Global Gulf Conference in 2016.

Bibliography

Abu Lughod, Janet (1989), *Before European Hegemony: The World System AD 1250–1350*, Oxford: Oxford University Press.

Adelaar A. (2009), 'Towards an Integrated Theory about the Indonesian Migrations to Madagascar', in I. Peiros, P. Peregrine and M. Feldman, *Ancient Human Migrations: A Multi-Disciplinary Approach*, Salt Lake City: University of Utah Press, pp. 149–72.

Anon (2009), 'The Cargo from the Cirebon shipwreck', <http://cirebon.musee-mariemont.be/home-6.htm?lng=en>

Beale, Philip (2006), 'From Indonesia to Africa: Borobudur Ship Expedition', *Ziff Journal*, 2006: 17–24.

Boivin, Nicole, Alison Crowther, Richard Helm and Dorian Q. Fuller (2013), 'East Africa and Madagascar in the Indian Ocean World', *Journal of World Prehistory* 26: 213–81.

Braudel, Fernand (1976), The Mediterranean and the Mediterranean World in the Age of Philip II, trans. Siân Reynolds, 2nd edn, 2 vols. New York: Harper & Row.

Broodbank, Cyprian (2013), *The Making of the Middle Sea: A History of the Mediterranean from the Beginning to the Emergence of the Classical World*, London: Thames & Hudson.

Burger, Pauline, Armelle Charrié-Duhaut, Jacques Connan, Pierre Albrecht and Michael Flecker (2010), 'The 9th-Century-AD Belitung Wreck, Indonesia:

Analysis of a Resin Lump', *International Journal of Nautical Archaeology* 39(2): 383–6.

Casson, Lional (1989), *The Periplus Maris Erythraei. Text with Introduction, Translation and Commentary*, Princeton: Princeton University Press.

Chaudhuri, K. N. (1985), *Trade and Civilization in the Indian Ocean: An Economic History from the Rise of Islam to 1750*, Cambridge: Cambridge University Press.

Chaudhuri, K. N. (1990), *Asia Before Europe*, Cambridge: Cambridge University Press.

Chittick, H. N. (1975), 'The Peopling of the East African Coast', in H. N. Chittick and R. I. Rotberg (eds), *East Africa and the Orient*, New York: Africana, pp. 16–43.

Chittick, H. N. (1977), 'The East Coast, Madagascar and the Indian Ocean', in R. Oliver (ed.), *Cambridge History of Africa Vol. 3*, Cambridge: Cambridge University Press, pp. 183–231.

Cox, M. P., Nelson, M. G., Tumonggor, M. K., Ricaut, F.X. and Sudoyo, H. (2012), 'A Small Cohort of Island Southeast Asian Women Founded Madagascar'. *Proc Biol Sci* 279 (1739): 2,761–8.

Crowther, Alison, Margaret-Ashley Veall, Nicole Boivin Mark Horton, Anna Kotarba-Morley Dorian Q. Fuller Thomas Fenn, Othman Haji and Carney D. Matheson (2015), 'Use of Zanzibar Copal (Hymenaea verrucosa Gaertn.), as Incense at Unguja Ukuu, Tanzania in the 7–8th century CE: Chemical Insights into Trade and Indian Ocean Interactions', *Journal of Archaeological Science* 53: 374–90.

Crowther, Alison, Leilani Lucas, Richard Helm, Mark Horton, Ceri Shipton, Henry T. Wright, Sarah Walshaw, Matthew Pawlowicz, Chantal Radimilahy, Katerina Douka, Llorenç Picornell-Gelabert, Dorian Q Fuller and Nicole L. Boivin (2016), 'Ancient Crops Provide First Archaeological Signature of The Westward Austronesian Expansion', *PNAS* 113(24): 6,635–40.

Cunliffe, Barry (2001), *Facing the Ocean: The Atlantic and Its Peoples*, Oxford: Oxford University Press.

Dissanayake, Samanthi (2014), 'The Wreck Detectives. This is the Story of the Coast that Sank 1000 Ships'. *BBC News*, <http://www.bbc.co.uk/news/special/2014/newsspec_8704/index.html>

Flecker, Michael (2000), 'A 9th-century Arab or Indian Shipwreck in Indonesian Waters', *International Journal of Nautical Archaeology* 29(2): 199–217, doi: 10.1006/ijna.2000.03 16

Flecker, Michael (2001), 'A Ninth-Century AD Arab or Indian Shipwreck in Indonesia: First Evidence for Direct Trade with China', *World Archaeology* 32(3): 335–54, doi: 10.1080/00438240120048662.

Flecker, Michael (2002). *The Archaeological Excavation of the 10th Century Itan Shipwreck*, Oxford: British Archaeological Reports.

Flecker, Michael (2008), 'A 9th-century Arab or Indian Shipwreck in Indonesian Waters: Addendum', *International Journal of Nautical Archaeology* 37(2): 384–6.

Fleisher, J. and LaViolette, A. (2013), 'The Early Swahili Trade Village of Tumbe, Pemba Island, Tanzania, AD 600–950', *Antiquity* 87: 1,151–68.

Freeman-Grenville, G. S. P. (1962) *The East African Coast. Select Documents from the First to the Earlier Nineteenth Century*, London: Clarendon Press.

Goitein, S. D. and M. A. Friedman (2011), *India Traders of the Middle Ages. Documents from the Cairo Geniza ('India Book')*, Leiden: Brill.

Guillain, M. (1856), *Documents sur l'Histoire, la Géographie, et la Commerce de l'Afrique Orientale*, Paris: Bertrand, 3 vols.

Guillot, Claude (n.d.), 'Épave de Cirebon; description des Pieces', <http://cirebon.musee-mariemont.be/home-6.htm?lng=en>

Guy, John (2004), 'The Intan Shipwreck: A 10th Century Cargo in South-east Asian Waters', in S. Pearson (ed.), *Song Ceramics. Art History, Archaeology and Technology*, London: Percival David Foundation of Chinese Art Colloquies on Art & Archaeology in Asia no. 22: 171–92.

Guy, John (2017), 'The Phanom Surin Shipwreck, a Pahlavi Inscription, and their Significance for the History of Early Lower Central Thailand', *Journal of the Siam Society* 105: 179–96.

Harkantiningsih, N., Wibisono, S. C. and Miksic, J. N. (2010), *Sunken Treasures from the Tenth Century; Catalogue of the Cirebon Wreck*, Jakarta: PANNAS BMKT.

Horden, Peregrine and Nicholas Purcell (2000), *The Corrupting Sea: A Study of Mediterranean History*, Oxford: Oxford University Press.

Horton, Mark (1987), 'The Swahili corridor', *Scientific American* 257(3): 86–93.

Horton, Mark (2017a) 'East Africa and Oman c.600–1856', in Abdulrahman al-Salimi and Eric Staples (eds), *The Ports of Oman*, Hildesheim: Olms, pp. 255–79.

Horton, Mark (2017b) 'Early Islam on the East African Coast', in Finbarr Barry Flood and Gülru Necipoglu (eds), *A Companion to Islamic Art and Architecture*, Hoboken: Wiley-Blackwell, pp. 250–74.

Horton, Mark (2018), 'The Swedish Corridor Revisisted', *African Archaeological Review* 2018: 1–6, doi: 10.1007/s10437-018-9294-2.

Horton, Mark (forthcoming), *Zanzibar and Pemba, the Archaeology of an Indian Ocean Archipelago*, British Institute in Eastern Africa/Routledge.

Horton, Mark, Nicole Boivin, Alison Crowther, Ben Gaskell, Chantel Radimilahy and Henry Wright (2017), 'East Africa as a Source for Fatimid Rock Crystal: Workshops from Kenya to Madagascar'. in A. Hilgner, S. Greiff and D. Quest (eds), *Gemstones in the First Millennium AD: Mines, Trade, Workshops and Symbolism*. vol. Tagungen 30, RGZM Tagungen 30, Römisch-Germanisches Zentralmuseum, Mainz, pp. 103–18.

Horton, M. Brown, H. W. and Oddy, W. A. (1986), 'The Mtambwe hoard', *Azania* 21: 115–23.

Horton, Mark and John Middleton (2000), *The Swahili: The Social Landscape of a Maritime Society*, Oxford: Blackwell.

Horton, Mark, Seth Priestman Seth, Nicole Boivin Nicole and Alison Crowther (forthcoming), *The Ceramics from Unguja Ukuu and Fuckuchani: A Quantitative Analysis of Early Swahili Assemblages on the East African Coast*, Oxford: Archeopress.

Hourani, A. (1994), *Arab Seafaring* (new edn by J. Carswell), Princeton: Princeton University Press.

Kervran, M. (2004), 'Archaeological Research at Suhār 1980–1986', *Journal of Oman Studies* 13: 263–381.

Krahl, R., John Guy, J. K. Wilson and Julian Raby (2010), *Shipwrecked. Tang Treasures and Monsoon Winds*, Washington: Sackler Gallery, and Singapore: National Heritage Board.

Kusuma, Pradiptajati, Murray P. Cox, Denis Pierron, Harilanto Razafindrazaka, Nicolas Brucato, Laure Tonasso, Helena Loa Suryadi, Thierry Letellier, Herawati Sudoyo and François-Xavier Ricaut (2015) 'Mitochondrial DNA and the Y Chromosome Suggest the Settlement of Madagascar by Indonesian Sea Nomad Populations', *BMC Genomics* 16: 191.

Liebner, H. H. (2014), 'The Siren of Cirebon. A Tenth-Century Trading Vessel Lost in the Java Sea', unpublished Ph.D., University of Leeds.

Lübeck, Irmin and Wiebeck Erno (1994), *Welt der Entdeckerschiffe in berühmten Nachbauten*, Berlin: DSV-Verlag.

Mackintosh-Smith, Tim and Montgomery, James E. (eds and trans.) (2014), *Two Arabic Travel Books: Accounts of China and India*, Abu Zayd al-Sirafi *and Mission to the Volga*, Ahmad ibn Fadlan, New York and London: New York University Press.

McLaughlin, Raoul (2014), The Roman Empire and the Indian Ocean, Barnsley: Pen and Sword.

McGrath, W. H. (1988), 'Some Notes on the Navigation of 1985 Trans-Indian Ocean Canoe Voyage', *Journal of Navigation* 41(2): 174–85.

Middleton, John (2004), 'African Merchants of the Indian Ocean', Long Grove: Waveland Press.

Pellat, C. (1962), *Mujuj al-Dhahab wa-Ma'adin al-Jauhar of al-Mas'udi* (text and translation by C. Barbier de Meynard and P. de Courteille, *Les Prairies d'or*, rev. edn) Paris.

Peters, Edward (2003), 'Quid nobis cum pelago? The New Thalassology and the Economic History of Europe', *Journal of Interdisciplinary History* 34: 49–61.

Preecharpeechacupt, Nareerat (2014), 'The Phanomsurin Shipwreck', *Silpakorn Journal* 57(2): 22–35 [in Thai].

Prestholdt, J. (2008), *Domesticating the World. African Consumerism and the Genealogies of Globalization*, Los Angeles: University of California Press.

Priestman, Seth (2013), 'A Quantitative Archaeological Analysis Of Ceramic Exchange in the Persian Gulf and Western Indian Ocean, AD c.400–1275', doctoral thesis, University of Southampton, Faculty of Humanities.

Priestman, Seth (2017), 'Quantitative Evidence for Early Long Distance Exchange in Eastern Africa: The Consumption Volume of Imported Ceramics', in Stephanie Wynne-Jones and Adria LaViolette (eds), *The Swahili World*. Abingdon and New York: Routledge, pp. 472–84.

Rapoport Yossef and Emilie Savage-Smith (eds and trans.) (2014), *An Eleventh-century Egyptian Guide to the Universe: the Book of Curiosities*, Leiden: Brill.

Rodney, Walter (1972), *How Europe Underdeveloped Africa*, London: Bogle-L'Ouverture Publications.

Rougeulle, Axelle (2015), *Sharma. Un entrepôt de commerce médiéval sur la côte du Hadramawt (Yémen, ca. 980 1180)*, Oxford: Archaeopress and British Foundation for the Study of Arabia monograph 17.

Severin, Tim (1983), *The Sindbad Voyage*, London: Putnam.

Shen, Hsueh-man (2017), 'Chinese Ceramics Circulating in the Middle East', in Finbarr Barry Flood and Gülru Necipoglu (eds), *A Companion to Islamic Art and Architecture*, Hoboken: Willey Blackwell, pp. 197–218.

Sheriff, Abdul (2010), *Dhow Cultures of the Indian Ocean*, London: Hurst.

Shepherd, G. M. (1982), 'The Making of the Swahili: A View from the Southern End of the East African Coast', *Paideuma* 28: 129–48.

Sinclair, P. J. J. (1982), 'Chibuene – an Early Trading Site in Southern Mozambique'. *Paideuma* 28: 149–64.

Staniforth, Mark (2012) 'First Wrecked, Now Pillaged: Vietnam's Underwater Treasure', *The Conservation*, 8 November.

Stilliman, S. (2010), 'Indigenous Traces in Colonial Spaces: Archaeologies of Ambiguity, Origins, and Practices', *Journal of Social Archaeology* 10(1): 28–58.

Tibbetts, G. R. (1971), *Arab Navigation in the Indian Ocean Before the Coming of the Portuguese*, London: Royal Asiatic Society.

Vérin, Pierre (1986), *The History and Civilisation in Northern Madagascar*, Rotterdam: Balkema.

Villiers, Alan (1940), *Sons of Sinbad*, London Hodder & Stoughton.

Vink, Markus (2007), 'Indian Ocean Studies and the "new thalassology"', *Journal of Global History* 2(1): 41–62.

Vosmer, Tom, Luca Belfioretti, Eric Staples and Alessandro Ghidoni (2011), 'The *Jewel of Muscat* Project: Reconstructing an Early Ninth-century CE Shipwreck', *Proceedings of the Seminar for Arabian Studies* 41: 411–24.

Wallerstein, Immanual (1974–80), *The Modern World System*, New York (3 vols).

Warmington E. H. (1974), *The Commerce between the Roman Empire and India* (1928 new edn), London: Curzon Press.

Whitcomb, D. (1975), 'The Archaeology of Oman: A Preliminary Discussion of the Islamic Periods', *Journal of Oman Studies* 1: 123–57.

Whitehouse, D. (2001), 'East Africa and the Maritime Trade of the Indian Ocean AD 800–1500', in B. S. Amoretti (ed.), *Islam in East Africa: New Sources (Archives, Manuscripts and Written Historical Sources, Oral History, Archaeology)*, Rome: Herder, pp. 411–24.

Wink, Andre (2002), 'From the Mediterranean to the Indian Ocean: Medieval History in Geographic Perspective', *Comparative Studies in Society and History* 44(3): 416–45.

Wood Marilee, Serena Panighello, Emilio F. Orsega, Peter Robertshaw, Johannes T. van Elteren, Alison Crowther, Mark Horton and Nicole Boivin (2017), 'Zanzibar and Indian Ocean Trade in the First Millennium CE: the Glass Bead Evidence', *Archaeological and Anthropological Sciences* 9(5): 879–901, doi 10.1007/s12520-015-0310-z.

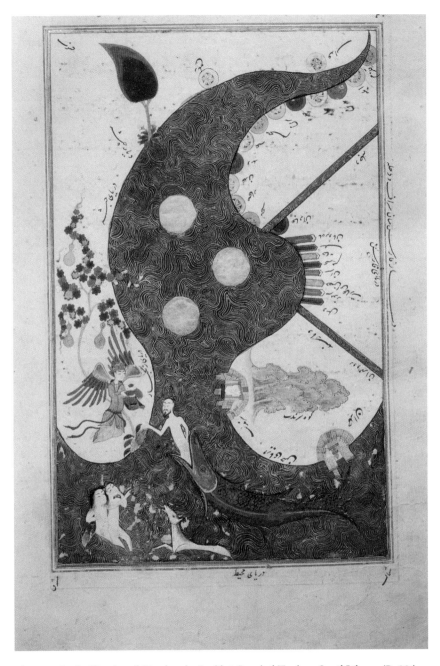

Plate 1 *Book of Roads and Kingdoms* by Istakhri, Istanbul Topkapı Serail Library (B. 334 Fol. 17 a.). Roland and Sabrina Michaud/akg-images.

Plate 2 Abraham Cresques, Catalan Atlas, fourteenth-century pearl fishers in Gulf. France National Library.

Plate 3 Two small date-shaped flasks (~6.2 cm in height) dated to the first century CE, made from mould-blown light amber and amber-brown glass: (left) from Mound 11 Tomb 20 of the Saar necropolis and (right) from Mound 1 Tomb 26 of the Shakhoura necropolis in Bahrain. Source: Bahrain National Museum, Manama, Bahrain.

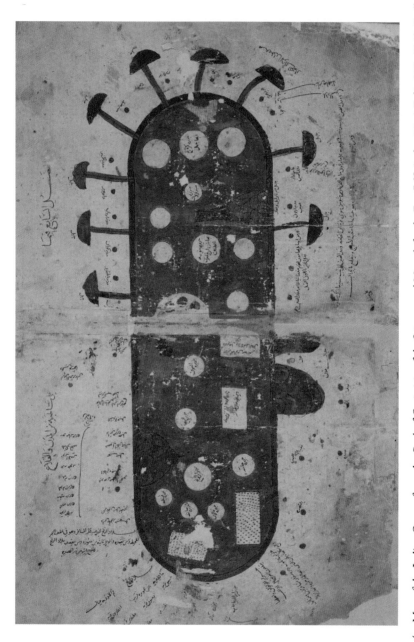

Plate 4 Map of the Indian Ocean, from the *Book of Curiosities of the Sciences and Marvels for the Eyes* (MS Arab c.90, A Folio 29B–30A). Bodleian Library, Oxford. Reproduced with permission.

Plate 5 Part of the Phanom Surin shipwreck, showing a section of main mast and the keelson.

Plate 6 Glass of Iranian origin, which travelled eastwards via the Gulf, found in the Cirebon ship. Qatar National Museums.

Plate 7 Turquoise-glazed ware (Sasanian-Islamic) of Gulf origin, found in the Cirebon ship. Qatar National Museums.

Plate 8 Rock crystal pieces, most likely from Madagascar, found in the Cirebon ship. Qatar National Museums.

Plate 9 Plan of the Oases of al-Ain and Buraimi showing sites mentioned in text.

Plate 10 A well-preserved house from the Early Islamic settlement at Hamasa.

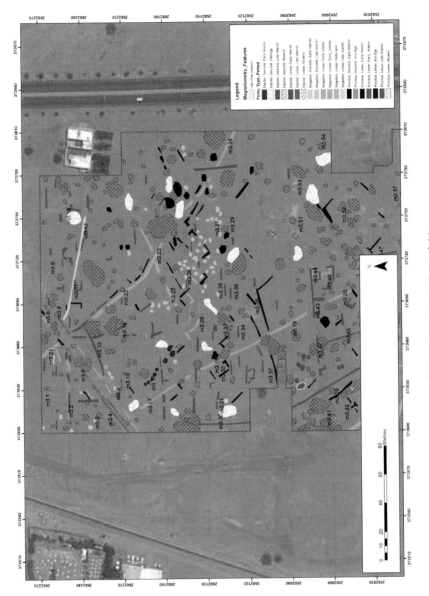

Plate 11 Geophysical survey showing overlaid Early and Late Islamic field systems.

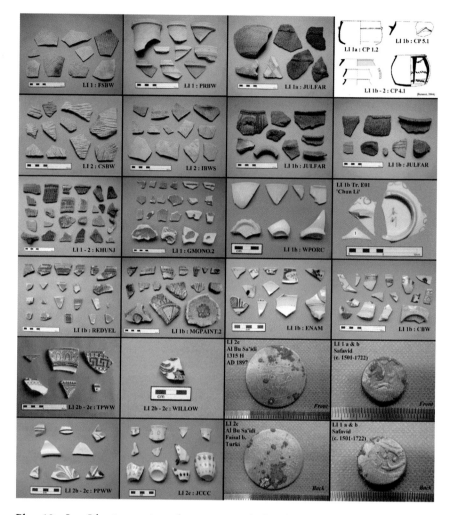

Plate 12 Late Islamic ceramics and coins commonly found in al-Ain.

Plate 13   Late Islamic date press from the Bayt Bin Ati in Qattara Oasis.

Plate 14 European 'China' from Muharraq excavations, late nineteenth–early twentieth century CE, with one likely Japanese imitation (left side no. 18). Left side: transfer-printed wares. Right side: painted and sponge-printed wares. Source: Robert Carter.

Plate 15 Porcelains excavated in Muharraq. Mainly late nineteenth–early twentieth century CE, but mid-twentieth-century examples likely include left side nos 16–23, and right side nos 23–4. Source: Robert Carter.

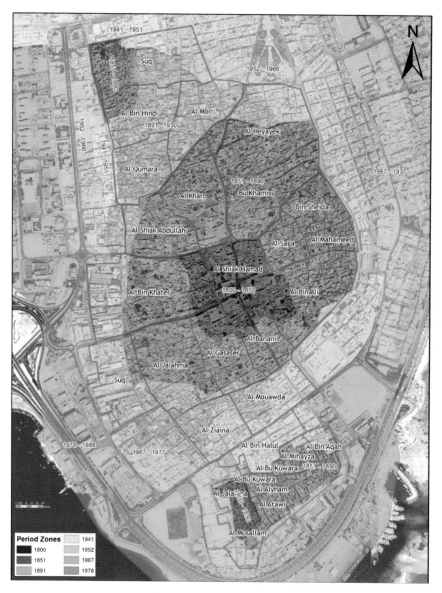

Plate 16 Nineteenth–twentieth-century expansion of Muharraq. Source: Al-Sulaiti 2009, with kind permission of Dr Abdullah Al-Sulaiti.

Plate 17 Two small 'Sidonian'-style mould-blown glass amphoriski (~ 6.5–7.2 cm in height) with scrollwork designs, dated to the late first century CE, from graves in the UAE and Bahrain: (left) bottle from collective tomb at Dibba in Sharjah, UAE (source: Sharjah Archaeology Authority), and (right) bottle from Mound 1 Tomb 17 of the Shakhoura necropolis in Bahrain (source: Bahrain National Museum).

Plate 18 A modern-day cuboid incense burner being manufactured by a potter from Mirbat. Photograph by W. Zimmerle.

Plate 19 Courtyard of one of the restored historic houses, location of Msheireb Museums, Doha. © EQRoy/Shutterstock.

PART IV

DIVERSITY AND CHANGE: BETWEEN SKY, LAND AND SEA

10

ASTROLOGY AS A NODE OF CONNECTIVITY BETWEEN THE PRE-MODERN MEDITERRANEAN AND GULF

Michael A. Ryan

Perhaps it is old-hat to begin a chapter focusing on the pre-modern Mediterranean with a quotation from Fernand Braudel. Nevertheless, one must always pay credit where credit is due, and one could do far worse than citing a scholar as indispensable as he. Regarding the climatic boundaries of the Mediterranean Basin, in his magisterial two-volume work *The Mediterranean and the Mediterranean World in the Age of Philip II*, Braudel remarked: 'The Mediterranean climate lies between the northern limit of the olive tree and the northern limit of the palm grove.'[1] Obviously, as Paolo Squatriti notes in his work on the vegetative Mediterranean, published in the indispensable *vade mecum* on trends and methodologies in Mediterranean studies edited by Peregrine Horden and Sharon Kinoshita, the Braudelian limits of olive and palm are simultaneously evocative and enduring. Granted 'historical respectability' on account of Braudel's scholarly legacy, they yet remain fundamentally incorrect.[2] Still, the attempt to impose boundaries on the Mediterranean – or on any maritime or terrestrial expanse allowing for significant exchange of multiple perspectives, ethnicities and ideas – is an eternal endeavour, albeit frustrating in the arena's inherent resistance to the deed. One must always be wary, especially when dealing with maritime histories, of falling into the trap of what Kären Wigen has termed 'basin thinking', of granting particular exceptional qualities to the Mediterranean, or the Gulf that centres geographically this present collection of essays, that elides the subtle intricacies of these regions' histories. Nevertheless, in the cases of both the Mediterranean and the Gulf, their specific geographic qualities, their peninsulas, their coves, and their islands, marked them as venues that provided the sailors, missionaries, colonists, pirates and merchants traversing their deep blue waters with relatively easy exposure to a multiplicity of languages, faiths, cultures and identities, thus permitting them to engage in centuries' worth of political, economic and cultural encounter and exchange.[3]

A singularly important study that has made a most profound impact on the study of the pre-modern Mediterranean is Peregrine Horden and Nicolas Purcell's 2000 publication *The Corrupting Sea*. For Horden and Purcell, the Mediterranean Basin must not be read via purportedly eternal qualities of unity or disrupture, as evidenced in earlier Mediterranean scholarship, therefore romanticising the Mediterranean Basin and technically engaging in the exact type of 'basin thinking' which Wigen warned against. It, along with Michael McCormick's 2002 publication *Origins of the European Economy*, has re-evaluated fundamentally how scholars study the history of the pre-modern Mediterranean. Especially for Horden and Purcell, 'connectivities' rooted in climatic and geographic particulars linking disparate parts of the Mediterranean Basin provide the unique characteristic crucial to understanding the history of the pre-modern Mediterranean Basin.[4]

But what of the sky that spans both the Mediterranean and the Gulf, an eternal expanse that defies all boundaries? Of course skies are mapped with the emergence of recognisable patterns via the position of the stars and the celestial courses they run, allowing imaginations to forge constellations. Unlike the Mediterranean or Gulf, however, which have coastlines that separate the waters from the lands, the pre-modern skies have no visible limits as the heavens cover all below. If one were to gaze at the midnight skies over what would become Abu Dhabi and, say, a Western Mediterranean city like Barcelona on 16 July 1348, during the period of the pandemic subsequently known to history as the Black Death and for which astrology functioned as a crucial tool for magical and medical prognostication alike, one would observe roughly the same celestial phenomena. Many of the stars that wheel in the night-time skies above the Gulf and the Mediterranean certainly appeared in both locations, as Abu Dhabi and Barcelona are located at 24 degrees north, 54 degrees east and 41 degrees north, 2 degrees east respectively. Stars, naturally, fill the expanse. Over Barcelona, the constellations of Pegasus, Cygnus and Aquila soar while Ophiuchus bears the Serpent. These signs appear in the skies of Abu Dhabi as well, and here Perseus joins the celestial gathering. Crucially, in the case of Abu Dhabi, the planets Jupiter and Mars, as well as the constellations of Aries and Pisces, the first and last astrological signs making up the zodiac, would have been visible above the celestial equa-tor, with Saturn below. The presence of Jupiter, Saturn and Mars was of no small importance; when, astrologically speaking, they were in great conjunc-tion, paradigm shifts would be imminent. These great conjunctions always portended great upheaval in astrological prediction, particularly for the later Middle Ages. As the spectre of pestilence initially loomed across Europe, it was reported that members of the Medical Faculty of the University of Paris had astrologically predicted its arrival. The Parisian physicians observed a great conjunction of Saturn, Jupiter and Mars that occurred within the house of Aquarius on 20 March 1345 at 1:00 p.m., a cosmological event that portended imminent and widespread pestilence, destruction and death.[5]

My present remarks regarding the depiction of these night skies must be received with the full knowledge that these skies were not observed via a precisely scientific test, nor do they factor in all the variabilities of local condi-tions that existed and that would have affected the observation of these skies, including weather conditions, the presence of particulates in the atmosphere, etc. at that specific historic moment. Still, the similarities between the skies over those locations at that specific time are far more striking than the differ-ences. The heavens and their stars bridge these two disparate parts of the Dar al-Islam ('Abode of Islam' – the Islamic world).[6]

In this chapter, I offer preliminary thoughts and suggestions regarding the role of astrology as a node of connectivity between these locations in the pre-modern Dar al-Islam. In David Abulafia's review of my book *A Kingdom of Stargazers: Astrology and Authority in the Late Medieval Crown of Aragon*, which was published in the *English Historical Review* in 2013 and which in a kinder moment he described as 'curious', he takes particular umbrage with my description of pre-modern astrology as a 'liminal' discipline.[7] Astrology, like other disciplines of privileged knowledge read as 'occult' in the pre-modern world, such as astrology, alchemy and, especially from the fifteenth century onwards in the Latin Christian tradition, Hermetic magic appealed to many segments of the pre-modern populace, due to their purported access to a large body of privileged knowledge. Medieval interest in the occult centred on the promise of accessing this body of hidden and privileged knowledge and a battery of arcane disciplines, including astrology, which constituted the occult and magical arts, and which tantalised and fascinated many from all levels of society, Jewish, Christian and Muslim alike.[8] Jewish, Christian and Muslim authorities – particularly theological ones – would attempt to construct precise definitions and explanations as to the nature of magic, future insight, prophetic revelation and their roles within a religious framework. For the vast majority of people, for whom the acquisition of systematic, rigorous and licensed intellectual training was provided through formal study, such rigid reading of these disciplines did not apply.

Michael D. Bailey, in his most recent and excellent study, *Fearful Spirits, Reasoned Follies: The Boundaries of Superstition in Late Medieval Europe*, relies exclusively on a range of scholastic treatises written by and for the fifteenth-century Christian intellectual elite regarding the discernment and application of supernatural power. Yet magic in the Middle Ages stood at a 'crossroads of culture', in the words of Richard Kieckhefer, and as Bailey has shown, fifteenth-century Latin Christian ecclesiastical authorities such as Johannes Nider and Jean Gerson were unable to come up with a hard-and-fast exact definition of magical superstition – which included astrological matters – to be applied equally and universally.[9] Magic was – is – as elusive as quicksilver. It, and by extension astrology in the service of magic, is inherently liminal, resistant to all impositions of boundaries.

The scholarship of Sarah Davis-Secord stands as a model by which one can – and should – conduct studies regarding cultural connectivities, of which astrology is a vital part, within and between disparate parts of the pre-modern Mediterranean, as well as the Gulf. Drawing upon the model espoused by Horden and Purcell, in her book *Where Three Worlds Met: Sicily in the Early Medieval Mediterranean*, published by Cornell University Press, Sarah Davis-Secord has written a groundbreaking study on the history of the island. Sicily's physical location within the Mediterranean Sea inherently privileged the island as a site of encounter and exchange among various peoples for centuries, thus making it the perfect case study for her analysis. Beginning by raising a series of significant questions about the location of Sicily – whether it was at the edge of Europe, the Byzantine World or the Dar al-Islam or at the heart of a system that connected these three societies, whether it was an island that divided the Christian from the Islamic worlds or united them – Davis-Secord shows how crucial medieval Sicily is for studying the connections within and among the pre-modern Mediterranean.[10] By studying this island's history over a period of six centuries, Davis-Secord shows how Sicily becomes a hub – cultural, economic and social – of the medieval Mediterranean. As a society that had significant connections to the shores of Latin Christendom, Byzantium and the Dar al-Islam, Sicily was literally well positioned to achieve such a shift. Astrological, alchemical and magical works were produced in the centres for translation and housed in libraries on the island and constitute a crucial component of this cultural connectivity within the Mediterranean.

But what of the connectivity between the *khalij* and *thalassa*? Do astrology and astrological thought themselves serve as effective connectors between these two disparate regions, especially in pre-modernity? After all, both the Gulf and the Sea comprised significant parts of the pre-modern Dar al-Islam where for centuries astral and scientific treatises were composed and copied, analysed and instructed, especially at the highest of levels. George Saliba's work on astrology demonstrates undeniably the liminality of the discipline in the pre-modern Islamic world.[11] As in Latin Christendom, astrology in the Islamic world was a discipline that overlapped with magic, science and religion, and bridged heresy and orthodoxy, licit and illicit knowledge. Yet it was in the Dar al-Islam that astrological sciences were refined to the point of being art, a development that would profoundly affect the study of the discipline in the medieval Christian world.

One particular set of writings shows a learned, yet accessible, understanding of astrology in medieval Islam. The writings of the Ikhwān aṣ-Ṣafāʾ, also known as the Brethren of Purity, a collective of Muslim mystics centred in tenth-century Basra, reference astrology and astral sciences among many other subjects in their massive encyclopedic work. Composed around 970 CE, over the course of fifty-two volumes they address an enormous range of subjects, all designed to expound upon and glorify the mysteries of Islam via a Neoplatonic lens in an exhaustive manner. In the twenty-second *Rasa'il*, or epistle, which largely deals with ethics, the reader is introduced to Bīwarāsp the Wise, the king of the branch of jinn who embraced Islam, and who adjudicates a case brought before him by the animals on the Green Sea island over which he ruled, Sā'ūn. The animals plead for Bīwarāsp's assistance due to the rapacious nature of a group of humans shipwrecked there. Appreciating the many positive qualities of such a *locus amoenus*, whose utopian nature was displayed via the abundance of natural resources and harmonious living among the members of the resident animal population, the humans settled down and soon began running roughshod over the island and its animals, hunting and enslaving them. Before the king of the jinn the humans argue that it is their right as humans to enslave animals and representatives from the human world address the jinn to showcase the many noble features, learned arts and sciences, and fine products of human ingenuity and industry. A 'man with a lean, brown body, a long beard, and a great mane of hair', hailing from Ceylon, but who represents India more broadly, mentions that God, whom he praises, 'raised up a swirling sea of light, compounded the spheres from it and set them spinning. He formed the stars in their courses, allotted the zodiac signs and let each one rise in its turn.'[12] Furthermore, the Indians achieved significant renown in the astral sciences, especially when those disciplines intersected with magic: 'He favoured us with the subtlest of sciences – astrology, sorcery, incantations, augury, conjuring, and divination.'[13] Another human, a Byzantine bearing an astrolabe, waxes eloquently about the Greeks' contribution to the rational sciences: 'He [God] made us natural rulers, for . . . our overwhelming intelligence, keen discernment, and deep understanding, our many sciences and wonderful arts – medicine, geometry, astronomy'. Like his fellow man from Ceylon, he notes that such sciences can be used magically: 'He gave us . . . the instruments of astronomy, and talismans.'[14]

Five representatives from the animal kingdom, the jackal, the nightingale, the bee, the parrot and the frog, also plead their case before the King of the Jinn against the injustices meted out to them by the humans.[15] Through the voice of the parrot, representative of the birds of prey, the Ikhwān clearly depict the perception of the stars as potential tools for divination. Bīwarāsp posed a question to the parrot that was grappled with by many a medieval

Christian and Jewish and Muslim theological authority: 'Tell me, what good is foreknowledge? . . . What use is there in all that is foretold by the masters of the many divining arts – the soothsaying, astrology, omens, sortilege, geomancy, palm reading, and like ways of seeking signs of impending disaster and the changes brought by the days, years, and seasons – if one cannot prevent or forestall them?'[16] At stake is the matter of free will. Should the stars preordain the course of one's future, the role of human will is nullified. Furthermore, humans' attempts to perceive future events by interpreting the position of the stars in the heavens could run dangerously close to an attempt to perceive the unknowable plan of the Divine. The parrot addresses this concern deliberately when, in response to the King's query, it says: 'Indeed . . . it is possible to avoid and guard against such misfortunes, but not in the ways sought by astrologers and other such folk . . . [but] By taking refuge in the Lord of the stars, who created and controls them.'[17] Indeed, the stars can only provide such information on account of their being created by Divine Will:

> For the signs of astrology and divination only foretell the acts of the Lord of the stars, who created and rules them and who gave them their form and their courses. To seek help from the Lord of the stars, the Power beyond the spheres and above the stars is better, more fitting and proper, than invoking the will of some star to ward off the fixed outcomes of astral events – intersections, revolutions, the dawn of the new years and months, and conjunctions and oppositions marking nativities.[18]

During times of crisis, one should turn to the stars by reflecting on the goodness of their creator in order to stave off disaster. 'That is how one should use the determinations of the stars and the foreknowledge their signs afford us of our fortunes and the shifts of destiny – not as they're used today by astrologers and those taken in by their words, who pick out a particular ascendant and seek its protection from the larger effects of astral influences . . . Better to turn to the Lord of the spheres for protection from them.'[19]

To get a sense of the scope and scale of the study of the astral sciences in the Islamic world, one can consult the reading of Arabic astrological authorities, especially the ninth-century Muslim authority *par excellence*, Abū Maʿshar al-Balkhī (d. 886 CE), known in the Latin West as Albumasar, among members of the intellectual elite existing throughout the entire geographic scope of the Dar al-Islam. That is, at first blush, the most evident method of determining astrological connectivities within and throughout the pre-modern Islamic world.

The certainly more intriguing, and more difficult, way of ascertaining astrological connectivities between disparate parts of the medieval and early modern Islamic world would be to identify and analyse claims to privileged and supernatural knowledge made by less authoritative astrologers with varying degrees of ability and training in the discipline. Crucial to this endeavour would be investigating how their claims were then subsequently received by segments of the larger population. As astrology was a discipline that found significant interest and receptivity among all members of pre-modern society, those who claimed access to that privileged knowledge could find their claims to be quite lucrative. Here the world of the astrologer intersects with that of the magical charlatan. By the end of the fifteenth century, in Latin Christendom, secular and ecclesiastical authorities, in addition to literary and artistic works, used the term 'charlatan' to refer loosely to quack physicians, popular magicians, alchemists, dream interpreters and sellers of fake relics and, of course, astrologers. This perception also occurred in the pre-modern Dar al-Islam. The Brethren of Purity's character of the parrot challenged humans' claims as to their elevated skill in medicine:

> For no one is seen at the physician or pharmacist's but one who is sick, ill, in poor health, just as no one is seen in the astrologer's doorway but one who is wretched, miserable, or afraid. And the astrologer only compounds his misfortune. He takes his coin but can't advance good fortune or put off trouble. He just offers flowery phrases, guesswork, and unfounded conjectures. Your so-called physicians do just the same.[20]

The thread binding these professions of the astrologer and the physician with the charlatan was their practitioners' claim to access privileged, specialised knowledge used to defraud others, offering false hopes and remedies, especially during periods of crisis.

I suggest two ways in which one might identify the popular reception of astrology and astral matters within a larger system of Mediterranean and/ or Gulf connectivities. The first centres around the figure of Abū Ma'shar al-Balkhi himself. As lofty an authority as Abū Ma'shar was for medieval and early modern astrology, he also figures as a character in works evidencing more popular perceptions and receptions of him and his sidereal legacy. In the tenth-century *Fihrist* of Ibn al-Nadim, Abū Maʿshar gets involved in a contest with his contemporary al-Kindi, the influential author on optics and the magical properties of rays. In the account, Abū Maʿshar incites a crowd against al-Kindi, in reaction against the Hellenistic sciences that were part of the astrology espoused and practised by al-Kindi, but the latter was able to stay the crowd's furor, and turn Abū Maʿshar's anger against the discipline to favour by seducing him with the complex mathematics underpinning its study.[21]

But Abū Maʿshar, as a character in various Islamic writings dealing with astrological themes, is not always so easily swayed by mathematics. ʿAli al-Tanuki's *Nišwar*, also from the ninth century, references a story involving Abū Maʿshar's exposing a charlatan-astrologer. The pre-modern charlatan-astrologer, whether Christian or Muslim, had significant loci at his or her disposal where he could choose to rob those whom he or she deemed a 'mark'. William Eamon has demonstrated how the culture in and of the public square, described in various vernaculars as the *place*, *plaça*, *piazza*, *campo* or *zoc*, not unlike the waters of the Mediterranean or Gulf, were spaces that permitted the great and mean alike to encounter each other.[22] In the *Nišwar* account, the charlatan-astrologer practised his craft *en plein air* in Samarra, producing primarily horoscopes for women, the predominant demographic of his clientele. Abū Maʿshar asked the charlatan to draw up his horoscope to divine what his present action was, which he guessed correctly, namely that he was on his way to meet an imprisoned acquaintance who would be released upon his arrival. Returning to the charlatan-astrologer's place in Samarra, Abū Maʿshar proclaimed, 'If I did not know how this charlatan predicted correctly I would lose my mind, tear up my books, and believe in the falsehood of astrology.' The charlatan recognised the authoritative heft of Abū Maʿshar, kissed his hands, and replied, 'I lie and deceive women and I place in front of me this *taht* (dust board), this astrolabe, and this *taqwīm* (ephemeris) in order to deceive people.'[23] The tools of the legitimate astrologer spread out before the charlatan legitimise his false actions and assist him towards duplicitous ends; put differently, the presence of the tools of the astrologer's trade earns, for this particular charlatan, the confidence of his marks. He admits to Abū

Ma'shar that the only way he could guess correctly was through his use of *zaǧr*, *fa'l* and *'iyāfa*, technically not illegal in Islamic religious law, as they are three modes of divination originating from pre-Islamic Arabia and not 'tainted' with Hellenistic astrology.[24] The charlatan told Abū Ma'shar he learned these approaches from Bedouins and would instruct the premier astrological authority in these styles of divination.[25]

The second method that I suggest scholars may consider as a way of identifying privileged and occult knowledge as a point of connection between disparate parts of the pre-modern Dar al-Islam is via their analysis of recipe books, which tantalisingly and seamlessly compile and blend bodies of elite and popular knowledge between their covers. *Recetarii* of medical, alchemical and astrological miscellanea have been especially intriguing sources to work with regarding the role of charlatans in pre-modern culture and society. *Recetarii* in general, and one of specifically Venetian provenance with which I have worked extensively and which exhibits clear influences of occult Islamic knowledge, Yale University's Mellon MS 6, are more than mere lists of medieval recipes and alchemical procedures. They can – and should – be read within a larger medieval magical tradition; *recetarii* like Mellon MS 6 could also serve as guides for the would-be charlatan and are crucial sources for magical-themed trickery and alchemical charlatanry in late medieval culture.

One fifteenth-century paper codex Venetian alchemical *recetario*, written in both Latin and the Venetian vernacular, is full of recipes and alchemical and astrological techniques designed to elicit wonder and surprise. This unstudied *recetario*, which is a course source material for my next manuscript-length project, the working title of which is *And You Will See Wonders: Magic, Fraud, and Deceit in Late Medieval Venice*, functions as a guide, I argue, for the prospective Venetian charlatan to use magical wonderworking to swindle someone. There are eight sections to this specific manuscript. The first and most authoritative is the *Liber lapidum preciosorum,* attributed to the eleventh-century scholar, Marbodus Redonensis or Marbodus of Rennes (c. 1035–1123 CE), discussing the magical and supernatural properties attributed to various stones and gems. The next and longest section, spanning folia 7 to 11v., written in the same hand as the copy of Marbodus' treatise, is a compendium of seventy-three miscellaneous magical and alchemical procedures. Some of these procedures drew upon a longer, more established and authoritative magical tradition to effect change whereas others were clearly designed to create a startling effect to dupe a potential mark. All the *experimenta* comprise the heart of the wonderworking contained between the covers of Mellon MS 6.

Other documents include various other bodies of information and practices that could be used to dupe others. These include an anonymous Latin account of the astronomical positions of the zodiac, their qualities, and the corresponding days when their influences would be most effective; a treatise attributed to one Zael, or Thelque, concerning the powers of astral signs and magical sigils etched on stones; a medical recipe attributed to the astrologer Michael Scot (c. 1175–c. 1234 CE) to create a salve against the ravages of worms in and on the body – an affliction the cure of which was particularly favored and touted by late medieval Italian medical charlatans – and, finally, a variety of anonymous medical and alchemical procedures written in both Latin and Venetian.[26] The presence of the 'authoritative' *lapidarium* and the medical recipes attributed respectively to Marbodus and Michael Scot legitimise the rest of the documents contained within the codex, even though those documents include the processes of making paste gems and false potions.

The wonderworking contained within Mellon MS 6 evokes similar rites from the most famous medieval treatise of astral magic of the Dar al-Islam, the *Ghāyat Al-Hakīm*, known in the West as *Picatrix*. King Alfonso X of Castile-León, known by his sobriquet 'El Sabio', or 'The Wise', had his scholars translate the work from the original Arabic, ascribed to the pseudo-Abū al-Qāsim Maslama ibn Ahmad al-Majrītī, into the Castilian vernacular between 1256 and 1258 CE.[27] Alfonso's translation of the *Ghāyat Al-Hakīm* contributed to the study of the theory and practice of medieval Arabic astral magic. Subsequent intellectuals translated *Picatrix* into Latin, whence it achieved larger circulation within medieval Europe. A compendium of the secrets of sages, *Picatrix* is a powerful tool that contains great volumes of hidden, occult knowledge, but that knowledge should only be used 'for good and toward the service of God'.[28]

The hidden knowledge contained within the four volumes of *Picatrix* appears to have directly influenced at least some of the magic found within

Mellon MS 6, as the texts share similar processes and rituals. In the fifth chapter of the first book of *Picatrix*, for instance, there are a variety of processes and rituals involved in making magical images for many ends, including beneficial ones, including producing harmony between two people, establishing an enduring love, repelling scorpions, and being a good subject to one's lord or sovereign and having said lord recognise you as such; as well as harmful ends, such as destroying an enemy or laying waste to a city.[29] In Mellon MS 6, there are similar rites that are beneficial, such as 'restoring corrupt wine', 'extracting a thorn' and 'conserving wine so that it does not spoil', and a scratched-out recipe for making melons and cucumbers ripen at an appointed hour (the recipe is scratched out because it directly relies on necromancy to effect its desired ends, as the melons and the cucumbers to be ripened are to be interred in soil from a graveyard), but the *libellum* also includes processes that are far from helpful.[30] No particularly harmful rituals exist in Mellon MS 6 as are found in *Picatrix*. Nevertheless, there are rites and rituals designed to elicit wonder in a mark. These include making an ass speak aloud, having letters vanish from a page, producing candle flame from one's hand without receiving any harm, crafting a stone-sized object that emanates continuous light and, most stunning of all, making it appear as if someone is dead without inflicting any harm whatsoever to the 'dead' person.[31] Analysing comparable recipe books hailing from the pre-modern Islamic world combining folk and elite magical, medical and astrological traditions would give the prospective scholar of pre-modern Islamic charlatanry much rich material with which to work.

Astrology and the astral sciences function as nodes of connectivity between the pre-modern Mediterranean and the Gulf, as well as for academic studies on the subject in those regions. The populace of the pre-modern world was receptive to the astrologer and their astrological claims and wonderworking, particularly during times of great and universally experienced crisis, such as political upheaval, economic uncertainty or withering pandemic. The stars, for the perspicacious astrologer in the Islamic or Christian world, represented much. More than just beautiful and fascinating points peppering a fixed sphere under which the other crystalline spheres of the planets spun within the system espoused by the greatest astrological authority of antiquity, Ptolemy, the stars provided much for those on earth. The 'legitimate' astrologer who worked with the high-level mathematics necessary for formal study of the discipline received a significant intellectual cachet that provided him with, at best, stable employment resident at court or in a noble patron's service. Less honest practitioners of the discipline, of course, had a variety of loci at their disposal where they could – and did – rob and cheat those whom they deemed 'marks' in their respective societies. The stars fascinate and they enchant. As such, they represent perfect points by which one can trace connections across and within pre-modern maritime societies, bathing and binding both *khalij* and *thalassa* with their soft glow.

Notes

1. Fernand Braudel, *The Mediterranean and the Mediterranean World in the Age of Philip II.* 2 vols, trans. Siân Reynolds (Berkeley: University of California Press, 1995), Vol. 1, p. 232.

2. Paolo Squatriti, 'The Vegetative Mediterranean', *A Companion to Mediterranean History*, ed. Peregrine Horden and Sharon Kinoshita (Oxford: Wiley-Blackwell, 2014), pp. 26–41, here p. 26.

3. Kären Wigen, 'Oceans of History', *AHR*, vol. 111, no. 3 (June 2006), pp. 717–21, here p. 720.

4. Peregrine Horden and Nicholas Purcell, *The Corrupting Sea: A Study of Mediterranean History* (Wiley-Blackwell, 2000) and Michael McCormick, *Origins of the European Economy: Communications and Commerce AD 300–900* (Cambridge: Cambridge University Press, 2002).

5. S. Jim Tester, *A History of Western Astrology* (Woodbridge: Boydell Press, 1987), p. 185.

6. My description of these skies come from images produced via <https://www.fourmilab.ch/cgi-bin/Yoursky> (last accessed 10 June 2016).

7. David Abulafia, review of *A Kingdom of Stargazers* in *The English Historical Review*, 128 (531), pp. 414–15. Despite the unimpeachable impact of Abulafia's impressive body of scholarship upon the study of the pre-modern Mediterranean, his outright dismissal of my reading astrology as liminal evidences his complete misreading, as well as his fundamental misunderstanding, of my essential argument regarding what astrology represented – what it *was* – within and for late medieval culture wracked by a series of profound political, economic, theological and demographic crises.

8. For introductions to the study of medieval magic, see Lynn Thorndike, *The*

History of Magic and Experimental Science, 8 vols (New York: Macmillan, 1932–58); Richard Kieckhefer, *Magic in the Middle Ages* (Cambridge: Cambridge University Press, 1989); and Michael D. Bailey, 'The Meanings of Magic', *Magic, Ritual, and Witchcraft*, vol. 1 (Summer 2006), pp. 1–23. For early modernity, see Keith Thomas, *Religion and the Decline of Magic: Studies in Popular Beliefs in Sixteenth and Seventeenth Century England* (New York: Oxford University Press, 1971). Jean-Patrice Boudet, *Entre science et nigromance: Astrologie, divination et magie dans l'Occident médiéval (XIIe–XVe siècle)* (Paris: Publications de la Sorbonne, 2006) provides a monumentally important survey of astrology and its role in medieval thought.

9. Michael D. Bailey, *Fearful Spirits, Reasoned Follies: The Boundaries of Superstition in Late Medieval Europe* (Ithaca: Cornell University Press, 2013) and Richard Kieckhefer, *Magic in the Middle Ages* (Cambridge: Cambridge University Press, 1989).

10. Sarah Davis-Secord. *Where Three Worlds Met: Sicily in the Early Medieval Mediterranean* (Ithaca: Cornell University Press, 2017).

11. George Saliba, 'The Role of the Astrologer in Medieval Islamic Society', *Bulletin d'études orientales*, vol. 44 (1992), pp. 45–67; repr. in *Magic and Divination in Early Islam*, ed. Emilie Savage-Smith (Aldershot: Ashgate Variorum, 2004), pp. 341–70.

12. *The Case of the Animals versus Man before the King of the Jinn: A Translation from the Epistles of the Brethren of Purity*. trans. Lenn E. Goodman and Richard McGregor (Oxford: Oxford University Press, 2012), pp. 205–6. See also Richard McGregor's chapter in this present volume, 'Chapter 2: The Cosmopolitan Figure as Ethical Exemplar: Notes from a Tenth-Century Gulf Encyclopedia'.

13. *The Case of the Animals versus Man*, pp. 206–7.

14. *The Case of the Animals versus Man*, p. 216.

15. *The Case of the Animals versus Man*, p. 101. Like the parrot, each animal is the representative of its particular branch of the animal world. The jackal represents the predators, whereas the nightingale speaks for the birds. The bee is the representative of all swarming insects and the frog represents aquatic animals.

16. *The Case of the Animals versus Man*, p. 282.

17. *The Case of the Animals versus Man*, p. 282.

18. *The Case of the Animals versus Man*, p. 283.

19. *The Case of the Animals versus Man*, p. 285.

20. *The Case of the Animals versus Man*, p. 289.

21. P. Adamson, 'Abū Maʿšar, Al-Kindī and the Philosophical Defense of

Astrology', *Récherches de théologie et philosophie médiévales*, vol. 69, no. 2 (2002), pp. 245–70.

22. William Eamon, *Science and the Secrets of Nature: Books of Secrets in Medieval and Early Modern Culture* (Princeton: Princeton University Press, 1996).

23. Saliba, 'The Role of the Astrologer', p. 55.

24. Saliba, 'The Role of the Astrologer', p. 47, n. 21, cites Toufic Fahd, *La Divination Arabe. Etudes religieuses, sociologiques et folkloriques sur le milieu natif de l'Islam* (Leiden: Brill, 1966).

25. Saliba, 'The Role of the Astrologer', p. 56.

26. Piero Gambaccini, *I mercanti della salute: le segrte vertù dell'imbroglio in medicina* (Florence: Le lettere, 2000), trans. and pub. in English as *Mountebanks and Medicasters: A History of Italian Charlatans from the Middle Ages to the Present* (Jefferson, NC: McFarland, 2004). For more on Mellon MS 6, see Michael A. Ryan, 'A Note on Magical Deception', *Magic, Ritual, and Witchcraft* 6:3 (Summer 2012), pp. 52–7.

27. For more on the Castilian translation of this work, see David Pingree, 'Between the *Ghāyat* and *Picatrix* I: The Spanish Version', *Journal of the Warburg and Courtauld Institutes*, vol. 44 (1981), pp. 27–56. For studies on the culture of Alfonso X's court, see Evelyn S. Procter, 'The Scientific Works of the Court of Alfonso X of Castille: The King and His Collaborators', *The Modern Language Review*, vol. 40, no. 1 (January 1945), pp. 12–29; idem, *Alfonso X of Castile, Patron of Literature and Learning* (Oxford: Clarendon Press, 1951); and the collection of essays ed. Robert I. Burns, *Emperor of Culture: Alfonso X the Learned of Castile and His Thirteenth-Century Renaissance* (Philadelphia: University of Pennsylvania Press, 1990). For more on Alfonso X as an unwise king, see Robert I. Burns, '*Stupor Mundi*: Alfonso X of Castile, the Learned', *Emperor of Culture*, pp. 1–13. A more recent and sympathetic treatment of Alfonso X's intellectual and legal legacies has recently appeared by Simon Doubleday, *The Wise King: A Christian Prince, Muslim Spain, and the Birth of the Renaissance* (New York: Basic Books, 2015).

28. *Picatrix: The Latin Version of the* Ghāyat Al-Hakīm, ed. David Pingree (London: Warburg Institute, 1986), p. 2: *Ego autem rogo altissimum ceratorem quod iste noster liber nonnisi ad manus perveniat sapientis qui intendere posit quicquid in eo sum dicturus et tenere in bono, et quicquid operabitur ex eo ad bonum et ad Dei servicium operetur.*

29. *Picatrix: The Latin Version*, pp. 14–25.

30. Mellon MS 6: *Ad conservandum Vinum ne corumpatur . . . Ad spinam extraen-*

dam . . . Ad conservandum vinum ne corumpatur . . . Ad faciendum maturare in eadem hora melones et cucumeros et cucurbitas.

31. Mellon MS 6: *Ad faciendum asinum tonare alta voce . . . Ad removendum litteras . . . Ut manus tua ardeat ad modum candele sine lesionem . . . Carbunculum continuo lumen praestantem sic facias . . . Si vis aliquem quasi mortuum et non habebit malum.*

11

SHIPS OF THE GULF: SHIFTING NAMES AND NETWORKS

Eric Staples

The 'dhow' of the Gulf has been an object of study for well over two centuries. In some ways, it is perhaps one of the best-documented aspects of maritime culture in the region. It often evokes romantic images of an almost timeless traditional vessel, plying the shallow waters of the Gulf and the Indian Ocean for centuries with little to no alteration. And yet hidden within this single English misnomer is a much more complex and contested diversity that reflects the widespread and integral connections that the Gulf has had with the rest of the world. These vessels were a dynamic aspect of the maritime material culture in the Gulf that integrated the region in profound ways with a much larger series of networks in the Indian Ocean world. This chapter will examine two aspects of Gulf shipping in particular, vessel typologies and construction materials, in order to explore these connections.

Before discussing these topics directly, a brief note on the 'dhow' is required. The dhow has long been viewed as a technological object, and as a vehicle of transport. More recently, scholars such as the Tanzanian Professor Abdul Sheriff have framed the dhow as a dynamic carrier of culture, religion and ideas: 'A dhow is not merely an inanimate transporter of goods, but an animated means of social interaction between different peoples who need to exchange those goods, and more.'[1] This theoretical framework builds on an established tradition within both maritime and world history that views maritime activity as instinctively more global and interactive.[2] The ship is seen in particular to be a primary agent of these processes, facilitating commerce, migration and empire. This discussion builds on the conception of the vessel as an animated vehicle of human interaction to include the classification and construction of the vessels themselves.

Vessel Types

In the English language, the word 'dhow' usually refers to any vessel from the north-west Indian Ocean. The term itself has no exact equivalent in the Arabic language, but is often translated into Arabic as *safina* (ship) or *markab* (vessel). The British first appropriated the word in the latter half of the eighteenth century, using a term (*daww*, *dau* or *daw*) that referred to a specific type to eventually describe all vessels from East Africa, Arabia, Iran or India. The exact word that the term stems from is debated, with various theories ascribing its origins either to a particular warship in Arabia, an East African vessel type, or to an early Persian term.[3] Regardless of its origins, the development of the term represents a linguistic homogenisation of what is in fact a rich diversity of watercraft. The term 'dhow' has referred to a considerable variety of vessel types over a significant period of time and a large geographical area.

Agius, in his trilogy on maritime terminology in the region, has amply documented the typological diversity found in the Arabic historical sources from the beginning of the Islamic era to the present.[4] A few terms show a remarkable degree of continuity, such as the relatively generic *markab*, *safina* and *qarib*, and certain roots with variant vowelling patterns, such as *sanbuq/sanbuk/sambuq/sambuk*, *zawraq/zaruk*, *tarida/tarada/tarrad* and *fulk/filka/faluka* have remained a part of the Arabic maritime lexicon for at least a millennium, and in some cases much longer.[5] However, the vast majority of vessel types are historically contingent terms that appear and then disappear from the written record. For example, in the seventh century, the *ghassaniyya*, *khaliyya*, *qadis* and *'udawliyya* are all mentioned as ship types in pre-Islamic and Early Islamic poetry.[6] However, these quickly fade from the literary record, and a host of alternative terms for different craft become more common in the historical chronicles and geographical works of the ninth and tenth centuries, terms such as *shadha'*, *sumayriyya*, *zabzab* and *barija*. By the Middle Islamic period (1000–1500), new types such as the *burma*, *jashujiyya*, *dunij*, *jafan* and *'aykari* appear.[7] There appears to be another shift in the Early Modern period (1500–1800), as new Ottoman and Portuguese forces brought new types to the Indian Ocean. The *ghurab, tranki, qit'a* and *qilyata* are mentioned sailing across the seas of the Indian Ocean in the sixteenth and seventeenth centuries, many of which previously existed in the Mediterranean. And then in the late eighteenth and nineteenth centuries, the modern typologies, such as the *baghla, ghanja, badan* and *battil*, that have been the subject of so much study, emerge.

Some of these types are distinctly regional, such as the Gulf *battil*, a craft with a long raking stem and a prominent stern-fin, often decorated in shells and leather), but others illustrate broader maritime relationships between the Gulf and the Indian Ocean. The *baghla*, for example, is a Perso-Arab reflection of the Indian *kuttiyya* and the Omani *ghanja* that had both regional and European influences. Its hull shape below the waterline is characteristically western Indian Ocean, with a strongly raked fine stempost, but its elaborate transom decoration, aft counter and false quarter galleries all mimic European decorative transom structures of the time. Nineteenth-century drawings by François-Edmund Pâris of different *baghla* also illustrate that it could use either an Indian Ocean settee or a European square-sail rig, a rare example of rig hybridisation within a single Indian Ocean type.[8]

Many of the Arabic terms for these vessel types often have Persian, Indian, East African and European connections. Small dugout canoes such as the *huri* were often shaped from mango logs, and primarily came from India. The term itself comes from the Sanskrit *hoda* via the Hindi *hori*. The term *mashuwa*, used to describe rowing boats and large tenders for most trading vessels in the Gulf, is derived from the Hindi *machu* or *machwa*.[9] *Jashujiyya* comes from the Persian term for sailor, *jashu*, and *qilyata* is an Arabic adaptation of the Portuguese *galeota*. The *kitar*, a common term for a small tender, was most likely derived from the English word 'cutter'. These are just a few examples of linguistic connections that these types have with the broader Indian Ocean and European maritime cultures, evidence of what Agius has referred to as 'the function of language contact in the multi-ethnic Indian Ocean and the borrowing of the terminology that took place over the centuries'.[10]

204 | THE GULF IN WORLD HISTORY

Hidden within these terms are other significant and fundamental shifts within the boat-building tradition that are difficult to discover from a linguistic perspective. Transitions from sewn to nailed construction and shell-first to hybrid frame-first construction were all taking place that dramatically altered the construction of these vessels themselves. The standard narrative of ship construction in the western Indian Ocean states that all vessels were sewn together with natural fibre cordage until the Portuguese arrived in 1498 and introduced nailed frame-first construction to the region, revolutionising ship construction in the process. However, within these broad brushstrokes, there are alternative histories that complicate and enrich this rather simplistic and linear narrative. For example, there is evidence for nailed construction of Chinese and potentially even Indian vessels prior to Portuguese entry into the Indian Ocean, just as there is also evidence in the Gulf for the strong continuity of the sewn-plank tradition several centuries after the Portuguese arrived in the Indian Ocean.[11] Over two and half centuries after Vasco da Gama first sailed to India, the Danish traveller Carsten Niebuhr noted in 1765 that commerce between Oman and Basra was mostly undertaken by sewn vessels known as *tranki*:

> The inhabitants of Oman, although not fond of sea-fights, are nevertheless the best mariners in all Arabia. They have several good harbors, and employ many small vessels in the navigation between Jidda and Basra. To this last town there come annually fifty such vessels, called Trankis . . . They are sewed together without nails, the planks being bound with cords.[12]

Even later, in 1835–7, Lieutenant-Colonel Chesney noted that *tranki* and *battil* were still being sewn primarily with coconut fibre in southern Iraq, commenting: 'This method, in consequence of the elasticity it imparts to the vessels, gives them, in points of sailing, some advantages over those fastened with nails; and the superiority is very observable in the war-boats used by the Arabs.'[13] These technological processes should not be viewed as simple linear evolutionary histories, but rather as complex non-linear developments that included a variety of counter-narratives and even hybridities. For example, even today, the fishing-boat type known as the *battil* in the Musandam Peninsula in the Strait of Hormuz utilises both nailed and sewn construction. The majority of the planking is clench-nailed to the frames, but the planking hood ends in both the bow and the stern are sewn with date palm fibre, as well as the through-beams, thus combining two seemingly distinct construction traditions within a single vessel.[14] This very brief overview of the historically contingent nature of these typologies and their construction illustrates that these 'dhows' were anything but static and timeless, but rather were technologically organic and diverse reflections of the specific context in which they were built and operated.

Materials

Such an organically diverse interpretation of the dhow can also be applied to the materials used to build these vessels. From an external perspective, the dhow appears relatively uniform in its material culture: a vessel made of teak planking nailed to hardwood frames, with cotton sails. However, a closer examination reveals a much wider range of materials used to build watercraft over the time. From reed and date palm rafts, to lashed, sewn and nailed wooden vessels, different materials have been used to construct vessels capable of crossing the waters of the Gulf and Indian Ocean. An essential element of this diversity within the Gulf is due to its timber-deficient environment, and its sparse ecology required the creation of *longue durée* trade networks with other ecological regions in order to construct watercraft.[15] Collectively, these networks sustained material connections with East Africa, as well as south and southeast Asia, producing ecologically hybrid representatives of material culture in the process.

Timber

Timber is an essential requirement for most ship construction. It has also historically been a constant challenge to obtain it in the Gulf region. As a result, a rich variety of species of timbers have been obtained from throughout the Indian Ocean and Eastern Mediterranean with which to build vessels in the Gulf. Although there are accounts of entire vessels being built out of a single type of wood, most vessels, in particular larger ones, used a variety of different timber species depending on the component being constructed. Certain timber species were used to construct planks, frames, heavy timbers and spars respectively, due to the specific requirements of each type of component. Planking required timber cut from relatively long, straight logs, while frames required shorter, curved pieces with natural crooks. Spars were perhaps the most difficult, as they required light, supple and straight logs of considerable length with interlocking grain. For this discussion, timber species used for planking, framing and spars will therefore be examined separately.

Regarding planking, teak (*Tectona grandis*) is the primary wood mentioned for most discussions of boatbuilding in the region. It is seen to be the primary timber used for millennia to build boats in the Indian Ocean. This is largely because teak is ideally suited to make the planking of the vessels. It is strong and durable and yet relatively easy to work with. Its natural oil makes it resistant to fungi, rot and, in particular, the teredo shipworm, a waterborne parasite that could consume the hulls of ships from within. Teak is a long, deciduous tree native to south and southeast Asia that grows relatively straight up to considerable lengths of 40 metres or more.

And yet, although teak in the modern period is definitely the primary wood used for the planking of boats in the Gulf and western Indian Ocean, it does not appear as dominant in past historical sources. A reference by Theophrastus in the third century BCE of planks lasting two hundred years in Bahrain has been suggested to have been to teak, but this is not definitive.[16] By the Islamic period, teak is mentioned in the historical sources in reference to ships. Al-Mas'udi specifically mentions ships' planking made with teak and sewn with coconut fibre in the tenth century,[17] and the lexicographers Ibn Durayd and Ibn Sida both provide the following verse of al-'Ajaj:

> The *qurqur* (a type of ship) [is made of] teak, and its teak
> are heavy planks covered in bitumen.[18]

The textual and archaeological evidence also illustrates that a diversity of timbers were being used for planking. Al-Sirafi, in the second volume of *Akhbar al-Sin wal-Hind* (History of China and India), in the tenth century mentions that entire vessels, including the planking, were being made out of coconut wood:

> Indeed, in Oman there are shipwrights who travel to these islands [the Lakshadweep Islands] where the coconut palms are, bringing with them carpentry tools and other equipment. They fell as much coconut wood as they want: once it is dry, it is sawn into planks. Next, using coconut fiber,

they twist enough cordage to sew together the planks that they have sawn, and use them to build the hull of a ship. Then they hew masts from the coconut wood, weave sails from its fronds, and use its fibre to twist what they call *kharabat*, which are cables in our parlance.[19]

The archaeological record provides perhaps the most accurate record of this diversity. The ninth-century ship that was wrecked off Belitung Island, Indonesia, and which was the basis for the experimental reconstruction, *Jewel of Muscat*, also varied in its timber composition. Timber identifications indicated that although its through-beams were teak, the planking was *Afzelia africana*, with *Afzelia bipindensis* for the keelson, rosewood (*Dalbergia* species) for the stem post and juniper (*Juniperus procera*) for the ceiling planks.[20]

The sewn timbers excavated in the southern Omani archaeological site of al-Balid, dating from the tenth to fifteenth centuries, allude to a similar variety. This is a collection of timbers, primarily sewn planks, discovered over the last ten years that had been recycled as construction timber for buildings at the site. Eight of the timbers have been submitted for species identification, seven of which are planking. Of the seven planks identified, three are teak, but others include two *Terminalia* and one *Calophyllum* species, as well as one non-identifiable timber.[21] All of this suggests that teak was just one of several different types of planking timber.

However, by the modern period, the narrative dominance of teak in the historical sources is more pronounced. Commander Rowand in Lorimer's *Gazetteer* mentions that vessels in the Gulf were built with 'roughly adzed planks of teak' at the beginning of the twentieth century.[22] Commander Wilson, a British officer who documented a variety of watercraft in Bombay at the beginning of the twentieth century, identifies teak as a major source of boat-building timber. In his description of a type of *sanbuq* from the Gulf, the Red Sea and the east coast of Africa, he states: 'The timbers or frames of the vessel are practically undressed logs of some kind of jungle wood, to which the teak planking is fastened by iron nails.'[23]

The oral evidence largely supports the assumption that teak is the main planking wood for ships in the region. Interviews and discussions with boat builders, sailors and fishermen in Oman all mention teak as the primary boat-building wood for planking. The Kuwaiti maritime historian Ya'qub al-Hijji, who provides perhaps the most depth in these linguistic inquiries during his interviews with the shipwrights of Kuwait, notes the prevalence of teak, although he does acknowledge that benteak (*Lagerstroemia lanceolata*) was used below the waterline since it cracked in the sun, and that pali (*Palaquium elliticum*) was used for thicker wale planking, due to its lack of expansion.[24] From the historical references, and the oral record, it would be safe to assume that teak was the primary wood used for planking, except for the two exceptions mentioned by al-Hijji above, at least in the modern period.

However, although teak is definitely the primary wood used for construction for planking, the more recent archaeological and textual evidence also alludes to a much greater diversity in planking in the modern period than oral interviews suggest. Timbers identified from a shipwreck recently surveyed on a beach in Dhofar show *Terminalia* species for planking. The planks of the sewn *sanbuq/kambari* of Dhofar are made of arir (*Delonix elata*). Timber identification of a plank of the *al-Dhi'b*, the last sailing *sanbuq* in Oman, show that it was *Tetramerista glabra*.[25] A partially reconstructed *badan* from Sur, Oman recently displayed in Paris was primarily planked with miranti (*Shorea* species). The *Sohar* reconstruction that sailed to China in 1980–1 used aini (*Artocarpus hirsutus*) for planking, as it is better suited for sewing boats together.[26] The ubiquitous dugout canoe (*huri*) is often made of mango (*Mangifera indica*) logs.

Today, vessels are being planked in teak in the wooden boatyards around the Gulf, but a brief survey of the few remaining wooden boatyards and timber yards in Oman, the UAE and Qatar also shows that a significant amount of afromosia (*Pericopsis elata*), iroko (*Milicia excelsa*), miranti (*Shorea* species) and even obeche (*Triplochiton scleroxylon*) are being used for planking. The variety of timber found in the archaeological and boat-documentation record further enriches the evidence found in the oral historical record.

A similar comment can be made for timber used to make the frames or ribs of a vessel. They can be made of teak, but usually shorter trees with longer curved branches are preferred because they have natural bends and crooks. Again, there are a variety of timbers that can be, and have been, used for framing. Archaeological frame timbers in the Belitung shipwreck and the al-Balid site have been identified as *Afzelia africana* and possibly *Anogeissus acuminata* respectively. The frames for the boat description provided by al-Sirafi above would most likely have been made of coconut, although it is not specified.[27] Within the twentieth century, local woods such as *sidr* (*Ziziphus spinachristi*) and *qarat* (*Acacia nilotica*) have been used for framing, as well as the 'jungle wood' (*jangali*) referred to by Commander Wilson above. Efforts have been made to identify this term with a single species, mostly Indian laurel (*Terminalia tomentosa*), but discussions with lumber suppliers suggest that it is a more diverse collection of tropical hardwoods, primarily from India, used for framing. This potentially included jackfruit (*Artocarpus heterophyllus*), karam (*Adina cordifolia*), white laurel (*Terminalia piniculata*) and even vaka (*Albizia lebbeck*). More recently, African woods such as bilinga (*Nauclea diderrichii*) and dabema (*Piptadeniastrum africanum*) have been used as well for framing in the Gulf. Thus, the framing timber is a combination of both local wood and tropical hardwoods from India and Africa, a clear reflection of routes that these ships were sailing.[28]

And then there are the kinds of timber used for the masts and yards. These require light, strong and long lengths of timber, preferably with an interlocking grain. Puna and cherapuna have historically been the preferred woods in the western Indian Ocean, as António Pessoa noted in 1548:

> In Ceylon as many masts and yards can be obtained as are wanted for galleons, galleys and ships, and all other things for which there is need, of puna and cherapuna, which is the best type to be found.[29]

However, they were not always as plentiful as they were in Pessoa's time, and other woods have been used. Al-Sirafi's previously-cited tenth-century passage indicates that masts were also being made out of date palm trunks, and in addition there are references to teak being used as well.[30]

Collectively, this brief survey of boat-building timber illustrates a considerable variety even with our limited evidence. This diversity is important, because it alludes to larger connections between the Gulf and the timber-rich regions of the Indian Ocean. As most of this timber was not indigenous to the Gulf, at least for the last several thousand years, almost all of these timbers had to be imported. This boat-building timber trade is one of the more ignored aspects of western Indian Ocean commercial networks that connected the Gulf with a much larger world. Luxury trade in spices, aromatics, ivory, textiles, pearls, gold, and human trafficking such as the slave trade, are all frequently mentioned in relation to maritime trade in the Indian Ocean, but the timber trade receives little focus, especially when considering the amounts of timber required to build a boat. The experimental archaeological ninth-century reconstruction *Jewel of Muscat* (based on the Belitung shipwreck), for example, was a mid-sized 18.6-metre trading vessel, and yet it required over fifty tons of timber for its construction. All of this wood had to be felled in the tropical forests of Kerala and East Africa, transported to a local port, loaded onto ships, and sailed across the seas.

This trade required a constant supply of timber flowing towards the shipyards of the Gulf in order to keep them stocked for construction and repair. The arsenal of Hormuz, for example, had a stock of timber sufficient to replace and repair the masts on demand, most of which would have had to come from the west coast of India and from East Africa. This trade was often considered so important that rulers controlled its trade, such as was the case in Hormuz in the fifteenth century, and for the Ya'rubids in Muscat in the seventeenth century.

A brief example illustrates the two main western Indian Ocean sources of this wood in the Ya'rubi period. The Dutch merchant Georg Wilmson's records of trade in Muscat in 1673 show a variety of boatbuilding materials arriving in Muscat. From Kerala, seven small ships delivered a total of 210 planks and 195 bundles of reeds, bamboo, conifers and other timber, as well as 123,000 coconuts, 170 *candis* of coir and 154 *candis* of iron. However, a ship from Pate also arrived carrying 250 planks and eight masts.[31] Unfortunately, the species are not identified, but such examples indicate that both South Asia and East Africa were significant sources for boat-building materials in the Gulf.

Rigging and Sails

This diversity is also apparent to a lesser extent with the materials needed to make the rigging and sails of the vessels. In general, the material composition of rigging and sails is less well documented in the historical record than that of timbers, largely because the rigging and sails are less likely to survive. However, a handful of textual references indicate that coconut fibre (coir) was the main material used for rigging. Tomé Pires noted in his description of Malabar: 'Nothing but coir is used in these is used in these parts for ship's rigging and cables, and it is an important trading item.'[32]

Coir was also the dominant fibre used to sew vessels together. Ibn Battuta (d. 1377) mentions this during his stay in the Maldives:

> This (coconut fibre) is the hairy integument of the coconut, which they tan in pits on the shore, and afterwards beat out with bars: the women then spin it and it is made for cords for sewing the [planks of] ships together.[33]

However, it was not the only material. The limited archaeological evidence we do have from the Belitung vessel, an ostensibly 'Arab' trading vessel that sank near Indonesia, suggests that hibiscus (perhaps sea hibiscus, *Hibiscus tiliaceus*) was also used to stitch planks together, with paperbark wadding (*Malaleuca*).[34] More recently, date palm coated in bitumen has also been used to stitch the *battil* of northern Musandam.

As for sails, a variety of materials were used. There are records of sails being made out of woven palm. Al-Sirafi mentions that sails were made of woven coconut palm. One of the images found in *Maqamat al-Hariri* illustrates a woven palm sail.[35] Palm sails were also frequently used in East Africa. The journal of Vasco da Gama's first voyage to East Africa records sails 'made of palm matting' in Mozambique in 1498.[36] The Portuguese writer Luís de Camões (d. 1580), who lived for a time in the Indian Ocean, describes the sails rather more poetically in the following verse:

> The boats appeared in a manner new
> long-built and narrow-beamed, for swiftness plan'd;
> mats were the wings wherewith they lightly flew,
> from certain palm-fronds wove by cunning hand.[37]

There are descriptions of East African *mtepes* using such sails as late as the early twentieth century in East Africa. Doum palm in particular was used to make sails for the *mtepe* reconstruction in the House of Wonders Museum, as well as the palm sail as an alternative experimental sail for *Jewel of Muscat* during its passage across the Indian Ocean in 2010, but other palm species sails such as date and coconut palm could also have been used.

Alternatively, cloth was also clearly being used for sail making. Arab lexicographers primarily define a sail (*shira'*) vaguely as cloth. Ibn Sida defines it as 'the curtain (*riwaq*) of a ship', and Ibn Manzur as 'that which is made of cloth (*thawb*) and raised aloft, so that the wind can fill it and make it move'.[38] Ibn Majid describes how to make a sail in his poem *Hawiya*, mentioning bolts of sail cloth (*shaqa'iq*) laid out on the ground and sewn together.[39] This echoes similar descriptions of sail-making found in more recent sources, such as Commander Rowand's description of sail cloth in the Gulf at the beginning of the twentieth century:

> The sail is made of cotton of various thicknesses and texture, suitable for the
> different sized craft. The natives weave the canvas by hand. It is made about 18'
> wide, and is sold by weight. It is made in Lingeh, Khamīr, Qishm, Dishkūn,
> Kung, Halīleh, and Bahrain, also possibly, at Kuwait and other places.[40]

In addition, the twentieth-century Kuwaiti mariner and lexicographer Ahmad al-Bashar al-Rumi states that different types of cotton canvas, in particular from north-west India and Pakistan, were also used to make sails. He distinguishes between two main types: the *al-bahrani*, a heavy canvas for larger vessels, and *al-marbu'*, used for lighter sails and smaller boats.[41] What is apparent from all of these accounts is that all of these sail materials were obtained from throughout the western Indian Ocean. Coconut palm from South Asia, doum palm from East Africa, and cloth from both the Gulf and Pakistan and north-west India created material connections with the Gulf and the broader western Indian Ocean.

Wood Preservatives

Unlike the timber and rigging and sail materials, preservatives were more readily available in the Gulf for regional consumption. A variety of regionally available substances were used to preserve the hulls both above and below the waterline. There is evidence for both bitumen and animal fat mixed with lime powder (*shuna*) being used to protect the hull beneath the waterline. Bitumen has been a prominent waterproofing substance for watercraft for millennia. The earliest evidence for sea-going watercraft is in fact bitumen fragments from the fifth millennium BCE site of al-Sabiyya in Kuwait with barnacles on one side and reed impressions on the other. By the third millennium BCE, bitumen fragments are found in several sites along the Gulf. The Girsu Ur III list of boat-building materials lists over 475 tons of bitumen being used for ship construction, indicating that it was a significant material for waterproofing ancient craft.[42]

This substance continued to be used in the Islamic period. Bitumen has been found on several of the planks from the Middle Islamic period in al-Balid. The lexicographer Ibn Manzur mentions that ships were coated with bitumen in the thirteenth century, using a specific term for the process of applying it to the hull (*damma al-safina*).[43] The anti-fouling on the vessel illustration in the *Maqamat al-Hariri* manuscript is a dark greyish brown, suggesting that it depicts a bitumen anti-fouling. In the nineteenth and twentieth centuries, a variety of sources, including British officers, Arab scholars and modern ethnographers all attest to the continued use of bitumen to waterproof vessels, in particular in southern Iraq. For example, the lexicographer al-Dujayli, in his section of vessel types in Iraq in 1912, lists multiple types, including the *duba*, *ᶜisbiyya* and *sammakiyya*, that were all coated with bitumen.[44] Collectively, this evidence indicates that bitumen has been used for waterproofing on vessels for at least the last seven thousand years in the Gulf.

However, vessels were also coated with an alternative compound, a mixture of animal fat and lime powder obtained from burning shells. Al-Masʿudi mentions this practice in the early tenth century: 'Vessels from the Arabian Sea do not use iron nails because the sea water dissolves the iron, and they become thin and weak. Rather, seafaring peoples use fiber rope instead, and coat the hulls with animal fat and lime (*al-nura*).'[45] This practice is found even today on wooden fishing vessels in the Gulf and Oman.

Another substance historically used to preserve the hull was fish/whale or shark oil. Al-Sirafi provides an account of this in his tenth-century description of Siraf, mentioning that whale fat was harvested from whale carcasses found washed up on the beach:

> The oil is also scooped out of the whale's eye with jars, once the eye has been melted in the sun. All this oil is collected and sold to the owners of ships; it is then mixed with various other ingredients that they use and daubed on the hulls of the sea-going ships to seal the seams in the planking and to seal any places where the seams have come apart. The oil of this whale fetches a considerable sum of money.[46]

In a more modern context, shark liver oil (*sal*), in spite of its pungent smell, has been the oil of choice for preserving the wood above the waterline. Commander Rowand in his comments on vessels in the Gulf at the beginning of the twentieth century noted that 'the topsides, outside are coated with two applications of shark oil every year; and the whole of the interior is given one coat during a similar period; this prevents the timbers from splitting and warping'.[47] The few remaining commercial wooden fishing vessels in Oman still coat their planking with shark liver oil, although this practice is declining as more and more fishing craft transition to fibreglass hulls.

Conclusion

Although a complete discussion of boatbuilding materials would include a more diverse range of substances such as metals, tree resins and ballast, this brief and selective discussion does illustrate that these material networks connected the Gulf with timber merchants in Africa and South Asia, rope makers in Kerala and the Maldives, cotton and doum palm weavers in the Kutch and Zanzibar, and bitumen suppliers in northern Iraq. And although the exact tendrils of these networks are often difficult to chronicle, particularly in the pre-modern period, due to the paucity of evidence, it is clear that this trade altered over time, as different materials became more or less valuable or accessible.

This process of material procurement and vessel construction in the Gulf generated a significant degree of cultural interaction, requiring long-distance trade and cultural negotiation in order to build these vessels. In spite of efforts to simply categorise Gulf watercraft within a single cultural or even linguistic label, these vessels were often in fact diverse material artefacts, reflective of both the regional and the broader social and economic western Indian Ocean networks that created them. Typology and materials are just two of a host of other facets of Gulf shipping, including technical terminology, naval design, musical traditions and crew and shipwright demographics, that reflect the Gulf's connections with other littoral societies. These vessels are perhaps some of the most materially explicit evidence of the Gulf's relationship with the larger Indian Ocean, and deserve to be understood as such.

Notes

1. Sheriff, Abdul, *Dhow Cultures and the Indian Ocean: Cosmopolitanism, Commerce and Islam* (Oxford: Oxford University Press, 2010), p. 1.
2. For discussions on these historiographical developments with the Indian Ocean specifically, see Wink, M., 'Indian Ocean Studies and the "New Thalassology"', *Journal of Global History*, vol. 2, no. 1 (2007), pp. 41–62; Mukherjee, R., 'Escape from Terracentrism: Writing a Water History', *Indian Historical Review*, vol. 41 (2014), pp. 87–101; Alpers, Edward, 'Maritime History, World History, Global History: Some Thoughts on Past, Present and Future', in A. al-Salimi and E. Staples (ed.), *Oman: A Maritime History* (Hildesheim: Olms, 2017), pp. 17–28.
3. Agius, D. A., *In the Wake of the Dhow: The Arabian Gulf and Oman* (Reading: Ithaca Press, 2002), pp. 33–4, 58–61.
4. Agius, *In the Wake of the* Dhow; Agius, D. A., *Classic Ships of Islam: From Mesopotamia to the Indian Ocean* (Leiden and Boston: Brill, 2008); Agius, D. A., *Seafaring in the Arabian Gulf and Oman: People of the Dhow* (London: Kegan Paul, 2005).
5. Agius, *Classic Ships*, pp. 280–5, 292–4.
6. Agius, *Classic Ships*, pp. 298–330.
7. Ibn al-Mujawir, Abu Bakr b. Muhammad b. Mas'ud b. 'Ali b. Ahmad, *Taʾrikh al-Mustabsir*, ed. Oscar Löfgren, 2 vols (Leiden: Brill, 1951–4); idem, *A Traveller in Thirteenth-Century Arabia*, trans. G. Rex Smith (London: Ashgate; The Hakluyt Society, 2008); Goitein, S. D. and Mordechai Akiva Friedman, *Indian Traders of the Middle Ages: Documents from the Cairo Geniza ('India Book')* (Leiden: Koninklijke Brill NV, 2007); Margariti, Roxanne, *Aden and the Indian Ocean Trade: 150 Years in the Life of a Medieval Arabian Port* (Chapel Hill: University of North Carolina Press, 2007), pp. 76–83; Ibn Majid, Ahmad, *Al-'Ulum al-Bahriyya 'inda al-'Arab. Al-Qism al-Thani: Musannafat Shihab al-Din Ahmad b. Majid b. Muhammad b. 'Amru b. Fadl b. Duwaik b. Yusuf b. Hasan b. Hussain b. Abi Mu'alliq al-Sa'di b. Abi Raka'ib al-Najdi. Al-Jiz'a al-Awwal: Kitab al-Fawa'id fi Usul al-'Ilm al-Bahr wa-al-Qawa'id*, ed. I. al-Khuri (Damascus, Matbu'at Majma' al-Lughat al-'Arabiyya bi-Damashq, 1971), pp. 310, 313; Tibbetts, G. R., *Arab Navigation in the Indian Ocean before the Coming of the Portuguese* (London: Royal Asiatic Society, 1981), pp. 225, 227.
8. See Agius, *In the Wake of the Dhow*, pp. 49–53; Burningham, Nick, '*Baghla, Ghanja* and *Kotia*: Distinguishing the *Baghla* from the Suri *Ghanja* and Indian

Kotia', *International Journal of Nautical Archaeology*, vol. 36, no. 1 (2006), pp. 91–111, for more discussion of the *baghla*.

9. Agius, *In the Wake of the Dhow*, p. 117.

10. Agius, *Classic Ships*, p. 372.

11. Ibn Battuta, *The Travels of Ibn Battuta*, trans. H. A. R. Gibb and C. F. Beckingham (New Delhi: The Hakluyt Society, 2004), IV, pp. 813–14; Tomalin, V., V. Selvakumar, M. V. Nair and P. K. Gopi, 'The Thaikkal-Kadakkarappally Boat: an Archaeological Example of Medieval Shipbuilding in the Western Indian Ocean', *International Journal of Nautical Archaeology*, vol. 33, no. 2 (2004), pp. 253–63.

12. Niebuhr, Carsten, *Travels through Arabia and Other Countries in the East*, trans. Robert Heron (Edinburgh: Morison & Son, 1792), p. 123.

13. Chesney, F. R., *The Expedition for the Survey of the Rivers Euphrates and Tigris carried on by Order of the British Government in the Years 1835, 1836, and 1837; Preceded by Geographical and Historical Notices of the Regions Situated Between the Rivers Nile and Indus* (London: Longman, Brown, Green & Longmans, 1850), II, p. 646.

14. Weismann, Norbert, Eric Staples, Alessandro Ghidoni, Tom Vosmer, Piotr Dziamski and Lilli Haar, 'The Battil and Zaruqah of Musandam, Oman', *International Journal of Nautical Archaeology*, vol. 43, no. 2 (2014), pp. 1–23.

15. Sheriff, *Dhow Cultures*, pp. 22–5.

16. Hourani George F. and John Carswell, *Arab Seafaring in the Indian Ocean in Ancient and Early Medieval Times* (Princeton: Princeton University Press, 1995), p. 90; Vosmer, Tom, 'The Development of Maritime Technology in the Arabian Gulf and Western Indian Ocean with Special Reference to Oman' (Ph.D. diss., Curtin University of Technology, 2007), p. 83; Agius, *Classic Ships*, p. 147.

17. Al-Mas'udi, Ali b. Husayn, *Muruj al-Dhahab wa-Ma'adin al-Jawhar*, ed. and trans. C. B. Meynard and P. De Courteille, 9 vols (Paris: À l'Imprimerie Impériale, 1861–77), I, p. 365; Hourani and Carswell, *Arab Seafaring*, p. 90.

18. Ibn Durayd, Muhammad b. Husayn, *Kitab Jamharat al-Lugha* (Beirut: Dar al-'Ilm, 1987), I, p. 199; Ibn Sida, Abu al-Hasan b. Isma'il, *Kitab al-Mukhassas* (Beirut: Dar al-Kutub al-'Ilmiyya), X, p. 26.

19. Al-Sirafi, Abu Zayd, *Two Arabic Travel Books: Accounts of China and India*, trans. Tim Mackintosh-Smith (New York and London: New York University Press, 2014), pp. 119–21.

20. Flecker, Michael, 'A 9th-Century Arab or Indian shipwreck in Indonesian waters', *International Journal of Nautical Archaeology*, vol. 29, no. 2 (2000),

pp. 199–217; Flecker, Michael, 'A Ninth-Century Arab Shipwreck in Indonesia. For the First Archaeological Evidence of Direct Trade with China', in *Shipwrecked* (Singapore: Smithsonian Institution, 2011), p. 117. For the *Jewel of Muscat* reconstruction, see Vosmer, Tom, 'The Jewel of Muscat. Reconstructing a Ninth-Century Sewn-Plank Boat', in *Shipwrecked* (Singapore: Smithsonian Institution, 2011), pp. 121–35.

21. Belfioretti, Luca, and Tom Vosmer, 'Al-Balid Ship Timbers: Preliminary Overview and Comparisons', *Proceedings of the Seminar for Arabian Studies*, vol. 40 (2010), pp. 111–18; also Vosmer, personal communication, 26 April 2015.

22. Lorimer, J. G., *Gazetteer of the Persian Gulf, Oman and Central Arabia* (Calcutta: Superintendent Government Printing, 1915), I, p. 2319.

23. Wilson, N. F. J., *The Native Craft: A General Description of the Native Craft visiting Bombay Harbour and Particulars as to their Survey, Registry, Measurement and Lighting* (Bombay: the Times Press, 1909), p. 50.

24. Al-Hijji, Y. Y., *The Art of Dhow-building in Kuwait* (Kuwait: London Centre of Arab Studies, 2001), pp. 38–40.

25. Alian, M. A., *In Memory of the Sambuq: Record of a Way of Life* (Muscat: Muscat Printing Press, 2006), pp. 7–8; and Vosmer, personal communication, 26 April 2016.

26. Severin, Tim, *The Sinbad Voyage* (Norwalk, CT: Easton Press, 1982).

27. Flecker, 'A 9th-Century Arab or Indian shipwreck', pp. 199–217; al-Sirafi, *Akhbar al-Sin wal-Hind*, pp. 119–21.

28. Al-Hijji, *The Art of Dhow-building in Kuwait*, pp. 38–40; Agius, *In the Wake of the Dhow*, 139; Semaan, Lucy, 'From Tree to Plank: A Multidisciplinary Approach to the Study of Wood Use in Boatbuilding in the Red Sea' (Ph.D. diss., University of Exeter, 2014), pp. 367–70.

29. De Silva, C. R. (ed.), *Portuguese Encounters with Sri Lanka and the Maldives: Translated Texts from the Age of the Discoveries* (Farnham and Burlington, VT: Ashgate, 2009), p. 32.

30. Al-Sirafi, *Akhbar al-Sin wal-Hind*, pp. 119–21.

31. Floor, Willem, *The Persian Gulf: Dutch–Omani Relations, A Commercial and Political History 1651–1806* (Washington, DC: Mage, 2014), pp. 193–5.

32. Coartesao, A. (ed.), *The Suma Oriental of Tome Pires, An Account of the East, from the Red Sea to Japan, Written in Malacca and India in 1512–1515 and The Book of Francisco Rodrigues, Pilot Major of the Armada that Discovered Banda and the Moluccas: Rutter of a Voyage in the Red Sea, Nautical Rules, Almanack and*

Maps, written and Drawn in the East before 1515, 2 vols (New Delhi, Chennai: Asian Educational Services, 2005), p. 84.

33. Ibn Battuta, *The Travels of Ibn Battuta*, IV, p. 827.

34. Flecker, 'A ninth-century Arab Shipwreck', pp. 117–18.

35. See the facsimile reproduction of the original manuscript in al-Hariri, Abu Muhammad al-Qasim, *Maqamat al-Hariri, Illustrated by Y Al-Wasiti. Thirteenth-Century Manuscript*, introd. Oleg Grabar (London: Touch Art, 2003).

36. Ravenstein E. G. (ed. and trans.), *Journal of the First Voyage of Vasco da Gama 1497–1498* (London: Hakluyt Society 1898), p. 26.

37. Burton, R. F. (ed. and trans.), *Camoens: His Life and His Lusiads* (London: Bernard Quaritch, 1881), I, p. 20.

38. Ibn Sida, *al-Mukhassas*, p. 26; Ibn Manzur, Muhammad b. Mukarram, *Lisan al-'Arab* (Cairo: al-Matba'a al-Kubra al-Miriyya, 1882), III, p. 127.

39. Ibn Majid, Ahmad, *al-Nuniyya al-Kubra ma'a Sit Qasa'id Ukhra*, ed. Hassan Salih Shihab (Muscat: Ministry of Culture and Heritage, 1993), pp. 213–14; idem, *Hawiyat al-Ikhtisar fi Usul 'Ilm al-Bahr*, ed. and trans I. Khuri (Ras al-Khaimah: Documentaries and Studies Centre, 2010), pp. 76, 78.

40. Lorimer, *Gazetteer*, I, p. 2,320.

41. Al-Rumi, Ahmad al-Bashar, *Mu'jam al-Mustalahat al-Bahriyya fi Kuwayt* (Kuwait: Markaz al-Buhuth wal-Darasat al-Kuwaytiyya, 1996), p. 57; al-Kasadi, B. A., *Qamus al-Bahri: Mu'jam al-Mustalahat al-Bahriyya fi Junub al-Jazirat al-'Arabiyya*, ed. Hassan Salih Shihab (Abu Dhabi: al-Majma' al-Thaqafi, 2004), pp. 110–15.

42. Carter, Robert, 'Watercraft', in D. T. Potts (ed.), *A Companion to the Archaeology of the Ancient Near East* (Oxford: Wiley-Blackwell, 2012), pp. 347–71.

43. Ibn Manzur, *Lisan al-Arab*, XV, p. 97; Belfioretti and Vosmer, 'Al-Balid Ship Timbers', p. 113.

44. Al-Dujayli, Kazim, *Lughat al-'Arab* (Baghdad: Wazarat al-A'lam, 1912), II, pp. 97, 102.

45. Al-Mas'udi, *Muruj al-Dhahab*, I, p. 365.

46. Al-Sirafi, *Akhbar al-Sin wal-Hind*, pp. 126–7.

47. Lorimer, *Gazetteer*, I, p. 2,319.

12

THE ROLE OF INDIAN OCEAN TRADE INLAND: THE BURAIMI OASIS

Timothy Power

Geographical Setting and Background

The historic Buraimi Oasis is situated on the border between the United Arab Emirates and the Sultanate of Oman. It consists of six discrete date-palm oases now divided between the modern towns of al-ᶜAin (UAE) and Buraimi (Oman) (Plate 9). The archaeology of the Buraimi Oasis is quite well-known, having been the subject of fifty years' research. Al-ᶜAin is now inscribed on the list of UNESCO World Heritage Sites. Although it has been occupied for at least five thousand years, permanent settlement in the landscape does not appear to have been continuous. It now seems that the Iron Age and Late Islamic periods represent peak occupations, with less intensive but still considerable settlement activity in the Early Bronze Age and Early Islamic period, and almost no evidence for occupation during the Late Pre-Islamic and Middle Islamic periods. Such settlement patterns can be interpreted as evidence for episodes of 'bedouinisation' and 'sedentarisation', in which societies occupying so marginal an environment adapted their subsistence strategies according to changing 'push' and 'pull' factors. This gives the pattern of human settlement in the Buraimi Oasis a cyclical character.

The 'push' and 'pull' factors driving settlement cycles in the Islamic centuries can be identified in the historical sources and archaeological record. 'Sedentarisation' in the Buraimi Oasis was, in both the Early and Late Islamic periods, stimulated by Indian Ocean trade cycles. Although somewhat far from the coast, the Buraimi Oasis was influenced by the cycles of Gulf and Indian Ocean prosperity. This was because powerful regional dynasties based in central Oman, the Second Ibadi Imamate (c. 793–891) and the Ya°rubids (c. 1624–1722) respectively, emerged in response to peaks in the Indian Ocean trade. Mercantile capital was invested in large-scale agricultural estates. The oasis landscape of Buraimi was a product of the organisational capacities of centralised states coupled with the windfall of booming maritime trade that made these states possible. A second wave of agricultural expansion began under provincial successor polities, those of the Bani Sama in the tenth century and Bani Nu°aym in the eighteenth century, as the centralised states dissolved into dynastic infighting. These provincial dynasties had a vested interest in increasing the profitability of their land and benefited by retaining tax revenues locally. However, they ultimately lacked the military resources to defend their agricultural wealth from the depredations of bedouin confederations, with the Qaramita confederation in the tenth century and Wahhabi raiders in the nineteenth century both using al-Hasa° in eastern Arabia as the base from which to launch invasions of the Buraimi Oasis. These devastating invasions precipitated episodes of 'bedouinisation' wherein field systems and palm plantations fell into ruin and the oasis villages declined or were abandoned.

Early Islamic Period (c. 750–1050)

Archaeological evidence for the Early Islamic period in al-°Ain and Buraimi (The Early Imamate) has come more sharply into focus in recent years. It may now be considered one of the main periods of sedentary occupation. The most important site yet discovered is Hamasa on the Omani side of the border.[1] We found that the remains of ten mudbrick buildings arranged around two streets were discovered in sand dunes truncated during the laying out of a road grid (Figure 12.1). However, the spread of surface ceramics across a much larger area suggests this is part of a potentially much larger site. More Early Islamic ceramics were reported from an archaeological evaluation in al-°Ain, immediately to the west and just beyond the border fence. About

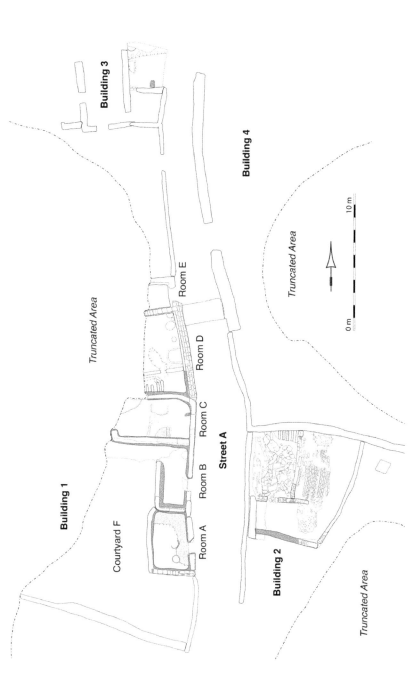

Figure 12.1 Plan of a street and buildings from Early Islamic Hamasa.

1.3 km to the south-west of the Hamasa excavations, at ᶜAwd al-Tawba in al-ᶜAin, a number of Early Islamic mudbrick square-plan buttressed buildings were found together with a small mosque and *falaj* channel system lined with baked bricks (Plate 10).[2] Another square-plan buttressed building, again in association with a *falaj* and Early Islamic ceramics, was unearthed during an archaeological evaluation at a proposed school in Jimi, about 1.8 km to the north-west of the Hamasa excavations. Further to the north-west, about 2.6 km from Hamasa, two phases of hearths, pits and post-holes associated with Early Islamic ceramics were discovered at Qattara and interpreted as an *ᶜarish*, reed hut settlement.[3] These sites raise issues about the extent and character of settlement. It is perhaps possible that Hamasa lay near the centre of a single large low-density settlement, stretching south to 'Awd al-Tawba and north to the Jimi school site, and surrounded by *ᶜarish* suburbs. Alternatively, these sites may represent smaller discrete settlements scattered across an otherwise rural landscape.

Further evidence for the Early Islamic landscape of Buraimi was found during a 2014 survey (Plate 11).[4] Geophysical surveying to the north of the Hamasa excavations located two *aflaj* irrigation channels, one of which can be identified with the Jimi school *falaj* and may accordingly be dated to the Early Islamic period. A network of field boundary walls was discovered on the same alignment as these *aflaj*, not visible on the surface and underlying the Late Islamic layers, which therefore likely belongs to an Early Islamic field system. When these features were targeted by a test pit, a thick silty deposit containing Early Islamic pottery was discovered, representing a possible cultivation horizon (Figure 12.2). No direct evidence for palm groves was found. However, the *madbasa* system for extracting date juice from Room D in Building 1 constitutes proxy evidence for the cultivation of palms. The Early Islamic landscape of al-ᶜAin and Buraimi was therefore most likely one of open fields and palm groves interspersed with clusters of mudbrick and *ᶜarish* reed houses.

The Early Islamic ceramics noted above may be dated to between 750 and 1050 CE. During this period the Gulf had become the major artery for Indian Ocean trade. Suhar (or Sohar) became an important port of embarkation for the voyage to India and China, and grew wealthy on the back of this lively trade, sending an enormous annual tribute of 300,000 *dinars* to

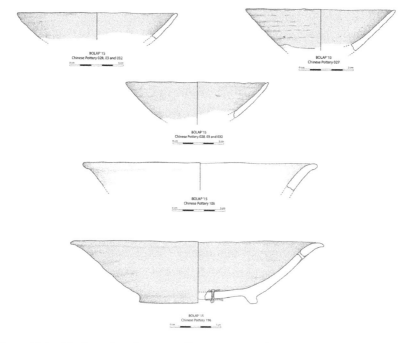

Figure 12.2 Ninth- and tenth-century Chinese ceramics from Early Islamic Hamasa.

the Caliph.[5] Its importance is reflected in the move of the Ibadi capital from Nizwa to Suhar during the reign of Imam Ghassan (r. 808–23), who is credited with ushering in a sort of 'golden age', later remembered as 'the days when the kingdom was in its prime and in the fullness of its power'.[6] A number of stories recorded in the Omani sources testify to his particular concern for agricultural development.[7] The labour needs for this agricultural expansion appear to have been met by the mass importation of East African slaves, for the Omani sources record anecdotes demonstrating the care with which Imam Ghassan treated them. It might, however, be objected that the maintenance of irrigation channels and fair treatment of slaves are *topoi* of the just ruler. Yet archaeological survey of the land behind Suhar attests to a maximum extent of cultivation (73 Ha) in the ninth and tenth centuries,[8] clearly demonstrating that there was a significant investment in agriculture. Parallels for the mass use of agricultural slaves are to be found in contemporary Iraq, where large numbers of East Africans were set to work in the Sawad, the rich agricultural region, culminating in the Zanj slave revolt of 872–82.

We can suggest that, beginning in the ninth century, the wealth generated by the 'India trade' passing through Sohar was reinvested in agricultural projects in the hinterland, which included the Batina and Buraimi Oasis.

Finds from Hamasa point to the importance of maritime trade with the Gulf and Indian Ocean to this inland site. For instance, the ceramic assemblage of Period I Hamasa was dominated by locally made cooking pots, with small quantities of black burnished ware from India.[9] Contacts with the subcontinent were to prove the most enduring, with Indian imports attested throughout the Hamasa sequence, recalling to mind the appellation of Oman as *Ard al-Hind*.[10] The appearance of turquoise alkaline glazed wares in Period II Hamasa demonstrated a renewal of contacts with Iraq. The circulation of Kennet's Type 72 rim profile between the mid-seventh and early eighth century points to the Umayyad conquest of Oman, sometime between 694 and 705, followed by the rise of the Muhallabid Dynasty and a strengthening of ties with Basra in Iraq.[11]

Period III Hamasa represented the peak of settlement, meaning more evidence in general and so more evidence for trade, though the spike in foreign contacts is nevertheless likely significant. Contacts with Iraq intensified and a wide range of pottery from the Samarra (the new capital of the Caliphs in Iraq) class emerged. These included some quite rare types, such as an opaque white glazed bowl with blue and yellow wedge motifs arranged in bands, and some finely painted polychrome lustrewares. It is also to Iraq that most of the sizeable glass assemblage should be attributed. Obvious parallels can be made with Siraf and Suhar, but identical forms have been found at Indian sites such as Sanjan, showing the integration of Hamasa into western Indian Ocean commercial networks. Links with India are demonstrated by the ceramics, with micaceous red ware from Maharashtra and red painted ware from Sind, this last found in large quantities together with Islamic ceramics at Sehwan Sharif.[12]

While material from India and Iraq were found in earlier periods at Hamasa, contacts with China constitute an innovation of Period III. About a dozen sherds were found with two distinct classes, namely Gongxian white stoneware from the ninth century and Yue green stoneware from the ninth or tenth century.[13] A full typological quantification of the ceramic assemblage is currently under way, but it is already immediately obvious that the vast majority of vessels were imported, and that trade links with the Gulf and Indian Ocean were fundamentally important to Early Islamic Hamasa.

This material was reaching the Buraimi Oasis through one or more of a number of local ports. The most obvious candidate is Suhar, which at a three-day journey through the Wadi al-Jizzi was the closest of the known Early Islamic ports of Oman, and was moreover the largest and busiest port of eastern Arabia in this period.[14] However, some material may have been coming south from Julfār, about five days' journey along the well-watered flanks of the Hajar Mountains. The nearby site of Hulayla appeared to have constituted the focus of settlement, and more likely corresponds with the Julfar of the historical sources.[15] Islamic ceramics from Period II Hulayla were similar to those of Period III Hamasa,[16] though the scarcity of high-end Samarra classes and lack of Indian or Chinese imports is significant, and serves to preclude Julfār as a port of the Buraimi Oasis. Another coastal site worth considering is Jumeirah, about a four-day journey from the Buraimi Oasis. This large settlement was characterised by rectilinear buttressed buildings which find ready parallels with those of ᶜAwd al-Tawba and the Jimi school site in al-ᶜAin.[17] Although the finds have never been published, the selection of ceramics on display in the Dubai museum includes Buraimi cooking pots, Samarran lustrewares and Chinese stonewares, again providing close parallels with the Hamasa assemblage. While the prosperity and proximity of Suhar would logically identify it as the primary entrepôt of Hamasa, strong comparisons are available from Jumeirah, a link which echoes in the regional settlement patterns and Arabic geographical sources considered below.

Early Islamic Hamasa may further be considered in the context of regional settlement patterns. The foundation of Suhar, which may be placed on the basis of archaeological evidence in the eighth century,[18] was associated with a boom in Indian Ocean trade under the early Abbasids. Chinese ceramics first appear at Siraf, on the Persian side of the Gulf, shortly before c. 750–75 and the first reference of the voyage to China in the Arabic sources pertains to the mid-eighth century.[19] Politically, this period corresponds with the Second Ibadi Imamate (c. 793–891), when much of the present UAE and Oman was integrated into a centralised state. The peak occupation of Suhar, Hamasa, Ḥulayla and Jumeirah is generally dated to the ninth and tenth centuries on

the basis of the Samarra Horizon. This is curious given that the evidence from
Iraq and Iran suggests the Indian Ocean trade began to falter in the second
half of the ninth century. The sack of Baṣra in 871 and the Ghangzhou massacre of 878 further undermined the infrastructure of maritime trade, and
it is telling that the Abbasid state in Iraq was bankrupt by the accession of
al-Muʿtadid in 892.[20] Seth Priestman's quantified typological study of Indian
Ocean trade ceramics demonstrates a corresponding drop in regional and
exotic imports from a peak in his Ceramic Period 4 (c. 825–900) to Ceramic
Period 5 (c. 900–1025).[21] One might suggest that while net Abbasid Indian
Ocean trade was declining, the Omani share of trade was in fact growing,
with merchants moving away from troubled metropolitan markets to more
secure regional markets. As al-Muqaddasi notes, referring to the period of
Siraf's peak prosperity before the earthquake of 977, 'in the period of its
prosperity . . . Siraf and not Oman was the transit port of China'.[22] The
general conclusion is that Suhar had overtaken Siraf by the time al-Muqddasi
was writing in 985. This transition from metropolitan to regional markets
beginning in the second half of the ninth century may be associated with the
growing number and rising affluence of settlements in the Omani Peninsula,
of which Early Islamic Hamasa is a noted example.

While the decentralisation of the Abbasid Indian Ocean trade was
undoubtedly to the benefit of regional markets, the continued fragmentation
of regional states left the less powerful local successor polities exposed to
the attentions of covetous neighbours. The powerful Second Ibadi Imamate
collapsed in 893 after a period of civil war culminating in an opportunistic
Abbasid invasion, to be briefly succeeded by the Bani Sama of Tuʾam who
established themselves in Suhar as the Wajihid dynasty (fl. 898–965), only to
be repeatedly invaded by the Qaramiṭa (or Qaramatians) of al-Hasaʾ between
896 and 965, then the Buyids of Shiraz between 962 and 984.[23] The tenth
century could therefore be identified as a period of encroaching decline. As
has been suggested, the only evidence for decline at Hamasa was the poorer-
quality building materials used for repair in the later occupational phases,
while the replacement of a putative ʿarish enclosure with a mudbrick wall
may point to unsettled conditions. Yet the quality of the finds from Hamasa,
including Samarran lustrewares and Chinese stonewares found together with
quantities of fine glass vessels, and al-Muqaddasi's glowing description of

Suhar in the late tenth century, suggest that whatever decline may be read into the architecture was not precipitous.

It is significant that Hamasa, Hulayla and Jumeirah were all abandoned at broadly the same time, around the mid-eleventh century, as indicated by the presence of hatched *sgraffiato*. This fits quite neatly with the last major invasion of Oman, that of the Saljuqs of Kirman in 1063, which ushered in a Turkish occupation lasting until 1141.[24] No evidence of destruction was found at Hamasa, Hulayla or Jumeirah, however, suggesting that abandonment should be attributed to systemic developments associated with the foundation of the Saljuq empire, rather than Turkish force of arms or the fear of barbarian invaders. Priestman's study of the Indian Ocean trade ceramics points to a major drop in regional and exotic imports in his Ceramic Period 6 (c. 1025–1250), again implying that broader economic factors were at work in the decline of the Omani Peninsula.[25]

Late Islamic Period (c. 1650–1800)

The medieval centuries of the Omani Peninsula constitute something of a 'dark age' to historians and archaeologists alike. It is known that the coasts were directly subject to the Kingdom of Hormuz and the interior variously owed fealty to the Nabhani dynasty of Bahla or the Banu Jabir of al-Hasaʾ. The impact of the Portuguese was perhaps less fundamental than has sometimes been supposed. The Kingdom of Hormuz continued under new management as the Hormuz Captaincy, with a greater emphasis on taxation generally deleterious to economic growth, while Portuguese mercantile ambitions were limited to exploiting the existing 'country trade' with India and East Africa. Certainly the wealth generated by the ports does not seem to have significantly stimulated the economy of the Omani interior. Alburquerque (fl. 1507) writes of Suhar that 'the interior parts here are of the dominion of the Benjabar . . . [and] the people of the interior are called Badens [= bedouins]'.[26] The explicit reference to the bedouin deserves serious consideration, since virtually nothing from the thirteenth through to the sixteenth century has been found in over forty years of archaeological work in the oases of al-ʿAin and Buraimi, suggesting that sedentarism in the hinterland of Suhar was not at that time well advanced. The political division of the Omani Peninsula throughout this period therefore served to divorce ports from their hinterlands and worked to impede economic and social development.

Archaeological evidence indicates that permanent occupation of the Buraimi Oasis was resumed between the late seventeenth and early eighteenth centuries, a date provided by key ceramic markers and Safavid (c. 1501–1736) coins (Plate 12). Excavations at the Bayt Bin ʿAti al-Darmaki in al-ʿAin suggest that Qattara Oasis was created sometime between the late seventeenth and early eighteenth centuries. It logically follows that Qattara *falaj* providing water for the oasis was dug at this time. To what extent the other oases of al-ʿAin and Buraimi conform to this chronology is the subject of ongoing investigation. Excavations associated at Bayt Bin Hadi al-Darmaki in Hili Oasis suggest that this oasis is probably contemporary with Qattara. In comparison to the resounding lack of evidence for the medieval centuries, the sudden appearance of palm plantations and tower houses between the late seventeenth and early eighteenth centuries represents a transformation of the landscape.

Historical evidence provides a context for the changes identified in the archaeological record. The career of Nasir b. Murshid al-Yaʿrubi (r. 1625–49 CE) marks a turning point in the history and historiography of the Omani Peninsula. The Persian and English expulsion of the Portuguese from Hormuz in 1622 CE offered the Omanis an incentive to unite and similarly expel the Portuguese from their homeland. So it was that in 1624 CE the Ibadi community gathered in al-Rustaq to elect Nasir b. Murshid as their Imam, 'to govern them in the approved manner and forbid them doing unlawful things'.[27] Imam Nasir moved against both the petty kings of the Omani Peninsula, taking the Buraimi Oasis early in his reign, before ejecting the Portuguese from Suhar in 1643, with Muscat shortly thereafter falling to his cousin and successor, Imam Sultan b. Sayf, in 1650. In the words of one eighteenth-century Omani historian, the Imam Nasir 'subdued all 'Omán and reduced to obedience all its districts, purging the land of tyranny and oppression, of infidelity and rebellion, and restoring to it justice and security, and governing the people with equity and kindness until God took him to Paradise'.[28] As such, he laid the political foundation for the remarkable economic expansion of the next century.

The creation of a centralised state and unification of the Omani Peninsula was the prelude to a remarkable expansion of the Ya'rubids into the western Indian Ocean.[29] The Omani conquest of East Africa began under the Imam Sultan b. Sayf (r. 1649–79 CE) with an attack on Zanzibar in 1653 and was then followed by the fall of Mombasa in 1665. Portuguese possessions in India were repeatedly attacked, beginning with Bombay in 1655 and 1661, then Diu in 1668 and 1676. The Portuguese were not finally expelled from East Africa until 1698, under the Imam Sayf b. Sultan (r. 1682–1711 CE), by which time the Omanis had established a powerful mercantile presence in the western Indian Ocean.[30] Ceramic evidence suggests that as the eighteenth century progressed, the Buraimi Oasis enjoyed a historic peak in Indian Ocean trade. East Asian imports include Chinese blue and white as well as enamelled porcelains, Batavian Ware from Indonesia and Imari Ware from Japan, dateable to the first half of the eighteenth century. Links with the Swahili coast are borne out by similarities in the ceramic assemblage. Manganese purple wares were found at Kilwa and Manda,[31] green glazed ware at Shanga,[32] with Bahla Ware from the interior of Oman also commonly attested.[33] The Ibadi chronicles dealing with this period contain numerous references and anecdotes relating to Indian Ocean commerce. Omani, Yemeni and Hindu merchants are mentioned, and connections to the Makran, Sindh and Malabar appear to have been close.[34] The wealth generated by the dramatically expanded Omani share of the western Indian Ocean trade was invested in agricultural projects, which worked to effect environmental change and population growth in the Omani Peninsula.

Archaeological evidence shows that the eighteenth century was the peak of pre-modern occupation and agricultural expansion. A remarkably undisturbed pre-modern field system was discovered in the open plain of desert scrub linking the Buraimi Oasis proper and the Jimi and Qattara Oases, covering an area c. 440 m N/W x c. 260 m E/W. When this is taken together with the less well preserved field boundary walls to the north, it soon becomes apparent that the Buraimi Oasis proper was once considerably larger than at present, apparently over half as much again. A sheikh of the Shawamis told us that the area is known as al-Bustan, meaning garden, and said it used to be planted with wheat and before that with palms. However, the sketch plans and aerial photographs from the '50s and '60s demonstrate that the field system was abandoned beyond living memory. None of the readily

identifiable European refined white wares was noted, suggesting that occupation had ended by the mid-nineteenth century. The relatively small number
of ceramics found scattered across the surface, although not systematically
collected or quantified, were clearly dominated by eighteenth-century classes
and types. Certainly the Yaʿrubids are known to have invested heavily in
agriculture elsewhere in the Omani Peninsula, as the sources make clear:

> [The Imam Sayf b. Sultan al-Yaʿrubi] improved a large portion of Oman
> by making water-courses and planting date and other trees . . . he had
> acquired one-third of all the date-trees in Oman [over the course of his
> reign, c. 1692–1711] . . . he repaired the al-Sayighy canal at al-Rastak,
> the al-Yazily in the Dhahira, the al-Kuthir at al-Hazm, and the also the
> Barazaman and al-Misfah canals . . . [He] planted at Naʿman Barkah
> 30,000 young date-trees and 6,000 cocoa-nut trees, besides which he
> planted at Biʾr al-Nashwa, al-Rassa and al-Mandzariya.[35]

Date production in the Oasis was geared to meet more than just the
subsistence needs of the population. Percy Cox put the population at around
5,000 with some 60,000 date palms in the early twentieth century,[36] and
by 1970 J. H. Stevens put the number of date palms at 65,000 and suggested that this actually represented a decline, with date gardens having been
replaced by more profitable cultivars in the second half of the twentieth
century.[37] Moreover, all the eighteenth-century houses so far excavated contained *madabis*, date-presses that allowed dates to be dried and compacted
before storage and transport and provided *dibbs* (date-syrup) as a by-product
of the process (Plate 13). Date cultivation was very likely stimulated by the
opening of new markets as the Buraimi Oasis was incorporated into the
Indian Ocean empire of the Omani Yaʿrubid Imams. The English traveller
John Ovington, who visited Muscat in 1689, observed that 'the staple commodity of the country is dates, of which there are whole orchards for some
miles together. They have so much plenty of this fruit, for which they have
so ready a vent in India, that several ships are sent thither loaded from hence
without any other cargo.'[38] Dates may therefore have been produced for
export as part of a monetised exchange: it is perhaps significant that coins are
first found consistently and in quantity during this period.

It is highly likely that this agricultural expansion was only made possible by slave labour.[39] The same Sayf b. Sultan is credited with the final expulsion of the Portuguese from Mombassa in 1698, an event which marks the beginning of uncontested Omani rule in East Africa. Ibn Ruzayq states that he personally 'had many male and female slaves . . . he possessed seven hundred male slaves and twenty-eight ships'.[40] The connection between slaves and ships in the mind of the author perhaps suggests that these ships plied the trade in East African slaves. No figures for the number of East African slaves imported to Oman are available for the seventeenth and eighteenth century, though the situation in the first half of the nineteenth century suggests something of the scale. A British naval captain active in Zanzibar around 1811 put the annual export figure at between six and ten thousand souls,[41] while an Italian physician living in Muscat between 1809 and 1814 observed that the tax on slave imports constituted the mainstay of government revenues, with other sources suggesting that in c. 1840 fully a third of Oman's 800,000-strong population was made up of black slaves.[42] It is, moreover, clear that slaves were set to work in the date gardens. In 1902, the Rev. Samuel Zwemer wrote of the Buraimi Oasis that 'the gardens are well kept, and all the labour is done by slaves, who form, I think, at least one-half of the population'.[43] The excavation of the many sunken date palm groves and associated *aflaj* was, arguably, only made possible after the seventeenth century by the ready availability of slave labour resulting from the expansion of the Omani maritime empire.

Conclusion

The available evidence for both the Early and Late Islamic periods appears to show that in each case sedentarisation, indicated by mudbrick settlements and date palm plantations, is associated with a peak Indian Ocean trade, indicated chiefly by imported ceramics, glass and coins. This situation is not limited to the Buraimi Oasis, as Derek Kennet's recent work in the great oasis of Rustaq in the Omani Batina demonstrates.[44] It is possible to identify a western Indian Ocean 'triangle trade', in which Arabian dates and horses were exported to India in exchange for textiles, which were then traded with East Africa for slaves who were set to work in Arabian oases. The oases of Omani Peninsula are therefore comparable with the contemporary plantations in the New World, wherein maritime trade networks supplied both the means of production and the export market.

Notes

1. Power *et al.* 2015, 2016.
2. al-Tikriti 2002, pp. 119–37; 2003, pp. 16–17; 2011, pp. 126–30.
3. Power and Sheehan 2011, pp. 275–6; 2012, p. 297.
4. Power *et al.* 2015, pp. 245–6.
5. Costa and T. J. Wilkinson 1987, p. 17; *cf.* J. C. Wilkinson 1973.
6. *Kashf al-Ghumma* 1984, p. 16.
7. Rawas 1990, pp. 234–6.
8. Costa and T. J. Wilkinson 1987, p. 88.
9. Kennet 2004, pp. 88–9.
10. Wilkinson 2009, pp. 145–6.
11. Miles 1919, pp. 57–9; Hinds 1991.
12. Kervran 1999, pp. 4–5; Figs 13–16.
13. Zhang, Ran, personal communcation.
14. Wilkinson 2009; Power 2014.
15. Power 2016.
16. Kennet 1994, pp. 169–70; Sasaki 1996, Fig. 2, Plate 4.
17. Kennet 2012 , p. 194; Potts 1990, pp. 298–300; Fig. 24.
18. Kennet 2007, p. 99.
19. Power 2014, p. 46.
20. Hodges and Whitehouse 1983.
21. Priestmans 2013, Fig. 8.3, p. 405.
22. Sheriff 2010, p. 158. The text reads *kānat ḥina'dh dihlīz al-ṣīn dūn ʿumān*, which literally translates as 'at that time it was the vestibule of China and Oman [Suhar] was inferior' (al-Muqaddasī, 1906: 126). Collins' translation, 'it was at that time the point of access to China, after ʿUmān' (2001, p. 378), misses the point which Sheriff's freer translation conveys, that 'in the period of its prosperity . . . Siraf and not Oman was the transit port of China' (2010, p. 158).
23. Piacentini 2005; al-Salimi 2009.
24. Bosworth 1968, pp. 86–8.
25. Priestman 2013, Fig. 8.3, p. 405.
26. Alburquerque, i, 92.
27. Ibn Qayṣar quoted by Bathurst, 1967, p. 54.
28. al-Izkawī 1986, p. 44.
29. Cf. Bathurst 1967: 'Ch. 4: War Overseas and Territorial Expansion', pp. 111–48.
30. Cf. Bathurst 1967: 'Ch. 5: Trade and Trading Relations', pp. 149–78.

31. Kennet 2004, p. 41; Chittick 1974, p. 305, Pl. II, Pl. 114 d, e; Chittick 1984, pp. 12, 84, Pl. 36.
32. Kennet 2004, p. 43; Horton 1996, Table 14.
33. de Cardi and Doe 1971, pp. 266–7.
34. Cf. Ibn Raziq, pp. 98–9.
35. Ibn Raziq 1986, p. 93. Cf. Mershen 2001, pp. 158–9.
36. Cox 1905, p. 207.
37. Stevens 1970, p. 414.
38. Ovington 1696, p. 423.
39. Cf. Costa and T. J. Wilkinson 1987, p. 220.
40. Ibn Raziq 1986, p. 93.
41. Alpers 1967, p. 8.
42. Segal 2001, p. 146.
43. Zwemer 1902, p. 62.
44. Kennet *et al.* 2016.

Bibliography

Albuquerque, A. (1875), *The Commentaries of the Great Afonso Dalboquerque, Second Viceroy of India*. Trans. W. G. Birch. London.

Alpers, E. A. (1967), *The East African Slave Trade*. Berkeley: University of California Press.

Bathurst, R. D. (1967), 'The Yaᶜrubi Dynasty of Oman', unpublished D.Phil. thesis, University of Oxford.

Bosworth, C. E. (1968), 'The Political and Dynastic History of the Iranian World (AD 1000–1217)', in Boyle, J. A. (ed.), *The Cambridge History of Iran. Vol. 5: The Saljuq and Mongol Periods*, Cambridge: Cambridge University Press, pp. 1–202.

De Cardi, B. and D. B. Doe (1971), 'Archaeological Survey in the Northern Trucial States', *East and West* 21: 225–89.

Chittick, N. (1974), *Kilwa, An Islamic Trading City on the East African Coast*, Nairobi: British Institute in Eastern Africa.

Chittick, N. (1984), *Manda. Excavations at an Island Port on the Kenyan Coast*, Nairobi: British Institute in Eastern Africa.

Costa, P. M. and T. S. Wilkinson. (eds) (1987), 'The Hinterland of Sohar: Archaeological Surveys and Excavations Within the Region of an Omani Seafaring City', *Journal of Oman Studies* 9.

Cox, P. (1925), Some Excursions in Oman, *The Geographical Journal* 66(3): 193–221.

Hinds, M. (1991), *An Early Islamic Family from Oman: al-ʿAwtabī's Account of the Muhallabids*, Manchester: University of Manchester Press.

Hodges, R. and Whitehouse, D. (1983), *Muhammad, Charlemagne and the Origins of Europe: Archaeology and the Pirenne Thesis*, New York: Cornell University Press, pp. 123–57.

Horton, M. (1996), Shanga. *The Archaeology of a Muslim Trading Community on the Coast of East Africa*. Memoirs of the British Institute of Eastern Africa, 14. London: British Institute in Eastern Africa.

Ibn Raziq, Humayd b. Muhammad (1986), (repr.) *al-Fatḥ al-mubīn fī sīrat al-sādāh Āl Bū Saʿīdīn*. Ed. and trans. G. P. Badger. 1871. *History of the Imams and Seyyids of Oman*. London.

al-Izkawi, Sirhan b. Saʿid (1984), (repr.) *Kashf al-Ghumma*. Trans. E. C. Ross. 1874. *Annals of Oman*. Introd. P. Ward. Cambridge: Oleander Press.

Kennet, D. (1994), 'Jazirat al-Hulayla – Early Julfar', *Journal of the Royal Asiatic Society* 4(2): 163–212.

Kennet, D. (2004), *Sasanian and Islamic Pottery from Ras al-Khaimah. Classification, Chronology and Analysis of Trade in the Western Indian Ocean*, Oxford: Archaeopress.

Kennet, D., W. M. Deadman and N. S. al-Jahwari (2016), 'The Rustaq-Batinah Archaeological Survey', *Proceedings of the Seminar for Arabian Studies* 46: 155–68.

Mershen, B. (2001), 'Observations on the Archaeology and Ethnohistory of Rural Estates of the 17th Through Early 20th Centuries in Oman', *Proceedings of the Seminar for Arabian Studies* 31: 145–60.

Miles, S. B. (1919), *The Countries and Tribes of the Persian Gulf*. 2 vols. London: Harrison & Sons.

Ovington, J. (1696), *A Voyage to Suratt in the Year 1689*, London: Jacob Tomsen.

Power, T. C. (2014), 'The ʿAbbāsid Indian Ocean Trade', in Sindbæk, S. M. and Trakadas, A. (eds), *The World in the Viking Age*, Roskilde: Viking Ship Museum, pp. 46–9.

Power, T. C. (2015), 'A First Ceramic Chronology for the Late Islamic Arabian Gulf', *Journal of Islamic Archaeology* 2(1): 1–33.

Power, T. C., al-Jahwari, N. S., Sheehan, P. D. and Strutt, K. D. (2015), 'First Preliminary Report on the Buraimi Oasis Landscape Archaeology Project (BOLAP)', *Proceedings of the Seminar for Arabian Studies* 44: 233–52.

Power, T. C. and Sheehan, P. D. (2011), 'The Bayt Bin ʿĀtī in Qaṭṭāra Oasis: A Prehistoric Industrial Site and the Formation of the Oasis Landscape of al-ʿAin, UAE', *Proceedings of the Seminar for Arabian Studies* 41: 267–82.

Power, T. C. and Sheehan, P. D. (2012), 'The Origin and Development of the Oasis Landscape of al-ᶜAin (UAE)', *Proceedings of the Seminar for Arabian Studies* 42: 1–18.

Power, T. C. and Sheehan, P. D. (2015), 'The Oasis Landscape of al-Ain and Buraimi', *Bulletin of the British Foundation for the Study of Arabia* 20: 43–4.

Rawas, I. A. A. (1990), 'Early Islamic Oman (ca. 622/280–893): A Political History', doctoral thesis, Durham University, <http://etheses.dur.ac.uk/1497/>

Sasaki, T. (1996), 'Umayyad and Abbasid Finds from the 1994 Excavations at Jazirat al-Hulayla', *Bulletin of Archaeology (The University of Kanazawa)* 23: 179–222.

Segal, R. (2002), *Islam's Black Slaves*. London: Atlantic Books.

Sheriff, A. (2010), *Dhow Cultures of the Indian Ocean: Cosmopolitanism, Commerce and Islam*, London: Hurst.

Stevens, J. H. (1970), 'Changing Agricultural Practice in an Arabian Oasis', *The Geographical Journal* 136(3): 410–18.

Strutt, K. D., Power, T. C. al-Jahwari, N. S. and Sheehan, P. D. (2014), 'Archaeological Survey at Buraymī Oasis, Oman. An Integrated Strategy for Geophysics, Surface Collection and Test Pitting', *The Newsletter of the International Society for Archaeological Prospection* 40: 4–8.

al-Tikriti, W. Y. (2002), 'The Southeast Arabian Origin of the Falaj System', *Proceedings of the Seminar for Arabian Studies* 32: 117–38.

al-Tikriti, W. Y. (2003), 'An Early Islamic Falaj from al-Ain, UAE', *Bulletin of the Society for Arabian Studies* 8: 11–19.

al-Tikriti, W. Y. (2011), *Archaeology of the Falaj. A Field Study of the Ancient Irrigation Systems of the United Arab Emirates*, Abu Dhabi: Tourism and Culture Authority.

Wilkinson, J. C. (2009), 'Omani Maritime Trade in the Early Islamic Period', in A. M. El Reyes (ed.), *New Perspectives on Recording UAE History*, Abu Dhabi: National Archive, pp. 145–54.

Zwemer, S. M. (1902), 'Three Journeys in Northern Oman', *The Geographical Journal* 19: n 1: 54–64.

PART V
RECENT GULF ARCHAEOLOGY

13

PEARL FISHING AND GLOBALISATION: FROM THE NEOLITHIC TO THE TWENTIETH CENTURY CE

Robert Carter

Introduction

In this chapter I will outline the ancient origins of the pearl fishery of the Arabian Gulf over seven thousand years ago, and will trace the progressive, albeit interrupted, expansion of its markets through time to encompass a truly global scale during the period from the eighteenth to the twentieth century CE. Following a brief pre-historical and historical overview, this chapter will focus on how pearls played a formative role in the creation of the Gulf that we see today, drawing the Gulf and its people into the wider world of communication, consumption and globalisation. From the eighteenth century, the pearl fishery shaped the Gulf's settlement pattern, urban landscape, politics, demography and societies. As well as historical sources, I will employ archaeological data and geographical techniques, focusing on two case studies: Doha (Qatar) and Muharraq (Bahrain).

Pearl fishing and the pearl trade of the gulf before the eighteenth century CE

Early Evidence for Pearl Fishing in the Gulf, Sixth to First Millennia BCE

It is impossible to give a detailed summary of the development of the Gulf's pearl fishery in the space of a single chapter, for which other publications must be used (e.g. al-Shamlan 2000; Carter 2012). Instead, I will briefly examine the consumption of pearls locally and in distant markets, from the Neolithic onwards, focusing on the observable spread of the distribution of Gulf pearls through the world, and knowledge of their source, over the last seven and a half thousand years.

The earliest evidence comes from the sixth millennium BCE, when pearl jewellery is found relatively frequently at human burial sites, both coastal and inland, along with collections of pearls and single finds at coastal settlements along the Arabian shore and Oman (Carter 2005; Charpentier *et al.* 2012). The burial sites clearly indicate that they were valued by local Neolithic populations, and it can be inferred that pearls were also traded into Iraq. At this time (6th–5th millennia BCE), a remarkable maritime trading relationship existed between the coastal Neolithic populations and the village communities of southern Iraq, manifested by the export of painted ceramics to the Gulf (Carter 2006). Possibly, pearls were one of the items traded into Iraq in exchange for the pottery, perhaps among other goods (Oates *et al.* 1977: 233; Uerpmann and Uerpmann 1996: 135; Masry 1997: 133; Carter 2010: 199; Kallweit 2003: 61). The presence of intensive shell jewellery manufacture (mainly of disc beads) at several of the coastal sites implies that pearls may have been part of a broader package of shell jewellery products intended both for local use and export (Carter 2010). Although still speculative, owing to the paucity of evidence for pearl and shell jewellery finds in their purported destination in Iraq, here we have the first stage in our expanding global cartography of pearls. At the very least, we are certain that they were fished and used locally by the Neolithic communities of eastern Arabia and Oman.

Evidence is sparser for the succeeding three millennia, though sufficient data exist to indicate continuing exploitation during the fourth, third and second millennia BCE, with rare finds of pearls from Bahrain, Oman, southern Iraq and Kuwait (Carter 2012: 5–8). It is not until the middle of the first millennium BCE that we see large quantities of pearls reappearing, with hundreds found in a hoard and elite burial in Achaemenid Iran, and smaller quantities known from the Assyrian world and the Gulf itself (Carter 2012: 9–10). It is most likely that all these pearls originated from the Gulf, which then had direct connections with the two regions, though connections with the pearl-producing areas of the Red Sea and India/Sri Lanka cannot be ruled out.

Trade in Gulf Pearls during the Classical and Late Antique Period

By the time of Alexander and his successors, the pearl riches of the Gulf were well-known to the Greeks, albeit initially conflated by the Greek writer Theophrastus with the Red Sea fishery. The Romans were well aware of the distinction between the Gulf, Red Sea and the Indian/Sri Lankan fisheries, and the first clearly identifiable localities of pearl fishing were named by Pliny: Bahrain, then known as Tylos; and a fishery off the Persian shore, Stoidis, which had been alluded to but not named by earlier Greek authors (Rackham 1942: 449; Carter 2012: 11–14). Abundant archaeological and historical evidence indicates that the Gulf was fully integrated into Roman and Late Antique maritime trading networks which connected Arabia and India to the Red Sea, and thence Egypt and the Mediterranean, as well as the overland route through Iraq and Syria to Anatolia and the Mediterranean via the kingdom of Charax (in southern Iraq, also known as the kingdom of Mesene) and Palmyra (Heldaas Seland 2011). We learn from the *Periplus of the Erythraean Sea* that pearls were exported from the Gulf to India (Casson 1989). During this time pearls became highly fashionable and much desired throughout the Roman world, worn by elites and middle classes alike, and eliciting disapproving comments from numerous authors, including Pliny, who equated them with wastefulness and vanity (Eichholz 1962: 173; Carter 2012: 16).

This phase indicates the first major extension of the market for Gulf pearls to the Mediterranean and Western Europe. The Roman craze for pearls, and the appearance of abundant Roman glassware in the settlements and graves of eastern Arabia, prefigure the much later pulse of globalisation and commodity exchange that linked the Gulf to the West in the early modern era.

The Iranian markets were also potentially huge during the Roman and Late Antique periods. Although we know little of Parthian consumption of pearls, the Sasanian monarchs gloried in pearls and are depicted wearing great pearls in their ears. We learn that a Sasanian monarch commissioned a Christian bishop of the Church of the East to lead a successful pearling expedition in the Gulf, and that pearling centres included Mashmahij, now the village of Samahij on the island of Muharraq in Bahrain, and Rishahr, on the Bushehr Peninsula (Beaucamp and Robin 1983; Carter 2012: 23). Records of the Church of the East add details about the conduct of the Christian pearl fishers of the Gulf, including an injunction from the year 585 CE, just a few decades before the coming of Islam to the region, urging pearl fishers not to work on Sundays unless compelled to do so (Chabot 1902: 448; Carter 2012: 22–5).

Pearl Fishing and Markets during the Early Islamic and Medieval Period

The coming of Islam did not appear to disrupt the fishery, or quell the international taste for pearls. Although pearl finds are relatively rare in the Islamic world (not being included in burials, and there being no Islamic equivalent to the elaborate pearl-encrusted religious vestments that characterised the medieval Christian world), the literary sources are exceedingly rich, particularly from the Abbasid period onwards. Scholars such as Al-Mas'udi, Al-Biruni and Al-Idrisi, and many successors, meticulously list the pearl fisheries of the world, often dwelling on those in the Gulf and singling out the fisheries of Bahrain and Qatar as the finest (Carter 2012: 38–45). A huge amount of detail is provided on the technology of fishing, the types and value of pearls and the markets, particularly by Al-Biruni. Also important are the poems and stories surrounding the pearls of the Islamic world and their courts; famous pearls had names, and their own stories and legends (Shalem 1997; Carter 2012: 36–7).

Western markets consumed pearls during the early and medieval Islamic period, and both Christian and Muslim courts in the Mediterranean used pearls as an elite signifier of luxury and status (Grabar 2006; Carter 2012: 52). Pearls coming to the Mediterranean via Egypt and Palestine might have combined the products of the Gulf, India/Sri Lanka and the Red Sea, the latter fisheries being less productive than the Gulf but nonetheless significant; it is not possible in most historical sources to distinguish Gulf pearls from those from the Indian and Red Sea fisheries, and neither can they be distinguished in the jewellery of the time (Carter 2012: 53–8). Nonetheless, by the thirteenth century we are aware of at least two partly overland routes that carried pearls from the Gulf, originating in the rival trading centres of Qays and Hormuz, crossing Iran to Tabriz and Trabzon on the Black Sea, and then passing by sea to Genoa and Venice respectively (Piacentini 2004; Piacentini and Maestri 2009). At various times between the tenth and fourteenth centuries, Bahrain, Qatif, Kharg, Julfar, Siraf, Qays and Baghdad, among others, were named as regional pearling centres and pearl markets (Carter 2012: 38–53).

Additionally, by this time the Chinese had become aware of the Gulf's pearls, perhaps owing to trading connections initially forged by the maritime merchants of the Persian port of Siraf. These merchants transferred themselves and their knowledge to Qays and Hormuz after the demise of Siraf in an earthquake. Various Chinese accounts of the tenth to thirteenth centuries refer to pearls from the Middle East and Gulf region, including Chau Ju-Kua (Zhao Rugua), a thirteenth-century customs inspector of Guangzhou (Canton), who cites a twelfth-century source to reveal detailed knowledge of the Gulf fisheries; and Ch'ang Te, an envoy dispatched to Fars in the mid-thirteenth century. Chau Ju-Kua notes that the best pearls come from islands in the land of the Ta-Shi (Arabs), specifically mentioning the pearl fisheries of Qays and Oman (which traditionally included the Arabian shore of the lower Gulf), while Ch'ang Te speaks of the pearls of Shiraz, that is, Fars, bordering the Gulf. Both give accounts of fishing methods that include both realistic details and fantastical elements. Significantly, Chau Ju-Kua mentions the presence of foreign traders bringing concealed pearls into China, in order to evade duties (Carter 2012: 58; Hirth and Rockhill 1911; Bretschneider 1888). The reach of the Gulf's pearls now extended from Western Europe to China.

Pearl Fishing during the Age of European Colonial Expansion, Sixteenth–Seventeenth Century CE

The next major alteration in the configuration of global markets occurred with the arrival of the Portuguese in the Gulf, ushering in the beginning of the modern age of globalisation, as well as the opening of rival New World sources of pearls, and in later centuries, lucrative North American markets. Even before their arrival, the Portuguese were well informed about the centres of the Gulf fishery, particularly Bahrain, which they specifically targeted for its pearl revenues, and which they recognised from the beginning as the source of the finest pearls (Carter 2012: 70, 77). Throughout their period of hegemony their attentions focused on Hormuz, Bahrain and Julfār, but they also collected pearling taxes from lesser centres, including Qatif, Qatar and a series of ports on the Persian shore (Aubin 1973; Fernandes 2009; Carter 2012: 69–74). Even after they had been expelled from their bases in the Gulf and Oman, the Portuguese still retained enough maritime power to make agreements with the Persian authorities to collect customs dues and boat taxes, well into the eighteenth century (Carter 2012: 72–3).

Subsequent European interests in the pearl fishery were shown by rival colonial powers, namely the Dutch and the English. Dutch missions were sent in the mid-seventeenth century to explore the value of the fishery in Bahrain and Bandar-e Kung (which briefly emerged as the Gulf's main pearl market), and in 1754 the Dutch East India Company (VOC) considered invading Bahrain in order to appropriate its pearling revenues (Floor 1982; Floor 1984). Having decided against this, the VOC's resident attempted unsuccessfully to launch his own fishery around the island of Kharg (Floor 1982).

It is possible that the Gulf fishery was depressed between the sixteenth and seventeenth centuries, with the Portuguese registering declining revenues, perhaps as a result of their taxation but also because of the discovery of extremely productive fisheries in the New World, particularly Venezuela (Carter 2012: 76, 84–6). The latter were quickly fished out, however, perhaps because of the use of dredges, and by the end of the seventeenth century a powerful demand for pearls existed throughout the Western world as well as the New World, with attention once again focused on the ancient and still productive fisheries of the Gulf and India/Sri Lanka.

The main centre for the international pearl trade under the Portuguese was Goa, which pooled the products of the Gulf and Indian/Sri Lankan fisheries, fulfilling a role taken later by Surat under the British during the seventeenth century, itself superseded after 1686 by Bombay. Shorter-lived local pearl markets came and went in the Gulf and Oman, including Bandar-e Kung (important as the Gulf's main clearing centre in the seventeenth century, when it relegated Bahrain to seasonal importance), Muscat (significant in the late 17th century, and again in the 19th) and Kangan (briefly important in the early 18th century). In the meantime, the ancient pearl market in Basra retained importance, presumably for pearls passing directly into the Ottoman domains, while other pearls passed through Persia to central Asia and Russia (Carter 2012: 99, 105–6). Little is known of the southeast Asian and Far Eastern pearl markets at this time, for which further research in the Portuguese, Dutch and local sources is required.

Global Markets and Consumption in the Gulf in the Eighteenth–Twentieth Centuries

The final stage of pearl market expansion and pre-oil globalisation in the Gulf spans the eighteenth to early twentieth centuries CE. During this time demand expanded hugely in the Americas (especially in the new market of the USA) and in Europe, as the industrialised and industrialising West generated new wealth, new commodities and new middle classes with a voracious appetite for consumption. Demand-led price rises stimulated a pearling boom in the Gulf, comprising a dramatic intensification of pearl fishing, unprecedented demographic movement to the coast, and a wholesale and permanent rearrangement of the settlement pattern and the political configuration of the entire region. While demographic growth and increased revenues became most intensive between c. 1890 and 1912, the archaeological and historical economic data combine to show a longer process of growth going back to the early eighteenth century CE.

As the pearling boom began to peak in the late nineteenth century, the pearl-producing economy of the Gulf became increasingly directly linked to major Western economies and patterns of global commodity exchange. Both the archaeological and economic records demonstrate that international goods entered local Gulf markets and material culture and consumption was directly and responsively linked to revenues from the pearling industry. This process was part of a wider pattern of globalisation which is well known to historians of the nineteenth and twentieth centuries, but has not yet been described in detail for the Gulf region.

New Foundations: the Birth of the Gulf Towns

The most prominent consequence of the pearling boom can be found in the very existence of Gulf towns and cities of today. Previous research has noted the foundation of a series of new pearl-fishing settlements during the eighteenth and early nineteenth centuries (Carter 2005, 2009, 2012). Historical, cartographic and archaeological sources show numerous new towns and villages (Figure 13.1) appearing in Qatar, most notably Zubara, Doha and Wakra, but also Freiha, Ruwaidha, Yusufiyya (possibly the same as Ruwaidha), Jumail, Khor Hassan, Fuwairit, Abu Dhuluf, Ruwais, Al-Khor, Sumaisma and others. The same is seen in Bahrain, chiefly Muharraq, at some point joined by Busaiteen, Hidd, Galali and others, with Budaiya founded around 1850; and in the UAE (Abu Dhabi, Dubai, Ajman, Sharjah, Umm al-Qaiwain, Jazirat Al-Hamra, with Al-Khan, Hamriyah and others also appearing at some point). In Saudi Arabia, older pearling centres expanded (e.g. Darin and other sites on Tarut island, Qatif), while Kuwait also saw

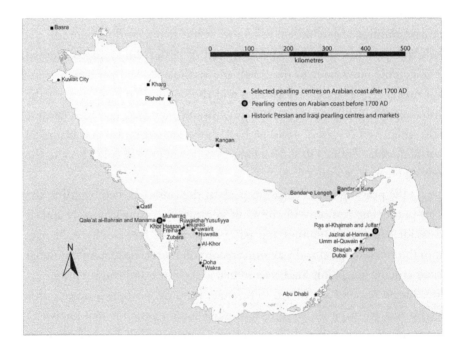

Figure 13.1 Pearl fishing settlements in the Gulf. Source: Robert Carter.

dramatic change, expanding from a tiny overland caravan station known as Qurayn to being the biggest city in the Gulf. Without exception, these new towns were founded and populated by people seeking to exploit the pearl banks of the Gulf, though some went on to develop additional major trading interests (most notably Kuwait, Zubara, Sharjah and eventually Dubai).

This new settlement pattern was in marked contrast to previous configurations on the Arabian littoral, which usually saw a very small number of permanent population centres located in agricultural areas. Since the advent of Islam these included the city of Julfār (succeeded during the 16th century by Ras Al-Khaimah, just a few kilometres away); an urban centre in Bahrain (namely, Qala'at al-Bahrain since the Bronze Age, followed by a possible town at Muharraq during the Early Islamic period, then Bilad Al-Qadim from the 9th century CE, then Qala'at Al-Bahrain again from around the 13th century, then Manama from the 16th century); and Qatif (sporadically). These places also specialised in pearl fishing, but they would not have existed as permanent settlements without their plentiful sweet water, good soils and agricultural potential. Productive pearl fishing required significant manpower, and this was provided by the agricultural hinterland that supported these towns. There was no question that pearl fishers from these towns and similar centres on the Persian shore created temporary settlements in arid areas of coastline during the pearling season (see e.g. the 16th-century testimony of Balbi), and in all likelihood fishers, bedouin and traders were familiar with, passed through and exploited the coasts and islands for centuries. This is amply borne out by the archaeological record showing small sites and campsite-like remains in almost all periods from the Neolithic onwards (Carter 2009: 270–3; 2005: 146, 168–78; 2012: 82).

Following the start of the eighteenth century a clear change occurs. Arid areas with extremely limited agricultural potential began to host large and permanent population centres, including the Qatari shore, large stretches of the coast of the UAE, and Kuwait. From this we can conclude that the revenues derived from pearl fishing had reached a point at which the low carrying capacity of the land could be overridden. The inhabitants of these towns were able to use their revenues from the pearl fishery to purchase imported food (mainly from India, Iraq and Iran), and even drinking water from relatively distant sources (bought from the Shatt Al-Arab in the case of

Kuwait, and from Dalma island in the case of Abu Dhabi). Moreover, almost the entire population of most of these towns was entirely reliant on the cash economy generated by pearls: other sources of income generation were extremely limited in all but a handful of places, and even those employed in handicrafts and service industries relied on a customer base and cash economy almost entirely generated by the pearl fishery.

It is almost impossible to underestimate the reliance of the Gulf towns on the global trade in pearls, even in the case of those with alternative sources of revenue. According to Lorimer's early twentieth-century survey of the Gulf pearl fishery:

> were the supply of pearls to fail, the trade of Kuwait would be severely crip-
> pled, while that of Bahrain might – it is estimated – be reduced to about
> one-fifth of its present dimensions and the ports of Trucial 'Oman, which
> have no other resources, would practically cease to exist; in other words, the
> purchasing power of the inhabitants of the eastern coast of Arabia depends
> very largely upon the pearl fisheries. (Lorimer 1915: 2,220)

Partial exceptions to this dependence on pearls can be found in Bahrain (where the agricultural sector remained important, as well as maritime trade in commodities, although both were dwarfed by pearling revenues); Kuwait (where boat building and maritime trade provided about half the city's revenues); Ras Al-Khaimah (which also retained an important agricultural hinterland); and Dubai (which remained a very major pearling centre but took on a role as a trading hub during the early 20th century).

Value of the Pearl Fishery

Statistical data on the value of the fishery were gathered sporadically by foreign observers up to 1873, and then annually by the British authorities until the mid-twentieth century (Figure 13.2). Notwithstanding short-term collapses in the 1770s–80s and 1830s, these show an overall trend of growth starting in the eighteenth century (between 1723 and 1770 the value more than doubled) which continued to the 1870s (nearly doubling again between 1770 and 1885), followed by an explosive increase starting in the 1880s that peaked in 1912 (with an eighteenfold increase in value between 1882 and 1912). The figures given here are for Bahrain only (the best-documented

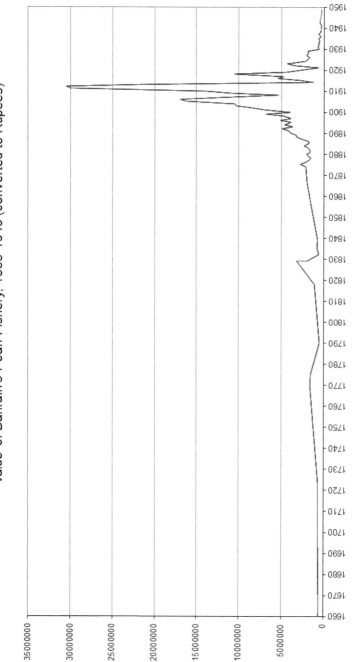

Figure 13.2 Pearling revenues in Bahrain, 1663–1949. For data sources and conversion rates see Carter 2012: 309. Source: Robert Carter.

fishery), but abundant other data indicate that they are indicative of the pattern throughout the Gulf towns.

The regional economic boom, and its consequent impact on settlement, was driven by international demand for pearls. Although the Western markets had always been important, as outlined above, and Indian markets had always provided a major outlet closer to the Gulf, a series of remarkable price rises began in the mid-nineteenth century, fuelled by the rise of wealthy middle classes in the industrial and industrialising West. According to Lorimer's account, the rate for each class of pearl doubled between 1852/3 and 1877/8, and more than doubled again between then and 1905 (Lorimer 1915, Appendix C: 2,239), while in the British Administration's Trade Report of 1911–12 it was stated that pearls sold 'for several times, even up to 10 times what they did a few years ago' (Anonymous 1987, Vol. 3, 1911–12: 6). At the time it was believed that up to 80 per cent of the world's fine pearls originated from the Gulf, a figure supported by modern calculations (Carter 2012: 179–80), and there is no question that these local price rises were predicated upon Western demand. The harvest of pearls was estimated at 40–50 million from the Gulf annually (Rosenthal 1984: 65), and nearly all travelled to Bombay, where major European (particularly French and British) and American pearl merchants and their agents scouted for the highest-quality pearls to take back home. In time, these foreign merchants, including Jacques Cartier, attempted to cut out intermediaries in Bombay by travelling directly to Bahrain and the other Gulf ports, to buy directly from the local Arab and Indian merchants (Carter 2012: 165–71).

The Expansion of the Gulf Towns

The rush of new foundations had largely halted by the late nineteenth century, but the new pearling towns continued to expand in size and population under the influence of the pearling boom. Some still appear to have been growing as late as the 1920s, including Doha and Muharraq, which we here examine as case studies.

In Muharraq, Bahrain a series of stages can be detected in the growth rings of the city. Abdullah Al-Sulaiti's analyses of architecture, mosque foundation dates and local and foreign (mainly British) historical sources and maps showed how the town grew outwards from two cores following its foundation in the early nineteenth century, the cores being located in the later town centre and to the south at Halat Bu Maher (Al-Sulaiti 2009: 133–6, Map 4.6). By 1851 these two cores had expanded significantly but had not joined, and a third core had been added in the north-west (Plate 16). By 1891, significant further expansion had occurred and the central and north-western cores had joined together. The gap between the main town and the southern core had narrowed considerably but not closed completely.

The town had not completely finished expanding in 1891, and on a more localised level, the final stages of growth are demonstrated by architectural studies conducted by Yarwood in the Suq Qayseriyyah sector of Muharraq (Yarwood 1988: 204; 2005), and by excavations in the same area, directed by this author (Carter and Naranjo-Santana 2010; Carter and Naranjo-Santana 2011). Having run out of land along its all-important coastal strip, Muharraq very literally expanded into the sea during the late nineteenth and early twentieth centuries, with near-continuous land reclamation creating a zone of ever-advancing coastal warehouses. Yarwood showed how four phases of expansion extended Muharraq's shoreline between the late nineteenth century and 1940, the first three of which precede 1925 (Yarwood 1988: 204).

While Muharraq's repeated and rapid phases of expansion up to 1930 clearly indicate how the town responded at the peak of the pearling boom, other economic forces were also at work in Bahrain: the final phase of extension (in the 1930s) actually occurred after the collapse of the pearling revenues, and illustrate Bahrain's developing role as a transhipment hub and centre of the British administration in the Gulf, and perhaps the early impact of oil concession revenues. Although the hardship caused by the collapse of the pearl market was very serious (particularly during the war years, when starvation occurred), indications were already being given of how Bahrain's engagement with global trading networks offered a degree of relief in some quarters, and of how oil would eventually come to rescue the local economy.

Doha, Qatar, also reveals a pattern of expansion, albeit differently configured because of local geography. Doha was a smaller and arguably more isolated town than Muharraq, with almost no expatriate population or visitors apart from an isolated garrison of Ottoman troops from the 1870s. There was also a population of enslaved Africans. The few resident British subjects (Indian merchants) were expelled in the 1880s. Although it was less visited

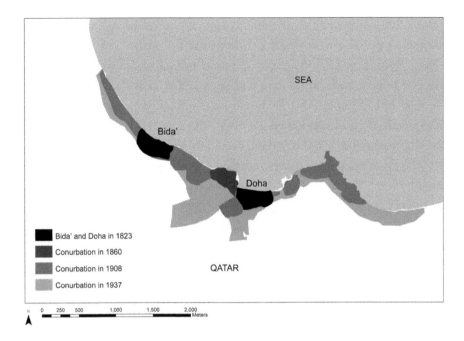

Figure 13.3 Expansion of Doha, 1823–1937. Source: Robert Carter; mapping by Richard Fletcher.

by outsiders, and thus possessed limited historical and mapping data, it is possible to trace its growth through an examination of British naval charts from 1823 and 1860, combined with a brief description and photographs of 1904 by a rare visitor (Burchardt), and by cross-referencing Lorimer's relatively detailed written account of Doha and its historical districts (*firjan*, s. *farij*) with the first aerial imagery and detailed maps from the 1930s (Figure 13.3). Excavation in central Doha and today's Msheireb district adds to our knowledge of the town's growth.[1]

The results show that two small cores existed in the 1820s (originally separately known as Bida' and Doha), which had started to grow together by 1860, with an extension of the eastern core (Dohat As-Saghira, later Dowaiha, and eventually known as Jasra). There was complete destruction of the whole conurbation in 1867 (a devastating joint raid by Bahrain and Abu Dhabi), rapidly followed by resettlement but subsequent depopulation in the 1880s due to instability and warfare with Abu Dhabi. Permanent recovery began in the 1890s, with both archaeological evidence[2] and historical data

(Burchardt, Lorimer, and sporadic reports on population size) indicating a dramatic extension of Doha along c. 4 km of the seashore before the end of the first decade of the twentieth century. This is despite a temporary abandonment in Spring 1893 owing to hostilities with the Turkish garrison (Tuson 1991: 363; Anonymous 1986, 1893/1894: 8). Further growth then ensued, but had halted some time before 1937, after which only decline and decay took place before the advent of significant oil revenues in 1950.

Notwithstanding certain differences in local economic contexts, and different histories of settlement and resettlement, both Muharraq and Doha exhibit similar patterns of urban and demographic growth, namely foundation in the early nineteenth century followed by expansion (interrupted in the case of Doha), which sharply accelerated towards the end of the nineteenth century in step with the dramatic increase in pearling revenues inferred from the economic data.

Moreover, as noted in previous publications, the foundation and florescence of new pearling towns in the eighteenth–nineteenth centuries was accompanied by a significant intensification of activities in the coastal and islands regions of the Gulf, visible archaeologically as an increase in seasonal and permanent village settlements and campsites (Carter 2009: 272–3; 2005: 169–78). The people who fuelled this coastal urban and rural growth on the Arabian shores migrated from all regions bordering the Gulf, particularly inner Arabia (Nejd) and the Persian coast; but also Oman, Iraq, India, Baluchistan, Dhofar, Yemen and East Africa (Carter 2012: 110, 159). Many were enslaved and brought to man the pearl fishery and serve the households of the wealthier members of local society, but many came freely to profit from the industry, often in mass migrations of families and tribal Arab groups.

Global Commodities in Pearling Towns

A clear demonstration of the local impact of increased revenues and intensified engagement with global networks can be found in the material culture recovered from archaeological excavation and survey. The excavated data from Doha reveal the changing degree of engagement with wider networks of trade and consumption, through the quantification of items imported from distant areas, across successive phases of the site. Ceramics are usually used for this purpose, but other classes of artefact can be equally revealing (e.g. glassware, construction materials). This approach provides tangible and quantifiable evidence of trading patterns which complements the historical data, and reveals patterns of behaviour and consumption that are almost absent from the historical sources.

The most notable change in Manama and Doha is a marked increase in the quantity of decorated European and Far Eastern ceramics. These include mass-produced semi-porcelain bowls and dishes, mainly from the Maastricht potteries but also from the UK, bearing either transfer-printed decoration in a limited range of standardised patterns or painted and sponge-printed decoration, also in a restricted range of patterns (Plate 14). Both the shapes and decoration indicate standardised and well-understood local requirements and tastes, and some patterns clearly show the deliberate targeting of local markets in the distant places of manufacture (e.g. a common type of large dish with a moon-and-star motif). In addition to these products, small fluted porcelain coffee cups become extremely common, again in a highly restricted range of styles, and some with Arabic mottoes, again indicating the targeting of local markets (Plate 15, right side). The origin of these is still uncertain, but Japan is a leading contender. Other porcelains (Plate 15, left side) largely originate from China, including low- and medium-quality blue-and-white wares from the Jingdezhen kilns and Dehua, being the tail end of a much longer tradition of imported Chinese ceramics, as well as polychrome wares. In addition, Japanese imports of bowls and dishes, some imitating earlier European designs, appear to become increasingly common during and after the 1920s (Plate 14, left side, no. 18; and also Plate 15, left side, no. 21, which bears an identifying stamp, and perhaps no. 16).

These wares may have begun to be imported as early as the 1870s (Sundblad 2011), but the clearest evidence for their occurrence at Doha and Muharraq comes from the 1890s onwards. Work on the finds from the Doha excavation is still in progress, but the emerging pattern indicates that the quantity of these 'global ceramics' increased dramatically from that time until the 1930s, rising from c. 4.5 per cent of the ceramic assemblage in pre-1890s levels to c. 10 per cent around the 1890s, to c. 32 per cent of the assemblage during the first two or three decades of the twentieth century.[3]

This rise marches just out of step with (and is slightly later than) the very high spike in pearling revenues seen in Bahrain between the 1880s and 1920s.

The slightly later pattern is to be expected from the nature of archaeological evidence: ceramics are discarded and enter the archaeological record some time after they are purchased. Remarkably, the economic data from Bahrain show that import levels of 'Chinaware' and porcelain (and by inference local demand and purchase) also track pearling revenues very closely, often with a lag of one or two years (Figure 13.4). These figures indicate how intimately Bahrain and the region's consumption of global trade goods was linked to the annual value of the pearl fishery.

Preliminary examination of other artefacts from the Doha excavation, especially glass and metalwork, supports the data gathered from the ceramics. This link between consumption and the booming fishery was noted by outside observers. A report of 1910 by the British Agent in Bahrain, Mackenzie (Burdett 1995: 83), drew attention to observable changes in consumption, specifically luxury goods among the wealthy classes:

> The increased use of luxuries during the last few years has been noticeable in the town of Manama and among the richer inhabitants of Bahrein, no doubt consequent upon their visiting Bombay in connection with pearl transactions. Among the poorer classes no such symptoms are visible (except perhaps as regards food).

Our archaeological investigations imply that the poorer classes were also participating in these changes by enriching their range and quantity of domestic possessions, a phenomenon which Mackenzie probably would not have observed. His comments about changes in food consumption, however, may eventually be supported (or otherwise) by ongoing work on the dietary evidence from the Doha excavation (faunal and fish bones, and botanical remains).

Conclusions

Although Western demand had been highly significant since Classical times, a qualitative and quantitative change took place during and after the eighteenth century, whereby Western markets became increasingly significant, and the Gulf region became progressively more integrated into global patterns of exchange and consumption. This process accelerated

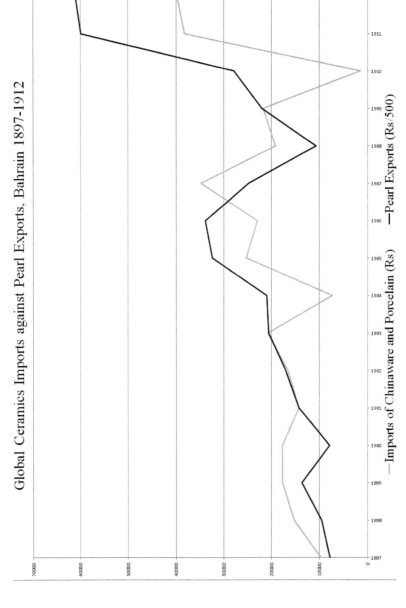

Figure 13.4 Value of ceramics imports in Bahrain against value of pearl exports (scaled to Rs/500). Source: Robert Carter.

and peaked during the last two decades of the nineteenth century and the first two decades of the twentieth (disrupted by the First World War), during which time the Western craze for pearls led to dizzying annual price increases and a corresponding spike in revenues throughout the Gulf region.

The pearl fishers themselves are generally considered to have benefited little from this boom, remaining impoverished and burdened by perennial debt, but the economic data and emerging archaeological record present a more complex picture of consumption and engagement with global commodity markets. Alongside the eighteenth- to nineteenth-century changes in settlement patterns and demographic movement to the coast, accompanied by the narrow specialisation of the productive economy, we can discern ongoing and accelerating impacts relating to late nineteenth- to early twentieth-century globalisation processes, manifested in the further expansion of the towns, and changes in material culture and consumption patterns.

The assumption that the towns in the Gulf were remote and isolated in the pre-oil era can therefore be shown to be false in several respects. Even the smaller and more inward-looking communities were engaged with global patterns of consumption, and pearls tied them intimately to global economic developments. It should be stressed, however, that although pearl fishing provided the regionally specific economic base that connected Gulf communities to the wider world, and although the choice and consumption of foreign goods were driven by very specific local needs and social mores, other communities in other parts of the world were experiencing similar developments, and consuming similar or identical trade wares. A close analogy can be found in the clove plantations of Zanzibar, connected to the Gulf through the Omani empire, where identical ceramics were used by plantation employees and slaves (Croucher 2011), apparently in similar commensal settings, and carrying similar values and meanings despite the distant locations, origins and circumstances of the consumer societies. To an extent, these similarities can be explained by the inclusion of Zanzibar in the political and cultural orbit of Oman, but it is also notable that the archaeological evidence from Zanzibar shows an increase in the occurrence of these global ceramics in the early twentieth century, comparable to the situation in Doha and Muharraq. Globalisation by its very nature incorporates broad, international and interlinked patterns of exchange and consumption, and rising demand for pearls from the Gulf was most likely matched by rising demand for cloves, while both areas were equally receptive to the manufactured goods of Europe and East Asia.

Finally, I note that the late nineteenth-/early twentieth-century peak outlined above is the culmination of an exceedingly long process of integration. Although it is not wholly appropriate to speak of globalisation as early as the sixth millennium BCE, and although the process was sometimes interrupted and reversed, the extent of the networks reaching into and out of the Gulf grew incrementally over a period of 7,000 years, a process we can clearly trace through a lens provided by the Gulf's pearl fishery. Although truly world-spanning networks may be relatively recent, the roots of globalisation are not.

Notes

1. This historical mapping work has mainly been undertaken by Dr Richard Fletcher of the *Origins of Doha and Qatar Project*, a QNRF-funded project directed by the author. This research was made possible by NPRP grant no. 5-421-6-010 from the Qatar National Research Fund (a member of Qatar Foundation). The statements made herein are solely the responsibility of the authors. The excavation was undertaken in partnership with Qatar Museums (QM).
2. Excavations took place in central Doha in December 2013 and February 2014. These were undertaken as a partnership between UCL Qatar and Qatar Museums (QM), as the Joint Qatar Museums-UCL Qatar Old Doha Rescue Excavation, co-directed by Dr Robert Carter and Dr Ferhan Sakal.
3. The assemblage from the Muharraq excavations are small, so the data from Doha are used here, specifically those from Area D, comprising around half of the total excavated material. Material from the other trenches in Doha, and analysis of overall site patterns, will be presented in future publications.

Bibliography

al-Shamlan, S. M. (2000), *Pearling in the Arabian Gulf: A Kuwaiti Memoir*. Trans. Peter Clarke, London: London Centre for Arab Studies.

Anonymous (1986), *The Persian Gulf Administration Reports. 1873–1947*, Cambridge: Archive Editions.

Anonymous (1987), *The Persian Gulf Trade Reports, 1905–1940*, Cambridge: Archive Editions.

Aubin, J. (1973), Le Royaume d'Ormuz au Début du VXIe Siècle, *Mare Luso-Indicum*, 2: 77–179.

Beaucamp, J. and C. Robin (1983), L'Évêché Nestorien de Mâšmahîg dans l'Archipel d'al-Bahrayn, in Potts, D. T. (ed.), *Dilmun: New Studies in the Archaeology and Early History of Bahrain*, Berlin: Dietrich Reimer Verlag.

Bretschneider, E. (1888), *Mediaeval Researches from Eastern Asiatic Sources*, London: Kegan Paul.

Burdett, A. (1995), *Records of the Persian Gulf Pearl Fisheries 1857–1962, Vol. 2*, Farnham Common: Archive Editions.

Carter, R. A. (2005), 'The History and Prehistory of Pearling in the Persian Gulf', *Journal of the Economic and Social History of the Orient*, 48(2): 139–209.

Carter, R. A. (2006), 'Boat Remains and Maritime Trade in the Persian Gulf during 6th and 5th millennia BC', *Antiquity*, 80: 52–63.

Carter, R. A. (2009), 'How Pearls Made the Modern Emirates', in Maitra, J. (ed.), *New Perspectives on Recording UAE History*, Abu Dhabi: Centre for Documentation and Research.

Carter, R. A. (2010), 'The Social and Environmental Context of Neolithic Seafaring in the Persian Gulf', in Andersen, A., Barrett, J. and Boyle, K. (eds), *The Global Origins and Development of Seafaring*, Cambridge: McDonald Institute for Archaeological Research.

Carter, R. A. (2012), *Sea of Pearls: Seven Thousand Years of the Industry That Shaped the Gulf*, London: Arabian Publishing.

Carter, R. A. and J. Naranjo-Santana (2010), *Amara Excavations 2009*. <http://ucl.academia.edu/RobertCarter/Papers/636236/Amara_Excavations_2009: Oxford Brookes Archaeology & Heritage>

Carter, R. A. and J. Naranjo-Santana (2011), *Muharraq Excavations 2010*. <http://ucl.academia.edu/RobertCarter/Papers/636240/Muharraq_Excavations_2010: Oxford Brookes Archaeology & Heritage>

Casson, L. (1989), *The Periplus of the Erythraean Sea*, Princeton: Princeton University Press.

Chabot, J. B. (1902), *Synodicon orientale, ou recueil de synodes Nestoriens*, Paris: Acade mie des Inscriptions et Belles-Lettres.

Charpentier, V., C. S. Phillips and S. Méry (2012), 'Pearl Fishing in the Ancient World: 7500 BP', *Arabian Archaeology and Epigraphy*, 23: 1–6.

Croucher, S. (2011), 'Exchange Values: Commodities, Colonialism and Identity on Nineteenth Century Zanzibar', in Croucher, S. and Weiss, L. (eds), *The Archaeology of Capitalism in Colonial Contexts*, New York: Springer.

Eichholz, D. (1962), *Pliny: Natural History. Volume X, Libri XXXVI–XXXVII*, Cambridge, MA: Harvard University Press.

Fernandes, A. P. (2009), 'Portuguese Cartazes System and the Magumbayas on Pearl Fishing in the Arabian/Persian Gulf', *Liwa*, 1.

Floor, W. (1982), 'Pearl Fishing in the Persian Gulf in 1757', *Persica*, 10: 209–22.

Floor, W. (1984), 'The Bahrain Project of 1754', *Persica*, 11: 130–48.

Grabar, O. (2006), *Islamic Visual Culture, 1100–1800. Constructing the Study of Islamic Art, Vol. 2*, Farnham: Ashgate.

Heldaas Seland, E. (2011), 'The Persian Gulf or the Red Sea? Two Axes in Ancient Indian Ocean Trade, Where To Go and Why', *World Archaeology* 43: 398–409.

Hirth, F. and W. W. Rockhill (1911), *Chau Ju-Kua: His Work on the Chinese and Arab Trade in the Twelfth and Thirteenth Centuries, entitled Chu-fan-chi*, St Petersburg: Imperial Academy of Sciences.

Kallweit, H. (2003), 'Remarks on the Late Stone Age in the U.A.E.', in Potts, D., al-Naboodah, H. and Hellyer, P. (eds), *Archaeology of the United Arab Emirates. Proceedings of the First International Conference on the Archaeology of the U.A.E.*, London: Trident.

Lorimer, J. G. (1915), *Gazetteer of the Persian Gulf, Oman and Central Arabia. Volume 1, Historical*, Calcutta.

Masry, A. H. (1997), *Prehistory in Northeastern Arabia. The Problem of Interregional Interaction*, 2nd edn, London and New York: Kegan Paul International.

Oates, J., T. E. Davidson, D. Kamilli and H. McKerrel (1977), 'Seafaring Merchants of Ur?', *Antiquity* 51: 221–34.

Piacentini, V. F. (2004), 'The Mercantile Empire of the Tibis: economic predominance, political power, military subordination', *Proceedings of the Seminar for Arabian Studies* 34: 251–60.

Piacentini, V. F. and E. Maestri (2009), 'Rise and Splendour of the Sahil 'Uman al-Shamal within a New Order (13th–16th Centuries AD)', in Anon (ed.), *New Perspectives on Recording UAE History*, Abu Dhabi: National Center for Documentation and Research.

Rackham, H. (1942), *Pliny: Natural History. Volume II, Libri III–VII*, Cambridge, MA: Harvard University Press.

Rosenthal, L. (1984), *The Kingdom of The Pearl*, London: Hodder & Stoughton.

Shalem, A. (1997), 'Jewels and Journeys: The Case of the Medieval Gemstone Called al-Yatima', *Muqarnas*, XIV: 42–56.

Sundblad, T. (2011), *Report on European Ceramics at Qatar National Museum*, Doha: Qatar National Museum.

Tuson, P. (1991), *Records of Qatar, Primary Documents 1820–1960. Volume 3: 1879–1896*, Slough: Archive Editions.

Uerpmann, H.-P. and M. Uerpmann (1996), 'Ubaid pottery in the Eastern Gulf – New Evidence from Umm al-Qaiwain (U.A.E.)', *Arabian Archaeology and Epigraphy*, 7: 125–39.

14

AN ARCHAEOLOGY OF GLASS AND INTERNATIONAL TRADE IN THE GULF

Carolyn M. Swan

Introduction

H istorians of glass are interested in understanding the role of glass objects within the social and economic life of people in the past, and in exploring glass as a material expression of culture. The ancient networks of glass were complex, involving the movement and exchange of raw materials, finished objects and craftsmen as well as specialised technical and artistic knowledge. Such networks were also far-reaching, and glass seems to have been regularly adopted into the material culture of those who came in contact with it.

Archaeological research in Bahrain, Qatar, the UAE and Oman, as well as coastal Iran, is revealing evidence for the trade and use of glass objects by people living on the shores of the Gulf. This history is largely one of import, as local glassmaking and glassworking seem to have occurred only on a non-existent or very limited scale: the vast majority of glass was carried as finished items overland or overseas from the Hellenistic, Roman, Parthian, Sasanian and Islamic glass centres located to the west, north and north-east of the region. During the Bronze and Iron Ages, there is a very limited use of glass in the Gulf, mostly for personal ornament in the form of beads. Glass vessels begin to appear in burials in a significant volume in the second century BCE, with small bottles and bowls imported from production centres bordering on the Eastern Mediterranean, namely Egypt and the Levant. Sometime in the third to fourth centuries CE, the Gulf experienced a shift from Mediterranean to Mesopotamian sources of glass. There was a second fluorescence of glass use by people living in the Gulf during the Early Islamic period, and emerging evidence suggests that at this time vessels were imported into the region from around the wider world and, in at least one instance, both raw glass and glass vessels were produced locally.

The study of glass recovered from archaeological sites within the Gulf is still in its infancy, and has to date focused primarily on the visually observable, typological aspects of glass (e.g. vessel shapes and functions). However, the examination of the invisible, technological aspects of Gulf glass (e.g. chemical composition revealing raw materials and sources) is growing, and when combined with typological work this new data is helping to clarify the shifting patterns of glass trade and distribution, relating this to the larger picture of life within Gulf communities.

Glass as Material Culture

Glass is one of several vitreous materials, and is part of a broad family of man-made items that consist mainly of silica (sand and powdered quartz or flint) combined in some way with alkali (soda, potash) and lime. Glazed stone, faience, frit and 'Egyptian Blue' are all vitreous materials, but there are important technological distinctions between these materials and true glass:[1] faience, for example, is sintered quartz covered with an alkali glaze, whereas a true glass has its raw ingredients completely fused together in a non-crystalline structure. It can be difficult to visually distinguish glassy objects from true glass – especially if an item has weathered to a significant degree – and this should be considered when perusing the published literature, as there is always a risk of the substitution of terms or misidentification of materials; some of the earliest examples of true glass are so altered in appearance and surface consistency that they might easily be confused with frit or faience.[2]

Glass is a relatively new innovation when compared with other man-made materials resulting from pyrotechnological processes, such as ceramics or metals and alloys. The earliest archaeological evidence currently available for vitreous materials indicates that glazed stone and faience began to be

made in Mesopotamia and Egypt sometime in the third or even fourth millennium BCE,[3] but it was not until the second half of the second millennium
BCE that true glass vessels were regularly produced. The production and use
of early glass in these regions was linked to the social elite, which underscores
the perceived value of glass according to those who made or encountered
the material: in Egypt, glass was meant to imitate precious stones and metals
like turquoise, lapis lazuli, gold and silver by means of its opaque colour
and shine;[4] glass objects were included as grave goods within elite burials in
Pharaonic Egypt,[5] and glass workshops were located near the palace complexes of Tell el-Amarna in Egypt;[6] in Mesopotamia, glass objects that were
symbolically linked to kingship have been found at Nippur;[7] glass ornaments
and jewellery were buried with the social elite in Mycenaean Greece, where
glass has also been found in several palatial complexes.[8] Even when glass
became a cheaper commodity that was more widely available to people of different social classes, it was sometimes still viewed as a miraculous substance.[9]

The global history of glass is as wide and varied as the manipulative
possibilities of the material itself, but the Eastern Mediterranean in particular
and its surrounding lands feature prominently in the early history of glass.
Textual, archaeological and chemical evidence attests to the high quality
of glass-making raw materials in this region, and Levantine and Egyptian
glass dominated production for many centuries beginning in the mid-second
millennium BCE.[10] This dominance only increased with the innovation of
glassblowing and the incorporation of the Eastern Mediterranean into the
Roman Empire during the first centuries BCE and CE,[11] and it continued
into the Late Antique and medieval Islamic eras with the development of an
industrial-scale glass production that produced many tons of raw glass at a
time, suitable for making millions of vessels.[12] High-quality glass continued
to be made in the Eastern Mediterranean by Islamic glassmakers, and high-
quality glassmaking raw materials were shipped by sea from the Levant to
Italy;[13] European glassmakers during the Renaissance regularly copied the
styles and techniques of the famed Venetian *cristallo* glass,[14] which relied on
Venice's privileged access to Levantine plant ashes. The importance of the
Mediterranean in glassmaking history is widely acknowledged, but it is also
just one part of a larger global story of glass.[15]

Approaches to the Study of Archaeological Glass

The specialist knowledge that was required to produce glass and to create glass objects, and the fragile nature of the material itself, positions glass as a unique form of material culture. Historians of glass are interested in understanding the place of glass objects within the social and economic life of people in the past, exploring glass as a material expression of culture. To that end, researchers employ typological and chemical evidence to identify the forms and styles, decorative manipulations and functional uses of glass vessels, in addition to reconstructing the technology, processes of production and networks of distribution. Such investigations are most successful when they are grounded in archaeological research, as glass objects in museum collections are overwhelmingly without context.

Typological analysis involves the close examination and classification of glass vessels based on the shape, style and forming methods of the various vessel components (e.g. rim, body and base). Such analyses also take into account the geographic and stratigraphic 'find spot' of an object in order to reconstruct the distribution of different types, as well as the chronology of production and use, and to broadly characterise or differentiate glass by culture, region or time period. Much of glass analysis relies on comparing objects to artefacts from other archaeological sites, looking for parallels with good excavation context in order to make or confirm the assignment of an object to a typological glass group.

Chemical analysis is used to identify and understand the materials, technology and production processes used to make the glass itself, as well as any manipulations done to alter the colour and degree of transparency. This is accomplished by means of a quantitative assessment of the elements and compounds that make up the glass matrix. This type of analysis aims to group glasses by their various raw materials, and seeks out patterns that can be related to geological, geographical, chronological, cultural and other factors (or a combination of these). Chemical analysis is a powerful tool when combined with typological analysis, and can potentially help differentiate glasses that are visually similar in appearance.

Analytical difficulties – both typological and chemical – particular to glass stem from the nature of the material itself and its preservation in the archaeological record. Vessel shapes, styles and forming methods were often so simple and long-lasting that it can be difficult to make meaningful chronological distinctions, and this ambiguity becomes more pronounced when glass objects are recovered in a fragmentary state. A serious limitation to both the typological and chemical study of archaeological glass is the deterioration of the material over time; this is an inevitable result of the interaction of post-depositional processes with the glass itself.[16] Just how much and how severely glass artefacts are altered depends upon the chemistry of the glass and that of its burial environment. Deterioration begins at the outer surface and proceeds inwards as the alkali and lime are leached out of the glass, leaving behind layers of siliceous 'weathering products' that vary in consistency from hard enamel-like encrustations to flaky iridescent sheets; in extreme cases, the glass is completely deteriorated to its core.

Glass in the Gulf

Tracing the history and significance of glass over time offers a way to understand the changing cultural, social and economic life within the Gulf. The study of glass in the Gulf is a research topic still very much in its infancy, and there is a great variety in the level of interest and published detail about the glass artefacts encountered during archaeological excavation in the region. This ranges from a passing mention of glass having been found,[17] to brief summaries with an illustration or two of the types present,[18] to full catalogues with discussions of the glass finds alone or in comparison with other types of material culture.[19] At present the only two archaeological sites in the Gulf with full studies of the glass finds are Ed-Dur and Kush,[20] both located in UAE; another highly valuable contribution is the comprehensive catalogue of glass objects from the burials of the so-called Tylos period (c. 300 BCE–600 CE) in Bahrain.[21]

In the text that appears below, some of the best-studied or most promising glass assemblages from the Gulf – especially Bahrain, Qatar, the UAE and northern Oman – are highlighted (Figure 14.1). Terms like 'Mesopotamian', 'Roman' and 'Sasanian' are used here when referring to glass with known cultural or regional affiliations, whereas terms like 'Bronze Age' and 'Late Pre-Islamic' are used more broadly to refer to archaeological periods.[22] In the Gulf, much of the glass suffers from a heavy deterioration that makes it

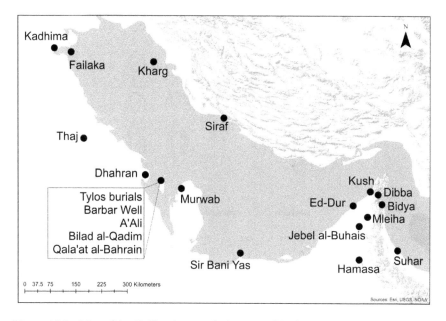

Figure 14.1 Map of the Gulf, indicating the location of the key archaeological sites with glass finds mentioned in the text. Sources for base map: Esri, USGS, NOAA.

challenging to identify glass colour and transparency, surface decorations or the type of vessel itself; the best-preserved glass artefacts are those that were placed in stone-built tombs during the Late Pre-Islamic era, but even these display some degree of deterioration. Despite this, the study of glass objects can still contribute to our historical reconstruction of the past. Patterns are beginning to emerge from the Gulf glass corpus, and it is hoped that these will become clearer with closer study of this material.

Glass in the Gulf from c. 3000 to c. 300 BCE (Bronze Age to Iron Age)

Glass is present in the Gulf during the Bronze Age primarily in the form of small beads. Two glass beads were recovered from a late third millennium BCE elite burial mound (BBM 20907) in the Wadi as-Sail, Bahrain,[23] and three more from late third–early second millennium BCE contexts at Qala'at al-Bahrain[24] (Figure 14.2); other beads made of glass from excavations in Bahrain likely exist but have not yet been published.[25] Glass beads have also been reported from two Bronze Age tells at Sa'ad wa Sa'aid on the island of Failaka, Kuwait, including nine beads from mid-to-late second millennium

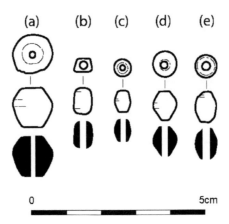

Figure 14.2 Glass beads from Bronze Age contexts: (a) blue and (b) gold glass beads from a 3rd millennium BCE burial at Wadi as-Sail in Bahrain (after Højlund *et al.* 2008: 152, Fig. 17), and (c–e) turquoise-blue glass beads from 3rd–2nd millennium BCE contexts at Qala'at al-Bahrain (after Højlund and Andersen 1994: 391–3, Figs 1,941, 1,942 and 1,963).

contexts of Tell F6.[26] The glass beads in the Gulf were likely imported from Mesopotamia, which is known to have been producing glass at the time, as ceramic and other imports from this region are plentiful at Gulf sites during the Bronze Age. Three patterns underline the probable high value of the glass beads: the colour of the glass, their relatively low abundance, and the raw materials of other beads. The colours of the glass beads shown in Figure 14.2 are described as blue, gold and turquoise-blue – colours that were meant to evoke precious stones and metal: lapis lazuli, gold and turquoise. Beads made of glass are notably quite rare in comparison to beads made from other materials – just nine out of 200 beads recovered from the 2008–12 excavations of tell F6 on Failaka are made of glass.[27] Glass beads are found alongside beads made from other materials – many of which are precious – such as faience, agate, carnelian, lapis lazuli, turquoise, quartz, gold, shell and mother-of-pearl.

Reports of glass vessels in such early contexts within the Gulf are even rarer than those of beads. A few glass fragments have been recovered from late second millennium BCE contexts on Failaka (c. 1300 BCE),[28] including seven small pieces and four irregular lumps of blue and dark blue glass recovered from Tells F3 and F6; preliminary chemical analysis of four samples has suggested that some of these may have a colouring chemistry similar to that of contemporary glasses from Egypt.[29] In the monumental building at Qala'at al-Bahrain, one very small and undiagnostic fragment from a red-brown glass vessel was reported from a c. 1600–300 BCE context.[30] Apart from these later, albeit broadly dated, fragments, there seems to be no evidence for glass in the Gulf during the Iron Age (c. 1300–300 BC); a deeper literature review is likely needed but, significantly, the author did not come across the mention of glass objects in the Gulf for the period. It should also be noted that other vitreous materials (e.g. faience and 'glass paste') are found in the Gulf starting at an early period, although these materials are not discussed here.

Glass in the Gulf from c. 300 BCE to 700 CE (Late Pre-Islamic and Late Antique periods)

Compared to the preceding millennia, glass vessels are present in the Gulf in a significant volume beginning in the Late Pre-Islamic period (c. 300 BCE–300 CE). The main vessel-forming methods of this era are all represented, including the techniques of core-forming, casting (slumping, pressing, and so on), mould-blowing and free-blowing.

The most extensive and best-preserved collection of glass in the Gulf comes from the so-called Tylos period (c. 300 BCE–600 CE) burial mounds of Bahrain. More than three hundred complete vessels and fragments date from the mid-first century BCE to the seventh century CE, and include 49 different vessel types.[31] Glass vessels feature prominently among the funerary objects buried with the dead at the necropoles of Shakhoura, Saar, Madinat Hamad, Abou Ashira, Al-Hajjar, Al-Maqaba, Dar Kulayb, Abou Saybi and Al-Maqsha. A pattern is discernible in the size, type, style and function of the glass: most are small containers (bottles, flasks, jars, and jugs of various form, including *amphoriskoi* and *aryballoi*) that served as *unguentaria* (containers for oils and perfumes). Drinking vessels (bowls, cups and beakers) were also buried with the dead but are less numerous. The earliest vessels within the graves were imported from the Hellenistic and Roman Eastern Mediterranean and are well-known in terms of both their distribution and dates of production; these include late second- to first-century BCE core-formed opaque *amphoriskoi* and a linear incised bowl, as well as first- to second-century CE pillar-moulded bowls, mould-blown date-shaped flasks (Plate 3) and 'Sidonian' mould-blown bottles (Plate 17, right).

Many of the glass objects excavated at the site of Ed-Dur in the Emirate of Umm al-Qaiwain also come from burial contexts, and the vessels date to the main period of occupation in the first century CE. Of the 227 complete and fragmentary vessels recovered from the Belgian and Danish excavations, almost all are typologically recognisable as imports coming from the Hellenistic and Roman Eastern Mediterranean.[32] Just fourteen vessels were deemed to be of 'indeterminate' provenance, as they share typological similarities with both Mediterranean and Mesopotamian glassware;[33] while a small number of glass objects may thus have been imported from Mesopotamia (making them Parthian rather than Hellenistic or Roman), the vessels at Ed-Dur have an overwhelmingly Mediterranean provenance. A large number of the beads recovered at Ed-Dur (565 of the 1228) have been identified as 'glass (paste)', and many of these also come from funerary contexts. The styles of the beads indicate that some were clearly imported from the Hellenistic-Roman world (e.g. mosaic flower and face beads) while others were notably imported from India (for e.g. turtle-shaped, hexagonal-bicone and collar beads).[34]

At the sites of Mleiha and Dibba in the Emirate of Sharjah, glass objects have also been recovered from tombs dating from around the first century BCE to the first century CE. Although heavily plundered, nine of the twenty-six tombs excavated at Mleiha contained glass vessels, and the described objects are certainly Roman imports (e.g. pillar-moulded bowls and mould-blown 'grape cluster' bottles).[35] The collective tomb at Dibba contained glass beads as well as jars, bowls, jugs, *amphorae*, *amphoriskoi*, *aryballoi*, pitchers and bottles, many of which are clear imports from the Roman Mediterranean (e.g. Plate 17, left).[36] One type of small, mould-blown bottle of opaque white glass with thick walls is reportedly a common type at Dibba; although this type is thought to have no close parallels elsewhere, there are similarities with a few first- to second-century CE bottles from tombs in Bahrain and with another from ed-Dur that have been speculated as originating in Mesopotamia;[37] however, there is also speculation that this type was a product of local glassworkers at Dibba.

Other finds from this period include a pillar-moulded bowl and *amphoriskos* reported from a first-century CE burial in Bidya in the Emirate of Fujairah.[38] A small amount of residual Roman and possibly Parthian glass dating to the first to third centuries was found in the Late Sasanian layers at the site of Kush in the Emirate of Ras al-Khaimah, including pillar-moulded bowls and mosaic glass.[39] Three small pieces of glass were reported from the site of Thaj in eastern Saudi Arabia,[40] including one 'millefiori' (mosaic) and two 'striped' (ribbon glass) fragments that are certainly late Hellenistic or early Roman imports.

Mesopotamian glass objects eventually replace Mediterranean imports into the Gulf. As noted, there may indeed have been some Parthian (1st–early 3rd century CE) imports at ed-Dur and on Bahrain,[41] but Parthian glass is something of an enigma and remains challenging to identify. Fortunately, Sasanian (early 3rd–7th century CE) glass is more readily recognisable. At Ed-Dur, the French excavations in Area F recovered glass vessels with clear Sasanian affiliations from third-to-fourth-century CE burial contexts: plain and mould-blown glass bowls as well as small bottles were common finds, with the number and variety of glass bottles increasing slightly in the fourth century.[42] Glass was also reported in second-/third- to early fourth-century CE levels of a fortified building at Mleiha (area CW) and within contemporary houses (area DA);[43] these finds are primarily bowls and small bottles that are also described as being similar to Mesopotamian examples. In the Tylos-period tombs of Bahrain there appears to be a hiatus in imported glass after the early second century CE, but people resumed interring glass vessels with the dead in the fourth century and then again in the sixth/seventh centuries,[44] but more likely extending into the eighth century;[45] the vessel types continue to include small *unguentaria* and drinking vessels, although the shapes are now reflective of Sasanian and Early Islamic wares from Mesopotamia and only a few examples of Western glass have been identified.[46] Glass has been reported from tombs 208–95 and B-16 in the tumuli fields near Dhahran in eastern Saudi Arabia, including what appears to be a Sasanian bowl.[47]

The bulk of the pre-Islamic-era glass at Kush is fifth- to early sixth-century Sasanian in date, and the assemblage appears to be dominated by tablewares that have good parallels with the common types found at contemporary sites in southern and central Mesopotamia.[48] At Jebel al-Buhais in the Emirate of Sharjah, three glass vessels were recovered from tombs BHS 29 and BHS 45, located in a small natural rock shelter: illustrations show a facet-cut bottle with a foot and narrow neck, a round-bottomed bottle with a folded or trail-wrapped mouth, and a deep bowl with pinched vertical projections and a base ring of pinched toes;[49] these finds were identified as Hellenistic, but they should be re-dated to the third–seventh centuries CE, as they appear to be blown, while their forms and decorations are Sasanian in character.[50]

Glass was recovered on the island of Kharg, off the coast of Iran, from tombs that have been broadly dated to after the sixth century CE. These objects are only briefly described, but photographs and line drawings are given: all of these items are small bottles, and their typology indicates they are Mesopotamian imports of Sasanian and Early Islamic date. Glass vessels were interred in three of the so-called 'Megalithic' tombs (tombs DI, DII5, and DII6) and in ten tombs in the necropolis known as 'the Plain' (tombs 3, 5, 13–14, 22, 36–8, 40, 45).[51] In tomb DII6 there is an early Sasanian bottle type with a pinched neck that has close parallels at Sasanian sites in Mesopotamia; four such vessels have also been found in the Tylos-period tombs on Bahrain.[52] The burials of 'the Plain' include examples of long bottles with narrow mouths and rounded bases, as well as small globular bottles with short flaring necks, two types that also have parallels with Sasanian vessels from Mesopotamia.[53] Many of the tombs on Kharg are quite wealthy, and glass items were evidently valuable: although tombs contain no pottery, glass vessels and copper or silver objects and jewellery are abundant; for example, in Tomb 13 a female was buried with eight small glass bottles, a necklace (of pearls, rock crystal, carnelian, opals, black stone and glass paste), a copper-alloy plate and a small statuette of a lion.[54] Almost all of the vessels within the Kharg tombs are described as being made of dark opaque grey glass ('verre opaque gris foncé'), but this mistakenly describes the weathered surface rather than the original colour and transparency of the glass, which would likely be light green and transparent. Sasanian glass typically has a significant weathering layer[55] that is usually white but also occasionally yellowish, brown and grey, and Early Islamic glass in the Gulf also typically has a dark opaque surface patina. It is highly likely that some of the vessels in the Kharg tombs are Early Islamic in date: the small globular bottles with short flaring necks are types that were also made during the Early Islamic period, while decorations like the applied ribbons around globular bodies and the horizontal ribbing or ridges on bottle necks are more characteristic of Early Islamic glass than Sasanian.[56]

Glass in the Gulf from c. 700 CE to 1300 (Early and Middle Islamic periods)

Glass vessel fragments were excavated within a Christian monastic complex on the island of Sir Bani Yas in the Emirate of Abu Dhabi, which has been re-dated to the late seventh–mid-eighth centuries;[57] although the glass assemblage has not been studied, the objects reportedly have similarities with Umayyad types,[58] and a published photo of a stemmed goblet fits neatly with this chronology: the stemmed goblet was a popular glass vessel type in the Late Antique Near East, while Sasanian to Early Islamic examples are also known.[59] A large collection of seventh- to eighth-century glass has reportedly been recovered from the excavation of a courtyard in the Early Islamic village of al-Qusur on Failaka,[60] and Early Islamic glass has also been reportedly recovered from excavations at the site of Kadhima on the coast of Kuwait.[61]

Early Islamic glass was also apparently found within the Nestorian monastery on Kharg, although no images or information about glass are given in the final publication.[62] The ceramics of the monastic complex have been dated to the ninth-century Abbasid period,[63] so it is reasonable to believe that any glass recovered from these contexts would be of similar date. Excavations at Bilad al-Qadim in Bahrain have uncovered a small amount of glass from the eighth- to tenth-century phases; the finds are very fragmentary and highly weathered, and objects include undecorated bowls and small bottles.[64] At Barbar in Bahrain, an estimated 12–15 glass vessels were recovered from a well that was filled with rubbish, from what appears to be a wealthy Abbasid-period household with strong ties to Samarra in Iraq based on its material culture:[65] most of the glass fragments come from plain bowls with relatively vertical walls that are characteristic of the glass repertoire of this period, as is a type of dark blue bottle with a narrow and irregular neck that was also recovered from the well. Abbasid glass has been reported from A'ali in Bahrain[66] and Hamasa in Oman,[67] and although these assemblages have yet to be studied, illustrations of some of the material largely suggest a ninth- to tenth-century date and include vessels with marvered trails and impressed geometric designs (Figure 14.3) that are characteristic of Early Islamic decorated glass. Glass vessels were also recovered from the ninth-century site of Murwab in Qatar,[68] including a few mould-blown vessels with a honeycomb pattern, molar flasks,

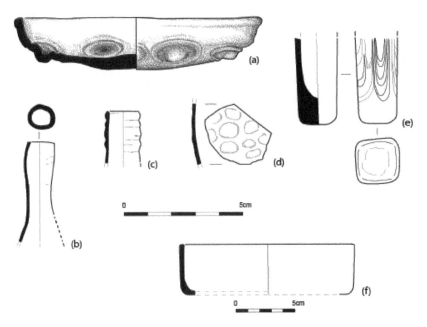

Figure 14.3 Examples of Early Islamic glass vessels from the Gulf, including (a) Hamasa in Oman (after P. Collet, courtesy of Timothy Power and the Buraimi Oasis Landscape Archaeology Project), (b and f) the Barbar Well in Bahrain (C. Swan), (c-d) Murwab in Qatar (C. Swan) and (e) A'ali in Bahrain (after Sasaki 1990).

small bottles with ridged necks and vessels with a pinched base ring; these types have been noted from Early Islamic sites across the Muslim world.

The Islamic glass from Kush is the best-studied assemblage for the period in the region, and the final publication is eagerly awaited.[69] On the basis of preliminary reports and discussions of the glass, the assemblage includes a variety of bowls, cups, beakers and bottles. Perhaps most interestingly, the Early Islamic glass at Kush does not seem to closely resemble contemporary glass in Mesopotamia: while some types from the late seventh- to early nineteenth-century contexts do show similarities of shape with Mesopotamian objects, they find closer parallels in terms of their unique turquoise and dark blue colour further east, for example at Merv in Turkmenistan.[70] Glass objects appear to be much more numerous at the site during the ninth–eleventh centuries than in previous centuries, and the assemblage is dominated by three main types: cylindrical bowls, mallet-shaped flasks and small unguent bottles with unworked rims – parallels for these types of vessels can be found all over the Islamic world. Another notable type of glass in the ninth–eleventh centuries at Kush is the colourless wheel-cut vessel.

A few Pre-Islamic glass fragments were reported from excavations of Suhar in Oman, one of the major Islamic ports of the Indian Ocean, but these objects likely date to the eighth century or later on the basis of a reassessment of the site's archaeology and the weathering patterns of the glass itself.[71] While a few fragments may represent residual fragments from the first–second centuries CE (including a vessel with trailed decoration), and others date to the fourteenth century and later, the majority of the glass at Suhar belongs to the Abbasid period. The collection is described as modest and displaying great variety, including various flasks, jugs, bottles, phials, bowls and beakers that are thought to have parallels with items from many other parts of the Islamic world. Of note are the shallow bowls with nearly vertical walls and the globular bottles with a narrow neck decorated with ridges,[72] which are ninth- to tenth-century types with good parallels from the Barbar well and Murwab.

On the north-eastern Gulf coast at the site of Siraf, another major port of the Early Islamic era, glass finds were reported to be second only to pottery in abundance – with more than a thousand fragments found in the first season of excavation alone.[73] The majority of the glass came from securely stratified contexts dating to the ninth–twelfth centuries CE, which was the settlement's greatest period of prosperity. Although the finds have not yet been published, an early examination of the glass notes that fragments fall into three categories: 'local glass', glass of an 'east Persian type' and 'Egyptian glass'. The local glass was found to dominate the site during the ninth–early eleventh centuries; vessel types include blown bowls, beakers, goblets, bottles, lamps, sprinklers and alembics. The 'local glass' was not usually decorated, whereas the 'east Persian' type include high-quality colourless glass beakers, bottles, and flasks with cut or carved decoration (and thus 'a family likeness' to glass from Nishapur). Glass with a supposed Egyptian origin was primarily identified by its mould-blown and carved decorations, and was rarer at the site.

Glass continued to be common and sometimes even more plentiful in the Gulf during the early part of the Middle Islamic period (c. 1000–1300 CE). At Bilad al-Qadim, glass bowls and bottles are more abundant during the eleventh–fourteenth centuries than they were in previous periods;[74] at Kush, however, there seems to be a decline in glass use during this same period, with a smaller range of types present.[75]

Glass Production Evidence

There is at present no evidence in eastern and south-eastern Arabia for glassmaking, that is, the primary production of glass from its raw materials. Evidence for local glassworking, that is, the secondary production of glass objects by melting chunks of raw glass or broken vessels (cullet), is rare, and this work seems to have occurred on a very limited scale at certain points in time. The most secure archaeological evidence for glassworking in southeast Arabia comes from the port of Dibba in the Emirate of Sharjah.[76] There, excavators have revealed a series of 52 small mudbrick rooms used as workshops in contexts dating to around the first century CE, while Room 2 has been identified as a glass workshop due to the large concentration of glass waste as well as broken vessels and broken ingots which are indicative of the secondary production of glass vessels at Dibba.

There is mention of an Early Islamic 'production site' from a small tell near A'ali in Bahrain, but no further detail is given.[77] Possible evidence for glassworking from Qala'at al-Bahrain dating to the Middle Islamic period (c. 12th–13th century) includes finds described as wasters, drops and mould fragments; one type of vessel base finish with a 'rope ring' is considered to be local work, with 'waster' fragments of this type discovered in connection with mould fragments.[78] Other reportedly local glass types at Qala'at al-Bahrain are small closed vessels of yellowish glass with mould-blown ribbing, which were also found alongside waste and mould fragments in excavations of the site.[79]

There is strong evidence that secondary glassworking activities took place at Siraf during the Early Islamic period, with primary glassmaking likely occurring in the hinterland if not at Siraf itself. An industrial area with large ceramic kilns was constructed on the coast near the western edge of the city (Site D), sometime in the tenth century. Large quantities of production debris such as glass slag, drops, trails and vessel fragments were recovered from one of the kilns as well as from a small pit, and much of the glass waste was found to correspond to the glass vessel types that were most common at the site.[80] Recent chemical analyses of glass vessels and working debris from the site further supports the notion that Siraf produced raw glass as well as glass objects for local use: the majority of the sampled glass has uniquely high levels of the trace element zirconium, which may indicate local primary production in southern Iran.[81]

Movement and Trade of Glass

The evidence suggests that there was very little use of glass by Gulf communities during the Bronze Age, and virtually no glass after that time until the arrival of Hellenistic glass from the Mediterranean. Glass vessels appear in significant numbers within southern Gulf settlements during the mid-second century BCE to the second century CE (Late Pre-Islamic B and C), at a time when there was a great deal of activity in eastern Arabia that was perhaps linked to the wealth of the incense trade from South Arabia.[82] The vast majority of the glass vessels in this period are imports from the Mediterranean. This sudden increase of glass in the Gulf, and its Mediterranean provenance, is not at all surprising given the increasingly widespread availability and use of glass vessels in the Greco-Roman Mediterranean in this very period, due to the technological innovations and trade connections of the time. Trade with the East seems to have enabled glass to easily make its way from Mediterranean producers to consumers living around the Gulf: trade between Rome and India is mentioned by the Roman authors Pliny (*Natural History*, 6.101 and 12.84) and Strabo (*Geography*, 17.1.13), and glass – both raw glass and finished vessels – is listed among the goods exported from Roman Egypt to India in the first century CE *Periplus of the Erythraean Sea*.[83] Apart from the Gulf, Late Hellenistic and Roman glass of Mediterranean origin has been found at archaeological sites located on the Red Sea,[84] Yemen,[85] Afghanistan,[86] northern Pakistan,[87] India[88] and Sri Lanka.[89]

Three possible routes have been proposed for the importation of Mediterranean glass into eastern Arabia and the Oman Peninsula:[90] (1) it was exported from Roman Egypt directly to the Gulf by means of Roman ships; (2) it was exported from Roman Egypt to India and then re-exported to the Gulf by means of Indian ships; or (3) it was carried by caravan overland through Syria to the Euphrates and down to the coast of Characene (the lower region of modern Iraq), from where it could then be shipped to the southern Gulf by sea or by land. It seems highly probable that all three routes were used. Textual and archaeological evidence shows that Egyptian ports on the Red Sea were engaged in long-distance trade during the Ptolemaic period, and this trade expanded after Egypt was annexed in 30 BCE.[91] Finds from Dura-Europos[92] and Palmyra[93] in modern Syria attest to Mediterranean glass reaching the Euphrates, from where it could easily continue south-east to the Gulf waters and then onwards by land or sea to the southern Gulf, while Thaj, in modern Saudi Arabia, was the capital of the prosperous ancient kingdom of Gerrha and the hub of long-distance trade in the area during the last centuries BCE. The re-export of glass from Roman Egypt to the Gulf via India could also explain the mechanism by which the few examples of Indian glass beads reached Ed-Dur.

Mediterranean trade with India is thought to have peaked in the mid-second century CE, declining by the third century.[94] This change in economic activity and trade is also made visible by the glass evidence, as the Gulf sees a shift from Mediterranean to Mesopotamian glass imports during the third century. Glass from Mesopotamian sources gradually enters into the corpus, beginning primarily during the third–fourth centuries (Late Pre-Islamic D), and there appears to be a drop in imports from the West at this very time. Imports from Mesopotamia continue in the following centuries, and an even wider network of glass trade was in place during the Islamic periods, with glass coming to the Gulf from Egypt, Mesopotamia and Persia, as well as from India.

Observations about the vessel types and relative volume of glass within the Gulf are starting to shed light on the patterns of import and consumption. If the history of glass within the Gulf is largely one of import, observations about the types of glass that are *not* present at Gulf sites are also of interest – although what such absences actually indicate is open to interpretation. At Ed-Dur, for example, two types of Roman vessels that were exported widely in the first–second centuries CE (colourless cast bowls and plates with overhanging rims, and colourless facet-cut beakers) are absent;[95] this absence has been used as evidence to support the interpretation that most of the glass came to Ed-Dur between 25 BCE and 75 CE, but it is also possible that it represents deliberate choices made by people involved in the export of the goods, or by the consumers within the region. Similarly, it was noticed that certain common types of glass found in Mesopotamia (thick-walled dropper flasks and stemmed vessels) were present in very small numbers or altogether absent in the Late Sasanian glass assemblage from Kush, which could possibly have been a choice on the part of consumers.[96] At many of the Early Islamic sites in the Gulf – for example Barbar and Murwab – the absence of distinctive decorative types such as scratch-decorated, metallic-lustre glasses and enamelled glass is of interest; other than at Hamasa, it appears that no examples of pincered or tong-impressed geometric decorations have been reported within the Gulf.

Glass chemistry helps to shed more light on the question of glass provenance and trade, and also shows patterns of glass consumption within the Gulf by means of a comparison of the compositional data from the different sites. While the publication of such work has been limited to date,[97] the results are promising. For example, chemical analysis of twenty-five fragments of first-century glass excavated at Ed-Dur supports the typological interpretation of this material, which concluded that the glass was imported from the Mediterranean; this interpretation is refined and expanded by the tight clustering of the compositional data, indicating that most of the sampled objects were probably made within the very same region,[98] which in turn may reflect an episodic glass trade or a direct (alternatively, a limited) trade partnership between regions or merchants. Compositional data have additionally suggested that there is a difference in the geology of the raw materials used to produce Sasanian-Islamic glass from Mesopotamia and Islamic glass from Syria,[99] and this detail can assist in the identification and quantification of imported glass from these regions to Gulf sites: at Kush, for example, glass from both Syria and Mesopotamia has been recognised.[100] The recent increase in trace element analysis (i.e. measuring the chemical components that are present in glass on the order of parts per million) has been particularly beneficial due to the discriminatory power of these elements compared to that of the major and minor components of glass (which tend to be quite similar across different glass types). Perhaps most significantly for the cultural and economic history of the Gulf, trace element analysis has identified a unique, high-zirconium glass that is little-known outside of the Gulf and appears to have been produced in or near to Siraf: a comparison of the chemical data from Siraf with those from contemporary Murwab, Kush

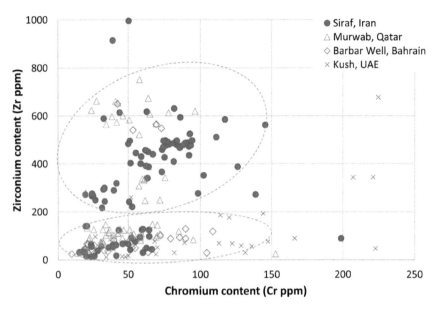

Figure 14.4 Scatterplot of the trace elements zirconium (Zr) vs chromium (Cr) in glass samples taken from four Early Islamic archaeological sites in the Gulf. The dotted ellipses highlight different chemical types: the larger, upper ellipse contains the high-zirconium glass that is thought to have been locally produced at Siraf (Swan *et al.* 2017 data, and Swan unpublished data).

and the Barbar well (Figure 14.4) shows that high-zirconium glass reached consumers on the western side of the Gulf, although not in great bulk; however, high-zirconium glass was traded as far as Sri Lanka and Thailand, nicely demonstrating Siraf's involvement in the eastward movement of material culture in the Indian Ocean trade network.[101]

Conclusions

This chapter takes an archaeological approach, considering the evidence for glass found within the Gulf from the earliest days to the end of the thirteenth century CE, when there appears to be widespread and general decline in the Gulf.[102] The glass evidence is largely typological, and more work needs to be done to identify and associate the object types from the Sasanian and Islamic periods in particular. The body of chemical evidence is also expanding, and synthetic discussion of this data will help to identify patterns of glass consumption and trade. This chapter does not claim to be exhaustive or complete, and there is much more work to be done – combing through excavation reports for references to glass artefacts and accessing museum storerooms to study the material itself, in particular.

Although glass from the late Middle Islamic (c. 1300–1500 CE) and Late Islamic (c. 1500–1800 CE) period is beyond the scope of the chapter, it should be noted that glass continued to be a prominent form of material culture within the Gulf. A consideration of these later eras will add much to the story of glass in the Gulf, for example identifying the arrival of new object types and newly prominent glass production zones and markets. One such example includes the introduction of thin glass rods (usually with a circular section and pointed tip), which served as applicators for cosmetics; such kohl rods are common starting in the fourteenth to fifteenth centuries, and are plentiful at sites like Bilad al-Qadim, Qala'at al-Bahrain, Siraf, and Julfar in the Emirate of Ras al-Khaimah.[103] Another type of object that becomes common in the Gulf during later periods are glass bangle bracelets, which were especially popular in the fifteenth to seventeenth centuries. These two glass types – kohl applicators and bangles – were largely produced in India and Iran, demonstrating once again the continually changing nature of glass production, movement and use in the Gulf over time, as well as the social and economic linkages of the Gulf within the wider world.[104]

Notes

1. For a clear description and complete discussion of the subtleties and nuances of glass and glassy materials, see esp. pp. 166–8 in P. R. S. Moorey, 'Working with Faience', 'Working with Egyptian Blue' and 'Glass and Glass-Making', *Ancient Mesopotamian Materials and Industries: the Archaeological Evidence* (Winona Lake: Eisenbrauns, 1999), pp. 166–215.

2. For example, 15th–13th century BCE glass objects from the sites of Ur and Nuzi in Iraq in the collection of the British Museum and Harvard University's Semitic Museum.

3. E. J. Peltenburg, 'Early Faience: Recent Studies, Origin, and Relation with Glass', in *Early Vitreous Materials*, ed. M. Bimson, M. and Ian Freestone (London: British Museum Occasional Papers 56, 1987), pp. 5–30; T. R. Fenn, 'A Review of Cross-craft Interactions Between the Development of Glass Production and the Pyrotechnologies of Metallurgy and other Vitreous Materials', *Cambridge Journal of Archaeology*, vol. 25, no. 1 (2015), pp. 391–8.

4. A. L. Oppenheim, 'The Cuneiform Texts', in *Glass and Glassmaking in Ancient Mesopotamia: an Edition of the Cuneiform Texts which Contain Instructions for Glassmakers with a Catalogue of Surviving Objects*, ed. A. L. Oppenheim, R. H. Brill, A. L. von Saldern and D. Barag (Corning: The Corning Museum of Glass Monographs 3), pp. 2–101; P. T. Nicholson and J. Henderson 2000, 'Glass', in *Ancient Egyptian Materials and Technology*, ed. P. T. Nicholson and I. Shaw (Cambridge: Cambridge University Press, 2000), pp. 195–224; C. N. Duckworth, 'Imitation, Artificiality and Creation: the Colour and Perception of the Earliest Glass in New Kingdom Egypt', *Cambridge Journal of Archaeology*, vol. 22, no. 3 (2012), pp. 309–27.

5. See e.g. B. Schlick-Nolte and R. Werthmann, 'Glass Vessels from the Burial of Nesikhons', *Journal of Glass Studies*, vol. 45 (2003), pp. 11–34.

6. W. M. F. Petrie, *Tell el-Amarna* (London: Methuen, 1894), p. 26; J. Henderson, 'Chemical Analysis of Ancient Egyptian Glass and its Interpretation', in P. T. Nicholson and I. Shaw (eds), *Ancient Egyptian Materials and Technology*, pp. 206–24; M. Smirniou and Th. Rehren, 'Direct Evidence of Primary Glass Production in Late Bronze Age Amarna, Egypt', *Archaeometry*, vol.53, no. 1 (2011), pp. 58–80.

7. T. Clayden, with G. Frame and S. Kirk, 'Glass Axes of the Kassite Period from Nippur', *Sonderdruck aus Zeitschrift für Orient-Archäologie*, Band 4 (2011), pp. 92–135.

8. E.g. K. Nikita and J. Henderson, 'Glass Analyses form Mycenaean Thebes and Elateia: Compositional Evidence for a Mycenaean Glass Industry', *Journal of Glass Studies*, vol. 48 (2006), pp. 71–120; K. Polikreti, J. M. A. Murphy, V. Kantarelou and A. G. Karydas, 'XRF Analysis of Glass Beads from the Mycenaean Palace of Nestor at Pylos, Peloponnesus, Greece: New Insight into LBA Glass Trade', *Journal of Archaeological Science*, vol. 38 (2011), pp. 2,889–96.

9. E. M. Stern, 'Roman Glassblowing in a Cultural Context', *American Journal of Archaeology*, vol. 103 (1999), pp. 441–84.

10 I. Freestone, 'Chapter 4: Pliny on Roman Glassmaking', in M. Martinon-Torres and Th. Rehren (eds), *Archaeology, History and Science: Integrating Approaches to Ancient Materials* (University College London: Institute of Archaeology Publications, 2008), pp. 77–100; P. Degryse (ed.), *Glass Making in the Greco-Roman World: Results of the ARCHGLASS Project* (Leuven: Leuven University Press, 2014).

11 Stern 1999 (n. 9).

12 I. C. Freestone and Y. Gorin-Rosen, 'The Great Glass Slab at Bet She'arim, Israel: an Early Islamic Glassmaking Experiment?' *Journal of Glass Studies* 4 (1999), pp. 105–16; I. C. Freestone, Y. Gorin-Rosen and M. J. Hughes, 'Primary Glass from Israel and the Production of Glass in Late Antiquity and the Early Islamic Period', in M.-D. Nenna (ed.), *La Route du Verre: Ateliers Primaires et Secondaires du Second Millénaire av. J.-C. au Moyen Âge* (Lyon: Maison de l'Orient Mediterranéen No. 33, 2000), pp. 65–83; F. Aldsworth, G. Haggarty, S. Jennings, and D. Whitehouse, 'Medieval Glassmaking at Tyre, Lebanon', *Journal of Glass Studies*, vol. 44 (2002), pp. 49–66; I. C. Freestone, R. E. Jackson-Tal and O. Tal, 'Raw Glass and the Production of Glass Vessels at Late Byzantine Apollonia-Arsuf, Israel', *Journal of Glass Studies*, vol. 50 (2008), pp. 67–80; R. H. Brill, 'Chemical Analyses', in G. F. Bass, R. H. Brill, B. Lledó and S. D. Matthews (eds), *Serçe Limanı: Vol. 2, The Glass of an Eleventh-Century Shipwreck* (College Station: A&M University Press, 2009), pp. 459–96.

13 E. Ashtor and G. Cevidalli, 'Levantine Alkali Ashes and European Industries', *European Journal of Economic History*, vol. 12 (1983), pp. 475–522; D. Jacoby, 'Raw Materials for the Glass Industries of Venice and Terraferma, About 1370–1460', *Journal of Glass Studies*, vol. 36 (1993), pp. 65–90.

14 C. Hess (ed.), *The Arts of Fire: Islamic Influence on Glass and Ceramics in the Italian Renaissance* (Los Angeles: The J. Paul Getty Museum); M. Verità, '6.2 Venetian Soda Glass', in K. Janssens (ed.), *Modern Methods for Analysing Archaeological and Historical Glass, Vol 2* (Chichester: John Wiley), pp. 515–36; K. Janssens, S. Cagno, I. De Raedt and P. Degryse, '6.3 Transfer of Glass Manufacturing Technology in the Sixteenth and Seventeenth Centuries from Southern to Northern Europe', in K. Janssens (ed.), *Modern Methods for Analysing Archaeological and Historical Glass, Vol 2* (Chichester: John Wiley), pp. 537–62.

15 For a concise overview see Th. Rehren and I. C. Freestone, 'Ancient Glass: From Kaleidoscope to Crystal Ball', *Journal of Archaeological Science*, vol. 56 (2015), pp. 233–41.

16 S. Davison, *Conservation and Restoration of Glass*, 2nd edn (Oxford: Butterworth-Heinemann, 2003).

17 E.g. P. Yule, 'Glasgefässe', *Die Gräberfelder in Samad al Shān (Sultanat Oman) – Materialien zu einer Kulturgeschichte* (Verlag Marie Leidorf, 2001), p. 79.

18 E.g. S. A. Jasim, 'The Excavation of a Camel Cemetery at Mleiha, Sharjah, UAE', *Arabian Archaeology and Epigraphy*, vol. 10 (1999), pp. 69–101;

A. Benoist, M. Mouton and J. Schiettecatte, 'The Artefacts from the Fort at Mleiha: Distribution, Origins, Trade and Dating', *Proceedings of the Seminar for Arabian Studies*, vol. 33 (2003), pp. 59–76.

19 E.g. D. B. Whitehouse, *Excavations at ed-Dur (Umm al-Qaiwain, United Arab Emirate), Vol. 1, The Glass Vessels* (Louvain: Peeters, 1998); D. B. Whitehouse, 'Ancient Glass from ed-Dur (Umm al-Qaiwain, UAE) 2. Glass excavated by the Danish Expedition', *Arabian Archaeology and Epigraphy*, vol. 11 (2000), pp. 87–128.

20 Whitehouse 1998 and Whitehouse 2000 (n. 19). D. Kennet, 'Glass', *Sasanian and Islamic Pottery from Ras al-Khaimah: Classification, Chronology, and Analysis of Trade in the Western Indian Ocean*, BAR International Series 1248 (2004), pp. 77–8. J. Price and S. Worrell, 'Roman, Sasanian, and Islamic Glass from Kush, Ras al-Khaimah, United Arab Emirates: a Preliminary Survey', *Annales du 15e Congrès de l'Association Internationale pour l'Histoire du Verre*, AIHV (2003), pp. 153–7. S. Worrell and J. Price, 'The Glass from Kush, Ra's al-Khaimah, U.A.E', in D. Potts, H. al-Naboodah and P. Hellyer (eds), *Archaeology of the United Arab Emirates: Proceedings of the First International Conference on the Archaeology of the U.A.E.* (London: Trident Press, 2003), pp. 248–52. D. Keller, 'Functional and Economic Aspects of Late Sasanian and Early Islamic Glass from Kush, United Arab Emirates', in B. Zorn and A. Hilgner (eds), *Glass Along the Silk Road from 200 BC to AD 1000*, RGZM – Tagungen 9 (Mainz: Römisch-Germanisches Zentralmuseum, 2010), pp. 71–80. D. Keller (forthcoming), 'Glass Vessels', in Simpson, St. J. *et al.* (eds), *Excavations at Kush: a Sasanian and Islamic Site in Ras al-Khaimah, United Arab Emirates II. The Small Finds and Glassware: Catalogue, Discussion, and Scientific Analyses* (Oxford: Archeopress).

21 S. F. Andersen, *The Tylos Period Burials in Bahrain, Vol 1: The Glass and Pottery Vessels* (Culture & Natural Heritage, Kingdom of Bahrain, 2007).

22 A note on the periodisation used in Gulf archaeology: 'Late Pre-Islamic' is a translation of archaeologist Michel Mouton's term 'Préislamique Récente' (abbreviated to PIR), which refers to the period c. 300 BCE–300 CE and is divided into four periods based upon a study of the ceramics from Mleiha: PIR A (c. 300–150 BCE), PIR B (c. 150–1 BCE), PIR C (c. 1–150 CE), and PIR D (c. 150–300 CE). See M. Mouton, 'Mleiha: Description and Dating of the Site', in M. Mouton (ed.), *Mleiha I: environnement, strategies de subsistance et artisanats* (Lyon: Travaux de la Maison de l'Orient Méditerranéen, 29), pp. 9–32.

23 F. Højlund, A. S. Hilton, C. Juel, N. Kirkeby, S. T. Laursen and L. E. Nielsen,

'Late Third-Millennium Elite Burials in Bahrain', *Arabian Archaeology and Epigraphy* vol. 19 (2008), pp. 144–55.

24 'Beads', in F. Højlund and H. H. Andersen, *Qala'at al-Bahrain Vol. 1 The Northern City Wall and the Islamic Fortress* (Moesgaard: Jutland Archaeological Society, 1994), pp. 391–3. The three glass beads come from Period Ib (c. 2100 BCE) and Period IIc (c. 1900–1700 BCE) contexts; the rectangular black glass bead with white wavy lines comes from Period V (Hellenistic) contexts.

25 Waleed Mohamed Abdulrahim Al-Sadeqi. *The Ancient Beads of Bahrain: a Study of the Ornaments from the Dilmun and Tylos Eras*, unpublished doctoral dissertation, Durham University, 2013.

26 A. Andersson, 'Beads, Pendants, and Other Ornaments from Late 3rd–2nd Millennium BC Occupation on Failaka, Kuwait', in A. Golani and Z. Wyganańska (eds), *Polish Archaeology in the Mediterranean 23/2, Special Studies: Beyond Ornamentation. Jewelry as an Aspect of Material Culture in the Ancient Near East* (Warsaw: Polish Centre of Mediterranean Archaeology, 2014), pp. 209–24; A. Andersson, 'The Beads', in F. Højlund and A. Abu-Laban (eds), *Tell F6 on Failaka Island. Kuwaiti–Danish Excavations 2008–2012* (2016), pp. 176–98, Figs. 906, 909–10 and 922; A. Andersson, *The Bead Material from the Danish Archaeological Investigations on Failaka, Kuwait*, forthcoming.

27 Andersson 2016 (n. 26): Fig. 831.

28 Flemming Højlund, personal communication, 2017.

29 A. M. Pollard, 'Report on the Analysis of Failaka Glass, Glazed Pottery, and Faience', in F. Højlund, *Failaka/Dilmun: The Second Millennium Settlements, Vol. 2 The Bronze Age Pottery* (Moesgaard: Jutland Archaeological Society, 1987), pp. 185–93, and Tables 1–2. Object numbers 881.AHJ and 881.BVD (tell F3), and 1129.FM and 1129.JJ (tell F6); there are no drawings or photos of these fragments.

30 F. Højlund and H. H. Andersen, *Qala'at al-Bahrain Vol. 2 The Central Monumental Buildings* (Moesgaard: Jutland Archaeological Society, 1997), p. 198 and Fig. 844.

31 P. Lombard and M. Kervran (eds), *Bahrain National Museum Archaeological Collections: A Selection of Pre-Islamic Antiquities* (Manama: Directorate of Museum and Heritage, Ministry of Information, State of Bahrain, 1989). M.-D. Nenna, 'La Verrerie', in *Bahrain: la civilization des deux mers, de Dilmoun a Tylos. Exposition présentée à l'institut du monde arabe du 18 mai au 29 aout 1999* (1999), pp. 181–91; S. F. Andersen 2007 (n. 16); M. I. Salman and S. F. Andersen, *The Tylos Period Burials in Bahrain, Vol. 2: The Hamad*

Town DS 3 and Shakhoura Cemeteries (Culture & Natural Heritage, Kingdom of Bahrain, 2009).

32 Whitehouse 1998 and 2000 (n. 14); for a review of these works see E. M. Stern, 'Early Roman Glass from the Persian Gulf', *Journal of Roman Studies*, vol. 13 (2000), pp. 693–7.

33 Whitehouse 1998, p. 59, cat. 62–4, 72, 94–7 and 106; Whitehouse 2000, pp. 116–17, cat. 33–8 (n. 19).

34 A. De Waele, 'The Beads of ed-Dur (Umm al-Qaiwan)', *Proceedings of the Seminar for Arabian Studies*, vol. 37 (2007), pp. 297–308.

35 S. Jasim 1999 (n. 18), Fig. 20.

36 S. Jasim, 'Trade Centers and Commercial Routes in the Arabian Gulf: Post-Hellenistic Discoveries at Dibba, Sharjah, United Arab Emirates', *Arabian Archaeology and Epigraphy*, vol. 17 (2006), pp. 214–37, Figs. 31–7.

37 Jasim 2006 (n. 36), p. 223, Fig. 34, 6–10 and Fig. 38. Compare Andersen 2007 (n. 21), pp. 34–5, Type 7 (see esp. Fig. 69–70, Cat. Nos. 7.1 and 7.2; one of these is described as whitish in colour, while another has an opaque white weathering crust overlying the green translucent glass) and Whitehouse 1998 (no. 19), p. 31, Cat. 72 (thick walls, annular pontil mark, and pale yellowish weathering looks like 'alabaster').

38. W. Tikriti, 'The Excavations at Bidya, Fujairah: the 3rd and 2nd Millennium BC Cultures', *Archaeology of the United Araba Emirates* vol. 5 (1989), p. 108 and Pl. 82a.

39. N. 20.

40. M. Golding, 'Artefacts from Later Pre-Islamic Occupation in Eastern Arabia', *Atlal*, vol. 8, no. 3 (1984), pp. 165–1,972.

41. Whitehouse 1998 and 2000 (n. 19). Andersen 2007 (n. 21), pp. 56 ff. and 96–7; although the publication states that the chemical analyses of glass samples from the Tylos burials identify eastern glasses (Appendix 2 in Andersen 2007, p. 251), the chemical data reflect highly deteriorated material rather than the original vessel glass: for example, 0.5–12 wt% Na_2O compared to the 13–18 wt% Na_2O of the Ed-Dur samples.

42. O. Lecomte, 'Ed-Dur, les occupations des 3e et 4e s. ap. J.-C.: Contexte des trouvailles et materiel diagnostique', in U. Finkbeiner (ed.), *Materialien zur Archäologie der Seleukiden- und Partherzeit im südlichen Babylonien und im Golfgebiet* (1993), pp. 195–218 and Fig. 14.

43. Benoist *et al.* 2003 (n. 18).

44. Andersen 2007, p. 97 (n. 21); Salman and Andersen 2009, p. 7 (n. 31).

45. S. J. Simpson, 'Sasanian Glass, an Overview', in D. Keller, J. Price and C. Jackson (eds), *Neighbors and Successors of Rome: Traditions of Glass Production and Use in Europe and the Middle East in the Later 1st Millennium AD* (Oxford: Oxbow, 2014), pp. 200–31.

46. Andersen 2007, p. 96 (n. 21), Type 37 and also Cat. 41.13.

47. J. Zarins, A. S. al-Mughannam and M. Kamal, 'Excavations at Dhahran South – The Tumuli Field (208–92), 1403 A.H. 1983. A Preliminary Report', *Atlal*, vol. 8 (1984), pp. 25–54, Pl. 50/10.

48. Keller forthcoming (n. 20).

49. S. A. Jasim, 'The Archaeological Sites of Jebel al-Buhais', in H.-P. Uerpmann, M. Uerpmann and S. A. Jasim (eds), *Funeral Monuments and Human Remains from Jebel al-Buhais* (Sharjah: Department of Culture and Information, Government of Sharjah, UAE, 2006), pp. 13–63; glass on pp. 55–6 and in Fig. 94: 1 (BHS 29) and 2–3 (BHS 45).

50. Simpson 2014 (n. 45), pp. 225–6.

51. E. Haerinck 'Le mobilier funérarire', written as part of 'Chapitre II: Les Tombs dite 'Mégalithiques' (pp. 69–77, Pl. 37 and 42) and 'Chapitre III: La Nécropole dite 'De la Plaine',' (pp. 79–84 and Pl. 44–50) in M.-J. Steve, *L'Île de Khārg: une Page de l'Histoire du Golfe Persique et du Monachisme Oriental* (Neuchâtel: Civilisations du Proche-Orient, 2003).

52. For Mesopotamian examples see Simpson 2014 (n. 45): Fig. 20.14, nos 1–8. For Bahrain examples see Andersen 2007 (n. 21), pp. 56–7, Type 24.

53. Simpson 2014 (n. 45), Fig. 20.8 nos 7–9; Figs 20.6–20.7.

54. Haerinck 2003 (n. 51), p. 80 and Pl. 45–7.

55. D. B. Harden, 'Excavations at Kish and Barghuthiat 1933: II. Pottery' *Iraq*, vol. 1, no. 2 (1934), pp. 131–6. For more on the colour and opacity of weathering layers for Sasanian glasses, see M. Gulmini, M. Pace, G. Ivaldi, M. Negro Ponzi and P. Mirti, 'Morphological and Chemical Characterization of Weathering Products on Buried Sasanian Glass from Central Iraq', *Journal of Non-Crystalline Solids*, vol. 355 (2009), pp. 1,613–21.

56. See e.g. S. Hadad, *Islamic Glass Vessels from the Hebrew University Excavations at Bet Shean* (Jerusalem: The Hebrew University, 2005), pp. 40–1 and Pl. 38 nos 762–79.

57. G. R. D. King, 'A Nestorian Monastic Settlement on the Island of Sir Bani Yas, Abu Dhabi: a Preliminary Report', *Bulletin of the School of Oriental and African Studies, University of London*, vol. 60, no. 2 (1997), pp. 221–35; see Fig. 10. For the re-dating of the site see R. Carter, 'Christianity in the Gulf during the

First Centuries of Islam', *Arabian Archaeology and Epigraphy*, vol. 19 (2008), pp. 71–108.

58. St John Simpson briefly examined the glass of Sir Bani Yas and noted similarities with Umayyad glass (during or after the second half of the 7th c.) with appliqué ribbons in wavy lines on the shoulder of miniature bottles; personal communication in Carter 2008 (n. 57), pp. 90–2.

59. Simpson 2014 (n. 45), Fig. 20.10. For Umayyad examples west of the Euphrates see S. Hadad (n. 56), pp. 28, 130–1, and Pl. 21 nos 400–12.

60. Karol Pieta, personal communication, 2017. See also K. Pieta, A. H. Shehab Shehab, J. Tirpák, M. Bielich and M. Bartík, 'Archaeological and Geophysical Survey in Deserted Early Islamic Village of al-Qusur (Failaka, Kuwait)', *ArcheoSciences*, vol. 33 (suppl.) (2009), pp. 155–7.

61. Derek Kennet, personal communication, 2015: this material is currently being studied typologically by Andrew Blair and chemically by Julian Henderson.

62. Despite the title, there is no mention of glass within the text, nor are there photographs or illustrations: C. Hardy-Guilbert and A. Rougeulle, 'La céramique et les verres du monastère', in M.-J. Steve, *L'Île de Khārg: une Page de l'Histoire du Golfe Persique et du Monachisme Oriental* (Neuchâtel: Civilisations du Proche-Orient, 2003), pp. 131–49.

63. D. Kennet, 'The Decline of Eastern Arabia in the Sasanian Period', *Arabian Archaeology and Epigraphy*, vol.18 (2007), pp. 86–122 (see p. 92); Carter 2008 (n. 57), pp. 97–8.

64. T. Insoll, 'Chapter 7: The Glass Vessel Fragments, Bracelets, Beads, Pendants, and Spindle Whorls', in *The Land of Enki in the Islamic Era: Pearls, Palms, and Religious Identity in Bahrain* (London: Routledge, 2005), pp. 281–302.

65. K. Frifelt, 'Early Islamic Material from Barbar', in *Islamic Remains in Bahrain* (Højbjerg: Jutland Archaeological Society, 2001), p. 32.

66. T. Sasaki, 'Excavations at A'Ali 1988/89', *Proceedings of the Seminar for Arabian Studies*, vol. 20 (1990), pp. 111–29 and Figure 8.

67. Timothy Power, personal communication, 2016.

68. C. Hardy-Guilbert, 'Fouilles Archéologiques a Murwab, Qatar', in R. Boucharlat and J.-F. Salles (eds), *Arabi Orientale, Mésopotamie et Iran Méridional de l'Age du Fer au Début de la Période Islamique* (Paris: Histoire du Golfe Editions Recherche sur les Civilisations, 1984), pp. 169–87. C. M. Swan, A. Guérin and F. A. Al-Na'imi, 'Abbasid Glassware in Eastern Arabia: Finds from Murwab, Qatar (ca. 805–885 AD)', forthcoming.

69. Keller forthcoming (n. 20).
70. Keller 2010 (n. 20), p. 78.
71. H. Morrison, 'Appendix I: The Glass from Suhar', in M. Kervran, 'Archaeological Research at Suhar 1980–1986', *The Journal of Oman Studies*, vol. 13 (2004), pp. 263–381. Kennet 2007 (n. 49), pp. 97–100.
72. Morrison 2004 (n. 71), Fig. 38 nos 10–13 and 6.
73. D. Whitehouse, 'Excavations at Sīrāf: First Interim Report', *Iran*, vol. 6 (1968), pp. 1–22.
74. Insoll 2005 (n. 64).
75. Keller forthcoming (n. 20).
76. S. Jasim and E. Yousif, 'Dibba: an Ancient Port on the Gulf of Oman in the Early Roman Era', *Arabian Archaeology and Epigraphy*, vol. 25 (2014), pp. 50–79.
77. Frifelt 2001 (n. 65), p. 32.
78. K. Frifelt, 'Medieval and Late Islamic Material from Qala'at al-Bahrain', in *Islamic Remains in Bahrain* (Højbjerg: Jutland Archaeological Society, 2001), pp. 156–8 and Fig. 338.
79. Frifelt 2001 (n. 78), pp. 156–9, figs. 338, 339, 340.
80. D. Whitehouse, 'Excavations at Sīrāf: First Interim Report', *Iran*, vol. 6 (1968), pp. 1–22.
81. Swan, C. M., Lankton, J., Rehren, Th., Gratuze, B. and R. H. Brill, 'Compositional Observations for Islamic Glass from Sīrāf, Iran, in the Corning Museum of Glass Collection', *Journal of Archaeological Science: Reports*, vol. 16 (2017), pp. 102–16.
82. Zarins *et al.* 1984 (n. 47), p. 41.
83. L. Casson. *The Periplus Maris Erythraei. Text with Introduction, Translation, and Commentary* (Princeton: Princeton University Press, 1989); see pp. 6, 7.17, 39, 49 and 56).
84. C. Meyer, *Glass from Quseir al-Qadim and the Indian Ocean Trade*, Studies in Ancient Oriental Civilization No. 53 (Chicago: Oriental Institute of the University of Chicago, 1992).
85. A. Lombardi, 'Glass Objects', in A. Avanzini (ed.), *A Port in Arabia Between Rome and the Indian Ocean (3rd c. BC–5th AD), Khor Rori Report 2* (Rome: L'Erma di Bretschneider, 2008), pp. 404–7.
86. M. Menninger, *Untersuchungen zu den Gläsern und Gipsabgüssen aus dem Fund von Begram/Afghanistan* (Würzburg: Würzburger Forschungen zur Altertumskunde, 1, 1996), pp. 16–22.

87. J. Marshall, *Taxila* (Cambridge: Cambridge University Press, 1951).

88. E. M. Stern, 'Early Roman Export Glass in India', in V. Begley and R. D. De Puma (eds), *Rome and India: the Ancient Sea Trade* (Madison, WI: University of Wisconsin Press, 1991), pp. 113–23.

89. R. Coningham, 'Glass Objects', in R. Coningham (ed.), *Anuradhapura: the British–Sri Lankan Excavations at Anuradhapura Salgaha Watta 2, Volume II: The Artefacts* (BAR International Series 1508, 2006), pp. 333–57.

90. Whitehouse 1998 (n. 19).

91. Whitehouse 1998 (n. 19).

92. C. W. Clairmont, 'The Glass Vessels', *The Excavations at Dura-Europos Conducted by Yale University and the French Academy of Inscriptions and Letters, Final Report IV, Part V* (New Haven, CT: Dura-Europos Publicaitons, 1963).

93. R. Ployer, 'Gläser', in A. Schmidt-Colinet and W. al-As'ad (eds), *Palmyras Reichtum durch Weltweiten Handel: Archäologische Untersuchungen im Bereich der Hellenistischen Stadt. Band 2: Kleinfunde* (Vienna: Holzhausen, 2013), pp. 127–205.

94. H. P. Ray. 'Early Maritime Contacts between South and Southeast Asia', *Journal of Southeast Asian Studies*, vol. 20, no. 1 (1989), pp. 42–54.

95. Whitehouse 1998 (n. 19).

96. Keller 2010 (n. 20).

97. Pollard 1987 (n. 29). Brill 1998 (n. 29). S. F. Andersen, 'Appendix 2', *The Tylos Period Burials in Bahrain, Vol 1: The Glass and Pottery Vessels* (Culture & Natural Heritage, Kingdom of Bahrain), p. 251.

98. Brill, R. H., 'Appendix, Chemical Analyses of Selected Fragments', in Whitehouse 1998 (n. 19), pp. 69–76.

99. I. C. Freestone, 'Glass Production in Late Antiquity and the Early Islamic period: A Geochemical Perspective', in M. Maggetti and B. Messiga (eds), *Geomaterials in Cultural Heritage* (London: Geological Society of London Special Publication 257, 2006), pp. 201–16. Simpson 2014 (n. 45).

100. I. C. Freestone and S. Lambarth, 'The Composition of Sasanian and Islamic Glass from Kush', in St J. Simpson (ed.), *Excavations at Kush: a Sasanian and Islamic Site in Ras al-Khaimah, United Arab Emirates II. The Small Finds and Glassware: Catalogue, Discussion, and Scientific Analyses* (Oxford: Archeopress); Swan, unpublished data.

101. Swan *et al.* 2017 (n. 81) and James Lankton (personal communication).

102. E.g. at Siraf, Kush, Suhar and Hamasa.

103. J. Hansman, 'Rings, Beads, and Kohl Sticks' (76–9), 'Glass Bangles' (80–3),

and 'Glass Containers' (84–7), *Julfar, an Arabian Port. Its Settlement and Far Eastern Ceramic Trade from the 14th to the 18th Centuries* (London: Royal Asiatic Society, 1985).

104. I am very grateful to those who generously shared their time and expertise with me during the course of this research: Flemming Højlund, Steffen T. Laursen, Derrek Kennet, Robert Carter, Timothy Power, Mark Beech, Mark Horton, Jose Carvajal Lopez, Fran Cole, Alexandrine Guerin, Faysal al Na'imi, Timothy Insoll, Pierre Lombard, Sh Khalifa Ahmed al-Khalifa, Nadine Boksmati-Fattouh, Mustafa Ebrahim Salman Jassim, Sabah Jasim, Hanae Sasaki and Fatma Marii. I also thank Thilo Rehren for his support of this research and for reading drafts of this manuscript. This publication was made possible by NPRP grant 7-776-6-024 from the Qatar National Research Fund (a member of Qatar Foundation). The statements made herein are solely the responsibility of the author.

PART VI

HERITAGE AND MEMORY IN THE GULF

15

FROM HISTORY TO HERITAGE: THE ARABIAN INCENSE BURNER

William G. Zimmerle

For most audiences, indigenous to the Arabian Peninsula, a cuboid incense burner probably does not need any explanation, or even a defence, as it has evolved into an iconic symbol of national heritage for most if not all of the Gulf States (Plate 18). However, how we define the cuboid incense burner – where it came from, and where it went, and how it evolved in its cultural identity – has been, of course, full of uncertainties in Western scholarship. In this brief overview, I dissect the history of the biography of the object in two parts. First, I highlight the background of this deep cultural heritage tradition, reviewing Western scholarship and research on the subject of cuboid incense burners. Secondly, I turn to discuss new ways of addressing the problems of interpretation for where and how these objects were once made inside the Arabian Peninsula, including my own ethnographic studies on its modern-day production in Dhofar, the southernmost region of the Sultanate of Oman. By casting a wider spatial and temporal net, I will bring the Arabian Peninsula into focus with southern Mesopotamia and the southern Levant in antiquity, highlighting two distinct trade patterns from the distribution percentages and cultural movement of the Pre-Islamic cuboid incense burner tradition in history. I conclude by summarising my ethnographic evidence from Dhofar to describe the manifold functions for these artefacts, which in turn has helped to clarify the relationship between incense burner users and incense burner makers in the past. In doing so, I hope to raise awareness of this important locally made artefact-type when found in our archaeological investigations and ongoing excavations across the Middle East.

Scholarly Interpretations

For over a century now, Western archaeologists have been intrigued by so-called cuboid incense burners since their discovery in the early 1900s at Tall Nuffar (ancient Nippur) in southern Iraq, when Hermann Hilprecht of the University of Pennsylvania Museum recorded them in the museum notes as diminutive 'four-legged troughs' while sitting in the Istanbul Museum of the Ottoman Empire (Figure 15.1). Shortly afterwards, when similarly shaped artefacts were found in the first field seasons at Tall al-Muqayyar (ancient Ur) in 1922, the expedition's excavator, the renowned Sir Leonard Woolley

Figure 15.1   A glazed terracotta cuboid incense burner from a first millennium BCE mortuary context at Nuffar (Nippur), Ancient Iraq. Photograph by W. Zimmerle in the Istanbul Archaeology Museum in Turkey.

of London, labelled the artefacts 'stands' (Field Number, U.238) and 'caskets' (U.846), and then, in 1923, 'stools' (U.1174) (Woolley 1962: Pl. 36). According to the field notes housed at the British Museum and his 1962 published excavation report, by the 1931–2 field season Woolley seemed to have progressed on their interpretation, and confirmed their identification as incense burners (U.17612) (Woolley 1962: 127). Although there was nothing of this specific type of object described by its descriptive categories of shape from any historical texts from Mesopotamia to assist him in understanding their interpretation, he must have been convinced of this fact then by Leon Legrain's 1930 study, *Terracottas from Nippur* (Legrain 1930: 10). In that book, Legrain identified the objects by the Sumerian NIG$_2$NA (*nignakkū*), one of the essential cultic objects of Mesopotamian witchcraft literature that were used to burn incense (Legrain 1930: Pl. LXV: 359).

In his 1962 report on the Neo-Babylonian and Persian material culture found at the site of Ur, Woolley would comment on the function of the incense burners, where there had been many more found at the site than those documented in the report. He wrote that cuboid incense burners were so common in the later periods that that fact alone 'suggests that some new ritual had been introduced'; judging from the ranges he supplied it was 'not a temple – but rather a domestic ritual that was affected' (Woolley 1962: 103).

Since the 1970s, however, much of the prevailing scholarship has been in response to the Syro-Palestinian archaeologist, William Foxwell Albright, and his suggestion that these artefacts were secular *toilettes* to enable women to perfume their bodies cosmetically (Albright 1974: 25). Albright applied a nineteenth-century ethnographic narrative by Samuel W. Baker (who had travelled to East Africa) to a limestone-cut block incense burner from the site of Tall ed-Duweir (ancient Lachish) in southern Palestine as a way of interpreting its function, and then he compared the artefact from Lachish to smaller stone-cut cuboid incense burners from Hellenistic sites in southern Arabian in Yemen (Albright 1974: 28). However sensible his suggestion might have seemed to scholars initially, his conjecture probably unintentionally led to the erroneous labelling of these objects by scholarship as secular 'Persian-type' burners for decades, despite the fact that their chronological distribution is attested as early as the late third millennium BCE. Nevertheless, one point was made clear by Albright: the incense burners had been found in domestic contexts, and that fact alone suggested that they were indeed objects which were part of an olfactory cultural milieu introduced from the famed frankincense trade of antiquity (Albright 1974: 25–8).

The Incense Burner Tradition

More recently, excavations conducted in the 1990s on the coast at Ra's al-Jinz (RJ), a seasonal fishing town along the north-east coast, have provided the earliest evidence for the four-legged form, which was crafted near the end of the third millennium BCE (2250 BCE) in the shape that was probably the most functional for burning frankincense (Figure 15.2). The fragments (DA 10850 and DA 11971) are not only the oldest known cuboid incense burners from Arabia, but one is a wholly intact exemplar (DA 12728), and all are from well-defined and clear archaeological contexts. The context has helped to define the overall functions for the cuboid incense burners, at least in Arabia.

Figure 15.2 Object number, DA 12728: four-legged sandstone incense burner from Ras al-Jinz, Sultanate of Oman (2250 BCE), National Museum in Muscat. Photograph by W. Zimmerle.

The intact incense burner was discovered in a deposit beneath and sealed by a layer of bricks and clay from the fallen walls surrounding it. The artefact is approximately twelve centimetres long, most likely made from locally made stone quarried from the nearby sandstone quarries. Its discovery from a daily domestic space as a plainly designed artefact without any decorative incised carvings suggested to the excavators that the artefact was indeed part of standard domestic equipment for the burning of frankincense in daily activities. The excavators, the late Serge Cleuziou and the late Maurizio Tosi, identified the object as 'an item of standard household equipment', and wrote that 'the burning of aromatics was an everyday activity performed with locally manufactured objects in common use' (Cleuziou and Tosi 2000: 54). They also wrote:

> Our calling the stone burner from RJ-2 'the earliest *mabkhara* of Oman' emphasizes the fact that the shape was already the one that has endured till the present day. The local Omani workers of Ra's al-Jinz did not hesitate to call it a *mabkhara*, and passed it to one another with the traditional formal gestures. (Cleuziou and Tosi 2000: 54)

When the excavators uncovered the fully intact incense burner along with two of its fragments from their excavations, they were unable to identify the object outright, but their Omani workmen were quick to recognise the square-shaped form as an incense burner.

Two Aromatic Trade Routes

Returning to Albright and his hypothetical chronological conjectures for the cuboid incense burners, the fact is that we can now map the object's chronology at least two centuries before the beginning of the Achaemenid Persian Empire since the discoveries at Ra's al-Jinz. Furthermore, after Ra's al-Jinz, similarly shaped forms manufactured from clay were found further afield geographically in significant numbers from excavations at the Middle Bronze Age levels of archaeological sites along the Middle Euphrates River conduit (Margueron 1982: 95–7). The second millennium BCE sites with cuboid incense burners include the following settlements: Tall Halawa, Mound A, Tall Bi'a (Tuttul) and Tall Meskene (Emar), all sites situated along the Middle Euphrates in Syria. Over the past five years, collections of incense burners were catalogued from comparative museum work in order to close the chronological gaps in history for this important artefact-type (Pruß 1994: 184; Margueron 1982: 95–7; Zimmerle 2014: 397).

After finding, sorting and mapping those cuboid incense burners to determine their distribution patterns, two distinct traditions distinctly surfaced. One major tradition was the stone cuboid incense burners that were found along short trade relays running out of South Arabia through the Arabian Peninsula and onward towards Gaza en route to the Mediterranean Sea markets such as to Rome. This later tradition of small stone incense burners found along this route involved burners that were usually made of limestone or chalkstone, and often incised with images from the natural environment including flora and fauna. The type of images *en miniature* that one can see on the small stone cuboid incense burners are akin to the engravings found on stones at rock art sites in Arabia and the Negev in antiquity. The repertoire of images ranges from plants and animals, human warriors and, occasionally, inscribed personal names and/or the names of aromatics in local languages including Aramaic and the ancient South Arabian languages and dialects such as Minaeic and Sabaic. For most of the incense burners from this tradition, the incised images were not from expected trading regions, but were images of the natural or local environments where the burners had been manufactured locally.

The second tradition from sorting and plotting the distribution of finds was a much earlier tradition of the aromatics trade roads that was presumably conducted via short, maritime relays along the Euphrates River and its nearby canals in Babylonia. This tradition included only clay incense burners. Terracotta clay cuboid incense burners were found chronologically running the opposite direction from north to south at sites along the Middle and Lower Euphrates River.

While the Levantine assemblage of incense burners were almost all made of stone, the southern Mesopotamian (Babylonian) first millennium BCE assemblage, including those from the second millennium BCE Middle Euphrates sites such as Emar and Halawa, Mound A, were almost all composed of clay, with some of the forms from sites such as Nippur being made from locally glazed polychrome that was technologically fashionable and unique at Nippur. At the sites along the Lower and Middle Euphrates, one finds the usual decoration that adorns the outside of traditional mudbrick houses taken from the built environment, thus making these small technological devices not only incense burners but also miniature architectural models, a point to which we shall return towards the end of this chapter.

The Values and Limits of Ethnographic Categories

Since material culture is often considered 'uninterpretable' by many textually-based scholars, making sense for how incense burners were used by people in the past has not always been easy for the interpreter, particularly when Western interpreters uncover unrecognisable artefacts in archaeological excavations, as was demonstrated above. For the workers at Ra's al-Jinz II, the four-thousand-year-old incense burner and its fragments that were discovered by Cleuziou and Tosi were easily recognised by the local inhabitants of the Sultanate, probably because the cuboid-shaped burner has had a long legacy in the Arabian Peninsula, making it knowable as an object of perfumery and frankincense-burning (Figure 15.3).[1]

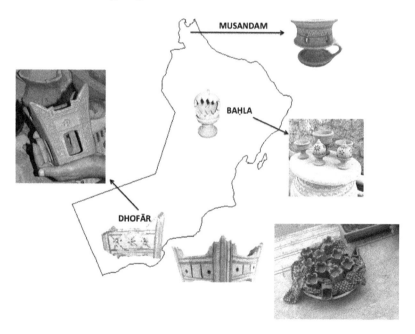

Figure 15.3. Map of the types of incense burners made in the Sultanate of Oman, including a photograph of incense burners arriving at the Mirbat Women's Association for firing in the co-operative kiln. Photographs and map by W. Zimmerle.

At that site, the local workers, unbeknownst to them, were involved in the process of ethnography when they quickly formed an analogy to identify the ancient artefact as an Omani incense burner. Ethno-archaeology, a sub-discipline of anthropological ethnography, refers to the study of contemporary cultures with the aim of creating analogies with which to understand the relationships that underlie the production of material culture (Ochsenschlager, 2004: 6; Zimmerle 2015: 337–52). While ethno-archaeology has often been contested since its development as a robust methodology in the 1970s, the argument against it in recent times has often been that the past cannot equal the present in historical reality. However, the method, when used properly, has helped us to recognise cultural nodes as patterns for ways of doing things, which were embedded within the cognition of traditional pottery communities and can be observed when specific conditions are met, as noted by Ochsenschlager in his ground-breaking study on Iraqi handicrafts and heritage culture in the ecological marshes:

> Through the restoration of the entire process involved in the manufacture of an artifact we can estimate the actual value of that artifact to the people who made and used it by measuring the skill and time required for its production . . . We can understand and better appreciate, for instance, the degree of coordination and skill required for everyday activities in ancient times because both modern and ancient peoples used similar artifacts for similar purposes. (Ochsenschlager 2004: 6)

For the ethno-archaeologist, by using observational methods and oral interviews, research-producing models are applied to the archaeological record as a means of creating analogies or links using comparative methods to interpret the multifaceted meaning of artefacts.

The idea behind the ethnographic interviews in Dhofar with potters who make modern-day incense burners was to conduct a study where the gum resin *Boswellia Sacra*, or frankincense, is cultivated, and to investigate how the ecology of the region might have influenced the development and shape of local incense-burning crafts which seem similar in shape as in the past. Like the Hadrawmaut of Yemen, and Socotra Island of the Indian Ocean, which are also known for their own locally made square incense burners where varieties of species of *Boswellia Sacra* and other gum-resins grow, Dhofar is a region where environmental and cultural factors seem to favour the development of a domestic ceramic specialisation of contemporary terracotta cuboid incense burners, which are crafted today in a similar form and style as in the past. In interviews conducted on the ground, cuboid incense burner makers revealed important information on how they selected and executed local architectural designs and impressed geometric patterns onto clays. Most importantly, data were generated about the people who made the incense burners, focusing on the history of production and the methods that have changed over the years.

For five years, ethnographic fieldwork focused on understanding the function of these devices, as well as examining the organisation of craft production, or how pottery manufacturing techniques and design selection might have differed regionally between the many villages of the Dhofar – the Wilayats Salalah, Mirbat and Taqah – all separated by roughly thirty-three to seventy-five kilometres respectively in eastern Dhofar from the rest of the handicraft centres of production in the Sultanate (Figure 15.4). By the third

Figure 15.4   Modern-day circular-perforated incense burner for burning frankincense from the Kechene Women's Cooperative in Addis Ababa, Ethiopia. Photograph by W. Zimmerle.

year, the project expanded to seek out the work of potters to study in the towns of western Dhofar, including Rakhyut and Sarfait near the border of Yemen, far beyond the major centres of Salalah in Dhofar. As greater trust developed between the potters and me, the project became a truly collaborative work with the potters from Dhofar, as I would spend some days travelling in the late mornings in the town of Mirbat, stopping inside the houses to visit the welcoming potters making incense burners. Multiple interviews and observations conducted with women, both in the home and at craft centres, helped to document the stages of craft production, which ranged from acquiring the clays from the *Jebel* (mountains) to firing and painting the forms (Figures 15.5 and 15.6). The potters were observed and selected because of their ability to construct and maintain the most traditional forms and designs that have been passed down from preceding generations.

From years of observations, it was noted that the social cohesiveness of the community was united at the household level. Women viewed themselves as maintaining social order and economic prosperity by crafting incense

Chaîne Opératoire

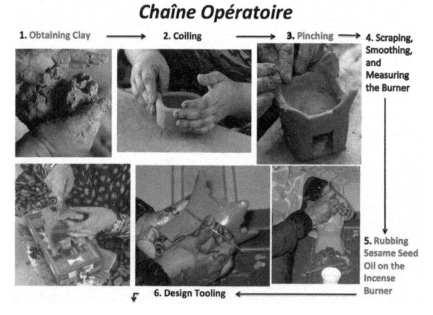

Figure 15.5 Documented ethnographic steps (nos 1–6) in the craft production of cuboid incense burners in Dhofar, Sultanate of Oman. Photographs by W. Zimmerle.

Figure 15.6 Documented ethnographic steps (nos 7–11) in the craft production of cuboid incense burners in Dhofar, Sultanate of Oman. Photographs by W. Zimmerle.

burners as a way of providing for their families. The vessel shapes in Dhofar were uniquely different from those of the rest of the Sultanate and were therefore cartographically specific in shape to the households where they had been made. The cuboid shape dominated all the assemblages in Dhofar; however, women also made other types of pottery vessels and incense burner shapes there. Nevertheless, if they wished to deviate from the cuboid shape, they did so only by modifying the bottom of the burner, as in the case of one household in Rakhyut, a seaside town near the border of Yemen (Figure 15.7).

Pottery Handicrafts

The transfer of methods of handicraft production between the modern world and the ancient one is obviously not always one-to-one. Different conceptions of the world around the ancients and around modern people living in the Middle East today lead to different descriptions of ideas, history, heritage and culture. Since the 1980s, revivalism of traditional culture in the Sultanate of Oman as a means of uniting all the tribes and people living in Wilayats of all the Sultanate has also led to an *elevation* in heritage status of handicraft

Figure 15.7 A modern-day cuboid incense burner from western Dhofar with its unusual bottom as the individual maker's mark of a household potter. Photograph by W. Zimmerle.

culture, especially in the case of pottery development (Valeri 2013: 146). As part of the educational impact of the Women's Associations development training in Dhofar, there are more women potters making incense burners in Dhofar than there were in Pre-Islamic times. Current quantitative observations record at least four hundred women potters alone in the seaside town of Mirbat making or learning to make incense burners.

On one occasion, while I was sitting and interviewing a potter in her house in Mirbat, the daughter of the potter, who was around four years old, emerged from sleep and began to work alongside her mother with her father watching. As she did this, her father exclaimed to me, 'Look, Look!' The young daughter rolled out some clay alongside her mother and began to repeat the first steps of pressing the clay flat with her thumbs. Although she was unable to complete all the steps in the process, it was clear that the process of learning how to make a cuboid incense burner was learned behaviour inside the home which started at a very young age. Many women who were invested in making cuboid incense burners also made their own *bahur* or perfume mixtures. The composite mixtures were trade secrets passed from

Figure 15.8   Crafting a modern-day cuboid incense burner using sesame seed oil by the hands of the potter Dallul from Mirbat. Here she uses the handle of a knife to measure the inside depth of the basin of the incense burner. Photograph by W. Zimmerle.

mother to daughter.

Furthermore, after rubbing sesame seed over the plastic of the clay to make the texture more malleable (Figure 15.8), Dhofari potters selected the design sets on their incense burners from the surrounding architecture – hand-carved doors and windows – of the older mudbrick houses in the villages in which the women potters lived, a fact that may help us understand how ancient potters selected their designs from either their natural or their built environment to manufacture incense burners as architectural models in miniature. Many of these designs were similar to the ones found on the ancient incense burners from southern Mesopotamia. Such geometric designs taken from the surrounding locally built environment were etched into the cognition of the potter's mind since childhood, and in the training practices and observations of children watching their mothers and grandmothers make incense burners inside the home.

The wider demand for tourism in Dhofar has invariably increased the number of experimental vessels for the market. What is true is that pottery made for the tourist and artisan market has adapted to become more creative in design and forms. While the tourist market may imply visitors and expatriates enjoying Salalah and its beaches while buying incense burners, many of those who want to procure incense burners with creative designs are Gulf citizens themselves. Glittery heel-shaped boots modelled as incense burners are among the latest designs sold on the market. Visitors, especially westerners, generally will request the traditional square form as an incense burner because they are told by the community of potters that it is indeed a traditional form.

The Question of Function

Not only were cuboid incense burner makers interviewed as part of the project, but also cuboid incense burner users, who were often the same individuals, in order to understand whether modern and ancient peoples used similar objects for similar purposes. In 1929, the famed British explorer Bertram Thomas wrote in his travel diary that he had photographed the use of a cuboid incense burner by the men of the mountain to expel evil from an animal at sunrise or sunset (Figure 15.9). He wrote:

> These mountain tribes are much afraid of the Evil Eye, not only for themselves, but equally for their flocks and herds. The ceasing of lactation is invariably ascribed to *Ain Balis*. The cure is frankincense . . . The incense

Figure 15.9 Explorations in the Dhofar Mountains, 1929. Courtesy of the Bertram Thomas Collection, UK.

burner was brought and wood introduced and lighted. The practitioner, the cow-owner, broke a fragment of frankincense about the size of a walnut into three pieces. Then spitting upon it three times he introduced it into the burner. While two other witnesses held the afflicted animal by head and led respectively, he waved about its head the burning frankincense, chanting a set sacrificial chant. (Thomas 1932: 88)

Today, the use of such kinds of cuboid incense burners by both genders of the older generation in the Dhofar reaffirms a ritual connotation for frankincense burning, which can be found in the following daily prayer chanted by many Dhofaris:

O, Frankincense (*Ya lubān*)! O, Frankincense (*Ya lubān*)! You the one who is going to the heavens; keep away from us, the enemy, and protect us from the hatred of the friend and enemy. (Zimmerle, August 2015)[2]

The prayer implies that the cuboid burner and its frankincense were used ritualistically inside the home. If the present can be used to restore the past by means of an analogy, it is clear that these enigmatic devices found in the archaeological record were indeed used for fumigation, but also, more importantly, were designed to purify, or to ward off evil and bring frankincense (and other kinds of incense as good scents) into private spaces. The historian Herodotus wrote:

Whenever a Babylonian has had intercourse with his wife, they both sit before a burnt offering of incense (*thymímēma*), and at dawn they wash themselves; they will touch no vessel before this is done. This is the custom also in Arabia. (Herodotus 1. 198)

Such an idea characterises the privatised rituals of a daily domestic lifestyle introduced into Mesopotamia and Mediterranean world from the Arabian Peninsula by both overland and maritime trade, as argued above. Regarding modern-day Dhofar, S. Tabook notes that newly-married individuals in Dhofar use frankincense daily, first to drive away the evil eye and secondly to benefit from its pleasant smell to perfume themselves (Tabook 1997: 130). The fact that so many of the incense burners have been recovered from mortuary and domestic contexts in antiquity, especially from Neo-Babylonian strata at sites in southern Mesopotamia (Babylonia), and at sites in the southern Levant from Iron Age II contexts, point to the idea that they were multifaceted and multifunctional as technological artefacts. This idea stresses the point that everyday fumigation is indeed a ritualistic activity. The cuboid incense burners from antiquity might not only have been used to beautify or fumigate the self, but also to purify the home and tomb from evil irritants and malodours, in tandem with the reciting of the prayers mentioned above.

Conclusions

Since the invention of cuboid incense burners about 2250 BCE, incense burners have become one of the most recognisable and important artefacts left behind by human beings in the Arabian Peninsula. They traditionally tell us about economic and social relationships and are useful for reconstructing ancient roads and pathways for the cultural movement of goods including aromatics and all kinds of spices, and the kinds of aromatics that were used to ward off evil for personal piety practices inside the home. Furthermore, cuboid incense burners are touchstones of heritage that serve as a reference point to a dynamic system of cultural exchanges that were transacted overland and via maritime relays since the third millennium BCE. More recently, the cuboid incense burner has become a symbol of national identify for all Omanis. For example, as I write this chapter at the time of Eid al-Fitr, Oman National Air displays an advertisement consisting of an image of a frankincense-inflamed cuboid incense burner. Since the current Sultan's reign, the cuboid-shaped incense burner has evolved into a touchstone for the image of hospitality and care for all Omanis, not only for Dhofaris but also for those citizens from the northern part of the Sultanate. Between the Women's Associations who serve the communities as handicraft training centres for teachers in Dhofar to learn how to make incense burners for tourists and locals alike and the commercial aspects of displaying oversized replicas of incense burners at roundabouts, or marketing the square form as heritage artefact in the *suqs* in all of the Sultanate, the cuboid-shaped incense burner has been elevated from history to patrimony for the preservation of national identity in the Sultanate today.

Notes

1. A similar example occurred in the February 2016. While teaching an 'Introduction to Sociology' as an Assistant Professor of Social Sciences at Dhofar University in the Sultanate of Oman, I asked my students to identify two objects for me: one was a Dhofari clay cuboid incense burner (Plate 18), and the other was a circular, perforated clay incense burner for burning incense during the coffee ceremony, made by the Kechene Women's Collective at Addis Ababa in Ethiopia (Figure 15.4). My Dhofari students identified the cuboid incense burner with horns easily without delay, while they struggled to make sense of or to identify the perforated incense burner from East Africa.

2. My thanks must be expressed to my colleague Mr Ali Aḥmad Al Shahri for the preservation and recitation of this prayer from the memory of his mother, who lived in the village of Salalah (personal communication, January 2013). I have abbreviated the prayer here because of space. Research for this project would not be possible without the funding support of the Sultan Qaboos Cultural Center, Diwan of the Royal Court of the Sultanate of Oman, US Fulbright Commission, the Metropolitan Museum of Art, Dhofar University, New York University-Abu Dhabi, and a Fairleigh Dickinson University's research grant. Thanks to the potters of Mirbat, Rakhyut, Salalah and Sarfait, especially Fatma Al Amri of Mirbat and Zamzam of Rakhyut.

Bibliography

Al Shahri, Ali A. Mahash (2016), 'The Dhofar's Handicraft Names in Shahri Language' (unpublished manuscript).

Albright, W. F. (1974), 'The Lachish Cosmetic Burner and Esther 2:12', in *A Light Unto My Path: Old Testament Studies in Honor of Jacob M. Meyers*, ed. H. N. Bream, R. D. Heim and C. A. Moore. Philadelphia: Temple University Press.

Cleuziou, S. and M. Tosi (2000), 'Ra's al Jinz and the Prehistoric Coastal Cultures of the Ja'alan', *Journal of Oman Studies* 11.

Legrain, L. (1930), *Terra-cottas from Nippur*, Philadelphia: University Museum Publications.

Margueron, J. (1982), 'Le Coffrets', *Mission Archéologique de Meskéné-Emar*, ed. D. Beyer. Paris: Editions Recherche sur les Civilisations.

Ochsenschlager, E. L. (2004), *Iraq's Marsh Arabs in the Garden of Eden*, Philadelphia: University of Pennsylvania Museum of Archaeology.

Peters, J. P. (1898), *Nippur or Explorations and Adventures on the Euphrates: The Narrative of the University of Pennsylvania Expedition to Babylonia in the years 1888–1890*, New York and London: G. P. Putnam's Sons.

Pruß, A. (1994), 'Räucherkästen', in *Ausgrabungen in Halawa: Die Bronzezeitliche Keramik von Tell Halawa A, Volume 3*, ed. W. Orthmann, 181–92, Wiesbaden: Otto Harrassowitz Verlag.

Shea, M. O. (1983), 'The Small Cuboid Incense Burner of the Ancient Near East', *Levant* XV: 76–109.

Tabook, S. B. S. (1997), 'Tribal Practices and Folklore of Dhofar, Sultanate of Oman', unpublished D.Phil. thesis in Arabic and Islamic Studies, University of Exeter.

Thomas, B. (1932), 'Anthropological Observations in South Arabia', *Journal of the Royal Anthropological Institute of Great Britain and Ireland* 62 (January–June).

Tufnell, O. (1953), *Lachish (Tell ed-Duweir): The Iron Age. The Wellcome-Marston Archaeological Research Expedition to the Near East*, Volume III, 2 parts. New York: published for the Trustees of the Late Sir Henry Wellcome by the Oxford University Press.

Valeri, M. (2013), *Oman: Politics and Society in the Qaboos State*, Oxford: Oxford University Press.

Woolley, C. L and M. Mallowan (1976), *Ur Excavations* Vol. VIII: *The Old Babylonian Period*, London: British Museum.

Woolley, C. L. (1962), *Ur Excavations* Vol. IX: *the Neo-Babylonian and Persian Periods*, London: British Museum.

Zettler, R. L. (1993), *Excavations at Nippur: Kassite Buildings in Area WC-1*. OIP 111, ed. T. A. Holland and T. G. Urban, Chicago: Oriental Institute.

Zimmerle, W. G. (2014a), 'Ethnographic Light on the Form, Function, and Decoration of "Arabian-Style" Cuboid Incense Burners from First Millennium BC Nippur', *Proceedings of the Seminar for Arabian Studies* 44 (Papers from the Forty-Seventh Meeting of the Seminar for Arabian Studies Held at the British Museum, London, 26–8 July 2013): 337–52.

Zimmerle, W. G. (2014b), 'Aromatics of All Kinds: Cuboid Incense Burners from the Late Third to the Late First Millennia B.C.', unpublished Ph.D. dissertation, University of Pennsylvania.

16

DOHA'S MSHEIREB HERITAGE HOUSE MUSEUMS: A DISCUSSION OF MEMORY, HISTORY AND THE INDIAN OCEAN WORLD

Karen Exell

Introduction

> None of the Arabian Peninsula states' national museums tackle the role or even the existence of minorities and other ethnic and religious groups . . . I am skeptical of claims that highlighting the 'other' will exaggerate differences and put them under the microscope. On the contrary, acknowledging and celebrating their roles and lives in a respectful manner would reinforce social cohesion and understanding. (Al Qassemi 2015, online)

The Msheireb Downtown Doha project, located on a 35-hectare site in the centre of Doha near the corniche,[1] will eventually encompass commercial, residential, cultural and government buildings, and has an agenda, according to the project website, to 'unite the Doha of yesterday with the vision of Doha tomorrow, restoring old ways of life, the traditional sense of community, and a strong sense of culture and heritage'. Incorporated into the redevelopment project are four museums housed in reconstructed or renovated houses dating to the first half of the twentieth century which opened to the public in September 2015. These museums are: Bin Jelmood House: The International Slavery Museum, focusing on Indian Ocean World slavery and contemporary human trafficking; Mohammed Bin Jassim (MBJ) House, presenting the urban history of the Msheireb area; Company House, which addresses the early oil industry in Qatar; and Radwani House, displaying the development of the house through archaeology, and traditional lifestyles in dioramic rooms. These museums have opened in advance of the new National Museum of Qatar (due to open in spring 2019), and other planned national museums such as the Oman National Museum (opened in 2016) and Zayed National Museum in Abu Dhabi (the project is currently paused), giving a foretaste of the contemporary construction of national histories in the region, and an introduction to the nature of the different Gulf states' conceptualisations of their relationship to the outside world, in particular their shifting relationship with the Indian Ocean World (Plate 19).

In this discussion, the Msheireb Heritage House Museums are used as a case study to examine the contemporary (re)construction of these relationships, considering the exclusions from the historical narratives of large elements of the Arabian Peninsula states' diverse populations and historical foreign interactions. The passage at the start of the chapter by Sultan Al Qassemi, a member of the Emirati ruling family and well-known cultural commentator, was used by John Thabiti Willis in his discussion of the representation of enslaved Africans in the pearling narratives in Arabian Peninsula museums (Thabiti Willis 2016). In this discussion, the author addresses the lack of reference to the ethnicity and social status of the pearl divers represented in archive images dating to the first half of the twentieth century in, for example, Dubai Museum, in a narrative that reclaims pearling history as purely a national (i.e. Emirati) pursuit without mention of the regional engagement in Indian Ocean World slavery. The Arabian Peninsula states acknowledge in their museums distant historical connections to the wider Middle East, Persia, India, Africa and further afield through trade routes,[2] arguably in order to construct a deeper and more legitimate time-depth, history and culture[3] while simultaneously devaluing the role of foreigners in the production of the modern nation through their exclusion from contemporary representation in museums, at public events such as festivals (Chalcraft 2012) and in official media (Gardner 2010: 96–114). The elision of foreign elements from the record of the nations' recent development allows the imagining of the contemporary mass migration as very new, requiring regimes of management such as *kafala* (Levitt 2015: 36) – the system whereby all labour migrants must be sponsored by a national citizen or state organisation.

While the Arabian Peninsula has for hundreds of years been home or a place of transit to people from many parts of the world, over the last forty years the foreign populations have increased dramatically, and today there are over fifteen million labour migrants at work in the region, with foreigners comprising a majority of the workforce in all of the Arabian Peninsula states, and an absolute majority of the population in Kuwait, where they make up 68 per cent of the population. In the UAE the figure is 81 per cent (Gardner 2014: 4) and in Qatar 88 per cent (Snoj 2017).[4] The dominance of foreign populations has resulted in existential anxiety among the national populations: Westerners are regarded as a threat in terms of the concern that secular Western culture will marginalise Islam, the Arabic language and traditional practices (Al Najjar 1991: 187), while the South Asian (and African) population is discursively constructed as culturally polluting, and through formal and informal practices of discrimination and chauvinism excluded from the public sphere (Dresch 2006; Gardner 2010).

The Museum and the Nation[5]

That museums construct knowledge, including national histories, rather than simply reflecting historical or scientific 'facts', is well-established (see e.g. Ames 1992; Arnold 1998; MacDonald 1998; 2002; Moser 2010; *cf.* Latour 2005). The necessarily selective curatorial processes required to create an exhibition, combined with the anonymous nature of the discourse produced, and the role of the museum as an authoritative public institution, are a potent combination that explicitly and implicitly communicates power structures (Exell, 2016b). Writing on national museums, Donald Preziosi has described the museum as a 'myth-making' technology that through '[t]he social management of memory and desire' produces the nation (2010: 58), an argument reflected by Simon Knell when he suggests that national museums 'provid[e] the scenography and stage for the performance of myths of nationhood' (2010: 4). New nations require a narrative – or myth – of homogeneity and unity (Sibley 1995: 110) and the Arabian Peninsula states are no exception; indeed, they provide a transparent example of the process of myth-making in museums less obvious in older nation states.

Since the establishment of the first Arabian Peninsula national museums in the 1970s,[6] the representation of regional history and society has focused on archaeology, traditional pre-oil lifestyles presented through dioramas populated by Arabs, and the ruling family; Kuwait, Bahrain and Dubai and Al Ain in the UAE are all good examples. Within representations of the national population – the citizens – social complexity (tribes, families, slavery, *ajam* and *hawala*, and so on) is absent, as are politics and the majority of military events (MacLean 2016). In terms of representing the foreign communities and their cultures and religions of the 'pre-oil' period (that is, before around 1950), the cosmopolitan and polyglot norm of Arabian Peninsula cities is omitted, aside from in Dubai Museum, where the displays include mention of recent links to Basra, India and East Africa, omitting Iran; the fact that the long-term-resident foreign communities and contact with foreign countries may form part of the ethnic inheritance of the Arabian Peninsula remains unmentioned (Simpson 2014: 40).

Elsewhere I have termed the unifying discourse under construction in museums and other forms of public discourse 'Arabisation' (Exell 2016a), a term referring to the presentation of the Sunni Arab identity of the ruling families in the public domain as the legitimate identity intimately connected to nationality at the expense of any other social, cultural, ethnic or religious identity category (see Gardner 2010: 123–33 for this process in Bahrain). The increasingly dominant foreign populations are a robust contributing factor to this racialised identity discourse, which can be traced back to the independence from the British from the 1960s and an emphasis on the nation state and 'Arabness' as a marker of identity. In Qatar, this process was strengthened through early tensions between Qataris and foreigners in the oil industry from the 1930s: according to Jill Crystal (1995: 141–5), Qatari oil industry workers in the 1930s demanded that the local arm of the oil company, Petroleum Development (Qatar) Ltd (later renamed Qatar Petroleum), hire Qataris over foreigners, resulting in strikes in 1951. A coalition of Qataris of diverse status was formed, united only by their emergent national identity, and in 1956 protective nationality laws were initiated. National citizenship is also an economic asset, realised through high-level public sector employment – over 90 per cent of Qataris are employed in the public sector (Commins 2012: 284; Ulrichsen 2011: 91) – and a generous welfare state, contributing to the perceived need to protect this status from outsiders (Dresch 2005: 2; Held and Ulrichsen 2012: 23; cooke 2014: 40–7). miriam cooke has noted that the idea of purity associated with national identity has extended to the genetic testing available in Qatar to prove an established Qatari lineage, guaranteeing status and benefits (cooke 2014: 47). Definition against the other, the foreigner, is therefore a central factor in the construction of Arabian Peninsula contemporary national identity.

The regional response to increased migration is articulated in policies and agendas of nationalisation and cultural protection, which acknowledge the necessity of the foreign populations alongside the need to control them.[7] This ethos was explicitly articulated in museological terms at a conference held at Sharjah Archaeological Museum in December 2013, entitled 'The Role of Museums and Cultural Institutions in Strengthening Identity'. The conference outline, circulated by email, explained that the focus was on managing the negative impact of globalisation, stating that 'there has never been a bigger need for protecting our Arab culture from the adverse consequences that have endangered our cultural identity' and that museums have a role in introducing the 'right definition of our cultural identity and the concept of belonging for generations to come'; within the outline, the Emirati national population is referred to as a 'racial minority'.[8] While the necessity of the foreign populations is pragmatically understood, allowing representation of these communities within the region's museums would contradict such state nationalisation policies while contributing to the more general social anxiety around the cultural and demographic dominance of foreigners – museums are spaces were power relations are constructed and enacted, and the museums of the Arabian Peninsula are no exception.

In the following section, the Msheireb Heritage House Museums are presented and their alignment with Qatar's agendas of nationalisation and concept of belonging to the nation considered, in particular given Bin Jelmood House's narration of the regional engagement with Indian Ocean World slavery and contemporary human trafficking, sensitive topics little discussed in the public domain in the region.

The Msheireb Heritage House Museums

The four Heritage House museums are located in the Msheireb area of downtown Doha, an area that began to be urbanised following the discovery of oil in 1939 during the period of the British Protectorate (1916–71). From the 1960s, South Asian migrant populations rented the properties from Qatari landlords who had moved out to suburban villas; in 2011, to make way for the redevelopment, many of the South Asian inhabitants were re-homed in a purpose-built village some distance from downtown Doha (King 2011). The following section presents a brief summary of each museum with a focus on the presentation of foreign communities within each narrative.

Bin Jelmood House: The International Slavery Museum

A visit to Msheireb Museums begins with Bin Jelmood House, located in the restored house of an ex-slave owner, with displays organised along the *liwan*, the open corridor (now glassed in) that runs around the central courtyard, and in the small rooms off the *liwan*. The interpretation utilises film, animation, expert interviews, images and text, with a limited number of objects. The first section addresses slavery in antiquity and elsewhere, then moves on to Indian Ocean World slavery, including the relationship of Islam to slavery; further along the *liwan* the visitor is introduced to a history of Qatar and Qatar's involvement with slavery, with the small associated rooms narrating the fictionalised journey of a family taken from East Africa to first Muscat and then Doha, using animation to narrate the dramatic journey and images and video to communicate the lost homeland, the repetitious domestic tasks enslaved people undertook, and enslaved men diving for pearls. The idea of being an oppressed, disempowered people is dramatically presented through a series of videos of individuals walking into the frame, heads bowed, and standing silently in front of the visitor. Overall, the narrative is vivid and poignant. The modern-day slavery section addresses human trafficking around the world; mention of Qatar and the *kafala* system is located at the bottom of a panel that also discusses migrant workers in the USA and UK ('contractual slavery'), illustrated with an image of workers on a lunch break in Doha captioned: 'Throughout the Gulf states, the abuse of the *kafala* (sponsorship) system directly affects large numbers of migrant workers'. The rest of the section presents local attempts to fight human trafficking, including information on Qatari organisations established for this purpose. The visit ends in the commitment room, where a pledge can be made to personally raise awareness of the issues.

In terms of locating Qatar in the world, the historic presentation of slavery in Bin Jelmood House situates the region within the Indian Ocean World, stating:

> The Gulf and its largely coastal communities were an important part of the Indian Ocean World. Great civilizations have expanded and contracted across the Indian Ocean World, most notably in India and the Middle East but also in Africa (Abyssinia) and Indonesia (Srivijaya).

Through this contextualisation, the Qatari engagement with slavery is geographically and historically contextualised, arguably normalising the practice and rendering the local situation more palatable – facilitating engagement with, rather than denial of, the narrative. The presentation discursively constructs the slavery experience as less detrimental than that of the Atlantic Ocean World, emphasising that many of those enslaved in the Gulf undertook domestic roles that were less arduous than tasks such as plantation work. There are numerous references to how Islam encouraged kindness and manumission, and that many enslaved people integrated into society and their master's family through converting to Islam, learning Arabic – or as noted on one panel, bearing the master's child; the circumstances that lead to this latter event remain undiscussed. On one panel an image shows an enslaved man with his owners, the caption explaining that he is dressed the same as his masters and also carries a weapon, indicating the trust and loyalty that was implicit in the relationship between master and slave. In addition, economic need in countries such as Baluchistan is presented as a driver for Baluchistani people to actively seek entrance into slavery for survival.

There are, however, some arresting images that belie the positive narrative: on one panel an image shows a group of chained African men being transported on foot in Zanzibar gesturing angrily at the camera; in another nineteenth-century image from Zanzibar, a child stands finger in mouth, his other hand balancing a large plank on his head which is chained to an iron loop around his ankle – his painful restraint from movement. Discussion of a connection of these enslaved people, or their cultural and ethnic contribution to contemporary Qatari society, is minimal: just one panel in the *liwan* display on historic Qatari slavery addresses social acculturation and cultural survival: the first section informs the visitor how enslaved people were held at Muscat for some time where they were taught the regional traditions, religion and language; the second section addresses the practising of African traditions in private, such as *zar-bori*, a form of exorcism, and *tanbura* and *laywa*, traditional African musical traditions (spelling as per the gallery panel text), as a way to manage the oppression of slavery. We learn that 'Belief in spirit possession in the Gulf is testimony to the resilience of African cultural traditions in the region' (gallery panel text). One image depicting black African men in Omani clothing is captioned 'Photograph of Arabs of African descent, in Muscat, early twentieth century', indicating that the designation 'Arab' is not ethnic but cultural.

Bin Jelmood House is the vision of Sheikha Mozah bint Nasser, wife of the Father Emir Sheikh Hamad bin Khalifa Al Thani (r. 1995–2013) and forms part of her agenda of addressing contemporary human trafficking issues, rather than social reparation for past wrongs, the case with museums and exhibitions relating to the Atlantic slave trade in the USA and UK which were created in response to public demands to acknowledge the slavery legacy (Smith *et al.* 2011). In Qatar, there has been no public call for representation of this history: the traditions of the enslaved communities – such as those connected to African spirit possession mentioned above – have been naturalised into 'Qatari' heritage and identity (see the MBJ House section below), or are presented as the result of trade connections or pearling traditions (Hopper 2014; Cooper and Exell 2016). Indeed, in the months since the museum's soft opening in September 2015, there has been limited local debate about Bin Jelmood House; instead attention has focused on Company House with its narrative of the early oil industry and Qatari industry 'pioneers', indicative of where contemporary historical value is located.[9]

Mohammed bin Jassim House

The next stop on the tour is MBJ House, just across the street. This museum presents the history of the Msheireb area in a suite of galleries that address the trajectory of the Msheireb area's urban history from development to decline to redevelopment. The first space gives the historic overview in a series of wall texts supported by personal testimonies in digital interactive panels set into central bench-seating. The second space, 'Memories of Msheireb', further humanises this story with oral history films of individuals who appear to step forward to meet the visitor and share their memories of different aspects of living in the Msheireb area – the early development, religious events and celebrations, the introduction of electricity, shopping and eating, and healthcare; these individuals are all Qatari nationals. The oral histories are supported by themed cases holding objects salvaged from the Msheireb area during the clearing and redevelopment of the site (Barbour 2012; Exell 2016b). The remaining spaces are dedicated to the urban renewal project and its sustainable architecture ethos, with a large interactive exhibit that allows different elements of the site to be highlighted.

As with Bin Jelmood House, the narrative begins by contextualising the museum topic within historic interregional connections and influences, informing the visitor that Doha's traditional architecture is similar to that of other parts of Arabia, as well as Asia and Africa, incorporating plaster forms from Iran, timber from Tanzania and reeds from the Euphrates. Foreign communities are introduced in the historic overview section: the Bismillah Hotel, still located in nearby Souq Waqif, is described as being a favourite among Indians and other foreign visitors in the 1950s, and the dramatic rise in population, from 20,000 in 1951 to 80,000 in 1975, is explained as being the result of foreign labour needed to support the growing economy. The text states that 'Msheireb became the vibrant heart of Doha, pulsing with locals and newcomers', and goes on to explain that Qatari families moved out to new suburban districts, to be replaced by foreign workers, and that the restaurants and shops now served 'a community of mostly Asian residents . . . Although Msheireb retained its enduring vitality and acquired fresh and vivid color, its houses became over-populated and its streets acutely congested. The district fell into a state of disrepair.' Having set up this multicultural histori-cal context, the Memories of Msheireb gallery then presents a purely Qatari (re-)imagining of the area through the oral histories and testimonies of Qatari nationals; meanwhile, many of the objects on display silently reference the South Asian community – an Indian peacock mirror, signs advertising samo-sas, and signs written in Hindi. Explicit reference to a positive connection to India is made in the section on healthcare where a local Qatari doctor is described as having 'studied well in India', while in the section on Islamic festivals Yusuf Abdullah Darwish describes how, on the occasion of Eid Al Fitr, 'In the old days . . . some danced tanbora and some danced laywa, fajery, haban, and others . . . These were the traditional [dances] that existed at the time' (quotation in the gallery panel text), indicating the reality of the 'resilience of African cultural traditions in the region' suggested in Bin Jelmood House; the source of these traditions is unreferenced in MBJ House. Towards the end of the visit, a text panel informs the visitor that, once complete, 'Msheireb Downtown Doha will once again be a place in which Qataris and non-Qataris wish to live' – though the non-Qataris will not be the re-homed South Asian communities, but white-collar expatriates wealthy enough to afford to live in the development, indicative of an elite neoliberal cosmopolitan vision of Qatar's near future.

Company House

Company House narrates the story of the early oil industry in the house that was the Qatari headquarters of the local oil company, Petroleum Development (Qatar) Ltd (later Qatar Petroleum). The entrance to the museum has a welcome statement in Arabic, and an installation that gives the names of the early 'pioneers' – Qatari oil-workers – again in Arabic; the lack of any English translation, unusual in Qatar's new museums, indicates that this is a museum about and for the Qatari community, rather than an international audience, such as Doha's Museum of Islamic Art. The museum presents a timeline of the discovery of oil and the industry's development, from the prospecting stage in the 1930s to the nationalisation of the industry in the 1970s and the development of the natural gas industry in the 1980s. An immersive cinema creatively narrates the same story, tracing the hardship of the early years for the Qatari workers to the impact of oil on the modern city of Doha. There is an object-handling space where early equipment can be examined, a room of interactive touch-tables that contain information on tools, oral histories, archive film, and the published account of an English man who worked as an accountant for the oil company in the late 1940s, 'Memoirs of a Company Clerk, Robert E. Hill'.[10] Small rooms offer the opportunity for visitors to record their own memories, and the final space contains the large Pioneers exhibit – the stories of six Qatari men who worked in the oil industry in its early years, with large images and personal memorabilia.

The role of the British in the development of the oil industry is central to the historical narrative, with reference made to the British geologists such as G. M. Lees, and a Mr Langham, and the quoting and reproduction of British source documents such as telegrams, reports and personal accounts such as Robert E. Hill's. The British are presented as technically useful, but there is ambivalence in the representation indicative of a tension between the need for foreign technical expertise and the necessity of tolerating those holding this expertise, a tension that has increased in Qatar in recent years. For example, in the immersive cinema voice-over reference is made to the big houses that the British lived in, compared to the living conditions of the Qatari workers. The nationalisation of the industry in the 1970s is presented as a key turning-point in the story. Aside from the technical role of the British, the role of other nationalities in the industry is almost entirely elided. Throughout, the museum text uses the term 'Qatari workers' or, occasionally, 'laborers' to refer to the workforce; it is only in the account of Robert E. Hill that we find reference to the ethnic diversity of the workforce, where he states at one point that 'the early workforce [of] Qatari, Indians, Pakistanis [and] Baluchi was honest, respectful and happy too', and in the Pioneers exhibit, where Hassan Kali recalls that in 1946 when a strike was threatened regarding rations, the quarter-master was an Indian called Mr Dass, who worked for English managers. The nation-building message of the museum is summed up in two statements, one towards the beginning of the timeline exhibit at the start of the museum, and one towards the end in the introductory panel of the final Pioneers exhibit. This first of these states that the museum is

> the complex story of a nation that managed with instinctive foresight to protect its resources from the self-interest of the world's great economic powers. It is also a straightforward story of a small country that lifted itself from poverty through the hard work, perseverance, and courage of ordinary men. (gallery panel text)

The second states: 'Although the West provided the technology required for its search and extraction, oil was secured as much through the hard work and commitment of the Company's Qataris workforce' (gallery panel text extract).

This is a story of Qatari success through hard work, aligning with ongoing government agendas of nationalisation and the 2030 National Vision's desire for 'a capable and motivated [Qatari] workforce' (GSDP 2008: 15) which will be realised, according to this Vision, through education and training so that Qatari nationals can take on leading workforce roles.

The final museum is Radwani House, which presents the archaeology of the house itself, and a series of rooms without interpretation re-creating the 'pre-oil' and immediately 'post-oil' lifestyles. The material culture on display indicates Qatar's ongoing connections with South Asia, including Indian textiles, peacock mirrors and furniture, as well as products from countries further afield such as the UK. This museum is used primarily for schools' educational programmes.

Concluding Discussion

In Qatar, and the surrounding Gulf states, the message of 'Arabisation', of the association of national identity with ideas of ethnic Arab purity and lineage, and Sunni affiliation, is promoted through government policies and agendas. The racialised construction of identity normalises an ethnic hierarchy that privileges Sunni Gulf Arabs above other identities and ethnicities, allowing if not endorsing prejudice in relation to the South Asian and African populations, which in turn informally validates control systems such as *kafala*. The message of homogeneity – the discourse of 'Arabisation' – is articulated in the older national museums across the region; while the narrative of the new National Museum of Qatar is not yet available for discussion, the Msheireb Heritage House Museums, also state museums, give an insight into the contemporary construction of national history and identity and the local imagining of Qatar's relationship with the rest of the world.

The analysis of the museum narratives reveals that, while the overarching agendas are established primarily through the written text, this is at times contradicted or undermined by the material culture, images and personal memories – an interesting disjunction exemplifying Pierre Nora's discussion of 'real memory – social and unviolated' and the organisation of the past by 'hopelessly forgetful modern societies, propelled by change' (1989: 7). In Bin Jelmood House, the text conveys a message that normalises Qatar's involvement in slavery, and emphasises that this was comparatively benign. However, the animated story of the enslaved family presents the enslavement's bleak emotional reality, and archive images of enslaved people in Zanzibar, en route to the Gulf, document a harsh and undignified experience. African cultural traditions are mentioned in both Bin Jelmood House and MBJ House; in the former practised by enslaved people in secret; in the latter incorporated (unexplained) into Eid Al Fitr celebrations, with the social mechanism that resulted in the integration of East African spiritual traditions into an Islamic festival remaining unexplained. The MBJ House testimony text panel recalls an undefined period in the past, probably the 1950s or 1960s, when many enslaved people had been manumitted and remained in Qatar following the official end of slavery in 1952. Elsewhere in the MBJ House narrative the decline of the area is implicitly connected to the increased inward migration of South Asian populations, and its subsequent salvation presented as a Qatari initiative intended for habitation by Qataris and wealthy expatriates. The South Asian period of occupation is described in passing as 'vibrant', but this long period (1960s–2011) is not equally represented through oral histories or testimonies – no South Asians tell their story. As with Bin Jelmood House, it is the non-textual content, in this case the material culture, that silently documents the South Asian history of Msheireb, a situation replicated in Radwani House, which presents a typical 'Qatari' house – filled with goods from elsewhere, including India. In Company House the role of the South Asian populations in the early oil industry is revealed by just one or two personal anecdotes that do little to counterbalance the narrative of Qatari national achievement.

The Msheireb Museums are working hard to promote a message of a predominantly Qatari past – even if the message is at times mixed – in order to construct such a future. As noted previously, national museums contribute to the construction of the nation rather than representing a pre-existing reality, selectively representing those people deemed to belong to the nation (see chapters in Knell, Aronssen and Amundsen 2010; see also e.g. Sokal 2008 and Jain 2011 on museums and Hindu nationalism). According to Western museology and museum practice, influenced by postmodernist thinking and in the context of postcolonialism, contemporary museums are expected to offer an inclusive space of representation (see the classic museological texts on this: Cameron 1971; Vergo 1989; Clifford 1997; Hooper-Greenhill 2000; case studies in Golding and Modest 2013), an approach that maps onto national agendas of multi-culturalism and equality (Crooke 2011). Qatar's national agendas define policies of exclusivity, and therefore it is unsurprising that its museums offer exclusive spaces of national representation. In addition, given the autocratic context, museums as public spaces do not have the freedom to present narratives that divert from this orthodoxy. A critique of such an exclusive approach solely from the perspective of European museological inclusivity is therefore inapposite, while the question remains, do these museums, through their selective representation, articulate a necessary stage for the construction of a national identity, or are they, in the context of the specific demographic circumstances of Qatar and its neighbouring Gulf states, and the regional nationalisation policies, contributing to a precarious ethical situation regarding race and prejudice? A study of the impact of these new history museums on local and regional perceptions of history, identity and belonging over the next few years would be revealing.

Notes

1. The site is in the Mohamed Bin Jassim District, bordered by the Al Rayyan Road to the north, Jassim Bin Mohamed Street to the east, Msheireb Street to the south and Al Diwan Street (part of the A Ring Road) to the west. The site is also adjacent to the redeveloped Souq Waqif and the historical Al Koot Fort.
2. For example, Ras Al Khaimah National Museum (UAE), which includes mention of the Sassanian Empire (3rd–6th century CE), as well as more recent interactions with the Dutch, Portuguese and British. The planned Zayed National Museum in Abu Dhabi emphasises on its website the connection of Abu Dhabi's history to the wider Middle East, in particular the Sumerian civilisation, and the Greeks.
3. At times the necessary reliance on foreign populations today is also publicly acknowledged, for example when Ali bin Abdulla Al Kaabi, the Minister of Labour in the UAE, observed to *The New York Times* in 2007 that if all the Indians went home the airports, streets and construction would shut down (quoted in Foley 2010, p. 251).
4. In 1970 non-Arabs made up 12 per cent of the Arabian Peninsula populations; by 1985 Asians, regarded as politically passive and cheaper, made up 63 per cent of the populations (Chalcraft 2012, p. 75; Naufal and Genc 2012, p. 48).

5. For an extended discussion of concerns surrounding the construction of contemporary national identity in the Arabian Peninsula states, see Chapter 3, 'Staging Identity in a Globalised World' in Exell 2016a.

6. Qatar National Museum, opened in 1975, was the first museum to use the word 'national' in its name. The first state museum to open was the Kuwait Museum in 1957 (replaced by the Kuwait National Museum in 1983), followed by Failaka Museum, on Failaka Island, Kuwait, in 1964. During the 1970s, museums were opened in Fujairah (1970, and redeveloped in 1991), Dubai and Al Ain (1971), Oman (The Oman Museum in 1974 and the Bait Sayyid Nadir bin Faisal bin Turki Museum in 1978) and Saudi Arabia (the Museum of Archaeology and Ethnography, 1978). In the 1980s, national museums opened in Kuwait (1983), Ras Al Khaimah (1987) and Bahrain (1988), and in the 1990s in Ajman (1991), Sharjah (Sharjah Archaeological Museum in 1993 – this serves as Sharjah's national museum) and Umm al Quwain (2000); see Bouchenaki 2011; Erskine-Loftus 2010; Hirst 2011.

7. For example, Dr Ali Al Khouri of the Emirates Identity Authority, who argues for

> the swelling influx of foreign residents and labour, threat of identity fraud, illegal immigration, international crime and global terrorism . . . While there is no doubt that migrant labourers have been integral forces behind the unprecedented pace of modernisation in the GCC countries, they have also been observed as a negative influence on the national cultures, identities and values as well as social structures. (Al Khouri 2010, pp. 6, 8)

Similarly, the Qatar National Vision 2030 states:

> Qatar must determine a suitable size and quality of its expatriate labor force. It must weigh the consequences of recruiting expatriate workers in terms of their cultural rights, housing and public service needs, as well as the potential negative impact on national identity, against the anticipated economic benefits that accrue from an increase in the numbers of foreign workers in the total labor force. (GSDP 2008: 3–4)

In addition, the conference 'The GCC Countries: Politics and Economics in the Light of Regional and International Shifts and Changes', organised by the Arab Centre for Research and Policy Studies in Doha in 2014, included the sessions 'National identity and society' and 'Foreign and Arab communities'; this latter addressed the 'challenge' of managing the dominant foreign populations.

8. The full outline is as follows:

> The world's countries have experienced a dramatic increase in globalisation woes over the past two decades. With limitless political, economic, social and cultural impacts on both urban and rural communities, cultural and social structures are affected worldwide, including our Arab communities. As today's challenges and negative impacts become ever greater, there has never been a bigger need for protecting our Arab culture from the adverse consequences that have endangered our cultural identity.
>
> Recently, there has been growing interest from researchers in museums as they showcase heritage, history and civilisation exhibits, which are main components of our identity. The researchers are endeavoring to create an active role for museums based on a comprehensive plan to promote and develop museums. The attempt seeks to introduce the right definition of our cultural identity and the concept of belonging for generations to come. It is a great opportunity to share experience with other nations with racial minorities who have managed to preserve their own identities amid a diversified community. Appreciation is given to the museums.
>
> The conference on 'The Role of Museums and Cultural Institutions in Strengthening Identity' has evolved from the need to preserve our identity. Sharjah Museums Department, represented by Sharjah Archaeology Museum, considers the conference to be a contribution to set a clear framework for the roles of the Arab museums in strengthening identity in line with modern age requirements. The program framework will be inspired by the successful experiences, which have allowed the museums to have an effective position in our community.

9. Sources are anecdotal conversations with Qataris and social media discussions.
10. More information on Robert E. Hill's life is available on a website created by his son: <http://www.robertehill.co.uk> (last accessed 28 March 2018).

Bibliography

Al Khouri, A. M. (2010), 'The Challenge of Identity in a Changing World: The Case of GCC Countries', in *Conference Proceedings: The 21st Century-Gulf: The Challenge of Identity*. University of Exeter, 30 June–3 July 2010.

Al Qassemi, S. S. (2015), 'Treasure Troves of History and Diversity', *Gulf News*, 25 January, <http://gulfnews.com/opinion/thinkers/treasure-troves-ofhistory-and-diversity-1.1137150>

Al Najjar, M. R. (1991), 'Contemporary Trends in the Study of Folklore in the Arab Gulf States', in E. Davis and N. Gavrielides (eds), *Statecraft in the Middle East: Oil, Historical Memory and Popular Culture*, Miami: Florida International University, pp. 176–201.

Ames, M. M. (1992), *Cannibal Tours and Glass Boxes: The Anthropology of Museums*, Vancouver: University of British Columbia Press.

Arnold, K. (1998), 'Birth and Breeding: Politics on Display at the Wellcome Institute for the History of Medicine', in S. MacDonald (ed.), *The Politics of Display: Museums, Science, Culture*, London and New York: Routledge, pp. 183–96.

Barbour, B. (2012), 'Salvaging Memory: The Msheireb Arts Centre (MAC) and the Echo Memory Project', unpublished essay.

Bouchenaki, M. (2011), 'The Extraordinary Development of Museums in the Gulf States', *Museum International* 63 (3–4, September–December): 93–104.

Cameron, D. F. (1971), 'The Museum, a Temple or the Forum', *Curator: The Museum Journal* 14: 11–24.

Clifford, J. (1997), *Routes: Travel and Translation in the Late Twentieth Century*, Cambridge, MA and London: Harvard University Press.

Commins, D. (2012), *The Gulf States: A Modern History*, London and New York: I. B. Tauris.

cooke, m. (2014), *Tribal Modern: Branding New Nations in the Arab Gulf*, Berkeley and London: University of California Press.

Cooper, S. and Exell, K. (2016), 'Bin Jelmood House: Narrating an Intangible History in Qatar', in P. Davis and M. L. Stefano (eds), *The Routledge Companion to Intangible Cultural Heritage*, London and New York: Routledge, pp. 371–84.

Crooke, E. M. (2011), 'Museums and Community', in S. MacDonald (ed.), *A Companion to Museum Studies*, 2nd edn, Oxford: Wiley-Blackwell, pp. 170–85.

Crystal, J. (1995), *Oil and Politics in the Gulf: Rulers and Merchants in Kuwait and Qatar*, Cambridge: Cambridge University Press.

Dresch, P. (2005), 'Introduction: Societies, Identities and Global Issues', in P. Dresch and J. Piscatori (eds), *Monarchies and Nations: Globalisation and Identity in the Arab States of the Gulf*, London and New York: I. B. Tauris, pp. 1–33.

Dresch, P. (2006), 'Foreign Matter: The Place of Strangers in Gulf Society', in J. Fox, N. Mourtada-Sabbah and M. Al Mutawa (eds), *Globalization and the Gulf*, new edn, London and New York: Routledge, pp. 200–21.

Erskine-Loftus, P. (2010), 'A Brief Look at the History of Museums in the Region and Wider Middle East', *Art & Architecture, special edition: Museums in the Middle East* 13 (Winter/Spring): 18–20.

Exell, K. (2016a), *Modernity and the Museum in the Arabian Peninsula*, London and New York: Routledge.

Exell, K. (2016b), 'Desiring the Past and Reimagining the Present: Contemporary Collecting in Qatar', *Museums and Society* 14(2): 259–74.

Exell, K. (2016c), 'Covering the Mummies at the Manchester Museum: A Discussion of Individual Agendas within the Human Remains Debate', in H. Williams and M. Giles (eds), *Dealing with the Dead: Mortuary Archaeology and Contemporary Society*, Oxford: Oxford University Press.

Foley, S. (2010), *The Arab Gulf States: Beyond Oil and Islam*, Boulder, CO: Lynne Rienner.

Gardner, A. M. (2010), *City of Strangers: Gulf Migration and the Indian Community in Bahrain*, Ithaca and London: ILR Press/Cornell University Press.

Gardner, A. M. (2014), 'Hosts, Migrants, Visitors, and the Enveloping Field of Relations: On Ethnography in the Contemporary Gulf', paper presented at the *Arab Gulf States: Authoritarian Regimes and Expatriates* workshop, Kyoto University.

Golding, V., and Modest, W. (eds) (2013), *Museums and Communities: Curators, Collections and Collaborators*, London and New York: Bloomsbury Academic.

GSDP (2008), *Qatar National Vision 2030*, Doha: General Secretariat for Development Planning, <http://www.gsdp.gov.qa/portal/page/portal/gsdp_en/qatar_national_vision/qnv_2030_documen>

Held, D. and K. C. Ulrichsen (2012), 'Editor's Introduction: The Transformation of the Gulf', in D. Held and K. C. Ulrichsen (eds), *The Transformation f the Gulf: Politics, Economics and the Global Order*, London and New York: Routledge, pp. 1–26.

Hirst, A. (2011), 'Museums in the GCC: Development for Whom?', MA dissertation, Durham University.

Hooper-Greenhill, E. (2000), *Museums and the Interpretation of Visual Culture*, London and New York: Routledge.

Hopper, M. (2014), 'The African Presence in Eastern Arabia', in L. G. Potter (ed.), *The Persian Gulf in Modern Times: People, Ports and History*, New York: Palgrave Macmillan, pp. 327–50.

Jain, J. (2011), 'Museum and Museum-Like Structures: The Politics of Exhibition and Nationalism in India', *The Exhibitionist*, Spring: 50–5.

King, K. A. (2011), 'The Heart of Doha? The Narrative of Qatari National Identity Offered by the Msheireb Urban Development Project', M.Phil. dissertation, Trinity College Dublin.

Knell, S. J. (2010), 'Introduction', in S. J. Knell, P. Aronssen and A. Amundsen (eds), *National Museums: New Studies from around the World*, London and New York: Routledge, pp. 1–10.

Knell, S. J., P. Aronssen and A. Amundsen (eds) (2010), *National Museums: New Studies from around the World*, London and New York: Routledge.

Latour, B. and P. Weibel (eds) (2005), *Making Things Public: Atmospheres of Democracy*, Karlsruhe: ZKM/Center for Art and Media.

Levitt, P. (2015), *Artifacts and Allegiances: How Museums Put the Nation and the World on Display*, Oakland, CA: University of California Press.

MacDonald, S. (1998), 'Exhibitions of Power and Powers of Exhibitions', in S. MacDonald (ed.), *The Politics of Display: Museums, Science, Culture*, London and New York: Routledge, pp. 1–24.

MacDonald, S. (2002), *Behind the Scenes of the Science Museum*, Oxford: Berg.

Maclean, M. (2016), 'Time, Space and Narrative in Emirati Museums', in P. Erskine-Loftus, M. Al Mulla and V. Hightower (eds), *Representing the Nation: Heritage, Museums, National Narratives, and Identity in the Arab Gulf States*, London and New York: Routledge, pp. 191–204.

Moser, S. (2010), 'The Devil Is in the Detail: Museum Displays and the Creation of Knowledge', *Museum Anthropology* 33(1): 22–32.

Naufal, G. and I. Genc (2012), *Expats and the Labor Force: The Story of the Gulf Cooperation Council Countries*, New York: Palgrave Macmillan.

Nora, P. (1989), 'Between Memory and History: les lieux de mémoire', *Representations* 26: 7–24.

Preziosi, D. (2010), 'Myths of Nationality', in S. J. Knell, P. Aronssen and A. Amundsen (eds), *National Museums: New Studies from Around the World*, London and New York: Routledge, p. 56.

Sibley, D. (1995), *Geographies of Exclusion*, London and New York: Routledge.

Simpson, I. R. (2014), 'Concern amid the Oysters as Pearling is Honoured: Nature and the Environment in Heritage Practice', in K. Exell and T. Rico (eds), *Cultural Heritage in the Arabian Peninsula: Debates, Discourses and Practice*, Farnham and Burlington, VT: Ashgate, pp. 33–49.

Smith, L., G. Cubitt, R. Wilson and K. Fouseki (eds) (2011), *Representing Enslavement and Abolition in Museums: Ambiguous Engagements*, Abingdon and New York: Routledge.

Snoj, J. (2017), 'Population in Qatar by Nationality – 2017 Report', *Priya Desouza: Making Sense of Qatar*, <http://priyadsouza.com/population-of-qatar-by-nationality-in-2017/>

Sokal, A. (2008), *Beyond the Hoax: Science, Philosophy and Culture*, Oxford: Oxford University Press.

Thabiti Willis, J. (2016), 'A Visible Silence: Africans in the History of Pearl Diving in Dubai, UAE', in K. Exell and S. Wakefield (eds), *Museums in Arabia: Transnational Practices and Regional Processes*, London and New York: Routledge, pp. 34–50.

Ulrichsen, K. C. (2011), *Insecure Gulf: The End of Certainty and the Transition to the Post-Oil Era*, London: Hurst.

Vergo, P. (ed.) (1989), *The New Museology*, London: Reaktion Books.

17

OMANI IDENTITY AMID THE OIL CRISIS

Lamya Harub

Introduction

With the establishment of the modern state of Oman in 1970, the government of Sultan Qaboos created and transmitted a national ideology based on 'shared' values, ideas and symbols embodied in the figure of Qaboos bin Said. This state project has sought to instil and cultivate an authentic national spirit among Omanis, who can recognise themselves as citizen-subjects of the 'old' country.[1] In line with this programme, many major infrastructure projects meant to display the power and legitimacy of the new order are named after the Sultan.[2] Hence, as many observers have noted, Oman's nation-building process is intimately connected to the personality of Sultan Qaboos. Yet, this link between national identity and the persona of the Sultan is not universally observed. In *Hatha Watani* (This Is My Nation),[3] a social studies textbook for Omani students in the eleventh grade, the Ministry of Education notes that the course aims to provide Omanis with a sense of national identity.[4] *Hatha Watani*'s focus was not to limit the *creation* of a national Omani identity to the sole character of Sultan Qaboos and *al-nahdha*, the 'renaissance'[5] of 1970, a period of prosperity brought about by his rise to power, but rather to appreciate the geology, geography, history, culture, diversity and so forth of the Sultanate's *constructed* past and present.

Analysing official government discourse and utilising personal inter-views conducted between December 2014 and March 2016,[6] this chapter's argument is twofold. First, contrary to expert claims on Oman and recent work by Omanis that Qaboos's presence and character constitute the pri-mary factor that upholds Oman's current national identity,[7] there are several other elements – for instance, the country's history, cosmopolitan culture, foreign policy, and so forth – that helped create an Omani national iden-tity.[8] These constructions, part of the awakening narrative, are represented as part of Oman's ancient past and hence naturalised for the national present. Secondly, and more pressing in view of current socio-economic challenges, is the role of energy in Oman. Since 1970, oil has played an integral part in grounding a brand of Omani identity promoted by the state. Therefore, contrary to countless analyses, the real crisis at hand is not the succession to Sultan Qaboos, as his legacy will continue after him, but that of oil, which has played a critical role in the social, economic and political structures of Oman from 1970.

Much of the existing literature on Oman can be organised into various clusters, ranging from foreign policy and history[9] to memoirs and accounts written by British officials who worked in Oman, and general studies con-cerning Arab Gulf states. More recently, however, works by Omani scholars have appeared on the phenomenon of Omani nationalism. Saif Al-Maamari dedicates his recent publication *Al-Muwatina fi 'Oman* (Citizenship in Oman) to the Omani employees working predominantly in the govern-ment sector.[10] It is not always clear whether Al-Maamari, adopting a unique style, is writing a novel, a poem, or an opinion piece; nevertheless, he begins his first two chapters with prose centring upon the month of November (Oman's National Day) and July (the month of the renaissance), suggesting to the reader that Sultan Qaboos is the centre of Omani citizenship. He uses the term *watani* (my nation), when expressing his love for the Omani *watan* (nation), and how Qaboos in 1970, through the Omani renaissance, made the Omani citizens dreams a reality.[11] Al-Maamari's main desire is for the youth and the people of Oman to have a greater appreciation for the values and national identity that were established in July 1970 with the accession of Sultan Qaboos. The centrality of Qaboos in Omani identity is further echoed in *Muwahad 'Oman*, where Emad Al-Bahrani begins Oman's historical narrative with *ashraqat el-shams* (the sun shines) on the day of the renaissance in 1970, with Qaboos moving the Omanis away from *al-dhalam* (the darkness) that they lived under for over a century (1856–1970).[12] The rest of the book offers praise to Qaboos and delineates the prosperous era established by the Sultan's leadership as he consolidated all Omani tribes under the banner of national unity.[13]

In contrast, Marc Valeri's *Oman* identifies inter-generational concerns considering Oman's diverse and tribal society. Accordingly, Valeri argues that the Sultan acquired his political legitimacy in 1970 through a 'modern tradition' known as *al-nahdha* (renaissance). He also demonstrates how the discovery of oil made *al-nahdha* possible.[14] Most suggestively, Valeri questions how the new generation – in the context of depleting oil resources and the increase of certain Omani population demographics – will adapt to the new social and economic challenges facing the Sultanate. While taking Valeri's arguments into account, this chapter also proposes an alternative, less pessimistic prognosis for Oman's future, and looks at the Sultanate's discursive national identity as varied and as dependent on other contextual elements independent of the persona of Sultan Qaboos.[15]

Like Valeri, an Omani journalist and doctoral student at the University of Bedfordshire, Hadil Moosa, explains how the Sultanate's nation-state is linked to the persona of Sultan Qaboos.[16] Moosa's ongoing doctoral research critically examines the relationship between women and entrepreneurship in contemporary Oman. Thus far, she has found that most of her interviewees look at Qaboos bin Said as the symbol of unity and *al-wataniya* (nationalism) in Oman, and therefore, he is equated with *al-wataniya*. Moosa explained that many people believe that without the current Sultan, Oman, as it currently exists, may find itself in a problematic situation in the future. She states: 'His Majesty has created the public space for nationalism. It is impacted by two dimensions: tribal unity and the persona of the Sultan.'[17] She goes on to explain how the Omani people trust Qaboos bin Said, yet the issue of tribal wars may arise after Sultan Qaboos's reign has ended, particularly due to the current drop in oil prices that may confront the Sultanate's economic stability.

To meet these economic challenges, Oman Vision 2040[18] was drafted to develop a long-term socio-economic plan that will ensure inter-generational equity. As a member of the committee for Oman Vision 2040, Mohammed Al-Rumhy, Minister of Oil and Gas in Oman, identified two key issues for the committee. The first was Oman's need for an energy policy,[19] and the second was 'to educate the Omanis to love to be Omani and to carry the Omani identity'.[20] He further emphasised that the Omani identity is important, and that Omanis should not have allegiance to their 'village, then region, then country; [they should] reverse it'.[21] That is, Oman the 'nation-state', as argued by Ernest Gellner (that the state was created without the nation), should come first.[22] The process of national formation in this scenario advocated by Al-Rumhy should therefore not begin with the 'village', or in other words tribal affiliation (*al-qabila*), but with the state.[23]

While extant research and literature demonstrate that Omani unity is based on Qaboos's renaissance project,[24] this chapter draws on existing historical narratives and personal interviews through the concept of 'banal nationalism' to show how Omani identity de-centres the Sultan from its own discourse. It argues that different understandings of Omani nationalism exist and are perpetuated through the active participation of individuals who shape and reproduce national values. Through an analysis of Oman's history after 1970 it will show how the Omani identity shifts and is context-dependent, and that the centrality of Qaboos's position in the invention of *al-nahdha* played a role in neutralising the national narrative. Before moving on to the first section, it briefly shows how Omanis identified themselves before Qaboos, and how diverse these senses of identity were.

Oman's History Prior to 1970[25]

During the early eighteenth century, Oman was governed by an Imamate system[26] – based on Ibadhism, one of Oman's dominant forms of Islam – and it had been for over a thousand years. This accordingly paved the way for Ibadhi-inflected concepts such as *shura* (consultation) and *imama* (sovereignty), as Hussein Ghubash argues, to be integrated as part of Oman's national consciousness.[27] In 1941, when Ahmed bin Said Al-Busaidi's accession took place,[28] tribal conflicts increased, often based on Al-Busaidi's alliance with the British. This continued for over a century until the British reduced tribal tension by forcing the opposition into signing the Treaty of Seeb in 1920. This agreement divided Oman into two political entities.[29] The treaty thus had a profound effect on the exploration efforts in the interior during the 1930s, as the tribes of the interior declared that Said bin Taimur (the father of Qaboos) did not have sovereignty over Oman.

Regardless of competing ideologies of the Imamate and the Sultanate – where the former demanded the removal of British troops and called for the establishment of an Islamic state, while the latter allied with the British – when the Saudis occupied al-Buraimi[30] in 1952 they united as Omanis against the foreign invaders. The British government also intervened in 1954 and attacked the Saudis with the Trucial Oman Scouts. Many tribes in the Imamate did not favour the close relationship of the British with Sultan Said; thus, they restricted the access of oil companies into the al-Buraimi territory.[31] The continual explorations on the frontier of the Imamate territory further infuriated the tribes, as they saw them as an infringement of the independence of Imamate sovereignty.[32] This was the beginning of what became known as the Imamate revolt of 1955, which dragged on intermittently until 1970.[33]

Military operations against the British and the Sultanate continued until 1958, which included frequent attacks on international oil companies. The political division between the Imamate and Sultanate allowed for an identity division, which later allowed for a British-backed Sultanate to rise at the expense of an Ibadhi Oman. By 1959, the British had occupied Jebel al-Akhdar and suppressed the Imamate revolts. Soon after, commercial quantities of oil were found, and Oman began exporting oil in 1967.[34] Although internal conflict in northern Oman subsided, the situation in southern Oman, Dhofar, was becoming unstable due to economic frustrations, extreme poverty and restrictions placed on personal mobility. Said bin Taimur was no longer able to handle the Dhofar revolution,[35] hence, on 23 July 1970, Qaboos with British assistance conducted a bloodless coup overthrowing his father, Sultan Taimur. On the day of his accession, Qaboos bin Said gave a speech to his subjects promising them that he would 'proceed forthwith in the process of creating a modern government', and work in unity to 'regenerate that glorious past'.[36] With this, the first part of the chapter explains how the process of national identity formation proceeded in the Sultanate.

Situating Omani Nationalism

This section lays out the theoretical framework that unpacks the different ways in which Omani nationalism was imagined and constructed. Through this, several assumptions about how the Sultanate was unified as a nation-state are revealed. The concept of 'banal nationalism', introduced later in the section, is the lens through which this chapter explains how Omanis are constantly reminded of nationhood.

Ernest Gellner argues that 'nations, like states, are a contingency, and not a universal necessity'.[37] They were created during the sixteenth century, known as the advent of 'modernity', and did not exist before that time, as neither 'nations nor states exist at all times and in all circumstances . . . Nationalism holds that they were destined for each other; that either without the other is incomplete, and constitutes a tragedy.'[38] For Oman the current tragedy, as Al-Rumhy points out, is the lack of a 'community' or a 'nation' that can be inserted into the Omani 'state'. The emphasis on 'shared traits' often appears essential in the process of nationalism. A nation, however, as defined by Benedict Anderson, is an 'imagined political community' that is sovereign since 'the members of even the smallest nation will never know most of their fellow-members, meet them, or even hear of them, yet in the minds of each lives the image of their communion'.[39] Anderson states three paradoxes that stem from the notion of nationalism: (1) the concept of nationalism stems from a new and created history, which nationalists adopt as a sacred concept; (2) it is universally accepted; and (3) its influence on a political level is powerful but its philosophical grounding is weak.[40] Given Anderson's paradoxes, Gellner thus delineates how the transition to modernity 'imposes homogeneity [that] surface[s] in the form of nationalism'.[41] Without homogenisation, nationalism ceases to exist. Therefore, when Sultan Qaboos came to power he 'injected' a political system, to use Anderson's term, into the country's weak and divided political foundation while homogenising the Omani people under the umbrella of his renaissance.

Therefore, to produce a national identity, a past must be invented. With a historical constructed past, elements of the 'modern' nation-state are placed in position. The necessity of this constructed past is echoed by Mohammed Al-Sawafi, an Omani working in Sultan Qaboos University, who contends that *al-wataniya* (nationalism) is a term attributed to the homeland – it should have cultural, social, historical and political links, etc. attached to it.[42] As will be further exemplified below, the Omani youth refer to this 'past' to substantiate Omani identity. This is also revealed in the textbook *Hatha Watani*, where Omani students are taught to appreciate the history of Oman that returns to the times of the Prophet Mohammad in Islam, which states that Oman welcomed the message of Islam with open arms, and thus the cultural production goes back thousands of years.[43] The role of energy, however, in assisting the creation of the *al-nahdha* is almost absent from the standard narratives of the country. Mandana Limbert explains that the Omani government 'both ignores the fact that a huge influx of capital enabled the new state to embark on massive infrastructure projects and naturalizes the projection of change'.[44]

Invented traditions can be renewed, replaced and disregarded. Eric Hobsbawm contends that to maintain a standardised national identity a 'historic continuity had to be invented'.[45] The invented tradition should be distinguished from 'customs'; the latter is a pre-industrial 'authentic' practice, while the former is an external construction that serves the development of a nation-state. Jeremy Jones and Nicholas Ridout argue that the process of 'modernisation' took place in 1749 with Imam Ahmed Al-Busaidi, the founder of what they call 'Oman's political dynasty'.[46] This, as Hobsbawm explains, asserts a historical continuity that assumes a teleological process until 1970. Partha Chatterjee challenges this temporality of nationalism.[47] He explains how 'modern' nationalist theorists propagate the idea that there is a universal understanding of the world that advocates an empty homogeneous time of 'modernity'. By conforming to a homogeneous understanding of time and nationalism, Jones and Ridout's narrative limits one's understanding of the process of nationalism in Oman, which is a recent development.

The transformative development that occurred with the reign of Qaboos emphasised the need for the Omani state to have a monarchy at the centre of the nation-state. Michael Billig, in stretching the term 'nationalism', introduced the concept of 'banal nationalism', which covers the ideological habits that enable established nations to be reproduced. These habits, Billig argues, 'are not removed from everyday life, as some observers have supposed. Daily, the nation is indicated, or "flagged", in the lives of its citizenry. Nationalism, far from being an intermittent mood in established nations, is the endemic condition.'[48] The banality of nationalism in Oman took two essential components: first, Sultan Qaboos was central in revitalising *al-sulta* (the Al-Busaidi monarchy); and second, the huge influx of oil revenues has been critical in this development. Qaboos integrated *al-sulta* into the new Omani state and made it part of Oman's premier national symbol. With *al-sulta*, an oil-based lifestyle emerged and became dominant, central to the social life of the country. This way of thinking about energy did not emerge naturally: it was propagated by *al-sulta* through *al-nahdha* in a subtle manner. Moreover, when Al-Rumhy linked the need for an energy policy with the importance of a national identity, what he was proposing was not a new energy policy, but rather, a new way of imagining social life in the context of the oil crisis.

Therefore, drawing from Billig's, Gellner's and Anderson's concepts of identity and nationalism, along with ethnographic interviews, this chapter illustrates the banal construction and performance of national identity among the youth population. The Omani identity, whether a construct or an invention, must find *something* with which to continue to shape the process of nationalism, and in the case of the Sultanate that something is in fact banal and is normalised through the enacted discourses and practices of Omanis. Nationalism in Oman thus took a subtle form and became a naturalised self-referential normalised product.

Al-Nahdha through the Prism of Banal Nationalism

As mentioned previously, many academics have argued that Omani nationalism is linked strongly, if not exclusively, to the figure of Sultan Qaboos. They have concluded that this may create a challenge in the future once his reign has come to an end. These scholars, however, have overlooked other constructed elements of Omani national identity, such as interpretations of Islam, foreign policy, economic stability and Oman's diverse and cosmopolitan history, that are reproduced and reconstituted as cultural products on a regular basis and have become part of the daily narrative of many Omanis. Using interviews with Omani nationals, this next section moves beyond an exclusive focus on the character of the Sultan and includes the diverse features of 'banal nationalism' in Oman.

Varied Perspectives

Oman's international position draws strong attention to its place in Omani identity. Abdulrahman Al-Maskary, a chemical engineering graduate, links Omani unity to the country's foreign policy and message of peace:

> I think that our foreign policy plays a significant role in uniting Omani people; which is why we always call for peace and do not meddle with other nations' internal issues. We, as individuals, have seen how this reflected positively on Oman, and helped in making almost all Omanis united in supporting this policy and the Sultan is behind it. Furthermore, this has managed to even eclipse the sectarian differences, which have caused violence or deep-rooted conflicts in most of neighbouring countries in the Middle East.[49]

The self-differentiation of Oman's foreign policy – that is, a policy of non-interference in other country's internal affairs and its role as mediator[50] – comes from the Sultanate's world view that 'reflect[s] His Majesty Sultan Qaboos' values and vision for Oman's role in the international arena'.[51] Oman's foreign policy is viewed as being distinct from those of its neighbouring countries, and thus, nation constructs are appropriated. As Al-Maskary has indicated, the Sultanate's foreign relations are inserted into a nationalist-inflected historical framework that is reflected in the country's maritime history, cultural diversity and cosmopolitan nature looking out to the Indian Ocean.

Oman's cosmopolitan culture[52] also played a part in creating a national identity for the Omani people. A first-year Omani student studying in the USA states: 'I feel like our history and diversity is part of our identity; for example, the different subcultures in Oman like the Swahili culture and the Balushi culture and all the different traditions found in various parts of Oman.'[53] The use of the term 'subcultures' indicates lines of division between the different forms of identity and association in Oman. While the diversity of cultures and tribes may cause inequality in some states, Sultan Qaboos initiated the integration of different tribes into government institutions by allocating the appointment of key ministerial positions to the various regions and tribes on an equal basis.[54] This deliberate and well-thought-of appointment system has become normalised and accepted as natural 'common sense' among Omanis.

The concept of *al-tasamuh*,[55] respect for others' beliefs, is another attribute banally produced, and invoked by Alice Ambusaidi, a Masters student and employee in the public authority for social insurance. Ambusaidi asserts how 'the right understanding of Islam by Omani people' assists in an understanding of Omani identity.[56] Ambusaidi is not talking here about a specific 'right' interpretation of Islam that comes from a particular school of thought, but rather the concept of *al-tasamuh*. This consequently eliminates prejudice or the favouring of one belief over the other.[57] In line with Al-Maskary, in which the concept of peace is essential for unifying Omanis, Ambusaidi explains how, granted an understanding that 'Islam means peace' and that therefore as a community you are able 'to love for others what you love for yourself', love for the Omani community automatically ensues if you follow the basic tenets of Islam.[58] *Al-tasamuh* thus provides Oman with a national identity that is distinct from the sectarian culture of the other Arab states. This is also produced daily in the Sultanate's official educational discourse. With the inflow of oil revenues, the attitudes, priorities and understandings of individuals vary and do not necessarily reflect the majority in a 'imagined community'; every individual unknowingly adheres to different aspects of nationalism.[59]

In other interviews, this study found that many Omani youths who answered the question 'What does the word "Omani" mean to you?' did not attribute the answer to the character of Sultan Qaboos; rather, the answers were mostly attributed to love for Oman, *al-watan*. For instance, an Omani medical doctor who graduated from the Sultanate stated that 'to be an Omani is to live in a peaceful country'.[60] The 'peaceful' position was further echoed, showing the importance of safety in Omani identity. The medical doctor further contended that '*hubb al-watan*' (to love one's homeland, i.e. patriotism) is what unites the Omani people today, 'because it is the only thing that brings peace and tranquility'.[61] This theme of the Omani identity belonging to *al-watan* (the nation) comes from the understanding that the relationship between land and identity is still very strong, to the point where the country's unity is predicated on the Omani nation. Al-Sawafi explains that the greatest example of Omani unity is associated with the way Omanis have dealt with past natural disaster.[62] He notes that 'the effects of the cyclone on Oman showed Omani unity and strong association with one another'.[63] Belief in the homeland itself, Billig argues, 'is situated within the world of nations. And, only if people believe that they have national identities will such homelands, and the world of national homelands, be reproduced.'[64] Nasir Alriyami, an Omani graduate from Izki, alternatively emphasises 'al-fakhar wa al-'iz' (pride and glory) when discerning what it means to be an Omani.[65] He explains that the Omani identity is 'to have a strong loving personality, to be sociable, and to be a pacifist internationally'.[66] Alriyami describes a form of nationalism based upon social equality and national self-determination; thus, the community is regarded as more important than the individual.

Another attribute brought forth by the interviewees was the current challenges considering the plummeting oil prices. An anonymous interviewee indicated that history has shown that the Sultanate has overcome the oil crisis of 1998, which acts as proof to him that the Omani people will stand together in times of future crisis.[67] In his opinion:

> [The] Omani identity will never change. Identity means loving the country's soil until the last second of being alive. There is only a small number of people that will try to create problems in order to be famous or for personal agendas, they will never make it. This is what happened in 2011. The demands were all economic, no one touched loyalty and unity. What unites the Omanis I guess are the values and principles they were brought up in.[68]

Here, nationalism is founded on the political boundaries of the state, that is, 'the country's soil' that ceases to change over time. Nonetheless, to the anonymous interviewee, while protestors during the Arab Spring made economic claims and were 'loyal' and united, some were arrested in Sohar in 2011 for being disloyal towards the Sultan.[69] Another anonymous interviewee contends: 'Oman was an empire before all these neighbouring nation-states were formed. The land is what attaches us to the nation.'[70] Tying nationalism to the land, and the pride harboured by many Omani citizens that the Sultanate was an 'empire' superior to its neighbours, is central to the discourse of nationalism and allows Omanis to define themselves in relation to their land. Alternatively, Hussein Al-Lawati, a successful Omani entrepreneur with several small enterprises, states that 'hardship is what unites Omanis', which was the essence of *al-nahdha* – the Omani renaissance.[71] Nonetheless, some Omanis feel that the country was rich, but that they personally have not benefited from development over the past generation or so, and this shows a sense of *relative inequality* that is in many ways much more important in relation to popular dissatisfaction than absolute inequality.[72]

In another vein, a young Omani businesswoman explained how Omanis do not comprehend what 'starvation' means and are 'lazy opportunists', and that the Government should apply 'zero tolerance to this', and if anything goes wrong, 'His Majesty will have a plan'.[73] She went on to say that because of 'His Majesty's sacrifices, and our parents [sacrifices]', we should 'be ready to fight for it'.[74] The businesswoman describes an appearance of patronage, whereby the Sultan has rewarded his citizens with wealth and thus political allegiance should be automatic. Her view, in this regard, connects nationalism to political loyalty to the state (the body of the Sultan is equated with the State) and to a quasi-religious belief in which Qaboos is equated with a divine figure who will know how to solve any problems that arise. Following this, I asked her what *al-nahdha* meant to her, to which she replied: 'I don't know.'[75] The unfamiliarity with, or disregard of, the Omani renaissance is, according to Al-Maamari, a loss of *wa'i* (awareness) and consciousness about what is essential in understanding Omani citizenship and identity.[76] This, paradoxically, illustrates the success of the renaissance project, which will have to be reimagined and re-produced considering the current global energy crisis.

The renaissance was thus the political and socio-economic development process that made Omanis more reliant on the state, and less on tribal, *'asabiyya*, affinity. 'When I think of the renaissance', Al-Maskary claims,

> it marked the transition from the dark ages to the modern era. We have made huge progress over the past 45 years, before which there was hardly any development. Moreover, we have to admit that the renaissance could not have made it this far without oil, which was a game changer for Oman as with other GCC countries. However, oil alone cannot bring a country to civilisation and modernisation without good leadership, which we got with our renaissance.[77]

The link between 'good leadership' and 'oil' in the process of unifying the country is emphasised by Al-Maskary above. In the official discourse, oil is not included in the definition of *al-nahdha*; the latter is solely attributed to Qaboos transitioning Oman to the 'modern era'. The connection of oil and nationalism and its impact on industry is in many ways important for understanding how Omanis identify themselves, and is in many ways evolving and changing. In addition, the continuation of this progress and development is essential; an Omani undergraduate claims that it is 'our responsibility as the new generation to keep the country moving forward'.[78] To be a nationalist, one must take on this responsibility. This, she explains, is why the renaissance 'makes me think of how oil was – and still is – a major factor in facilitating our progress'.[79] The process of nationalism and Omani unification has yet to be complete, and while many are sceptical of its progress, the Omani youth are educated enough to understand that 'His Majesty was one man; so why can't we make a difference too?'[80]

Many of the constructs that structure the way Omanis identify themselves reveal the success of the renaissance project. However, given its varied applications, Omani identity has been produced through individuals that have adopted national values through 'banal nationalism'. The ethnographic data above show that the *al-nahdha* project with the huge influx of oil revenue has successfully allowed for the continual reproduction of normalised national values by Omanis daily. Therefore, even if oil or gas runs out, it will not simply revert back, as some analysts contend. Nonetheless, there remain socio-economic challenges that need to be addressed that move beyond the issue of Omani identity.

Conclusion

The varied national attributes are part of an assemblage that converges and produces a single and distinct base for the people of Oman. The Omani national identity emerges out of the 'political nation' established by Sultan Qaboos to lay a foundation that replaces the tribal framework that existed prior to 1970. As such, Qaboos created a government wherein respect was given to all Omani tribes and cosmopolitan society. His personality is imprinted as it were on the state, through various naming practices and a developmentalist vision promoted by energy. The personal interviews conducted illustrate the success of the Omani Renaissance project, and show how these national values were reconstituted under the aegis of the energy complex.

The Sultanate's efforts towards 'modernisation' and nationalisation have focused on projects that in many ways have not provided the Omani people with suitable employment, projects that hence have increased the number of non-Omani nationals in the workforce. What is more, the issue of unemployment is not one that can easily be remedied; Omanis are willing to work if and when they are provided with a 'good job' that fits the profiles of the youth with high 'expectations' and aspirations for a career. Therefore, even if Oman no longer has oil, the Omanis will be able to loosen dependence on oil, and through hardship and 'creativity' they will unite to invent a new 'tradition' representative of their generation. The belief in the new generation and their capabilities in projecting 'banal nationalism' beyond the framework set out by Sultan Qaboos, I argue, is of great importance; it is up to the older generation to believe in the capabilities of the youth.

Finally, despite the dominant perspective of Qaboos' centrality in the formation of nationalism in Oman, the above findings demonstrate that the varied national values constructed through 'banal nationalism' provide a strong foundation that will assist the Omanis in moving beyond the galvanising character of Sultan Qaboos when re-imagining an Omani identity in the future. The belief in the new generation (and their capabilities in reproducing national attributes beyond the framework set out by Qaboos) is of great importance, as 'challenges can be avoided . . . if the current young generation realises the future responsibilities they have to take for their country'.[81]

This chapter has shown how everyday national representations of Oman are in fact naturalised self-referential products that play a significant role in constructing a nationalist Omani identity. These taken-for-granted attributes are artefacts of the state, elements as it were of the *al-nahda* ideology, but have achieved a certain dynamic that propels them beyond the figure of Sultan Qaboos. Moreover, this chapter has shown how these discursive representations are supported by Oman's energy complex, thus signifying the underlying importance of oil to this ideological formation.

Notes

1. Acknowledgements: I would like to express my deep gratitude to my dear friends Feras Klenk, Jessie Moritz, Anahi Alviso Marino, Sara Moradian, Mehammed Mack, Bushra Al-Maskari, Abdulla Baabood and Allen Fromherz, and to my

beloved family, for always providing me with hope, love, support, encouragement, guidance and valuable insight for this chapter.

Due to the orientalist undertones of the terms 'modern' and 'modernity', this chapter will, where possible, simply use 'the period of 1970' (pre-1970 or post-1970) to indicate the historical period discussed. However, in many instances when quoting or referring to other works, the word 'modern' and 'modernity' will be used. It is useful to add that the concept of 'modernity' is contested by many since it is defined by a claim to universality that promotes a false unity that assumes that there cannot be alternative modernities and therefore promotes ethnocentrism. For more on this see Timothy Mitchell (ed.), *Questions of Modernity* (Berkeley and New York: University of California Press, 2002).

Debates as to what constitutes 'authenticity' can be found in Charles Taylor (1994), *Multiculturalism*, Gayatri Spivak (1990), *The Post-Colonial Critic* and Penelope Ingram's article 'Can the Settler Speak?', to name a few. In this specific context, according to Taylor, it is interesting to point out the collective versus the individualist feature of 'authenticity'. In Oman there is a constant refrain of the new generation abandoning the old traditional values: a form, therefore, of reclaiming the authenticity imposed by the Sultanate upon the society. One cannot have an authentic self unless others perceive one's authenticity.

2. Sultan Qaboos University, Sultan Qaboos St, Sultan Qaboos Grand Mosque, Madinat al-Sultan Qaboos, Sultan Qaboos Sports Stadium, and so forth.

3. Ministry of Education (2013) *Hatha Watani: Fi Al-Sirat al-Hadariyya li'Oman* [This is My Nation: The Path of Civilisation for Oman], Ministry of Education of the Sultanate of Oman.

4. Hmoud bin Ali Al-Aaisari conducted an analytical study identifying national values included in the social studies textbooks for the secondary level in the Sultanate of Oman. His Masters thesis *Al-qiyam al-wataniya al-mutadhamina fi kutub al-dirasat al-ijtima'iya lil-marhala al-thanawiya fi Sultanate 'Oman* [National Values Included in the Social Studies Textbooks for the Secondary Level in the Sultanate of Oman] was submittted to the University of Jordan in 2001.

5. The 'renaissance' is a very specific term used locally to describe a specific time in Omani history. This is the day Sultan Qaboos acceded to the throne, 23 July 1970, which, for those who invoke the term, led Oman towards a path of prosperity, security, unity and development. For other understandings of the term 'renaissance' in the Omani context see Anita Rita Coppola, 'Oman and Omani

Identity during the Nahdahs: A Comparison of Three Modern Historiographic Works'. *Oriente Moderno*, vol. 94, no. 1 (2014), pp. 1–55.

6. In the second part of this chapter, I utilise qualitative interviews conducted (in both English and Arabic) between December 2014 and March 2016. The interviews provided an insightful way to view understandings of Omani nationalism and show that Omani national identity has multiple forms and meanings for Omanis. In order to provide varied and contrasting perspectives, the interviewees consisted of government officials, decision-makers and non-officials from different generational groups, mainly focusing on youth, that is, the 17–39 age group. The focus on youth (whether professionals or students) is rarely encountered, and since Omani youth make up over two-thirds of the country's population, this paper attempts to reflect a majority perspective. It should be noted that the author of the conducted interviews was approved by the guidelines to ensure research ethics offered by the College Research Ethics Committee.

7. Marc Valeri (2009) *Oman: Politics and Society in the Qaboos State*, p. 5. Similar claims are made in Saif Al-Maamari (2016), *Al-Muwatina fi 'Oman: Hawiya wa Qiyam wa Tahadiyat* [Citizenship in Oman: Identity, Values, and Challenges], Emad bin Jasim Al-Bahrani (2010), *Muwahad 'Oman: Al-Sultan Qaboos bin Said* [Unifier of Oman: Sultan Qaboos bin Said] and Christopher M. Davidson (2012), *After the Sheikhs: The Coming Collapse of the Gulf Monarchies*, to name a few.

8. The concept of identity in this chapter, whereby the discursive constructs of national identity are varied, is defined as context-dependent and dynamic. See ch. 2 in Ruth Wodak, Rudolf de Cillia, Martin Reisigl and Karin Liebhartp (2009), *The Discursive Construction of National Identity*, pp. 7–48.

9. Book-length studies on the history of Oman written before the 21st century include Robert G. Landen (1967), *Oman Since 1856: Disruptive Modernization in a Traditional Arab Society*; Miriam Joyce (1995), *The Sultanate of Oman: A Twentieth Century History*; and Carol J. Riphenburg (1998), *Oman: Political Development in a Changing World*.

10. Saif Nasir Al-Maamari (2016), *Al-Muwatina fi 'Oman: Hawiya wa Qiyam wa Tahadiyat* [Citizenship in Oman: Identity, Values, and Challenges].

11. Al-Maamari (2016), p. 89.

12. Emad Jasim Al-Bahrani (2010), *Muwahad 'Oman: Al-Sultan Qaboos bin Said* [Unifier of Oman: Sultan Qaboos bin Said].

13. Al-Bahrani published the book to coincide with the celebration of Oman's 40th national day, which is celebrated on Qaboos's birthday.

14. Valeri (2009), p. 73.

15. It is worth mentioning that this chapter does not deny that Sultan Qaboos – for better or worse – has created a state apparatus and an ideology around his body, both of which will outlast him, and probably the Al-Said dynasty. However, there are other factors and dimensions that assisted in the invention of an Omani national identity that will be discussed subsequently.

16. Interview with Hadil Moosa, an Omani journalist and doctoral student at the University of Bedfordshire (25 February 2016, Muscat). She is from Muscat and is in her mid-thirties.

17. Ibid.

18. Oman Vision 2040 aims to succeed Oman Vision 2020, which is a long-term plan for the country to boost private-sector activity, diversify away from oil and educate Oman's workforce so that they have the skills to fill the jobs that are created. The aim is to prepare Oman's large youth population to take on the jobs that Sultan Qaboos's plans will create, and to give employers the skilled local workforce they need. The committee for Oman Vision 2040 is chaired by the Minister of Culture and Heritage Sayyid Haitham Al-Said (who is rumoured to be the next Sultan of Oman).

19. Oman currently does not have an energy policy, and the reason for this, according to Al-Rumhy, is the lack of consensus in the Council of Ministers for having one. However, efforts to create a national energy strategy are currently under way.

20. Interview with Mohammed Al-Rumhy, Minister for Oil and Gas (18 February 2015, Muscat).

21. Ibid.

22. Ernest Gellner (1983), *Nations and Nationalism*.

23. Despite the assertion of some authors that national unity existed in Oman under the Abbasids, during the time of the 1964 Zanzibar revolution the region was in a state of political stagnation. See Robert G. Landen (1967), *Oman Since 1856*.

24. See *supra*, n. 6.

25. For detailed discussion of nationalist feelings/sentiments in the Omani diaspora prior to 1970 see the subsection 'Royalist Culture', ch. 9 in Abdel Razzaq Takriti (2013), *Monsoon Revolution*.

26. The word 'Imamate' derives from *Imam*, which means ruling. The Imamate is a 7th-century religious ruling system that comes from one of the dominant Islamic sects in Oman, Ibadhism. The name 'Ibadhism' came from the sect's founder, Abdullah ibn Ibadh, and was brought to Oman by Jabir bin Zayd,

who came from a city close to Nizwa in Oman. Interpretations of Ibadhism are based upon the Islamic sharia. For more details see Valerie J. Hoffman (2012), *The Essentials of Ibadi Islam*.

27. Hussein Ghubash (2006), *Oman: The Islamic Democratic Tradition*, p. 2.

28. His election as Imam was the beginning of a dynastic Al-Busaidi (Al-Said) succession as opposed to the traditional election tradition set out by Ibadhi doctrine.

29. For more on this see John Wilkinson (1987), *The Imamate Tradition of Oman*.

30. Buraimi is a town in the north-west of Oman and is bordered by the UAE (Al-Ain).

31. This disapproval runs right through Oman's history from the late 19th century to the 1950s.

32. Hussein Ghubash (2006), *Oman: The Islamic Democratic Tradition*, p. 181.

33. Robert G. Landen (1967), *Oman Since 1856: Disruptive Modernization in a Traditional Arab Society*, pp. 58–70, 388–414.

34. Sir Terence Clark (2007), *Underground to Overseas: The Story of Petroleum Development Oman*, p. 38.

35. For a detailed account on the Dhofar rebellion see Abdel Razzaq Takriti (2013), *Monsoon Revolution*.

36. Ministry of Foreign Affairs, Oman (2016), *MOFA Official Website* (last accessed 6 March 2016), <https://www.mofa.gov.om/?p=1034&lang=en> (added emphasis).

37. Gellner (1983), p. 6 .

38. Ibid (added emphasis).

39. Benedict Anderson (1991), *Imagined Communities*.

40. Anderson (1991), pp. 6–7.

41. Gellner (1983), p. 39.

42. Interview with Mohammed Hilal Al-Sawafi, an administrator working in the management and information division at Sultan Qaboos University. He is a graduate who studied in Oman and is 25 years old (5 March 2016, via email).

43. Ministry of Education (2013), pp. 110–13.

44. Mandana Limbert (2001), 'The Senses of Water in an Omani Town'. *Social Text*, p. 38.

45. Eric Hobsbawm (1983), 'Introduction: Inventing Traditions', *The Invention of Tradition*, p. 7.

46. Jeremy Jones and Nicholas Ridout (2015), *A History of Modern Oman*, p. 75.

This argument – that Oman's state foundation post-1970 comes from Imam Al-Busaidi – is also found in Valeri (2009), p. 25.

47. Partha Chatterjee (2003), 'The Nation in Heterogeneous Time', in Umut Özkirimli (ed.), *Nationalism and its Futures*, p. 36.

48. Michael Billig (1995), *Banal Nationalism*, p. 6.

49. Interview with Abdulrahman Al-Maskari, who works as a process engineer in British Petroleum from the interior city of Ibra and is 26 years old (2 January 2015, Muscat).

50. Oman's mediation-role efforts can be traced in recent history starting from the Iran–Iraq wars of the 1990s, the Sultanate's active part in the Madrid Peace Conference in 1991 and its neutral stance on the 2003 Iraq war, through to its current role in the Iran Nuclear Deal 2015, the ongoing Syrian crisis and war against Yemen, and the relocation of Guantanamo prisoners.

51. Ministry of Foreign Affairs, Oman (2014), 'Foreign Policy', *MOFA Official Website*, <http://mofa.gov.om/?cat=159&lang=en> (last accessed 19 March 2012).

52. As noted in Ministry of Education (2013), pp. 20–39.

53. Interview with an anonymous 19-year-old Omani undergraduate student from Bahla studying in the USA (26 February 2016, WhatsApp).

54. J. E. Peterson (2013), 'The Construction of the New Oman', in Abbas Kadhim, *Governance in the Middle East and North Africa: A Handbook*, p. 322.

55. The interviewee used the word 'tolerance' to translate *al-tasamuh*. However, 'tolerance' is an inaccurate translation for the word, even though officially the Omani Government uses the term 'tolerance'. The word actually means 'respect for others'.

56. Interview with Alice Ambusaidi from Nizwa, who works in the Public Authority for Social Insurance and is 32 years old (27 February 2016, WhatsApp).

57. Sectarian census is not applied in Oman to avoid disunity among the various schools of thought found in the country.

58. Interview with Ambusaidi (27 February 2016, WhatsApp).

59. Anderson (1991).

60. Interview with an anonymous Omani female doctor who obtained her degree in the Sultanate. She is from Seeb and is 28 years old (4 March 2016, via email).

61. Interview with an anonymous Omani female doctor (4 March 2016, via email).

62. This is in relation to Cyclone Gonu (2007) and Cyclone Phet (2010), which caused intensive damage in Oman whereby many people lost their lives.

63. Interview with Al-Sawafi (5 March 2016, via email).

64. Billig (1995), p. 8.

65. Interview with Nasir Alriyami, a graduate from Oman working as an information technology technician. He is from the interior, Izki, and is 24 yars old (4 March 2016, via email).

66. Ibid.

67. Interview with an anonymous individual from al-Sharqiya region (28 February 2015, Muscat).

68. Ibid.

69. For further details see Marc Valeri (2012), *Jadaliyya* (last accessed 19 March 2014),
<http://www.jadaliyya.com/pages/index/8430/%E2%80%9Cqaboos-can-make-mistakes-like-anybody-else_-the-s>

70. Interview with an anonymous Oman in his seventies (26 February 2016, Muscat).

71. Interview with Hussein Al-Lawati from Mutrah, an entrepreneur and CEO of Al-Qabas Printing Press in his mid-thirties (27 February 2016, Muscat).

72. See Khalid M. Al-Azri, *Social and Gender Inequality in Oman: The Power of Religious and Political Tradition* (Durham Modern Middle East and Islamic World Series) (London: Routledge, 2012).

73. Interview with anonymous businesswoman from Muscat in her mid-thirties working in the private sector (24 February 2016, WhatsApp).

74. Ibid.

75. Ibid.

76. Al-Maamari (2016), p. 26.

77. Interview with Al-Maskari (2 January 2015, Muscat).

78. Interview with anonymous Omani undergraduate (26 February 2016, WhatsApp).

79. Ibid.

80. Interview with anonymous businesswoman (24 February 2016, WhatsApp).

81. Interview with Abdullah bin Said Al-Ajmi, working as a senior translator in the Directorate of Planning and Studies at the Sultan Qaboos Higher Centre for Culture and Science, from the north of Oman (1 March 2016, via email).

Bibliography

Primary Sources

Ministry of Education (2013) *Hatha Watani: Fi Al-Sira al-Hathariya li'Oman* [This is My Nation: The Path of Civilisation for Oman], Ministry of Education of the Sultanate of Oman.

Personal Interviews

Interview with unnamed senior-ranking employee in PDO in his late thirties from south of Oman (24 December 2014, Muscat).

Interview with Abdulrahman Al-Maskari, working as a process engineer in British Petroleum from Ibra, 26 years old (2 January 2015, Muscat).

Interview with unnamed high-ranking official working in The Research Council (14 January 2015, Muscat).

Interview with Mohammed Benayoune, a non-Omani, of President of Kanata Chemical Technologies Inc., Benayoune & Associates International and The Achievement Centre – Middle East, who was formerly advisor to the Omani Minister for Oil and Gas (29 January 2015, Muscat).

Interview with high-ranking employee in the public authority for investment promotion and export development (10 February 2015, Muscat).

Interview with anonymous individual who worked in the government sector (15 February 2015, Muscat).

Interview with Mohammed Al-Rumhy, Minister for Oil and Gas (18 February 2015, Muscat).

Interview with Raoul Restucci, PDO Managing Director (19 February 2015, Muscat).

Interview with anonymous individual from al-sharqiya region (28 February 2015, Muscat).

Interview with unnamed Omani businesswoman from Muscat in her mid-thirties, working in the private sector (24 February 2016, via WhatsApp).

Interview with unnamed Omani lawyer aged 27 from al-Batinah region, working in the UK (24 February 2016, via WhatsApp).

Interview with unnamed senior-ranking Omani diplomat in his forties, from al-Batinah region in Oman (24 February 2016, via WhatsApp).

Interview with Hadil Moosa, from Muscat, an Omani journalist and doctoral student at the University of Bedfordshire who is in her mid-thirties (25 February 2016, Muscat).

Interview with unnamed Omani undergraduate student from Bahla who is studying in the USA and is 19 years old (26 February 2016, via WhatsApp).

Interview with unnamed Omani student from Muscat who is studying in the USA and is 26 years old (26 February 2016, via WhatsApp).

Interview with an anonymous Omani in his seventies (26 February 2016, Muscat).

Interview with Shadha Al-Kharusi, from Muscat, a first-year Omani undergraduate studying law in the UK who is 18 years old (27 February 2016, via WhatsApp).

Interview with Alice Ambusaidi, from Nizwa, who is working in the public authority for social insurance and is 32 years old (27 February 2016, via WhatsApp).

Interview with Hussein Al-Lawati, from Mutrah, an entrepreneur and CEO of Al-Qabas Printing Press in his mid-thirties (27 February 2016, Muscat).

Interview with unnamed entrepreneur from Muscat who is working in the private sector and is in his early thirties (28 February 2016, Muscat).

Interview with Abdullah Said Al-Ajmi from the north of Oman, who is working as a senior translator in the directorate of planning and studies at the Sultan Qaboos Higher Centre for Culture and Science (1 March 2016, via email).

Interview with unnamed Omani female doctor from Seeb, who obtained her degree in the Sultanate and is 28 years old (4 March 2016, via email).

Interview with Nasir Alriyami, from the interior, Izki, who graduated in Oman and is working as an information technology technician (4 March 2016, via email).

Interview with Mohammed Hilal Al-Sawafi, a 25-year-old Omani graduate working as an administrator in the management and information division of Sultan Qaboos University (5 March 2016, via email).

Interview with a 25-year-old anonymous student from al-Mawaleh studying in Oman (10 March 2016, Muscat).

Interview with a 24-year-old anonymous student from Muscat studying in Oman (10 March 2016, Muscat).

Interview with a 19-year-old anonymous student from Muscat studying in Oman (10 March 2016, Muscat).

Interview with Samaha Al-Harasi, a 22-year-old Omani medical graduate from Nakhel (14 March 2016, via WhatsApp).

Interview with Suha Al-Kindi, a 29-year-old Omani medical graduate from Nakhel (14 March 2016, via WhatsApp).

Books and Chapters in Books

Al-Azri, Khalid M. (2012), *Social and Gender Inequality in Oman: The Power of Religious and Political Tradition* (Durham Modern Middle East and Islamic World Series), London: Routledge.

Al-Bahrani, Emad Jasim (2010), *Muwahad 'Oman: Al-Sultan Qaboos bin Said* [Unifier of Oman: Sultan Qaboos bin Said], Beirut: al-Dar al-Arabiya Lil-mowsu'at.

Allen Jr, Calvin H (1987), *Oman: The Modernization of the Sultanate*, Boulder, CO: Westview Press.

Allen, Jr, Calvin H. and Rigsbee II, W. Lynn (2000), *Oman Under Qaboos: From Coup to Constitution, 1970–1996*, Portland: Frank Cass.

Al-Maamari, Saif (2016), *Al-Muwatina fi 'Oman: Hawiya wa Qiyam wa Tahadiyat* [Citizenship in Oman: Identity, Values, and Challenges], Muscat: Dar al-Waraq.

Anderson, Benedict (1991), *Imagined Communities: Reflections on the Origin and Spread of Nationalism*, London: Verso.

Billig, Michael (1995), *Banal Nationalism*, London: SAGE.

Chatterjee, Partha (1993), *The Nation and Its Fragments: Colonial and Postcolonial Histories*, Princeton: Princeton University Press.

Chatterjee, Partha (2003), 'The Nation in Heterogeneous Time', in Umut Özkirimli (ed.), *Nationalism and its Futures*, New York: Palgrave Macmillan, pp. 33–58.

Clark, Sir Terence (2007), *Underground to Overseas: The Story of Petroleum Development Oman*, London: Stacey International.

Funsch, Linda Pappas (2015), *Oman Reborn: Balancing Tradition and Modernization*, New York: Palgrave Macmillan.

Gellner, Ernest (1983), *Nations and Nationalism*, Ithaca: Cornell University Press.

Ghubash, Hussein (2006), *Oman: The Islamic Democratic Tradition*, London and New York: Routledge.

Hobsbawm, Eric (1983), 'Introduction: Inventing Traditions', in Eric Hobsbawm and Terence Ranger (eds), *The Invention of Tradition*, Cambridge: Cambridge University Press.

Hobsbawm, Eric (1990), *Nations and Nationalism since 1780: Programme, Myth, Reality*, Cambridge: Cambridge University Press.

Hoffman, Valerie J. (2012), *The Essentials of Ibadi Islam*, Modern Intellectual and Political History of the Middle East, New York: Syracuse University Press.

Jones, Jeremy and Ridout, Nicholas (2012), *Oman, Culture and Diplomacy*, Edinburgh: Edinburgh University Press.

Jones, Jeremy and Ridout, Nicholas (2015), *A History of Modern Oman*, Cambridge: Cambridge University Press.

Joyce, Miriam (1995), *The Sultanate of Oman: A Twentieth Century History*, Westport, CT and London: Praeger.

Landen, Robert G. (1967), *Oman Since 1856: Disruptive Modernization in a Traditional Arab Society*, Princeton: Princeton University Press.

Limbert, Mandana (2010), *In the Time of Oil: Piety, Memory, and Social Life in an Omani Town*, Stanford: Stanford University Press.

Mitchell, Timothy (2002), *Rules of Experts: Egypt, Techno-Politics, Modernity*, Berkeley and New York: University of California Press.

Mitchell, Timothy (ed.) (2000), *Questions of Modernity: Contradictions of Modernity*, Vol. 11, Minneapolis: University of Minnesota Press.

Peterson, J. E. (1978), *Oman in the Twentieth Century: Political Foundations of an Emerging State*, London: Croom Helm.

Peterson, J. E. (2003), *Arabian Peninsula Background Note*, <www.JEPeterson.net>

Riphenburg, Carol J. (1998), *Oman: Political Development in a Changing World*, Connecticut: Praeger.

Spivak, Gayatri Chakravorty and Sarah Harasym (eds) (1990), *The Post-Colonial Critic: Interviews, Strategies, Dialogues*, New York: Routledge.

Szücs, Jenö (1981), *National und Geschichte*, Budapest: Corvina Kiadó.

Takriti, Abdel Razzaq (2013), *Monsoon Revolution: Republicans, Sultans, and Empires in Oman, 1965–1976*, Oxford: Oxford Historical Monographs.

Taylor, Charles and Amy Gutmann (eds) (1994), *Multiculturalism: Examining the Politics of Recognition*, Princeton: Princeton University Press.

Valeri, Marc (2007), *Oman: Politics and Society in the Qaboos State*, London: Hurst.

Valeri, Marc (2011), 'Oman', in Christopher Davison (ed.), *Power and Politics: In the Persian Gulf Monarchies*, New York: Columbia University Press.

Valeri, Marc (2013), 'Oligarchy vs. Oligarchy: Business and Politics of Reform in Bahrain and Oman', in Steffen Hertog, Giacomo Luciani and Marc Valeri (eds), *Business Politics in the Middle East*, London: Hurst.

Wilkinson, John C. (1987), *The Imamate Tradition of Oman*, Cambridge: Cambridge University Press.

Wodak, Ruth, de Cillia, Rudolf, Reisigl, Martin and Liebhartp, Karin (2009), *The Discursive Construction of National Identity*, 2nd edn, Edinburgh: Edinburgh University Press.

Journal Articles

Al-Maamari, Saif (2014), 'Education for Developing a Global Omani Citizen: Current Practices and Challenge', *Journal of Education and Training Studies* 2(3): 108–17.

Coppola, Anita Rita (2014), 'Oman and Omani Identity during the Nahdahs: A Comparison of Three Modern Historiographic Works'. *Oriente Moderno* 94(1): 1–55.

Gray, Mathew (2011), 'A Theory of "Late Rentierism" in the Arab States of the Gulf', *Center for International and Regional Studies*, Georgetown University School of Foreign Service in Qatar, Occasional Paper 7: 1–44.

Ingram, Penelope (1999), 'Can the Settler Speak? Appropriating Subaltern Silence in Janet Frame's "The Carpathians"', *Cultural Critique* 41: 79–107.

Jones, Jeremy and Ridout, Nicholas (2005) 'Oman Democratic Development', *Middle East Journal* 59(3): 376–92.

Limbert, Mandana (2001), 'The Senses of Water in an Omani Town', *Social Text 68*, 19(3): 35–55.

Online Articles

Ministry of Foreign Affairs, Oman 'Foreign Policy', *MOFA Official Website*, <http://mofa.gov.om/?cat=159&lang=en>

Ministry of Foreign Affairs, 'Speech by His Majesty Sultan Qaboos bin Said to His People on the Day of his Accession', *MOFA Official Website* (last accessed 6 March 2015) <https://www.mofa.gov.om/?p=1034&lang=en>

Ministry of Foreign Affairs (2014) 'Speech of His Majesty Sultan Qaboos bin Said on the Occasion of His First Arrival in Muscat after Assuming the Reins of Power', *MOFA Official Website*, <https://www.mofa.gov.om/?p=1031&lang=en>

Valeri, Marc (2005) 'The *Omanisation* Policy of Employment: An Omani Economic Dilemma', *Colloquium CERI* (last accessed 15 May 2014) <http://www.ceri-sciences-po.org>

Valeri, Marc (2012) 'Qaboos Can Make Mistakes Like Anybody Else: The Sultan of Oman De-sacralized, *Jadaliyya*, <http://www.jadaliyya.com/pages/index/8430/%E2%80%9Cqaboos-can-make-mistakes-like-anybody-else_-the-s>

INDEX

Note: *italic* page numbers signify illustrations